Readings

in

Nonbook
Librarianship

Edited by

Jean Spealman Kujoth

The Scarecrow Press, Inc.
Metuchen, N. J.   1968

To my parents

Acknowledgments

Great appreciation goes to those who have contributed to the writing of this book. Chief among these persons are the authors whose articles appear in the book, and the editors who have so kindly granted permission to use copyrighted material. Thanks also to the librarians at the University of Wisconsin-Milwaukee Library and at the Milwaukee Public Library, who have provided assistance on many occasions.

Table of Contents

(Note: The authors' positions listed below are not necessarily their current ones. They are the posts held at the time the articles were published and are included as clues to the authority and viewpoint of each article.)

Page

Introduction   13

Section I. Not for Reading
    A. Lights, Camera, Action! (Films, Film-
            strips and Slides)
        Films in the Large Public Library. George M.
            Holloway (Head, Educational Films Depart-
            ment, Free Library of Philadelphia). Edu-
            cational Screen and Audiovisual Guide 42:
            620-1, November 1963.   16
        Films for a Purpose. Ray E. Howser (Assist-
            ant Librarian, Peoria Public Library). Ill-
            nois Libraries 44:109-12, February 1962.   20
        Slides and Filmstrips Add Service. F.A. White
            (Director, Bureau of Audio-Visual Instruction)
            and Jane Younger (Adult Services Consultant,
            Division for Library Services). Wisconsin
            Library Bulletin 62:162-3, May 1966.   24
        Film Evaluation and Criticism. James L. Lim-
            bacher (Audio-Visual Director, Dearborn Pub-
            lic Library, Michigan). Illinois Libraries
            46:121-5, February 1964.   27
        The Why and How of Film Circuits. Ida Gosh-
            kin (Coordinator of the Group Service Depart-
            ment, Akron Public Library; Administrator of
            the Ohio Valley Regional Film Circuit). ALA
            Bulletin 55:545-8, June 1961.   34
    B. What's That I Hear Now, Ringing in My Ear?
            (Phonograph Records)
        The LP and the Well-appointed Library. Paul
            Henry Lang (Professor of Musicology at Co-
            lumbia University, Chief Music Critic of the
            New York Herald Tribune, and Editor of the

Musical Quarterly). Library Journal 88:
1809-12, May 1, 1963.   39

First Steps Toward a Record Collection. Mrs.
Edna Frances Hanna (Director, Northern
Illinois Regional Library, Illinois State
Library, De Kalb. Formerly Head of
the Recordings Unit of the Illinois State
Library). Illinois Libraries 44:134-50,
February 1962.   44

The Establishment and Care of a Library Record Collection. Don L. Roberts (Librarian,
Fine Arts Library, University of New Mexico). New Mexico Library Bulletin 35:322-8,
Spring 1966.   66

A Concept of Recordings for Public Libraries.
Ruth Stines (Audiovisual Director, Danville
Public Library). Illinois Libraries 48:97-
103, February 1966.   72

Folk Music in the Library. Jerome Cushman
(Director of the New Orleans Public Library).
Library Journal 88:1833-4, May 1, 1963.   77

Jazz. Robert Wedgeworth (Assistant Librarian
at Park College, Parkville, Missouri). Li-
brary Journal 88:1830-2, May 1, 1963.   80

The Sound of Poetry. William Ready (Librarian
of Marquette University, Milwaukee). ALA
Bulletin 56:153-4, February 1962.   84

The Record Review. Kurtz Myers (Chief of the
Music and Drama Department of the Detroit
Public Library). Library Journal 88:1813-17,
May 1, 1963.   86

A Music Critic Looks at Basic LP Collections.
Sandor Kallai (Music Critic of the Kansas
City "Star" and a former professional musician). Library Journal 88:3802-3, Oc-
tober 15, 1963.   94

Classification Chaos. Gordon Stevenson (Head
of the Art and Music Department at the Kansas City, Mo., Public Library). Library
Journal 88:3789-94, October 15, 1963.   97

C. Loud and Soft Learning (Tape Recordings)
Radio Active Library. Floyd M. Cammack
(University Librarian at Oakland University,
Rochester, Michigan). Library Journal 90:
4300-2, October 15, 1965.   106

Oral History: A New Horizon. Elizabeth I.

Dixon (Librarian, Office of Oral History, University of California Library, Los Angeles). Library Journal 87:1363-5, April 1, 1962. 110

Language Lab in the Library. James H. Smith (Librarian, Highland Park High School, Highland Park, Illinois). Library Journal 86: 1656-7, April 15; Junior Libraries 7:20-1, April 1961. 114

Language Courses on Magnetic Tape: A New Reference Service. M.J. Harkin (Librarian, Language and Literature Library, Manchester Public Libraries). Library Association Record 68:161-5, May 1966. 116

World Tapes for Education--a Resource for Elementary School Libraries. Walter W. Williamson. Top of the News 21:311-17, June 1965. 125

Reading for the Blind at a New Frontier. Lee E. Grove (Director of Publications, Council of Library Resources). ALA Bulletin 55:744, September 1961. 133

Classification of Four-Track Tapes. Allen Cohen (Fellow in the Music Library, City College of New York). Library Resources & Technical Services 6:360-1, Fall 1962. 136

A Proposed Information Retrieval System for Sound Recordings. C.B. Hagen (Head of the Map Library at U.C.L.A.; owner and operator of a recording studio). Special Libraries 56:223-8, April 1965. 139

Section II. The Printed Word and Non-Word
A. Gems in Small Packages (Pamphlets)
Pamphlets: Problem or Blessing? I. Elizabeth Stafford (School Library Supervisor, Port Chester, New York). Top of the News 18:21-3, May 1962. 149

The Information File in the Secondary School. Sister M. Thomas Eulberg, O.S.F. (Mount St. Francis, Dubuque, Iowa). Catholic Library World 33:101-2+, October 1961. 153

Keeping Up with Pamphlets. Ruth B. Ferguson (Librarian, Mapleton Branch, Brooklyn Public Library) and Elizabeth Ferguson (Librarian, Institute of Life Insurance, New York City). Library Journal 86:1642-3,

Page

April 15; Junior Libraries 7:6-7, April
1961.   157

Building a Vocational Information File. Marianne Schmidt (Reference Librarian of the
Dearborn, Michigan, Public Library). Wilson Library Bulletin 33:231-2+, November
1958.   162

The Pamphlet in the University Library. Jack
King (Serials Cataloger, University of Min-
nesota; formerly Assistant in the Special
Collections Department, University of Iowa).
Library Resources & Technical Services
10:51-6, Winter 1966.   167

Don Mills Uses Dewey to Classify Pamphlets.
Reginald A. Rawkins (Head Librarian of the
Don Mills Regional Branch of North York
Public Library). Ontario Library Review
50:14-15, February 1966.   175

Dewey Pamphlets. Ruth Corner (Head, Adult
Services, York Township Public Library).
Ontario Library Review 50:84-5, June 1966.   178

A Survey of Vertical Files in California Public
High School Libraries.   Marie L. Graycar
(Librarian at Lynbrook High School, Sunny-
vale, California). California School Libraries
37:26-7, May 1966.   180

B. Wordless Wonders (Art Works)
A Picasso in Every Library. Donald L. Foster
(Cataloger at the University of Illinois Li-
brary). Wilson Library Bulletin 37:58-60+,
September 1962.   183

Aurora Loans Art Pictures. Eleanor Plain (Librarian, Aurora Public Library). Illinois
Libraries 44:151-3, February 1962.   188

Circulating Art Collections. Gordon Bebeau
(Director, Appleton Public Library). Wisconsin Library Bulletin 62:168, May 1966.   191

Eskimo Art in a Community College Library.
Bernard C. Rink (Librarian of Northwestern
Michigan College). College and Research Li-
braries 25:113-4, March 1964.   193

Experimentation with an Image Library. Dr.
Stanley T. Lewis (Art Librarian of the Paul
Klapper Library, Queens College of the City
University of New York).   Special Libraries
56:35-8, January 1965.   196

Regional Art As a Library Service. Michael
Ligocki (An artist and writer; has published
articles in magazines as diverse as American Mercury, Popular Science Monthly, and
Grade Teacher). ALA Bulletin 55:882-4,
November 1961. 201
Picasso in the Nursery. Oscar Teller (Director of Art Education Inc., Greenwich,
Conn.). Library Journal 89:4986-8, December 15; School Library Journal 11:36-
8, December 1964. 205
The Original Print. Robert E. Cain (Supervisor of Reference Services at the Cary
Memorial Library in Lexington, Mass.;
previously in charge of the exhibits and
public relations program of the Library).
Library Journal 91:5323-6, November 1,
1966. 209
C. The Built-In Teacher (Programmed Learning
Courses)
Programmed Learning '64. Philip Lewis (Director, Research, Development and Special
Projects, Chicago Public Schools). Illinois
Libraries 46:109-15, February 1964. 215
Agorithmic Mathetical Reinforcement; the
Implications of Programmed Instruction for
the Librarian. Ralph D. Gee, F. L. A.
(Technical Librarian, The National Cash
Register Company). This is the Library
Association prize essay, 1965. Library
Association Record 67:228-32, July 1965. 220
D. Music for the Making (Printed Notes)
Bibliography's Stepchild: The Printed Note.
Donald W. Krummel (Associate Librarian
at the Newberry Library, Chicago). Library Journal 90:1249-54, March 15, 1965. 230
Music in Medium-sized Libraries. Gordon
Stevenson (Head of the Art and Music Department at the Kansas City, Mo., Public
Library). Library Journal 90:1255-8,
March 15, 1965. 238
The Cost of Imported Scores. Gordon Stevenson (Head of the Art and Music Department
at the Kansas City, Mo., Public Library).
Library Resources & Technical Services
6:320-31, Fall 1962. 245

E. Worlds at Your Fingertips (Maps)
The Problem of Maps. Lloyd A. Brown
(Author of Early Maps of the Ohio Valley
and Notes on the Care and Cataloging of
Old Maps). Library Trends 13:215-25,
October 1964.   260

The Management of Map Collections and Libraries in University Geography Departments. A.M. Ferrar, B.Sc. (Department
of Geography, University of Leeds). Library Association Record 64:161-5, May
1962.   271

Problems in the Map Room. Theodore H.
Layng (Chief of the Map Division of the
Public Archives of Canada). Canadian Li-
brary 18:63-6, September 1961.   280

Geography and Map Cataloging and Classifica-
tion in Libraries. Dr. Arch C. Gerlach
(Chief, Map Division, Library of Congress,
Washington). Special Libraries 52:248-51,
May 1961.   286

Section III. Research Rarities
A. Verbatim! (Ephemeral Materials)
On Ephemera: Their Collection and Use.
Richard C. Berner (Curator of Manuscripts,
University of Washington Library, Seattle).
Library Resources & Technical Services
7:335-9, Fall 1963.   292

"File 13." L.O. Lewton (Head, Technical
Literature Section, Riker Laboratories Inc.,
Northridge, California). Special Libraries
57:58, January 1966.   298

Snipping Is No Snap. John R. Snider (Director
of News and Public Affairs, Radio Station
WTTS, Bloomington, Indiana). Focus on
Indiana Libraries 20:7-8, March 1966.   300

B. In the Original (Manuscripts)
Manuscript Collections. Robert L. Brubaker
(Curator of Manuscripts at the Illinois State
Historical Library, Springfield). Library
Trends 13:226-53, October 1964.   303

Some Fundamentals in Arranging Archives and
Manuscript Collections. Jean L. Finch (Reference Librarian, New York Public Library;
formerly of Bancroft Library of the University of California and of Manuscript Staff,

University of Washington). Library Resources & Technical Services 8:26-34,
Winter 1964.   332

Cataloging Small Manuscript Collections. Michael Jasenas (Rare Book Librarian, Cornell
University Libraries, Ithaca, New York).
Library Resources & Technical Services
7:264-73, Summer 1963.   342

C. The Lasting Likeness (Pictures, Photographs)

Pictures in Your Company's Archives. Betty
Hale (Information Researcher, Public Relations Department of Socony Mobil Oil Company, Inc., New York City). Special Li-
braries 56:41, January 1965.   354

Cataloging a Photograph Collection. Jane Howe
(Division of Manuscripts, University of Oklahoma). Oklahoma Librarian 13:8-12, January
1963.   356

Pictures for Public Relations. Irene Simpson
(Director of the History Room at Wells Fargo Bank, San Francisco, California). Spe-
cial Libraries, 56:39-40, January 1965.   364

May We Use This Picture?--Rights and Permissions. Helen Faye (Chief Art Editor at
Harcourt, Brace and World Inc. and Chairman of the Picture Division of S.L.A.).
Special Libraries 56:23-6, January 1965.   367

Section IV. Synthesis for Service

A/V: Has It Any Future in Libraries? Harold Goldstein (Professor of Library Science
at University of Illinois; Chairman of ALA's
Media Research and Development Committee).
Wilson Library Bulletin 36:670-3+, April
1962.   373

Fear of the Newer Media. A.W. VanderMeer
(Associate Dean of the College of Education,
Pennsylvania State University). ALA Bulle-
tin 55:798-802, October 1961.   381

Organizing Library-based A-V Materials. Joan
Pressler (Librarian at the Jefferson Junior
High School in Mt. Lebanon, Pa.). School
Libraries 14:43-6, March 1965.   389

Cataloging Nonbook Materials. Doris M. Car-
son (Cataloger and Assistant Professor,
Wichita State University). Wilson Library
Bulletin 39:562-4, March 1965.   396

Page

Filing Miscellaneous Materials. June Berry
(Librarian at the Laboratory School at Brig-
ham Young University, Provo, Utah). Library Journal 87:818-20, February 13;
School Library Journal 8:18-20, February
1962.   402

Get the Monkey Off Your Back!! Thomas W.
Roberts (Audiovisual Director, Wayne State
University, Detroit). Educational Screen and
Audiovisual Guide 44:25+, May 1965.   407

Choosing Audio-Visual Equipment. Wendell W.
Simons (Assistant University Librarian, Uni-
versity of California, Santa Cruz, California).
Library Trends 13:503-16, April 1965.   410

Recent Developments in Instructional Technology.
Philip Lewis (Director, Bureau of Research,
Development and Special Projects, Chicago
Public Schools). Illinois Libraries 47:107-
13, February 1965.   424

Author Index   429
Subject Index   431

Introduction

Though perhaps the first thing the word "library" calls to mind is books, in order to do its job well the library must provide other materials as well. Public Library Service; A Guide to Evaluation, with Minimum Standards states: "In addition to books, the public library selects and provides pamphlets, documents and other nonbook sources in printed form, and films, tapes, discs and other nonprint recording of knowledge and opinion."[1]

Objectives and Standards for Special Libraries states: "Physically, the collection may include a variety of forms and types of materials, not all of which are appropriate to a particular special library; books, pamphlets, preprints, reprints, translations, dissertations and theses; periodicals, newspapers, press releases, indexing, abstracting, and other services, transactions, yearbooks, reports, directories of organizations; external and internal technical reports; research and laboratory notebooks, archival materials; patents, trademarks, specifications, and standards; audio-visual materials (photographs, slides, pictures, motion pictures, filmstrips, tape and disc recordings); or special collections (maps, sheet music, manuscripts, catalogs, legislative materials, clippings, microforms)."[2]

Standards for College Libraries states: "The library's collection of books, periodicals, pamphlets, documents, newspapers, maps, microfilm, microcards, microprint, and other materials must be so constituted and organized as to give effective strength and support to the educational program of the institution... Printed, manuscript, and archival materials pertaining to the institution of which the library is a part should be collected and preserved... Audiovisual materials including films, filmstrips, recordings and tapes are an integral part of modern instruction, and every college library must concern itself with them. The library should take the initiative for providing them, if no other agency on campus has been assigned this responsibility."[3]

A statement about audio-visual materials in Standards for Junior College Libraries is similar to that above, but the list of types of materials is slightly more detailed: "...Audio-visual materials may include films, filmstrips,

13

slides, tapes, recordings in music, drama, speech, and foreign languages..."[4]

Standards for School Library Programs states:
"[The collections of printed materials should include]...an
extensive collection of pamphlets covering a wide range of
subjects... [The audio-visual collection should include] a
sufficient number of all types of audio-visual materials for
use in the classrooms, in the school library, and for home
use; films used six or more times a year are purchased;
filmstrips and recordings used more than once a year are
purchased."[5]

Nonbook materials, like books, are provided for a
broad range of purposes: to facilitate informal self-education; to support educational curricula and to enrich and further develop the subjects on which individuals are undertaking formal education; to meet informational needs; to support
the educational, civic, and cultural activities of groups and
organizations; to encourage wholesome recreation and con-
structive use of leisure time; to meet the highly specialized
needs of researchers, scholars, businessmen and professionals.

In order to make an intelligent decision about including a given type of nonbook material in the collection and
services of a given library, the librarian needs to have some
knowledge of the specific type of material: What are its
idiosyncrasies, its potential uses? What problems have been
encountered with it and how have such problems been solved
effectively? What are its values and costs, its sources of
selection and acquisition, methods of cataloging, classifying,
and storing? For what types of library, library purposes,
and library users has it been found worthwhile? What experiments have been or are being conducted with it? The
articles in this book, selected with these questions in mind,
cover the following types of materials: films, filmstrips,
slides, phonograph records, tape recordings, pamphlets, art
works, programmed learning courses, printed music, maps,
clippings and other ephemeral materials, manuscripts, and
pictures and photographs.

It is hoped that librarians who are considering a possible addition of nonbook materials to a library, or who are
faced with some problems in collecting and administering
such materials, or who just want to survey possibilities with
a view to the future, will find this book helpful. The articles relate the experiences of librarians in various types of
libraries and the conclusions drawn from them, as well as
the observations of a few non-librarians. The aim is to offer a broad perspective on many nonbook materials while al-

so treating each one in sufficient depth to be of practical
value to librarians.

Jean Spealman Kujoth
Milwaukee, Wisconsin
March, 1967

Notes

1. American Library Association. Public Library Service;
   A Guide to Evaluation, with Minimum Standards. Chicago, American Library Association, 1956. P. 3.
2. "Objectives and Standards for Special Libraries." In
   Bowker Annual of Library and Book Trade Information, 1966. New York, Bowker, 1965. Pp. 132-3.
3. "Standards for College Libraries." In American Library
   and Book Trade Annual, 1961. New York, Bowker,
   1960. Pp. 119-121. (This set of standards was approved by the Board of Directors of the Association
   of College and Research Libraries, and is now an official document of the American Library Association.)
4. "Standards for Junior College Libraries." In American
   Library and Book Trade Annual, 1961. New York,
   Bowker, 1960. P. 129. (These standards were prepared by the Committee on Standards, ACRL, and approved by the ACRL Board in 1960.)
5. "A Summary of the Major Quantitative Standards for
   School Library Programs." In American Library and
   Book Trade Annual, 1961. New York, Bowker, 1960.
   P. 115. (Standards for School Library Programs was
   published by the American Library Association in 1960
   to replace the National Standards for School Libraries
   set in 1945.)

The articles in this section deal with audio-visual materials, whose chief value lies in the immediacy of experience that they register upon the eye and the ear. Included
in this group are films, filmstrips, slides, phonograph records, and tape recordings. These media serve educational,
recreational, and archival purposes, as is shown in the articles in this section, which describe and evaluate the experiences of public, school, university, and college libraries.

Films in the Large Public Library
George M. Holloway

From Educational Screen and Audio-visual Guide 42:620-1,
November 1963. Reprinted by permission.

The responsibilities of the public library in the field
of adult education continue to multiply with each new learning
aid and technological discovery. Nevertheless, libraries,
particularly large city libraries, must continually justify their
existence in the audio-visual field. Sixteen-millimeter motion picture film, being the most costly of the audio-visual
media, is with very few exceptions the last to be added to
the public library's collections. Joseph Wheeler and Herbert Goldhor, in their recent text on public library administration,[1] advise spending five percent of the materials budget on audio-visual materials. Known to be conservative in
recommending the use of films in the public library, they
add that libraries of cities over 50,000 persons should have
a total annual budget of at least two dollars per capita support before venturing into a film library. This is still well
below the ALA's recommended $3.50 per capita for merely
adequate library support. There may be some significance
to this. There is no better means of promoting good will
and focusing attention on the library in a positive way than
through an active films service. This activity promotes
great interest in the library and may often result in increased
appropriations.
The public library does not advance new ideas in the

16

field of communication; however, it recognizes the value to
society of tried-and-true methods in this field and makes
good use of them.   Establishment of film collections in
eighty-one U.S. cities of over 50,000 population is an example of such alertness on the library's part to community
needs. [2]
     The most important role of the film librarian is in
the selection process.   Although more involved than book selection, film selection is also an individual process; however,
it is more effective when group selection methods are used,
such as screening committees.   Not only is a thorough
knowledge of the library's objectives and philosophy required
of a film selector, but he must appreciate the artistic qualities of film production and must understand the roles films
are to assume in the community.   In cities where screening
committees have not been organized, librarians rely heavily
on the ALA's Audio-Visual Committee selections, which appear in The Booklist and the committee's recent publication,
Films for Libraries. [3]
     In selecting films, the public librarian looks for films
which convey information, arouse discussion, and provide
stimulating experiences.   He avoids the classroom approach
film (the slow, deliberate narrator, and printed titles for
clarity and emphasis).   There is some evidence that straight-
forward teaching films may relinquish their position in the
classroom to closed-circuit television and programmed learning, while the professional teacher's job is supplemented by
imaginative, stimulating films.   The insatiable appetite of
Philadelphia elementary and secondary school teachers for
the Free Library's films partially supports this viewpoint.
In order not to compete with the School District's collection
of classroom films, and to hold down the service to a manageable degree, we allow elementary and secondary schools
to use our films only in assembly programs and for extra-
curricular activities.
     We do not mean to imply that our films are only for
entertainment and do not give information, nor that they are
technically better than those films which follow the standard
classroom format.   We do say that culturally stimulating
film produced in a new, often experimental, manner is primarily intended for adult audiences.   Nevertheless, the elementary and secondary schools account for twenty percent of
our film use.   College and other formal adult education
classes borrow seventeen percent; churches borrow eighteen
percent; the business community borrows three percent.
     Librarians are concerned with proper use of their
films.   We require written reports from borrowers; we talk

to program chairmen before and after their programs; we
sponsor workshops on the use of film with adults; and we
try to set an example of good programs in the library itself.
There is probably no other library department that keeps
such close contact with its borrowers as does the film lending service.   This relationship provides valuable insight into program needs and so provides a guide for the film selector.   We can also familiarize ourselves with the borrowing
agencies through their annual reports, feature articles in the
local newspapers, and radio and television interviews.   In a
large city the service agencies are numerous and varied,
and often very specialized in their community goals.   They
account for almost half of our film use here in Philadelphia.

While other service agencies borrow library films to
enhance and extend their own objectives (often combining a
library film with their own public relations film), the library
plans film programs in its own buildings for several reasons:
to accent some special collection; to join in celebrating historic events; and most often for adult education through film
and book discussion.   The latter program's format consists
of a short book talk related to the subject of the film or
films, or a film which presents a topic of current social
significance and a guest expert to lead discussion.   The object of all the library film programs is to lead the person
to interesting books to enrich his experience.

Film programming and film selection require a thorough knowledge of the cultural life of the community.   The
film librarian is concerned with other film sources in the
city and compiles a local availability file or a union catalog
of films, as the Free Library has done in Philadelphia.
We discovered approximately 5200 16mm film titles and over
15,000 prints available in fifty local film libraries.   The aid
provided by the union catalog is obvious.   Films are expensive.   In a small city the local film resources will very likely be known to the film purchaser; in the large city, a union
catalog can save unnecessary duplication of expensive titles.
In Philadelphia there are several highly specialized film collections.   For example, there are three on automobile safety alone.   The Free Library purchases very little in such
fields.   On the other hand, no collection of children's story
films exists in Philadelphia; therefore the Free Library has
emphasized the purchase of such films, which now constitute
ten percent.   The union catalog is on 3 x 5 cards and is
available to the film user through personal visit to the department or by phone.

Public librarians can expect extra benefits from providing an active films service: good public relations and

frequent publicity; a focus for community attention on library services; pride and satisfaction in contributing to the cultural development of the community.

Through the creative use of films, librarians play an important role in advancing specific community concerns, in increasing one's understanding of the world around us, and in influencing people's opinions. The film librarian, while equipped with the skills of specialization, has the opportunity of a wide view of the world.

Notes

1. Practical Administration of Public Libraries. New York, Harper, 1962.
2. U.S. Department of Health, Education, and Welfare. Key Audio-visual Personnel Washington, Govt. Print. Off., 1961.
3. Chicago, American Library Association, 1962.

Films for a Purpose
Ray E. Howser

From Illinois Libraries 44:109-12, February 1962. Reprinted by permission.

Now that more than forty public libraries in Illinois have established film service, it is desirable to reflect on the reasons why librarians entered into this activity.

There is a need in most communities for some agency to provide films on serious subjects for adult education utilization. What agency is better suited to that purpose than the public library? Films for films' sake is not a valid concept, but films which provoke and stimulate thinking, discussion, and action are important to a society that is being required at every turn to assume world leadership. It was the serious use of films by adults that, preceding World War II, sparked the drive within ALA to encourage film service in public libraries. According to an ALA Adult Services Division Report, Film Utilization, published in June, 1960, it would seem that many public libraries have lost sight of this original purpose and consequently their film service lacks a definite orientation toward adult education. We can assume this report does not reflect on film service in downstate Illinois, since the findings were based on research conducted in 1954-1955, a time when only a handful of Illinois libraries were involved and, to the best of my knowledge, were not included in the sample of libraries studied. If the sampling had included the Quad City Film Cooperative (headquarters at Moline) and the Peoria Public Library, the findings would have been considerably altered. Nevertheless, the report should serve as a warning not to lose sight of our main objective in public library film service--that of serving the adult education needs of our communities.

The key to the effective use of films with adult groups is training and experience. To be realistic, one must admit that training facilities are lacking. Most audio-visual courses are offered by teachers' colleges and these classes are designed to assist teachers in the use of nonbook materials in the formal classroom situation. The courses offered

20

in Illinois through our graduate library schools do not emphasize the group dynamic techniques of film use with adults.
Some librarians may find that agencies in their community,
namely the YMCA and YWCA, may offer a leadership training course which includes a unit on using films with adults.
Much of the literature on this subject needs revision, but
there are plenty of sources where basic instructions are
spelled out in clear, easy-to-understand terms.   One such
reference is Madeline S. Friedlander's Leading Film Discussions; A Handbook To Help Discussion Leaders To Use Films
and To Set Up and Conduct a Film Discussion Workshop,
League of Women Voters of the City of New York, 1958.   A
good bibliography is included in the ALA, Adult Services Division publication, Film Utilization, prepared by Margaret
Commiskey, June, 1960.

It is important to remember that librarians may not
actually be the ones who lead film discussions, but they
must know how in order to counsel intelligently those who
are responsible for such community programs.   As a member, I will recommend to the Audio-Visual Committee of the
Illinois Library Association that future conference program
time be allotted for workshops where the group dynamics of
film use can be discussed and demonstrated.

Adult education use of films in a community depends
on the right kind of films being available.   First purchases
need to include good general information films, plus some
titles for use with children's groups, in order to establish
rapport with the community.   Is it not, however, the more
serious provocative film that should receive priority?   A
quick look at the Recommended Basic List of Films for Public Libraries, published in this issue, will show that it mentions a sampling of titles that are powerful tools for serious
adult education use when put into the hands of a skilled discussion leader.   Titles such as Challenge of Ideas, Preparation for Later Years, Community Responsibilities, The Key,
Roots of Happiness, and the Ages and Stages series, along
with others, are all excellent adult films designed to stimulate thinking.   The discussion will come after a film showing, but it does not happen as spontaneous reaction--at least
not often.   How then can audiences be led into meaningful
discussion?

We start with the showing of the film itself.   There
is a technique and a correct procedure for arranging the
projector, speaker, and screen.   All of these items are not
mere refinements, but are basic to a correct film showing
and make the difference between an attentive audience and
one that is distracted by annoyances to the point where effec-

tive communication breaks down.   I recommend that all librarians working with films see and follow the instructions
given in these two films, <u>Facts about Projection</u> and <u>Facts
about Film</u>.   Both are available for sale or rental from the
International Film Bureau, Inc., 332 So. Michigan Avenue,
Chicago 4, Illinois.   The general audio-visual textbooks and
many special manuals and handbooks devote considerable
space to this subject.

The film production itself has much to do with the
discussibility index of the film.   A good discussion film does
not attempt to provide all the answers; in fact, many provide no solutions at all to the problems posed.   Many will
depict two opposing points of view and leave the audience to
identify itself with one or the other, or bring out other
points of view.   Sometimes a provocative film will almost
lead its audience to a conclusion, then suddenly end, or perhaps neglect to mention a seemingly obvious solution to a
problem.   These remissions on the first hand seem irresponsible, but they often provoke sudden, decisive discussion
when the room lights come on.   With all problematic films,
authoritativeness is a must and the action must not seem to
be contrived.   Films which use the documentary approach
strive hard to relate to the actualities through imaginative
insight.   If they achieve this, they are also works of art.

Truthfulness, explicitness, and fairmindedness are
three qualities of a good discussion film.   An overemphasis
on artistic synthesis can ruin what might otherwise have been
a good discussion film.   This is not to be confused with good
camera and editing techniques or a dramatic approach if it
is needed.   In the film <u>The High Wall</u>, for example, the subject of prejudice is handled with powerful and dramatic impact, well conceived to cause its viewers to think, to question, and to form a definite opinion.   A film such as <u>Picture
in Your Mind</u>, which also deals with prejudice, is artistically
a beautiful work of animation, but loses some of its force
because of its sophisticated artistry.   The desirable length
for a discussion film is a matter for further research, but
audiences can be overtaxed if a lengthy film introduces too
many details, too many points of view, too many contributing
factors.   I have heard some argue that <u>Face of Red China</u>
is too long for effective group discussion; others argue that
the subject warrants the film's fifty minutes of power-packed
documentation.   In my opinion it is a valuable information
film, but too long, too involved, to provoke effective discussion.

Preparing an audience for serious consideration of a
film lessens the risk that they will settle back in their seats

with the attitude, "I will now be entertained." This necessitates preview and study of the film beforehand on the part
of the leader. The introduction can and will be varied, depending on each leader's techniques, but it should not be a
synopsis or a preconceived opinion. The introduction should
state the reason for the group's coming together, the purpose in seeing a film on the subject, and words to the effect
that follow-up discussion is desirable. The film's title and
credits can be given and some general descriptive remarks
can be made, but these should be brief and should not be
all-revealing. Present, if at all possible in the introduction,
any known facts about the film which verify its authorship.
Who are its sponsors; who, if any, were the collaborators
or consultants; who produced the film?

After the film has been shown, discussion can be
stimulated by referring to essential points made in the film,
by posing a question, by using various methods of dividing
the group into smaller groups, assigning specific roles to
each group with a report-back time limit. There are many,
many more discussion leadership techniques that librarians
need to master, and the literature of adult education can supply much of this, but practice--actually doing, making mis-
takes, and correcting them--is the only way to become an
effective film discussion leader. Start with smaller groups
first, maybe with a few people you know. This will build
your confidence and give you practice for those larger groups,
and the confidence in your own ability to lead makes the
most unfriendly face in the audience look harmless.

The intelligent use of serious films with adults can be
a major contribution to the total adult education role of the
library. Going through the motions is not enough--much
more is expected of us at a time when the very best may be
too late.

Slides and Filmstrips Add Service
F. A. White

From Wisconsin Library Bulletin 62:162-3, May 1966. Reprinted by permission.

Filmstrips and slides, if properly prepared, selected, and used, can aid almost every teacher in communicating with students and can contribute to programming for public library and community groups.

There is a wide range of material available, from children's literature to flower growing, covering many aspects of the school curriculum. Filmstrips or slides on gardening, travel and history, for example, make excellent supplementary programming devices for public library borrowers such as study clubs, church groups, and youth organizations.

The preparation of filmstrips and slide sets is usually the responsibility of professionals who work carefully in assembling the combination of visual materials and appropriate verbal symbols. The professional also has access to wider resources than the amateur, such as photographs and art work, and can field test the filmstrip to determine needed visuals and captions. The result is an arrangement which is literally certain to be a logical and complete informational or recreational sequence.

Filmstrips are often more useful than slides, since they are series of slides organized for ease of showing, handling, and continuity of information. In the field of art, however, slides might be more practical. Because of variation in the quality of filmstrips available, it is advisable to compare like productions on a subject before purchasing.

Many public libraries which cannot, because of limited financial resources, provide film service, find it possible to supply these less costly audio-visuals. As with any new service, however, the budget must provide funds for the proper selection, utilization, storage, and maintenance of these items.

Instructional materials staff members work with teachers in making slides and filmstrips available for teaching purposes. They must be selected for a particular teaching

situation where specific learning is expected to occur, and
be completely curriculum oriented.   Previewing is a must.
        Since the mechanics of presentation are important,
materials center or library staff members who supervise
equipment should be sure that equipment is in good order,
and that users know how to operate and handle it properly.
        Students can use filmstrips and slides individually
with a minimum of assistance by the librarian.   They can
operate the equipment, and individual carrels are often provided for this purpose.   Sometimes the equipment and the
materials are in open shelf storage, sometimes at a control
desk.   The open shelf method is the logical and preferred
method from the standpoint of use and administration.
        The use or nonuse of filmstrips and slides is deter-
mined by both the awareness teachers, students, and library
patrons have of materials available to them, and the ease
with which they can find what they want.   Having filmstrips
in open racks reminds everyone of their availability and
makes scanning of titles easy.   Likewise, the storage of both
sets and individual slides in plastic pocket sheets makes it
very easy to see 25 slides at a time against the slide sorter
and thus to arrange a sequence quickly.
        Many libraries have found it convenient to house strip
collections in standard filmstrip file cases with simple numerical indexing.   Very frequently colored subject and title
cards for filmstrips are inserted in the card catalog beside
cards for printed materials.   Instead of a Dewey class number, the drawer number and the numerical assignment of the
strip within the drawer, or a simple numerical sequence, indicates location of the strip.   On the other hand, many libraries prefer to classify filmstrips as they do books.   If
printed catalogs are made, they can be organized under the
standard Sears or Library of Congress subject headings and
thus related closely to the catalog for books.
        Maintenance of filmstrips is far simpler than that for
films; damage occurs less frequently; damaged filmstrips
can be replaced at low cost; and strip projectors and previewers are simple to operate.
        Methods of circulating strips and slides vary.   One
common method in public libraries is the visible file, which
becomes unwieldy as the collection grows.   A better method
is inexpensive reproduction by mimeograph or other means
of a simply designed card form, possibly of a distinctive
color, which for circulation purposes can be handled like a
book card.
        With good preparation, convenient storage, curriculum
or community-based selection and wise utilization, filmstrips

and slides can increase the efficiency of educational communication.

Film Evaluation and Criticism
James L. Limbacher

From <u>Illinois Libraries</u> 46:121-5, February 1964. Reprinted by permission.

I am not a librarian working in audio-visual, but rather an audio-visual person working in a library. My statements result from my personal observations made in the course of a long career in this field. Ever since I began working as a high school projectionist, I have been involved in the audio-visual field.

In the last few years, there have been such rapid developments in the field that audio-visual work has become a profession, almost without our realizing the fact. Yet only a few years have passed since that time when a person who was tired of working on the reference desk could become an audio-visual librarian by default. When most of our present libraries were built, few people suspected that films, records, projected books, filmstrips, and related material would become part of so many public libraries.

In view of the growing importance of audio-visual aids, we audio-visual people are now in a position to strive for equal status with other library departments in such matters as higher professional standards, improved facilities, and increased budgets. And how do equal status and higher professional standards relate to evaluation and criticism? The answer is that with better financial support, better facilities, and professionally trained staffs, we audio-visual directors will be able to more effectively perform the basic tasks of serving the public and developing good collections.

Many of us tend to forget that we have a public to serve. Matters that are second nature to us are completely cryptic to our patrons. In fairness to our patrons, there is no reason why audio-visual materials cannot be cataloged more simply and made available to the borrower more quickly. No matter what care we take in the selection and evaluation of materials, our efforts are ineffective if the public, not understanding what we are doing, is unwilling to utilize our service.

Jack Ellis, of Northwestern University, speaking in Chicago at the Educational Film Association Workshop last

year, stated that reviewers, critics, and evaluators are dif-
ferentiated thus: a reviewer is concerned with his personal
tastes and his own emotional reactions; a critic works out
standards and analyzes the medium as a form of expression;
the evaluator follows the general principles of a critic but
analyzes and evaluates each film in terms of general or specific use and audience.

The majority of us, as audio-visual directors, fulfill
the function of evaluator, and it is an important responsibility. We must have a set of basic criteria to use in making
our selections, and we must, at the same time, allow some
flexibility for our own tastes and those of the community.
The same films will not necessarily appeal to every community which has audio-visual materials available. Here, then,
are twelve points which experience has taught me to use as
guideposts in the evaluation and selection of film for inclusion in public library collections.

Is It Best Presented As a Film? Is the medium used
creatively and strongly? Does it use the unique power of the
medium to good advantage? Can it best be done on film, or
would it be more effective as a filmstrip? Does the narration tell everything? In this case, might the material have
more value as a phonograph record?

I do not mean that a film made up of still pictures
would be better as a set of slides. The artistry of presentation determines whether the work is creative or merely a
movie made from slides. A well-made film can arouse a
response in the viewer that the printed page cannot duplicate.
The same film can stimulate the viewer to consult other media in order to develop or reinforce an idea arising from a
film. Thus, it is important that we realize the unique values of the motion picture.

Subject. Is the film similar to other films in the collection? Does it present an entirely different approach to
the same subject? Are there other films available, which
give the subject better treatment? Is the subject worth including in the collection?

The importance of having a well-rounded library of as
many different subjects as possible cannot be emphasized too
strongly, especially for smaller libraries, which cannot afford to have too many films dealing with one subject. In
viewing several different films on the same subject, consider
which one best fits the needs of your particular community.
It is a real mistake to fill the library with films of great
similarity, and it is a waste of the taxpayers' money. Obviously, several prints of one title deprive the community of
several other films on equally interesting subjects.

Interest. Is the film interesting? Does it "feel" theatrical or instructional? Will the community enjoy having this film available?

A public library is not a school, but rather a center of information. For this reason most audio-visual departments should be directed toward the interests and needs of the mature teen-agers and the adults. Few adults are interested in seeing films which are graded for school use, and not many of them will knowingly accept being "educated" by a film. Only the most creative and interesting films of a general instructional nature belong in the public library film collection. Those who select films for public libraries must also ask: who will use this film? The school which uses films has a captive audience, and the teacher and pupils share a common interest. Members of the community are likely to have any number of different interests. Ideally, the library collection should have a film to satisfy each one.

Techniques. Is the film well photographed? Is the sound audible? Do optical and visual techniques clarify transition from one idea to another? If narration is necessary, is it good? Does it synchronize with the visuals? Has color been so well used as to justify the additional cost? Can a film fail to meet these criteria and still be a valuable film?

Of course it can. Pow Wow is an unsynchronized, crudely photographed film--made for fifteen dollars. It is a joy to watch, a biting commentary on contemporary life. Primary, Lonely Boy, and Sunday feature shaky, hand-held cameras, overlapping dialogue, and cluttered sound tracks, yet they provide the viewer with images of such on-the-spot excitement, that they will probably become documentary classics. In other words, there are times when the subject is more important than the technique or lack of it.

Content. Is the film saying something you would like to know? Is it telling you something you did not know, or does it tell it in a new way? Is the presentation accurate and unbiased? What does it contribute to you as a person?

A film called Operation Abolition was so distorted in its presentation as to force libraries which bought it to buy two other films to counteract it. A good film must be basically truthful in order to interest all viewers without raising the cry of "bias." If the picture is one-sided, the commentary should indicate the fact. Otherwise, the audio-visual director must describe the film in his catalog as one-sided, but so technically excellent that it was acquired for the library collection.

Censorship. No one appreciates being pressured,
threatened, or persecuted over film selection. The best defense when this happens is to state that all films purchased
fill existing needs in both the library and the community.
Actually it is a high compliment to have some pressure
group become irate about a certain film; it indicates that the
library's film collection has become an important force in
the community. When a library purchases a controversial
film, an irate citizen will sometimes protest that his tax
money is being misused. This type of pressure--whether
from individuals or groups--should be resisted whenever possible. In order to fight censorship, the audio-visual director needs the backing of a strong head librarian as well as
that of the library board. Without this he might as well
change his profession. The film librarian who must worry
constantly about offending his audience is of no value to his
library or to the audio-visual field in general. The Dearborn Public Library contains films dealing with a great many
controversial subjects, yet none of the citizens has questioned their use. Frequently the same person who objects to
films on controversial subjects finds no fault with books on
the same topics, another indirect compliment to the impact
of the motion picture in comparison to that of the printed
page. One fact does emerge about censorship: an individual
has the right to avoid any film he does not wish to see, but
he has no right to prevent others from seeing it, if this is
their wish. To quote from the EFLA Film Evaluation Conference, "The question arose concerning any situation in
which a member of the community might blame the librarian
for showing an immoral film . . . arbitrarily immoral, that
is. The group thought that a librarian should not be a bland
individual and that he must assert himself concerning his
convictions as to the films he has chosen. "

Prejudice. Is a worthwhile film being ignored because of the personal philosophies of the film librarian?

The personality of the director is evident in the film
collection of every public library. Reading the film catalog
is an easy way to tell whether or not the audio-visual director has freedom of choice and whether he really enjoys the
films or merely tolerates them. It is necessary to put
aside personal feelings in order to provide films that present
both sides of a question. If a film tackles a subject in conflict with personal philosophies or prejudices, then they must
be sublimated in order to serve the best interests of the public.

Expense. How much does the film cost? Is it worth
the price? Are there less expensive films which are equally

good?

We must be always aware of our budgets and stay within them. If there is a good general film on a subject for $300 and an equally good one the same length for $150, then there is no reason whatsoever to choose the more expensive one. No public library has sufficient budget to allow for all the excellent films it needs; all film librarians must be bargain hunters without sacrificing quality and integrity in the process.

Appreciation. Does the film add to the viewer's appreciation of the picture as a medium of expression and as a visual art? Does it make a valuable contribution to the art of the film?

We must always remember that films are basically visual media. Every library should have a generous sprinkling of films whose images speak for themselves without dialogue or narration. Such films as Glass, Pacific 231, The Hunter and the Forest, Autumn Pastorale, A Divided World, Corral, Panta Rhei, Water's Edge, Swamp, Liquid Jazz, and the Norman McLaren films all give primary importance to the image. They speak volumes without uttering a single word.

Audio-Visual Diseases. There are several ailments to which audio-visual librarians are often exposed. Unless the director is inoculated with common sense and courage, they are highly contagious.

One such disease is "committeeitis." There is a vast difference between calling in experts to view a film and creating a committee to screen all films for possible acquisition. There is no justification for the existence of some film evaluation committees. Some members resent being on the committees, others are simply incompetent. Often a film becomes outdated before everyone has approved its purchase; sometimes a film never does get into a collection because the committee cannot agree on its usefulness.

"Age-levelitis" is another dread disease. If the librarian has been brainwashed in too many education classes, there is no cure. That long string of tags--elementary, junior high, senior high, college--in a public library film catalog shows that the librarian is "thinking school." Slotting and pigeonholing of films prevents their use by the largest number of viewers and hampers the creative programing that one should expect in a large audio-visual department. A good film, like a good painting, has no age level, and it will not look the same to any two people. The borrower should be given a chance to break away from the hamstringing influences of age levels. We should promote films on

their own merits.   For those who must know the age level
of a film, there are EFLA cards and producer's summaries
to use as guides.

Another audio-visual disease is "gripeitis." Instead
of taking advantage of what we do have, we tend to complain
about that which we lack.   Actually, we should be thankful
that our libraries have the foundation of an audio-visual department.   Using our present facilities creatively will help
to develop the kind of department we would like to have.

Audio-Visual Reference Aids.   Do we have all the
aids we need to answer our patrons' questions?   Can we
help a smaller library with information?

We study about audio-visual reference aids, but we
often ignore them when they are close at hand.   We should
do our best to get the most from the reviews and information on EFLA cards, in the Film Review Digest, Landers
Film Reviews, Educational Screen and Audio-Visual Guide,
Film World, Film News, The Booklist, and the New York
Times.   The value of the Film Daily Yearbook and the Educator's Guides to Free Films and Filmstrips cannot be ignored.

Participation.   There are times when the audio-visual
director must participate in activities which will broaden his
outlook.   He should try to attend the ALA audio-visual workshops, the EFLA workshops, the American Film Festival,
the audio-visual section of his own state library association.
Once in a while he must go to the movies.   There is no
reason to ignore theatrical films.   These are more familiar
to most of our patrons than the 16mm instructional films.
Audio-visual people who insist that they have not seen a good
Hollywood movie since Trader Horn must not have tried very
hard.   We can afford to be critical, but there is no need to
be snobbish regarding the influence of the theatrical film on
our society.   It is our responsibility to know what is showing at our local movie theaters and to give our patrons the
information by posting the Green Sheets and special information from Hollywood and the world film production centers.
We should have copies of Sight and Sound, Films and Filming, Film Daily, Film Culture, Film Quarterly, Film Society, Film Facts, Films in Review, Screen Facts, Variety,
and others on our shelves for the information of the public.
We should also gladly accept filmstrips on current Hollywood
productions.   If there is much interest in films in the community, the librarian should do everything possible to encourage this interest.   Organizing film forums or a film society, arranging for adult film showings under library spon-
sorship, are just two means of developing a critically en-

lightened public which is able to use library films more intelligently.

I believe that audio-visual directors and film librarians should never give the public what it wants. The public
does not really know what it wants, and it wants only that
to which it has been previously exposed. The real job of
the audio-visual director is to expose his community to the
different, the beautiful, the controversial, and the brilliant
films that are available. We are not simply suppliers of
films, we should also see that the films are used as con-
structively as possible by as many people as possible.

The Why and How of Film Circuits
Ida Goshkin

From A. L. A. Bulletin 55:545-8, June 1961. Reprinted by permission.

The film circuit, a cooperative system of providing films for small libraries, is one of the best things that has happened in libraries in a long time.

A film circuit usually consists of a group of libraries that have pooled their resources to provide film service for their communities. The films, 16mm sound, belong to the group, and the film collection is divided into as many sets as there are libraries. Each library uses a set of the films for a specified time, usually a month, then sends it on to the next library and gets a new set to circulate. In this way each library has the use of every film in the collection for a limited time each year. This round-robin schedule keeps the films rotating and in constant use.

The film circuit has advantages and disadvantages, and each library must weigh the factors involved. The most important advantage is that it makes films available in small libraries for use in small communities at a minimum fee. Film service is expensive, and many small libraries could not afford to have films unless there was some cooperative system for sharing the cost. By pooling resources they can provide films, constantly adding new titles to keep the collection alive and exciting. By rotating the films and having a large collection they avoid the saturation point that a small permanent collection reaches in a very short period in small communities.

A film circuit makes it possible to pay for the services of an experienced film librarian to administer the collection. This provides professional service in selection, processing, and maintenance of the collection. It makes possible lists, guides, and catalogs that are prepared and duplicated at a saving in time and library expense for the member libraries.

But film circuits also have their limitations. Each film is available in each library for a limited time. This means that groups may not have a specific film when they need it most. It also makes programing with films more difficult, but not impossible. It should invite more and better planning ahead, but of course this does not always follow. A film catalog that tells what titles will be available and on what dates is a good tool for urging patrons to plan their programs ahead. However, it does not provide for special needs or for special and frequently unplanned programs.

Another grave limitation is that films are selected on the basis of the general interest of many different communities. They cannot be selected for the needs of any specific community. Although most films selected are useful in most libraries, they may not be the ones needed most by a specific library, and it may be that some titles are never used in certain communities. Communities have different interests and needs. The individual community, I believe, suffers from this kind of mass film selection.

It is also much more difficult to maintain films in good condition when they are scattered in various libraries. Libraries vary as to their experience in the inspection and care of films, and the films get much harder use in a circuit than in a one-library collection.

How do film circuits operate? They vary in size, number of members, membership fee, cost of operation, policies, and administration. What follows is a description of the policies, methods, and administration of the film circuit I know best--the Ohio Valley Regional Film Library.

The Akron Public Library has a contract with the member libraries of our film circuit but is not a member of the circuit. This contract lists our responsibilities as the administering library, and those of the eleven member libraries. It specifies exactly what services we are to provide and it spells out to the members what they must do. The contract states the fee per library, the amount to be paid to the administering library for services rendered. See Cooperative Film Service in Public Libraries (ALA) by Patricia Cory and Violet Myer for sample contracts and budgets.

One of the first things the administering library did when it took over the film circuit was to present a written film selection policy to the members for approval. The members approved this policy, and it is used to evaluate films that are added to the collection. We consider this preselection of films our most important responsibility and contribution to the circuit, for the selection of films carries with it even more importance than the selection of books, if that is possible. Films affect the individual with the impact of visual images and sound. This makes it very important that we select films carefully and intelligently. We must be

able to distinguish the shoddy and dishonest from the significant and important. This is not easy. It takes many hours
of looking and studying to be able to understand what makes
a film good. A good film must have integrity, have something to say, and express it clearly and intelligently.

Film previewing goes on all through the year. In
January we begin preparing a list of films for possible purchase. This list is made up of films previewed and approved
during the year, and suggestions and requests from the librarians. The film collection is studied for gaps. What important subjects are not covered? Where does the collection
need to be strengthened? Does the collection have good balance between the information film, the opinion film, and
films that invite aesthetic appreciation?

A tentative purchase list, arranged by topics, is prepared and two copies are sent to each member library, one
to be returned to the administering library headquarters,
checked with preferences, the other for the library's own
file. As soon as the lists are returned, we cumulate the information on a master list. We then ask for a meeting of
representatives of the members to make the final selections.

This procedure points up one of the weaknesses of a
film circuit. Some of the members have an opportunity to
see some of the films, but not enough have the time to preview as many films as they should in order to do a good job
of selection.

Repairs during the circuit year are usually made by
the member libraries. Films needing major repairs, such
as replacement footage, are returned to headquarters. At
the end of the circuit year, which begins September 1 and
runs to August 1, the films are returned to headquarters.
After inventory, there begins the very time-consuming task
of film inspecting and screening to decide what to repair,
what to discard, and what to replace. We go over the condition cards (a file which gives the history of the film) after
the inspection, watch for recommendations of member libraries, and review the films that need re-evaluation. The
decisions are frequently difficult to make. Is the condition
of the film too poor for showing? Is it worth repairing, if
this means buying footage? Is the material too dated to replace? Should we just wait and "wear out"? Should we replace the title? Is there another film on the subject available and is it good enough to add? Or shall we wait for a
better film?

The new films are processed, the old films repaired,
cleaned, and inspected. As soon as we know the titles that
will be in the collection we prepare a tentative box list, a

list of titles that are selected to be used in each library for
a specific time.   The films in each box are different than in
past years, but still cover as many different subjects and
age levels as possible.   Each box contains films on travel,
child study, biography, science, children's films, at least
one film for teen-agers, and a few on important topics such
as the United Nations, race relations, and automation.   This
list permits the libraries to take bookings on films they expect to have for a certain period--routing schedules tell them
when they can expect a certain box of films.

As soon as the final decisions have been made on
what is to be discarded, replaced, or repaired, the final box
list is prepared and sent to the members.   This is usually
available toward the last of August.   Each box has a logbook
listing the films and their condition.

A film catalog is compiled, consisting of unassembled
sheets listing the films by box, including a title and subject
index.   The catalog gives the length, age level, states whether the film is in color or black-and-white, and has a descriptive annotation.   Each year a completely new catalog is
prepared.   The member libraries order the number of catalogs they want to purchase for distribution.

A monthly publication called <u>Circuit Lines</u> is another
means of communication.   It contains information on the
films, statistics on film circulation, and announces meetings
to be held.

The members have their own organization, with of-
ficers who call meetings to discuss their mutual problems.
They make the decisions on policy, consider and pass on the
allocation of the budget presented by the administrator, and
the financial statement presented at the end of the year.
They decide on the best type of insurance for the circuit,
what charges shall be made for damage to films, and the
service fee each shall charge.   The members decide on the
type of films and titles that shall be purchased for the collection.   The administrator carries out these policies.

On the whole, this circuit works very well.   It does
have certain weaknesses: 1) The members should be able to
preview more of the films they purchase.   2) There should
be some way for them to have more say in the discarding and
replacement of the films.   3) There should be more emphasis
on more effective use of films.   Workshops or programs of
various kinds should be developed to give those booking the
films an opportunity to get more training in their use.

I am impressed by the ability of librarians to work together.   The members of this film circuit have strong personal opinions about the films they want in their collection.

They express themselves freely with vigor and vehemence, but they also know how to compromise their differences for the good of the whole.

Originally my attitude toward film circuits was one of great skepticism, but I have changed my mind. I believe film circuits are important and serve a real need, especially in the small communities. It is important that people have access to a carefully selected film collection to counteract television and the "unscreened" free films that are used so much in club and organization meetings. These films fill the club programs with trite, unadorned advertisements to sell a product or a point of view. Members of a circuit can provide films that are accurate as to facts and imaginative in presentation, in order to help us better understand ourselves and our world.

Film circuits are playing an important part in bringing films into the small library. We need to be sure that they continue to develop with the same regard for high standards for which libraries are noted in their other services.

The LP and the Well-Appointed Library
Paul Henry Lang

From Library Journal 88:1809-12, May 1, 1963.   Reprinted by permission.

The book is the greatest symbol of culture and one of its most powerful voices, able to preserve and communicate ideas across time and space.   But while the book preserves the word, its own preservation is assured by the library. There was a time when books and the library were for many identical with human wisdom, and there still are some quiet circles where this piety is alive.   But it is difficult to maintain this devotion while our advancing industrial civilization saturates our minds with experiences and problems which preclude that inner calm the reader of earlier years could enjoy.   Now that the book is no longer the only source of wisdom, the variety of our life demands a vast extension both in the holdings and the services of the library.   The modern library helps us to understand the spiritual, historical, and cultural essence of man, but no longer in quite the old humanistic sense.

One of our great libraries carries the following inscription over its main entrance: "To provide enlightenment, to foster the prized traditions of human culture and achievement, to lead the minds of men and women."   A very excellent inscription this is, but no sooner do we start to elaborate on it than we run into difficulties of definitions and notions.

What are our great traditions of human culture and achievement?   Judging by the display of pulp magazines, soap operas, and so-called popular music, that is, the overwhelming commercial entertainment industry, we might have no traditions at all.   On the contrary, we appear to be creating new and questionable traditions for the future.   This argument may be countered by saying that these things represent neither science nor art, therefore they cannot be cited as indicative of our contemporary civilization.   Well, let us see.

The modern media of communication constitute today one of the most intensely cultivated fields of scientific endeavor.   Our radio, television, and phonograph sets become obsolete before their original tubes are worn out; our printing

presses, our photographic equipment, etc., are all improving
by leaps and bounds because the best scientific brains procur-
able are put to work on them. Thus we cannot say that this
mammoth industry is not representative of modern science.
However, the picture does change when we inquire into the
use this superbly contrived equipment is put to, for that, indeed, has only too often nothing to do with our prized traditions or with culture. In addition, the new mass media of
communication have altered our social life, virtually chal-
lenging the very concept of a "public."

Nowhere is this more apparent than in music, where
a concert audience used to be a group with a well-defined
code of behavior and ritual--even of dress. Now with the
modern phonograph all this has changed, the public has, so
to speak, melted around the edges as individuals take on a
whole symphony orchestra or opera house single-handed,
right in their own living rooms. A vast musical literature
in sound has been created, with its own system of classification and cataloging, and it was inevitable that the library
should be called upon to house this literature. Like the acceptance of the microfilm as a legitimate branch of library
activity, the arrival of the phonograph record created many
new problems of storage and service, the only difference being that besides novel library techniques, the phonograph
record brought with it a warehouseful of social and esthetic
problems unknown to other divisions in the library.

Music is a relative newcomer to the modern American library. To be sure, books on music were present in
some of our earliest libraries; if they had Pythagoras, or
Boethius, or Descartes, or Kant, they had tracts on the nature and the reasons for existence of music. Musical scores
were another matter. When the great edition of Bach's collected works was announced a century ago there were only a
handful of subscribers from the United States, and of these
only three were libraries. Yet today every sizable library
has a music division, the shelves groaning under the weight
of the large folio editions of the masters, the giant anthologies known as the "Monuments," and innumerable single
scores. Since America has become the virtual center of the
musical world, with large and famous musical establishments,
there has been a corresponding academic expansion, attract-
ing many students to our universities, and causing a parallel
growth in library holdings and services. Serious scholarly
literature on music, practically unknown in this country at
the turn of the century, has developed with phenomenal rapidity, and today the writings of American musicologists enjoy an international reputation.

The general public, also many practicing musicians--
even some college instructors--still look with amazement at
all this, maintaining that music is simply to be listened to.
This attitude was once voiced by the painters and sculptors,
whose opposition to the establishment of art history and ar-
chaeology as an academic discipline is now happily a thing
of the past. We must quote Constable, the great British
painter, whose insistence on the role of the intellect in art
is equally applicable to music: "Painting should be understood, not looked on with blind wonder, nor considered only
a poetic aspiration, but a pursuit, legitimate, and scientific."
    A corollary to the scholarly literature is the growth
of popular publications whose titles usually begin with "What
to, " "Whom to, " or "How to" listen, etc. Innumerable instruction books have sprung up on how to freshen the face of
dear old masterpieces or how to enjoy opera without understanding a word of it, and also largely fictionalized biographies of musicians. So many aids for the weaker brethren
in the appreciation of music have been written and published
that one would think that every possible type of listener must
by now have been provided for. Unfortunately, this popular
literature is a world in which little men handle--or fail to
handle--great issues; the preoccupation with the trivial is excessive. But something more than books, whether good or
bad, is needed to make music come to life--it must be heard.
This is the point where the phonograph record becomes an
invaluable interpreter, especially for the layman.
    Our libraries now are laying in stores of recordings.
One would think this to be a simple matter; just buy them,
catalog them, and--but then what? A phonograph recording
is like a score, a mute document; it must be played before
the inanimate plastic disc becomes a living reality. But
where is it to be played? In the reading room?
    I am afraid I am a little ahead of my story. Before
we can play the records we must select them, and before we
select them we must decide what system of reproduction to
favor: 78, 33, mono, stereo, tape--or perhaps all of them.
The economics of a record collection are annoyingly complicated. The 78's are gone, the LP monos are going, the
record itself is likely to be supplanted by the tape. But
there are many old 78's that are considered "classics, " constituting a sort of reference library, therefore a goodly number of them must be retained, together with the equipment
capable of playing them. In their turn the LP's are going
through a constant and endless process of rejuvenation, some
popular items being offered in dozens of different recordings.
    What is a library to do, set up a panel of judges to

select the "five best, " or should it simply acquire all 38 recordings of the Pathetique? The "five best" won't do because the Hi-Fi fraternity is a pistol-packing lot; acquisitive,
combative, shrewd, but also informed and comradely.   They
won't take Ormandy when they want Klemperer, and they
won't even listen to Tebaldi when they want Callas--and vice
versa.   The true-blue record lover does not see other people's point of view but feels aggrieved that some dare to disagree with his opinions, opinions which seem to him always
perfectly reasonable in every way.   The manufacturer con-
tributes to the confusion by labeling every new release as
"definitive" (as if such a thing were possible) and then just
as surely the next one comes out with the SRO sign.   This
Hi-Fi world is indeed a fantastic world, swayed by taboos,
prejudices, and young traditions.

      Then there is the extremely touchy question of the
large domain of music called "popular. " Does jazz belong
in this category or is it, as some maintain, the sole valid
expression of American creativity in music? Where does
folk music end and popular (i. e. commercial) music begin?
What is a "semiclassic" and a "light classic"? While we
leave the philologists to wrangle over the meaning of these
terms, the libraries will have to decide how far inland they
can or should proceed.

      But make no mistake; if they decide that Johann
Strauss and Offenbach composed "light operas" and thus are
accreditable, whereas Broadway musical comedy is out of
bounds, they will have a fight on their hands.   The Jerome
Kern and Richard Rodgers fans will rise in wrath at such
slighting of genuine American "light classics. " In my own
home I can easily draw the lines for my record collection--
at worst my children may consider me an old fogey--but an
institutional library is held accountable by the musical Watch
and Ward Society, and did not Danton say that public opinion
was a harlot? All these notions, divergent and not easy to
reconcile, are certainly not brought near to reconciliation; I
am not going to stick my neck out by advancing criteria for
classification.

      The question of "service" looms large in a library's
record collection.   Should the library offer facilities for
listening in the form of soundproof cubicles or silent machines with earphones, or should it simply circulate the records? The rub is that if they are played with ordinary styli
they will be ruined in no time, and if they are not handled
with care, the grooves being allowed to fill up with crumbs
and spilled coffee, the results may be just as deplorable.
Clearly, the 38 varieties will have to be multiplied several

times over to take care of the replacements.

Finally, we must come to what is perhaps the most difficult part of the game: the reference and counseling service. In the university library this is easy: the instructor makes the decision on what he is going to use or assign, but what about the public library? The librarian cannot go by the "literature" printed on the back of records--most of it is by rank amateurs and of very poor quality. He can of course study, and even compile, reviews by competent critics, but then, as in all the arts, even the expert critics may violently disagree.

These are some of the weighty problems of maintaining and administering a record collection in a library. How these problems can be kept in hand--let alone solved--is for the knowledgable library specialists to decide. There can be no question that a record collection is not only a legitimate but a necessary function of a well-appointed library, but apparently it belongs in that category of ambitious plans which includes the Tower of Babel. I am confident that the technical problems of maintenance and administration will be solved by our able library technicians; the listener's problems are quite another matter. If we ask how the listener is to know when the composer has attained to that condition of totality in imagination, when he speaks indeed with the voice of life itself, the answer must be that that is each listener's concern. It depends on how fit his soul is to be at home among masterpieces.

First Steps Toward a Record Collection
Edna Frances Hanna

From Illinois Libraries 44:134-50, February 1962.   Reprinted by permission.

This article is dedicated to librarians and board members who, faced with an increasing demand for recordings,
would like to learn more about the problems a collection presents.   It assumes that they are already aware of the demands imposed upon budget and staff by the book collection.
An added service implies adjustment or increase in budget,
staff, and physical arrangement.   Recordings can be a bane
or a blessing.   They may put a voice in your library's image, calling new patrons who come to listen and stay to read.
They may be a source of irritation or friction if the public
is unaware of its responsibility for using them with care.
Much depends upon interpreting in advance the policies of
selection, acquisition, and circulation.   There is healthy
variety in the types of services developed by librarians, who,
with imagination and a comparatively small budget, have en-
riched their collections with recordings of music and the
spoken word.   Their combined experiences offer no panaceas,
but many have learned to avoid the pitfalls and are savoring
the pleasures.   May this potpourri of their methods help your
records go 'round more successfully.

The Precedent for Recordings

Although mounting sales testify to the public's interest
in recordings, many librarians believe that libraries are for
books alone.   School libraries are fast changing from book
depositories to materials centers with films, recordings, and
art prints.   It is natural that young people who have been exposed to the values of these materials will continue to use
them after leaving school.   A few large libraries in the
country have music and drama collections which are reasonably complete.   However, many smaller libraries, faced with
the necessity for providing limited service in music or drama,
have considered it logical to provide material in a form com-
prehensible to professional and layman alike.   Recordings,
having the additional quality of aural interpretation, have
seemed a logical answer.

The first collection in an American library was a gift received by the St. Paul, Minnesota, public library in 1914.[1] In 1923 a circulating collection was begun in the Springfield, Massachusetts, library.[2] Although the United States Office of Education requested statistical information on miscellaneous stock in public libraries in only the 1950 and 1956 reports, 1,133 libraries indicated holdings of 321,000 recordings in 1950. When 1,651 libraries responded in 1956, the total was 897,000.[3]

The circulation report from 1,844 public library systems in the continental United States listed 3,452,000 musical and nonmusical titles in 1956, as compared with 1,967,000 in 1950. Hawaii reported a circulation of 7,013.[4] Unfortunately, no breakdown is available on the size of the libraries or the size of the cities reporting.

Assistance in Planning

Some state libraries offer consultant service in planning a record collection. More provide supplementary material by individual title or long-term loan. Illinois lends a small experimental collection for a period of up to one year, in order that the local library may gauge community interest and support before investing in a collection. By an alternative plan, it stands ready to assist several libraries in a natural service area in establishing a cooperative. Initially, each participant receives a small collection of records, which is exchanged at three-month intervals with another member. At the end of a year, the libraries may agree to continue the collection by joint purchase of recordings and provision for administrative staff.[5]

If you believe that consultant service is unavailable from your own state library, write anyway. It is by demonstration of stated needs that agencies, associations, and foundations are able to secure funds and support for their programs. Your letter, together with those of other librarians faced with similar problems, may lead to improved staff, additional research, publications based on practical needs, or the establishment of programs and services of inestimable value to library development in your community and in the United States. Since the passage of the Library Services Act in 1956, state libraries have additional funds and an unusual opportunity to provide professional leadership beyond mere distribution of materials. These funds have been extended for the next five years. You, the smaller libraries, have an obligation to interpret local problems and to share in planning programs which are consistent with the requirements of the people in your own community and geographical area.

Gifts and the Giver
         Because of the large number of selections required
for a basic collection, which will fill the needs of many borrowers with varied tastes, many libraries have gladly accepted gift collections, [6] with their attendant advantages and
disadvantages. When a group or an individual offers a collection for general use, some dissatisfaction with the content
may be outweighed by the continued interest of the donor and
by the opportunity to introduce the service to the public. Its
popularity may insure its inclusion as a permanent item in
future budgets. As with books, the gift encumbered by special strictures on shelving or use may prove costly in the
long run.
         The revolution in methods of sound reproduction and
the many improvements in equipment have forced audiophiles
to convert to long-playing monophonic or stereophonic recordings. The old "standard" or 78 rpm discs have been
discontinued by most manufacturers. In attics or basements
of hundreds of homes there are standard discs which are
"much too good to throw away." The library's record collection will appear to be the obvious place for these recordings to receive tender loving care. They roll into the library, brittle from storage in heat or mildewed from rest-
ing in basements; only the collectors' items and the titles
unavailable on LP discs remain at home. It is fascinating
to speculate that the donor may have overlooked the gold in
his attic, but hours spent in sorting, cleaning, and cataloging obsolete materials may represent an investment in terms
of staff time which the library can ill afford. The circulation of standard records is steadily decreasing, since most
patrons are reluctant to carry heavy albums and to assume
responsibility for easily broken discs. The 78 rpm disc has
definite value in a noncirculating reference collection, since
there are still outstanding artists and composers whose works
have not been transferred to long-playing discs and the library does have an obligation to collect archival material. [7]
         Most librarians will welcome recorded material of
local interest. Poets and musicians are often more honored
outside their own communities, but it is usually in their
home towns that privately recorded discs may be located. It
is to local sources that the research scholar will turn first
for material by these celebrities. Officials and committee
members often have all-but-forgotten recordings and transcriptions of centennials and special celebrations, which
should be rescued and stored properly for future generations.

At least one foundation, the Harry Futterman Fund, Inc., 1270 Avenue of the Americas, New York 20, New York, is organized to assist organizations which are empowered to create and run lending libraries of musical recordings in the United States and which are not operated for private profit. [8]

Why Not Cooperate

When the library budget is inadequate, there are decided advantages in cooperation. Small libraries near a municipal, county, or regional library may be able to arrange for contractual service. The payment of an annual fee for the use of recordings, which arrive cataloged and ready for distribution, is a decided economy in terms of staff time. Samples of contracts which could be adapted for provision of this service may be borrowed from the American Library Association. [9] The PLD Reporter, No. 5 (1956) and No. 6 (1958) are valuable studies with bibliographies. [10]

Libraries in a natural service area may agree to share collections through reciprocal borrowing privileges, by rotation of recordings in a common pool, or they may simply arrange for informal meetings in which they draw up selection lists, with each librarian assuming responsibility for one aspect of the collection. Distributors give larger discounts to libraries ordering cooperatively and often arrange to bill each library separately. Cooperative cataloging is probably the area in which the greatest saving is possible. A trained music librarian might be hired by several libraries to supervise administrative procedures, prepare lists, exhibits, and publicity, and provide assistance in specialized reference requests. The circulation in each library would be the responsibility of the general staff.

Free Service

Because recordings are subject to many varieties of wear and damage when circulated, some libraries have limited their use to the library. Although the recordings themselves suffer less abuse, it is doubtful whether savings from less frequent replacement offset the necessity for supplying soundproof listening rooms, record players, and supervisory staff, in addition to the cost of maintenance of equipment. Chicago and Philadelphia, faced with the problem of circulation to large populations, follow this system. Detroit, after providing the original collection, has financed its entire service by charging a rental fee on all recordings.

Wilmette, Illinois, found that the rental system made more sense to its tax-paying patrons than the free loan. When Gilbert and Sullivan fans presented a particular prob-

lem of wear and tear on the collection, a high rate of fifty
cents per album solved the difficulty.   The librarian adds
that a point in favor of rental service, albeit a negative one,
is its tendency to hold down circulation to a point at which
service can be handled by the existing staff. [11]

In Peru, Illinois, a yearly deposit or fee helped fi-
nance an active circulating collection. [12]   This type of fi-
nancing may have its advantages when frequent use is made
of supplementary material from the state agency.   It is advisable to ascertain what legal restrictions may affect the
use of state materials in a rental collection.   A service fee
may be permissible to cover mailing, whereas a rental fee
may be prohibited.

About Sound Reproduction

Closely allied to record selection is the seemingly
endless proliferation of discs and equipment.   In the early
days of the industry, record manufacturers produced discs
for use on turntables revolving at varying speeds.   At the
turn of the century a standard rate of seventy-eight revolutions per minute was agreed upon.   The discs of shellac
compound were either ten or twelve inches in diameter and
the playing time was three to five minutes.   A stylus or
needle of three or four-thousandths of an inch radius was
used.

In 1948 the long-playing record, played at thirty-three
and one third revolutions per minute, revolutionized the industry.   Finer grooves (micro-grooves), a needle point of
one one-thousandth of an inch in radius, and a lightweight
pickup of five to ten grams weight on the needle resulted in
a performance lasting twenty to thirty minutes.

A 45 rpm disc only seven inches in diameter, utilizing the microgroove, was an innovation, with a playing time
similar to a standard disc.   A subsequent development in
this speed, called the "extended play," lengthened the playing time to about eight minutes.   It requires less storage
space and represents certain advantages when a recording of
a single aria, a short overture, or other brief selection is
needed on a single disc, since these shorter selections are
usually grouped together on twelve-inch discs in a recital
type of program which is not always pleasing or useful in
all its parts.   A disadvantage is the larger center hole (one
and one-half inches), which requires adapters for each record or an adapter to be placed on the spindle.

Although simplification seemed a possibility when manufacturers abandoned the ten-inch disc, they devised still another speed.   The 16 rpm is used principally for spoken re-

cordings, since there is some distortion of musical tone at
this rate.   Talking Books for the Blind are being planned on
an 8 rpm disc.

The most recent players are adjustable for all speeds
from 78 down to 16 rpm, and a flip-needle apparatus holds
a standard and a long-playing stylus.   An adapter is also
available for converting 33 1/3 rpm to 16 rpm.   Some libraries have included adapters with the albums of 16 rpm
records, but damage and loss seem to indicate that the patron should be required to furnish his own, just as he furnishes his own player.

And now we have stereo!   It is not the purpose of
this article to explain the phenomenon, which reproduces
sound as we actually hear it--"binaurally" or with both ears.
On a monophonic record the same sound is engraved on both
walls of the groove.   In a stereo record the sounds coming
from two separate points are recorded one on each side of
the groove at forty-five degree angles.   Records so recorded
require equipment with a turntable, two-amplifier speaker
system, and a stereo cartridge.   The stereo cartridge trans-
forms into an electric signal the vibrations picked up by the
needle as it travels the record groove, keeping separate the
two sound messages and producing a three-dimensional effect. [13]

Of importance to the librarian is the fact that although the stereo cartridge plays monophonic as well as
stereophonic records, the ordinary cartridge used for long-
playing monophonic records is too stiff to follow the vertical
movements caused by the varying depth of the stereo groove.
Because it is capable of only slight vertical movement, it
cuts and seriously damages stereo record grooves.   Sound
becomes distorted and the needle may skip from groove to
groove.   Stereophonic effect cannot be achieved on monophonic equipment, since a second speaker is required to keep
the two audio channels separate until they are presented as
stereo sound.

Stereo recordings are in use in some libraries, but
since many patrons do not have the equipment, the monophonic disc, costing about a dollar less per record, is still
better suited for general circulation.   A conspicuous marking
device is used to distinguish stereo recordings, and they are
often shelved separately in the collection.   Some libraries
require a special deposit or a written statement from the patron that he will use only stereo equipment.[14]

Selection Policy

"Every library should have a written statement of pol-

icy covering the selection and maintenance of its collection
of books and nonbook materials."[15] A written statement,
published and freely circulated, is an advantage at all times,
particularly in the early stages of building a collection, when
requests for individual favorites will be so varied that it
will be impossible to heed every patron's suggestion. A cursory glance through the Schwann Long Playing Record Catalog
shows over 125 pages devoted to classical selections on
monophonic or stereophonic discs. Composite discs, spoken
and miscellaneous titles, musical shows, popular and folk
music of America and foreign countries, jazz, and children's
selections bring the catalog to over 250 pages. It is assumed that standard classics in renditions of outstanding technical excellence will be acquired as recommended in Public
Library Service, and that the other sections will be accumulated gradually as the collection grows.

Vincent Duckles has stated in a paper presented to
the International Association of Music Libraries:

> Music in a public library is of course not the same
> thing as a public music library... There are
> things which can be done at the small community
> level which cannot be accomplished on a large mun-
> icipal scale. The educational effectiveness of a
> public library is not determined by its size or
> even by the strength of its collection, but by the
> kind of relationship it has to its community. The
> librarian in the small public library is in the best
> possible position to know the musical resources
> and interests of his community. The amateur or-
> chestras and choral societies, the chamber groups,
> the local private music teachers, the music pro-
> gram of the local schools--these are the channels
> through which the library must work in fulfilling its
> role in modern musical education. Its effort should
> be to assist, to supplement, and to invigorate those
> agencies already established in the community for
> the purpose of music education, and also to pro-
> vide a place where the interested individual can
> pursue his own line of self-education in the music
> field.[16]

In the initial stages, supplementary service implies
avoidance of duplication of materials already available within
the community. Materials required in the school curriculum
may reasonably be considered within the province of the
school library, while recreational materials such as folk

dances may be provided for groups by the recreation commission. The local Council of Churches may already own
and furnish to religious groups its excellent albums of hymns
cleared for broadcasting or its transcriptions of radio broadcasts of interest to religious groups. A file of local resources and of material available through other channels may
do much to establish the library as a clearing house of information on recorded and allied materials. Where to rent
multiple copies of orchestral scores or purchase theatrical
sound effects are only two of the questions which naturally
seem to fall in this service category. The answers will be
as gratefully received as if you were able to produce the recording of a barking dog or the "sounds of a Roman arena,"
as one patron confidently requested.

Hit Parade and juke box favorites are so readily available by the turn of a radio dial that the library may feel secure in omitting these ephemeral selections from the collection. On the other hand, the FM station, with its large collection of classical and standard recordings, can be a guide
to some of the best musical materials. Its programs are
generally arranged to cover a particular period, form of composition, or composer. The FM and Fine Arts Guide lists
programs weekly. Program notes of the New York Philhar-
monic concerts and the Metropolitan Opera Guild's Opera
News keep the librarian informed and ahead of requests stem-
ming from these broadcasts.

The managers or directors of local symphony orchestras and choral groups often submit their programs for the
year, for group members as well as listeners are sure to
be among the library's patrons. Plays to be produced in the
community create a rash of requests from thespians hoping
to emulate Gielgud or McKenna.

The catalogs or acquisitions lists of other libraries,
from which one may secure interlibrary loans, assist patrons
who find the selections of the local library too limiting. A
consistent check of their requests often reveals notable gaps
in the collection. The opportunity to listen to an expensive
album under consideration for purchase may save the library
more pennies than the small borrowing fee.

Discographies and Indexes
Keeping in mind the limitations of the recordings and
the needs of the community, the process of selection begins.
Discographies are numerous. The term has only recently
been admitted to the dictionary, nudged there by its acceptance as a subject heading by the Library of Congress, which
uses it much as it uses "bibliography." The earliest ones

appeared in the 1930's in three separate countries almost
simultaneously: R.D. Darrell's Gramophone Shop Encyclopedia, in New York, 1936; Delaunay's Hot Discography in
Paris, 1936; and Roberto Bauer's Historical Records, in
Milan, Italy, 1937.   The Darrell work was revised in 1942
and 1948, carrying it to the brink of the LP era.[17]
        In 1952, Francis F. Clough and G.J. Cuming, of
Wales, brought forth the most ambitious publication yet attempted, The World's Encyclopedia of Recorded Music, af-
fectionately known as "WERM." Its three supplements bring
the work up to 1955, with the promise of future additions.
Its tables of works and meticulous identifications make it invaluable to the cataloger and reference assistant alike.
        Myers refers to the familiar monthly catalogs as ex-
tensions of Darrell and as "poor men's bibliographies."[18]
Two of the best known are the Schwann Long-Playing Record
Catalog and the Long Player, usually available in record
shops across the country.   Both list long-playing monophonic
and stereo records under a variety of categories, with the
composer, title, artist, manufacturer's number, and a price
guide.
        Record reviews in books and periodicals are legion.
A guide to them is Music Library Association's quarterly,
Notes, which includes "Index of Record Reviews," compiled
by Kurtz Myers.   The opinions of the reviewers are indicated by symbols.   The first section is listed by composer,
with a few subject entries bringing together folk and diction
records.   The second section, arranged alphabetically by
manufacturers, then serially by the manufacturer's numbers,
contains works by more than one composer.   Record Ratings
is a cumulation of earlier issues of the Index.   They are as
useful for tracing contents of composite discs as for their
evaluations.
        The Readers' Guide to Periodical Literature recently
indexed twenty-two magazines with record sections, and International Index includes a number of the more scholarly
journals in the Humanities.   Music Index, the only index to
the field of music, is rather slow in appearing.   Education
Index is a guide to educational periodicals which sometimes
review recordings of smaller companies issuing specialized
materials.   It is a particularly fertile source of information
about language records and nonmusic selections.
        Specialized discographies cover a single composer, a
subject, performers, or types of music.   They frequently appear in periodicals or are appended to books.

Children's Records

Although many recordings have been issued for children, the quality of content, performance, and sound reproduction is uneven. Good productions are frequently issued by smaller companies, which cannot afford to cut prices as low as some of the larger manufacturers. Such records are not intended to be played on toy record players with worn needles, and libraries often restrict their use to listening hours within the library or circulate them to adults.

Howard Taubman's excellent little book, How To Bring Up Your Child to Enjoy Music, lists a number of selections generally found in the adult collection, which are enjoyed by children. The gay wrappings in which children's discs appear sometimes conceal trite, cute, renditions which contribute nothing to the aesthetic or educational development of the child and too often fail to amuse. Although the discographies are out of date, the philosophy of selection expressed in such books as Emma Dickson Sheehy's There's Music in Children and Beatrice Landeck's Children and Music is still valid.

There are two reviewing services. Children's Record Reviews (Elizabeth Thomson, Woodmere, New York), issued five times a year, includes some filmstrips with recorded sound tracks. Louisville Free Public Library issues Children's Record Critique, prepared by staff members of the Children's Department in cooperation with a review committee from the Junior League of Louisville. The records reviewed have been tested by parents with their children. It is issued six times a year.

Ruth Tooze and Beatrice Krone include recordings in Literature and Music as Resources for Social Studies. Although many numbers are for 78 rpm records, the selections are in many cases available on LP's. The aim of the book is "to help those concerned with children find richer ways of aiding them in becoming good citizens of the world."

Acquisition

Many public libraries patronize their local dealers from choice or because library policy demands it. If the local dealer recognizes the opportunity which the library's collection affords his customers to listen to records which they eventually purchase for their own collections, he may offer a very favorable discount. In turn, the librarian may browse and audit at the local shop. A local dealer is usually generous in providing manufacturers' catalogs, display material, and even reference service. One enterprising young man offered to consult the Phonolog, a rather expensive

dealer information service, whenever the record librarian
could not locate a record or song title, while another, using
the One-Spot Record Finder, a similar service, turned over
his outdated issues to the library, where they were still very
useful for their title indexes.

Although most dealers sell at standard prices, some
cut-rate shops regularly price their stock about 30 percent
below advertised price. Some have records of excellent
quality in factory-sealed packages. Others are merely outlets for salesmen's samples. Caveat emptor! Manufacturers' specials are often advertised, particularly after the
Christmas rush, when sales are slow. They are a real opportunity when replacements are needed and one already
knows the value of the recorded selections.

The economy reprints of leading manufacturers are
sometimes windfalls. Camden (Victor), Richmond (London),
and Harmony (Columbia) are among these labels, which usually retail at $1.98. Lists of outstanding titles recently
appeared in Library Journal[19] and Hi-Fi/Stereo Review.[20]

Two distributors offering substantial discounts are
Sam Goody and The Chesterfield Shops. The former sends
The Long Player and Abner Levin's Basic Library of Classical LP's to mail order customers, while Chesterfield distributes the Schwann catalog. Children's Reading Service
has an annotated listing of phonograph records from kinder-
garten through senior high school. The Children's Record
Center has catalogs for elementary and high school. Its
listings include some labels more familiar in the West than
in the Central states. Directories of manufacturers are included in several audio-visual textbooks, certain issues of
Library Journal, and in the "Blue Book of A-V Materials, "
usually in the July issue of Educational Screen and Audio-
Visual Guide.

Record Care

From the moment recordings reach the library, the
strictures imposed by their form become apparent. Ideally,
records, films, and books on similar subjects and identical
titles in the three different media should be shelved together
in order that each may supplement the other. Since this is
not feasible, it is simplest to keep all recordings together
until the collection becomes large enough to warrant subject
division. A self-contained operation eliminates duplication
of special shelving and allows for the maintenance of the
proper climate in which records survive longest.

A technical but fascinating research study, The Preservation and Storage of Sound Recordings; a Study Supported

by a Grant from the Rockefeller Foundation, by A. G. Pickett
and M. M. Lemcoe, is recommended to those responsible for
the care of a collection.   It specifically eliminates consideration of playback deterioration.   It suggests that the optimum
storage environment for types of discs found in library collections should:

> (1) Prevent fungal damage by not providing an environ-
> ment suitable for fungal activity.   This can be accom-
> plished by:

>> (a) Reducing fungal nutrients to a minimum by keep-
>> ing discs clean and not using nutrient packaging ma-
>> terials for storage.

>> (b) Reducing moisture on disc surfaces below
>> amount required by fungi.

> (2) Keep moisture content of disc environment at a
> satisfactorily low value which is, at the same time,
> not so low as to cause undesirable changes in certain
> materials.   A moisture content in equilibrium with
> 50 percent R. H. at 70° F. seems to be satisfactory.

> (3) Keep temperature reasonably constant and at as
> low a figure as is compatible with human activity.

> (4) Deny access of ordinary sunlight or artificial light-
> ing of the shorter wave lengths (such as certain mer-
> cury vapor fluorescent lights).

> (5) Store all discs in the vertical attitude, keep them
> clean, do not use rough surfaced packaging materials,
> and do not permit sliding contact of disc surface with
> other surfaces.

> (6) Provide a vapor and gas barrier between the disc
> and the ambient atmosphere.   Inert gas purging of
> package prior to closure is feasible in a large opera-
> tion, but is probably not necessary as just prevention
> of the renewal of oxygen and atmospheric contaminants
> in the disc environment should reduce the attack by
> the agents to a tolerable level. [21]

It is further recommended that the library be air-con-
ditioned and kept dust free, at 50± R. H. and at 70± F., or,
where this is not possible, the playback and packaging facil-

ity environments should meet these standards and the stacks
should meet the temperature standards. [22]

It is obvious that these conditions are being met neither by the manufacturers of albums nor by most libraries,
but they suggest interesting possibilities for the comfort of
librarians as well as for the preservation of discs.

Because the report is recent, its implications for the
administrator have not yet been fully explored in print.
Many libraries which treat recordings in the same manner
as books, routing them through the technical processes division, pay little heed to climate and storage until the records
reach their permanent destination. Future recommendations
may stress the complete separation of books and records or
the erection of a new building which can meet specifications
in all departments!

The report also directs, "The technique of handling
discs should be carefully supervised. Discs should be kept
clean both for playback and storage."[23] Two commercially
available systems are recommended: (1) prior to playback
or packaging, a sparing application of detergent solution with
an applicator of sheared acetate fibers;[24] (2) during playback,
an ethylene glycol solution sparingly applied with a brush and
mohair applicator pad.[25]

In the laboratory, drastic cleaning was accomplished
only when necessary by washing the disc in a lukewarm detergent solution, rinsing with distilled water from a wash
bottle, quick drying in warm air from a hair dryer and conditioning the disc in the 70° F, 50 percent R.H. environment. The grooved surfaces were never handled with bare
hands, and the discs were inserted into and removed from
their packages without allowing the grooved surfaces to be
touched by the packaging material.

Shelving in a vertical position without pressure on the
disc surface and with no opportunity for an off-vertical attitude is recommended in addition to the following specifications: (1) a compartmental shelf, with each compartment of
a size to accommodate from one to two dozen packaged discs,
or fillers to keep them upright without requiring use of force
for insertion or removal of a packaged disc; and (2) shelves
very little larger than the package dimension, with well-
aligned slotted metal strips on both top and bottom of the
shelves to support each packaged disc independently of other
discs.

Although many of the findings are related only to permanent storage operations over which a library has no control, as when records are kept in a warehouse for many
months before being distributed, those libraries with archival

material or a reference collection which does not circulate
are faced with the same problems in a lesser degree.   In a
circulating library the recommendations for shelving, supervision in handling, and cleaning of discs are highly important.
Since library conditions will not be duplicated in the homes
of borrowers, about all the librarian can do to preserve records from harm is to carry on a continuing program of public education through the example of library practice in handling records at circulation points, through exhibits pointing
out the horrible results of leaving discs stacked in a hot,
sunny car or in front of an open window on a rainy day, and
by printed notices, such as that used by the Monterey (California) Public Library, on each circulating album.   Replacement of damaged discs is required by most libraries.   For
this reason, it is fair to examine the discs with the patron
before and after circulation, at the same time acquiring an
opportunity to suggest approved methods of care and checking
of needles.

Processing
        When records are received they should be checked
carefully for blemishes, warpage, and scratches, and assurance that the proper recordings are included in the albums.
(Even sealed packages may contain a factory error.)   The
desk on which the librarian works should be provided with a
smooth dust-free covering or surface, in order that discs
removed from the album may be processed without becoming
scratched.   The dust from ink erasers is highly abrasive and
clings to the plastic surfaces of the disc.   The same care in
handling is required and the same provisions for temporary
shelving in vertical position should be provided during processing as is provided in the permanent record area.
        Plastic album covers are beautiful, durable, and ex-
pensive.   If used, they should be attached with a small
amount of jacket cover adhesive; regular paste, glue, and
many of the plastic glues do not adhere to the laminated
sleeves.   If a card pocket is applied to the outside of a single record sleeve, it is less likely to be torn off by another
record being slipped into the shelf next to it if it is placed
on the left side of the front or the right side of the back.
Then it can be read easily while standing on the shelf.
        Markings on the sleeve are difficult to apply, since
highly enamelled stock or a laminated plastic is often used.
The latter may peel off in time.   The new press-on labels,
which come in long strips, are easily typed and quickly applied, also fairly durable.   The press-on luna label for long-
playing discs may be purchased printed with the library's

name and address.   There is usually enough space left for
the call number to be added. [26]   Gummed disc labels are
less satisfactory, since they do not always adhere to the record label and they must be moistened before application.

Cataloging and Classification

E.T. Bryant gives a comprehensive picture of the
problems of cataloging and classification in his chapter on
Gramophone records in Music Librarianship: A Practical
Guide. [27]   Asheim, too, discusses the subject in The Humanities and the Library. [28]   He points out that there is no one
"best way."   Most libraries attempt to keep the classification simple.   Some arrange alphabetically by composer or
numerically by accession number or manufacturer's number.
Others use a three-figure Cutter number, while a few have
devised a color code to group selections by form.   Library
Literature indexes numerous systems with enthusiastic ad-
herents.   Although some are deceptively simple, they are in-
capable of expansion after the collection grows to three or
four hundred records.   A simplification of the system used
for the library's books may prove less confusing to cataloger
and to patron.   The shortcomings of Dewey and the Library
of Congress systems are frequently pointed out, but their
advantages should not be overlooked.   Both may be expanded,
eliminating the expense of eventual reclassification.

An interesting report of a special committee of the
ALA Division of Cataloging and Classification is based on a
questionnaire to determine cataloging procedures in 176 college, university, and school libraries.   What these librarians
do and wish they could do differently is valuable information
for the library approaching cataloging of these materials for
the first time. [29]

The Library of Congress prints catalog cards for
Phonorecords (the term by which it designates all sound recordings).   Volume twenty-seven of the National Union Catalog, 1953-1957, is a cumulated list of works represented by
the Library of Congress printed cards.   It is available as a
separate.   The Code for Cataloging Music and Phonorecords,
prepared by the Music Library Association and the ALA Division of Cataloging and Classification, is available from the
American Library Association.

Although very brief cataloging is recommended by
some writers, descriptive cataloging is of great assistance
when the patron is expected to use the card catalog or when
assistants are unfamiliar with the intricacies of those few
indexes which exist.   Circulation will be facilitated by the
use of extensive analytics.   Although the Schwann catalog

gives an expanded entry for each record the first time it is
printed in the catalog, succeeding issues give only the date
of original entry. If the new library does not have back issues, the content of a record is difficult to locate. The
Schwann Artist Listing appears at irregular intervals, but
title listings are hard to find unless the library subscribes
to one of the expensive dealer services or maintains a large
supply of dealers' catalogs, many of which list by number
and not by title.

Whether to file colored cards for records in the main
catalog with books or whether to keep them in a separate
file depends upon the location of the records. Another consideration is whether to file all speeds in one or in separate
catalogs. If stereo records are purchased, there might be
less danger of using them on improper equipment if the patron were informed of the distinction between stereo and
long play by being required to consult a separate file. However, long-playing and 78 rpm discs have been filed together
for some years in libraries; if different colored cards were
used, a single file should be satisfactory.

Housing the Collection
Few libraries are lucky enough to have a new record
collection and a new building simultaneously. Of those who
have experienced the joy of new quarters for their collection,
Karline Brown, of the Cincinnati Public Library, has been
most generous in sharing the experience. Her articles in
several library periodicals reflect her enthusiasm as well as
her willingness to help others avoid the few errors which are
bound to occur in planning and equipping a new building. In
Notes, [30] her description of the recordings service of the
Films and Recordings Center is accompanied by a floor plan
and a number of attractive photographs.

Whether the records occupy a room of their own or
a corner in another department, the major consideration is
the placement of shelves to avoid damp walls, proximity to
heat pipes, and direct sunlight. Miss Brown mentions her
dissatisfaction with the adjustable metal separators suspended
from the shelf above to keep discs vertical in the metal
shelving. Wooden dividers at six to eight-inch intervals help
keep records erect. Shelves should be thirteen inches deep,
with at least thirteen inches between shelves to accommodate
the albums, which seem to grow bulkier and more elaborate
each season. The Urbana (Illinois) Free Library, using undivided shelves, substitutes a corrugated filler the size of
an album for each record removed from the shelves, in order to keep those which remain in vertical position. Since

records are larger than most books, adequate aisle space
should be planned between stacks.

The size of the records and the necessity for removing them from the album for inspection require that the
charging and return points provide desk space adequate for
the operation. Since record inspection is more time-consuming than checking out a book, separation of the two charging
functions, whether at different points at one desk or at separate desks, will eliminate delaying those with books. A
linoleum or rubber desk top is satisfactory and it should be
kept dust free at all times. Plenty of storage space is
necessary behind the desk for reference tools, carrying bags,
damaged and reserved records, earphones, adapters, and
other equipment. A player for testing should be accessible
to the desk. For the library with only one record player, a
transcription player with multiple outlets for earphones, usable independently from the loudspeaker, is practical. If it
is equipped with a microphone input, it may also be used as
a public address system. Mounted on a truck, it will have
multiple uses throughout the building. Although they are
more expensive, earphones designed to prevent sound leak
are better and seem more sanitary than those equipped with
a button which fits in the ear.

Browsing bins like those used in record shops are
available mounted on wrought iron legs, or reasonable facsimiles may be produced by a handyman somewhat less expensively. They provide excellent temporary storage for
records to be shelved and frequently eliminate the necessity
for shelving, since patrons seem convinced that the best records have just been returned.

An attractive small chair is not guaranteed to keep
toddlers from pulling records from the shelves while their
parents browse, but it offers temporary distraction. If library stools must be kept in view, the non-tip variety is
recommended for the safety of these same young climbers.[31]

Above all, non-glare lighting and plenty of outlets
should be provided, with an inspection lamp for checking
discs. Even a slight accumulation of dust cuts down lighting
efficiency. If a dust-free environment is not provided, a
janitor who has been alerted to the peculiar requirements of
records is just as valuable as the librarian.

Geared for Action

And now the recordings are ready to make their de-
but. Publicity inconsistent with the size of the collection
will bring patrons who are sure to want just what the library
does not own; they must be advised in advance of the scope

of the collection.   Album notes frequently suggest interesting
news stories about the recordings and the composers.   The
selection policy, the borrowing rules, the library's position
on the acceptance of gifts, and a clear statement of fees,
fines, or replacement charges will do much to avoid initial
misunderstandings.

An introductory series of library concerts, story
hours in which records are used in conjunction with books,
and exhibits which correlate the new service with other materials in the library will stimulate interest.   In order that
reaction may be favorable, the library not acoustically
equipped to protect those who do not want to listen should
approach "music in the air" with caution.   Background music
of the type used in industry to combat boredom and fatigue
is engineered to avoid modulations, changes of mood or tem-
po, and tricky arrangements or attention-getting solos.[32]
Library recordings have been chosen to be listened to as
well as heard.   The decision to listen should be made by
both patrons and staff members, never inflicted upon them
when they are engaged in concentrative activities.

Patrons are sure to come--serious students, those
who seek relaxation or enjoyment, those who have a specific
program to be developed.   Whether they seek a Vivaldi concerto, a Mantovani concert, or the poems of Dylan Thomas,
they are confident that the librarian will share their fervor.
They know that she will translate their request for "the music of the future with records to illustrate, " into a program
on concrete music or a rendition of the Illiac Suite.   She
will meet their challenge; for new ideas, new demands, and
new materials with which to meet them are the heart and
soul of a library's continuing effort to add new dimensions
to the aesthetic and intellectual life of the community it
serves.

Notes

1.   American Library and Book Trade Annual: 1961 (New
        York: R. R. Bowker Co. , 1960), p. 212.
2.   Ibid.
3.   U. S. Department of Health, Education and Welfare, Of-
        fice of Education, Biennial Survey of Education in the
        United States, 1954-56; Chapter 5.   Statistics of Pub-
        lic Libraries, 1955-56 (Washington: U. S. Govern-
        ment Printing Office, 1959), p. 24.
4.   Ibid. , p. 27.
5.   Edna F. Hanna, "Recordings on a Shoestring, " Illinois

Libraries, XL, September, 1958, p. 588.

6. Lester Asheim, The Humanities and the Library. Chicago: American Library Association, 1957, p. 176.

7. Edward E. Colby, "Sound Recordings in the Music Library: With Special Reference to Record Archives," Library Trends, VIII, No. 4 (1960), pp. 556-565.

8. The Foundation Directory (New York: Russell Sage Foundation, 1960).

9. Gretchen K. Schenk, County and Regional Library Development (Chicago: American Library Association, 1954), p. 33.

10. Available from Publishing Department of the American Library Association, 50 East Huron Street, Chicago 11, Illinois.

11. Helen Siniff, "A Rental Record Library," Illinois Libraries XXXVIII (1956), pp. 303-4.

12. Dorothy Bieneman, "Mighty Oaks," Illinois Libraries XXXVIII (1956), p. 300.

13. Adapted from sleeve of stereo disc produced by Capitol Records.

14. Irene H. McDaniel, "Stereo's Here to Stay," Library Journal, LXXXV, October 1, 1960, pp. 3381-3.

15. Public Library Service: A Guide to Evaluation with Minimum Standards, Chicago, American Library Association, 1956, p. 32.

16. Vincent Duckles, "The Role of the Public Library in Modern Music Education; an American Appraisal," Fontes Artis Musicae, 1956, p. 141.

17. Kurtz Myers, "For the Collector: Discographies Help Him Become an Expert," The New York Times, Sunday, April 19, 1959, section 11.

18. Ibid.

19. Chester K. Davis, "Economy Reprints in Sound," Library Journal 85; October 1, 1960, 3384-6.

20. "Guide to $1.98 Records" advertised in May, 1960, issue as available as a reprint.

21. A.G. Pickett and M.M. Lemcoe, The Preservation and Storage of Sound Recordings; a Study Supported by a Grant from the Rockefeller Foundation (Washington: Library of Congress, 1960), p. 47.

22. Ibid., p. 48.

23. Ibid.

24. Lektrostat Cleaning Kit, Dexter Chemical Corporation.

25. ESL Dust Bug.

26. Demco Library Supplies, Madison, Wisconsin.

27. E.T. Bryant, Music Librarianship: A Practical Guide (London: James Clark and Company, Ltd. 1959), 242-

262.
28. Ibid., 178-186.
29. "Bibliographic Control of Audio-Visual Materials: Report of a Special Committee," Library Resources and Technical Services, I, No. 4, 1957, 180-197.
30. Karline Brown, "From Low Estate to Hi-Fi," Notes, 2d. Series, XIII, No. 3 (June, 1956), 406-420.
31. "Kik-Step" or "Step-Up."
32. Jerome K. Levy, "Music to Be Heard--or Listened To," Musician's Guide, New York, Music Information Service, Inc., 1957.

Bibliography

Books

American Library and Book Trade Annual: 1961. New York:
      R.R. Bowker Co., 1960.
American Library Association, Public Libraries Division.
      Public Library Service: A Guide to Evaluation with
      Minimum Standards. Chicago: American Library As-
      sociation, 1956.
Asheim, Lester, and Associates. The Humanities and the
      Library. Chicago: American Library Association,
      1957.
Bryant, Eric Thomas. Music Librarianship: A Practical
      Guide. London: James Clark & Co., Ltd., 1959.
The Foundation Directory. New York: Russell Sage Founda-
      tion, 1960.
Schenk, Gretchen K. County and Regional Library Develop-
      ment. Chicago: American Library Association, 1954.
Taubman, Howard. How to Bring Up Your Child to Enjoy
      Music. Garden City, New York: Hanover House,
      1958.

Articles and Periodicals

"Bibliographic Control of Audio-Visual Materials: Report of
      a Special Committee," Library Resources and Techni-
      cal Services, I, 4:180-197, Fall, 1957.
Bieneman, Dorothy. "Mighty Oaks," Illinois Libraries, 38:
      300, December, 1956.
Brown, Karline. "From Low Estate to Hi-Fi," Notes, 2d.
      Series, 13:406-420, June, 1956.
Colby, Edward E. "Sound Recordings in the Music Library,
      with Special Reference to Record Archives," Library
      Trends, 8:556-565, April, 1960.
Duckles, Vincent. "The Role of the Public Library in Mod-
      ern Musical Education, an American Appraisal,"
      Fontes Artis Musicae, 3:140-143, July, 1956.
Emerson, Caryl. "Music Services in a Medium-Sized Li-
      brary in Richmond, California," Library Trends, 8:
      595-603, April, 1960.

Hanna, Edna F. "Recordings on a Shoestring," Illinois Libraries, 40:587-594, September, 1958.

Larrabee, Bernice B. "The Music Department of the Free Library of Philadelphia," Library Trends, 8:574-586, April, 1960.

McDaniel, Irene H. "Stereo's Here to Stay," Library Journal, 85:3381-3, October 1, 1960.

Myers, Kurtz. "For the Collector; Discographies Help Him Become an Expert," New York Times, April 19, 1959.

PLD Reporter: Contracts and Agreements for Public Library Service. No. 6, 1958.

PLD Reporter: Co-operative Practices among Public Libraries. No. 5, 1956.

Siniff, Helen, "A Rental Record Library," Illinois Libraries, XXXXVIII, December, 1956, 303-4.

Public Documents

Pickett, A.G. and Lemcoe, M.M. The Preservation and Storage of Sound Recordings: A Study Supported by a Grant from the Rockefeller Foundation. Washington: Library of Congress, 1959.

U.S. Department of Health, Education and Welfare. Office of Education. Biennial Survey of Education in the United States, 1954-1956, Chapter 5. Statistics of Public Libraries: 1955-56. Washington: United States Government Printing Office, 1959.

Unpublished Material

Marlin F. Joyce. Administrative Problems of Music Librarianship. January, 1958 (Library Science 405, University of Illinois: Master's Project).

The Establishment and Care of
a Library Record Collection
Don L. Roberts

From New Mexico Library Bulletin 35:322-8, Spring 1966.
Reprinted by permission

Since the advent of sound recordings, librarians have
been faced with the problem of whether they should offer
these materials to their patrons. In the early days, the physical nature of the cylinders and 78 rpm discs made the
heavy use of these recordings undesirable, since they were
so susceptible to unintentional damage. Now that long-playing discs and tapes are available at a nominal cost, many
people own the equipment necessary to reproduce the selections on these discs and tape. This being true, a number
of libraries have decided to add a record collection to their
holdings. So far, only a few attempts have been made to
provide pre-recorded tapes to library patrons, and consequently, even though tapes are likely to have a much greater
usage in the near future, the scope of this article will be
limited to phonograph recordings in public libraries.

Ideally, libraries should offer a circulating record
collection as one of their public services. However, small
libraries should beware of developing a record collection
without considering whether they have the qualified personnel,
the necessary storage facilities, and an adequate budget to
make the collection worthwhile. It is imperative that these
libraries have someone on their staffs who has a good knowledge of recordings to be in charge of the collection. Otherwise chaos is likely to occur.

Record Selection

When the planning for a record collection is initiated,
two basic decisions must be made: should monophonic or
stereophonic recordings be acquired and what areas should
be covered in the collection? The recent trend has been towards stereo recordings, since more realistic reproduction
is available through two channels than with only one. Hi-Fi
"bugs" will demand stereo records, but one should realize
that a stereo record must be played with a stereo stylus.

A monoaural stylus, which can move only vertically in the record groove instead of horizontally like a stereo stylus, will ruin a stereo record, and patrons need to be constantly warned of that fact.

It must also be remembered that there is no such thing as a "permanent" needle. All needles, including diamond ones, will eventually become worn. They need to be subjected to a periodic examination under a microscope. A worn needle has jagged edges that tend to abrade the delicate contours of a record groove. This not only wipes out the high frequencies, but also creates jagged areas that produce noise in subsequent playings.

Careful consideration should be given to the scope of a library record collection. Will only classical works be purchased, or will the jazz and popular fans find something that pleases them? What about plays, speeches, and poems? A well-rounded collection would include selections from all of the above areas. Also, especially in areas that are rich culturally, a sampling of "ethnic" records should be in the collection. Care must be taken when classical records are selected or else the collection may end up with only Bach, Beethoven and Brahms represented. The classical record collection should cover the whole spectrum of music history, from Gregorian chant to new compositions by contemporary American composers.

The basic methods and tools used for record selection are similar to those used for book selection. The most important bibliographical tool is the Schwann Long Playing Record Catalog, which is the record librarian's BIP as it lists all records currently available, their prices and the manufacturer's serial number. This catalog is issued monthly and contains a separate section which notes the new records listed for the first time. Records about to go out of print are also designated. Unfortunately, it is not possible to place a subscription for the Schwann catalog with its publisher. It is mainly considered to be an aid to record dealers, and copies must be purchased from a record shop.

The National Union Catalog's volume on "Music and Phonorecords" can also serve as a bibliographic tool. Its format is similar to the volumes which deal with books and it lists only those recordings for which Library of Congress catalog cards are available.

There are several excellent sources for reviews of newly-issued records. The American Record Guide, HiFi/ Stereo Review, and High Fidelity are the three major United States periodicals devoted to record and tape reviews and articles of interest to "sound buffs." Each has a very com-

petent reviewing staff and each is published monthly. It is,
therefore, difficult to say that any one of these periodicals
is more important than another. Since reviewers have their
individual tastes, a record will often receive a variety of reviews, ranging from excellent to poor. However, if a public library can afford only one or two of the guides, either
High Fidelity or HiFi/Stereo Review is probably better suited
to their needs than the American Record Guide.

Current record reviews can also be found in a number of other publications. The accuracy of these reviews
varies considerably but certain standard sources, such as
Library Journal and the Sunday edition of the New York
Times, are reliable.

Two standard indexes to record reviews exist. One
is the "Index of Record Reviews," which appears in each issue of the Music Library Association's quarterly journal
Notes. The record reviews in twenty-eight periodicals are
indexed and the tenor of each review is noted by a symbol
in a manner similar to that formerly used by Book Review
Digest. The other standard index is the Polart Index of Record Reviews. It indexes reviews in fourteen periodicals but
does not indicate the opinion of the reviewer.

Several guides for building a basic record collection
are currently available. One of the best is issued by the
W. Schwann Company and is available from them at 137 New-
bury Street, Boston, Massachusetts, 02116. This guide lists
only the works that should be represented and not a specific
recording of a work. Since a large number of new recordings appear each month, it would be impossible to keep such
a list of preferred recordings up-to-date unless it was revised monthly. Consequently, the various books that offer a
comparative survey of the different recordings of individual
works are usually obsolete before they are published. Such
books are valuable for a retrospective survey and not for use
as current purchasing guides.

The final step in record selection is the choice of a
dealer. Several leading record dealers advertise in the various library journals and all offer good service. Record
clubs are other possible sources for records. However, it
is most important to remember that almost all records can
be purchased for about 30 percent less than the list price.
Only on rare occasions should the full list price be paid.

Cataloging of Records

The cataloging of phonorecords is a rather complex
matter, since there often are as many as twenty different

selections on a single disc.   Theoretically, enough entries
should be made to direct the patron to any piece on a given
record.   This is often rather time consuming, but what good
does it do to have a record if the catalog does not inform
the patron just what is on the record?

Composer, performer, subject (form) and certain title
entries should be made for each record.   Conventional titles
must be used to bring all of the main entries for the various versions of the same work together in one place.   Cross
references should be made to the conventional title from the
other titles by which a work is communly known.   For example, if conventional titles were not used, four different
recordings of the Beethoven Third Symphony might be filed
in four separate places under Beethoven if the entries were
made from the titles as they were given on the record jackets.   One might be under S for Symphony Number 3, another
under T for Third Symphony, another under D for Dritte
Symphonie, and finally one under E for Eroica Symphony.
The conventional title would bring all of these together under
Beethoven, Ludwig van, 1770-1827.   Symphony, No. 3, Op.
55, E flat major.   Basic rules for record cataloging can be
found in the Code for Cataloging Music and Phonorecords,
which was published by the American Library Association in
1958.

Although Library of Congress catalog cards are available for phonorecords, many records are not covered by
this service.   Even when Library of Congress cards are
used, it is often necessary to add more entries than those
listed in the tracings on the cards.

The manner in which records are classified should
relate to how they are shelved.   Many different systems are
used.   Some libraries try to assign a Dewey number to a
record, while others attempt to arrange the records alphabetically by composer, without a call number.   Problems in
these systems arise when the works of more than one composer are put in a single album or when two types of works,
such as an overture and a concerto, are paired.   In this
case, some arbitrary decision must be made concerning how
to classify and shelve the recordings.   Perhaps the best
classification and shelving system is simply to file them by
accession numbers.   If the records are well cataloged, the
patron should have no trouble finding what he wants when
they are shelved in this manner.

Circulation of Records

Many libraries limit the use of recordings to a lis-

tening facility within the library. Some circulate records in
the same manner as books, while others limit the circulation
period to one week due to the heavy demands on the collection. Another procedure is to rent the records for five or
ten cents a day. This charge usually writes off the expenses
incurred in acquiring new recordings.

Each library needs to decide what is the best type of
circulation for its specific situation. However, it is imperative that all records which have been used be cleaned and
checked for damage before they are returned to the shelves.
Often charges are assessed for unnecessary damage to a
record.

Care and Housing of Records

It is not an easy matter to keep a recording in top
playing condition. A single speck of dust in the groove will
cause a crackle when the record is played. Hence, it is
extremely important that all recordings be carefully treated.
It is desirable to have directions on proper record care
available for each patron who uses the record library.

Fingers must never touch the grooved area of a record! Oil left on the surface by fingers will collect dust,
which will be ground into the grooves each time the record
is played. Records should be handled on the edges and
label only. This is an easy habit to master, and perhaps
each record user should be asked to demonstrate the proper
handling of records before he is allowed to check out a recording.

Dust must be removed from a record before each
playing. When a record is turned over, it should be cleaned, since the bottom side of the record may have picked up
some lint from the turntable while the top side was being
played. The best way to remove dust and dispel the static
charge usually found on records is to use a velvet-covered
cylinder with an internal moisture wick that dampens the
velvet. The nap of the velvet removes the dust from the
grooves, and the moisture de-staticizes the record. Other
de-staticizers, such as those in aerosol cans, are not recommended, since they leave a residue in the grooves that
often derails the light cartridges now widely used.

When a recording has finished playing, it should be
cleaned and immediately placed in a plastic cover and returned to the record jacket. It is advisable to place another
plastic cover over the record jacket to further lessen the
chance of dust getting on the record surface.

When not being used, records should be shelved on

their edges and not lying flat.   The shelving area must not
receive any direct sunlight, or excessive heat from radiators
or waterpipes.   Any of the above will warp a record, as
will leaving a record locked up in a car which is in the sun.
Badly warped records are unplayable and usually must be
discarded.   If the warping is not too serious, it can sometimes be corrected by placing several heavy books on the
record to flatten it out.   If this procedure is followed, it is
necessary to place a foam rubber cushion, or some similar
cushioning material, between the record and the objects
weighting it.

    Phonorecords can be just as temperamental as the
primadonnas who appear on them.   However, if they are
given the proper care, many hours of excellent, distortion-
free listening will result.

    There is little doubt that all public libraries with ade-
quate facilities, funds and personnel should offer a record
collection to their patrons.   Libraries that do circulate records have found their recordings are heavily used and much
appreciated.

A Concept of Recordings for Public Libraries
Ruth Stines

From Illinois Libraries 48:97-103, February 1966. Reprinted by permission.

At one time the sole function of the public library
was the dissemination of knowledge through the medium of
the printed word. The role of the public library in America,
with the rise in income, shorter work week, more leisure
time, development of hobbies, the surge of adult education,
and the technological change toward mechanization, has
brought about a change in the library's function. With the
introduction of various new services, the library has become more than just an assortment of books and a place to
browse.

As a result, librarians have assumed an important
function in making new materials and devices available to patrons of the library. Since the library is an educational institution, all types of materials should be available to make
learning a pleasure. Libraries, and especially public libraries, are becoming more and more involved with nonbook materials, both in securing and maintaining collections and
stimulating their use in the community. Nonbook materials
do not compete with but complement the printed materials.

In the field of recorded materials there is a particular audience who is not reached by books. With the advent
of the hi-fi and stereo record, a rich new world has been
opened for lovers of music and the recorded word. Millions
of homes are filled with hi-fidelity and stereo equipment and
the many recordings which are available.

The first Edison cylinder (1877) was a poetry recording ("Mary Had a Little Lamb") recited by Thomas A. Edison. Later, popular songs, monologues and dialogues, instrumental music, and political speeches were recorded.
The period 1900-1925 is associated with the age of opera
singing, with the voices of Caruso, Hempel, and others establishing the recording as a document of artistic value. [1]
Today video tape and other similar electronic devices are
being used to record and store sound.

With the growth of new libraries and special services,
music rooms and record departments with record players

and earphones for listening are being made available to the
public.   Music and the recorded word are now recognized as
part of our heritage.   In many instances the record department has no special quarters but has been assigned to any
available place not taken up with printed materials.   From
a small beginning some library record collections have now
grown into large collections with thousands of items.   Many
small libraries are attempting to develop collections and
services with limited space, budget, and staff.

There are many thousands of phono recordings released each year.   The Schwann Long Playing Catalog alone lists
35,000, and it does not include 45 rpm records, children's
records, and popular music of other countries, or the heavy
releases of records in September and December.   Also listed are 489 mono recording labels and 292 stereo labels.
This is exclusive of the foreign labels and the number of
new tape recordings released each month.

Our cultural explosion has developed thirty-seven million Americans who are amateur musicians--even Mother and
Dad are learning to play a musical instrument.[2]   The electronic revolution has produced the home experimenter and
the "build-it-yourself" hi-fi buff, the electrical engineer
checking acoustical standards for tonal values and orchestral
balance, and the collector of discographic data who browses
through old records looking for collectors' items.

All of these have produced the patron who borrows
discs for home listening, either for learning or enjoyment,
and the patron who uses the library listening room.   This
type of activity probably accounts for the greatest use of the
library collection.   While the musical recording is by far
the most popular, use of the recorded or spoken word in libraries and homes is increasing rapidly.   A record made
by a famous actor, poet, novelist or political figure may be
popular for many decades.   A disc featuring Robert Frost
reading his own works is more effective than one made by
an amateur.   With the development of summer theatres, amateur shows, light opera groups, choral and oratorio societies, drama and poetry groups, audio programs for radio
and television, language study and shorthand there is increasing use for discs for educational as well as recreational purposes.

The problem of classification of recordings is still
with us.   Most libraries prefer accession numbers or a modified Dewey.[3]   The Phonolog system recommended by the
Illinois State Library is proving satisfactory, but probably
because of the subscription cost public libraries are reluctant to use it.[4]   There is a serious need for some form of

standardization for cataloging, as most librarians find the
necessary amount of typing so time consuming as to create
a backlog. It may be possible to work out some form of
standardization with central processing.

The administration of a record collection is more
costly than that of a book collection, and records must be
handled more carefully than books. In a recent time and
motion study, the results proved that the average librarian
takes four times as long to discharge a recording than to
discharge a book.[5] The quality of some recordings is questionable, but with cleaning and care many recordings can be
played 50-150 times without noticeable wear. Phono discs
are fragile and will warp or break with improper usage.
This may account for some libraries' reluctance to add this
service.

If the record collection of the public library is of any
size, the administrating librarian needs a special musical
background. Patrons of the library come from all backgrounds, with their taste in music already determined. Some
are critics, who want all nineteen recordings of Mozart's
Symphony No. 41. Others are composers, vocalists, in-
strumentalists. Teachers and students will ask for English
polyphony. Include the engineer with his twelve speakers,
the choral director who wants an Agnus Dei, the folk singing
crowd, the "How to Play Your Own Guitar by Record" en-
thusiast, the minister who wants Charlton Heston reading
The Five Books of Moses, and the romantic who likes the
music of André Kostelanetz. With such a diversity of needs,
the record librarian must be prepared. Without specialized
training practical experience will not easily be acquired.
The library profession does not require the librarian to have
any musical knowledge, but if the profession were to promote musical librarianship as a career it would raise the
status of the record librarian. Tactful handling of all patrons is the best asset of a librarian. As a whole, most of
the public is cooperative when it comes to following rules
and regulations for record collections.

Few libraries have any tape recordings in the record
department. Possibly the added cost of tapes is the primary
consideration; also, fewer people have tape recorders, and
few libraries have any. If the library is housing a large
collection of old 78 rpm recordings, these might easily be
recorded on tapes for future use, preserving the musical
heritage and adding much needed space.

In the preparation of this article, a questionnaire was
sent to Illinois libraries. One section of the questionnaire
dealt with the use of library records for programs of various

types. Replies showed that four libraries sponsored special
listening programs in the library at Christmastime, and one
at Easter. One library reported the patrons violently opposing noontime concerts except at Christmas. Four libraries sponsored a regular radio program, one of them for
twelve years. Three reported special concerts during the
year, one in stereo, one in FM, one in cooperation with
community concerts. There was also a broadcast of recorded plays by a Friends-of-the-Library drama group. One library reported a television program for one year. Others
used spot announcements and newspaper listings as publicity
for new recordings.

The discography or bibliography of recordings and
evaluation criteria must be known to the professional librarian and the sources are vast. Lester Asheim has a good
list of reference tools in his book Humanities and the Library; Schwann Long Playing Catalog is a must. Add to
these such periodicals as American Record Guide, Educational Screen AV Guide, Film News, Film World and AV News
Magazine, Hi-Fi and Stereo Review, High Fidelity, Musical
America, Saturday Review, Library Journal, and The New
York Times. The Library of Congress also publishes a list
of recorded sound.

Many recording companies publish a basic list of library recordings in all fields. There are several record
clubs available to libraries, which give discounts up to
thirty-eight to forty percent. Sometimes a local distributor
will give a good discount to educational institutions. A few
major recording companies give outright gifts to public libraries. One library questioned obtained all its records by
gifts from a local organization. Many record collections
have been started by this method.

The final issue for discussion is a point of contro-
versy--does a record collection reach new patrons of the
community, or does it serve primarily people who already
make use of the book service? Fourteen libraries stated
that the patrons who use their record collections are already
users of the library, while nine stated that the collections
brought in new users. Three voted for both sides of the issue and four did not reply. By these answers, the people
who already make use of the public library are the heavy
users of the record collection.

This discussion has touched a few of the many facets
of a public library record collection. For more detailed
reading Mary Pearson's Recordings in the Public Library
(American Library Association, 1963) and Edna Frances
Hanna's First Steps Toward a Record Collection cover a

spacious area.[6]
    Is the public library making full use of recorded
sound? Public library services need to be expanded and a
way needs to be found to draw the patrons out of their environment and encourage them to use what the library has
to offer. Only about ten percent of the medium-sized public
libraries in America today have utilized to the full their opportunities for service, the resources of their staff members,
the potential for informal education, and the utilization of
new methods which are within reach of their budget.[7] In ten
years the median age of the population of this country will
be under twenty-five years. The population and information
explosions have forced libraries of all kinds to expand, and
the librarian must learn to keep abreast of all the rapidly
expanding technical data.

Notes

1.   Edward E. Colby, "Sound Recordings in the Music Li-
       brary: With Special Reference to Record Archives,"
       Library Trends, April 1960, p. 557.
2.   "They Laughed When I Sat Down to Play," Forbes Maga-
       zine, July 1, 1965, p. 36.
3.   Gordon Stevenson, "Classification Chaos," Library Jour-
       nal, October 15, 1963, pp. 3789-3794.
4.   Betty Ohm, "Here's One for the Record," Illinois Li-
       braries, February 1965, pp. 120-131.
5.   International Association of Music Libraries, Phonograph
       Record Libraries: Their Organization and Practice,
       p. 42.
6.   Illinois Libraries, February 1962, pp. 134-149.
7.   Carnovsky and Winger, The Medium-Sized Library: Its
       Status and Future, University of Chicago, Chicago
       Press, 1963, p. 112.

Folk Music in the Library
Jerome Cushman

From Sing Out! The Folk Song Magazine, v. 12, no. 3,
Summer 1962. Copyright 1962 by Sing Out! Inc. Reprinted
by permission.

Folk song surges from the wellsprings of mankind's
experiences and no matter what happens to him along his
tortuous journey toward civilization, he cannot forget that
part of his heritage, which is so much an intimate part of
him.

Besides being a real part of the fabric of man's experience, folk song is an expression of his deepest feelings
and emotional reactions of every shade ranging from love
through hate.   Therefore, no amount of sophistication can
entirely cover up man's desire to express both his experiences and his emotions.   Clever popular songsmiths have
dug into the folk song tradition for "modern" songs, which
swing along with a current beat but have their origins in
man's past.

A library is a natural institution for preserving, playing, and hearing folk song--listening with a view to learning
and understanding.

We always think of the library as an educational institution and so it is.   Folk song can be educational in both
the narrow and the broad sense.   When we get to the stick-
ing point, the library must also be considered a preserver
of the ways of mankind--more so in this frightful age in
which we live than ever before, because mankind will either
realize its unity, or it will cease.   The library can very
well, by making adequate use of its preservation facilities,
be a living example of man's need to preserve his unity.

When we think of folk song, we usually think in terms
of literary scholarship, textual criticism, literature, or of
the humanities.   Folk song does include all of these, but I
can see how its use with science can be most specific.   One
must bear in mind that the important case in point is in
what fashion folk song can help the library as a preserver
of the unity of man.

Is it not feasible when studying glaciers for students
to hear the music of the Eskimo who lives on these glaciers?

Science is always more than just fact, and the greatest scientists are those with the creative kind of imagination that
is far-reaching. I know of an agricultural scientist who is
working in a field of future protein food sources. His re-
searches have taken him to the beginnings of man, and he
has explored how man has handled his food problems down
through time. A Vedic hymn to the Sun, giver of life and
source of food, might not have a direct connection to the
searching and the results of this scientist's investigation,
but I maintain that the hearing of a Vedic hymn may provide
insight conditioning that could in turn lead to a "Eureka, I
have found it" reaction. Who knows what turns an insight
into scientific reality?

To reduce this to a school or library level of difficulty: the importance of the science teacher is his exploration
of man's experience, and man's feelings through folk song,
always in relationship to the thing he is teaching, whether it
be biology, physics, or botany, should not be underestimated.

Another important use of folk song in the library is
to give young people the feeling of language and its rhythms.
Language is never accidental; it is a part of the pulse and
rhythm of our lives. When we use the word "phooey" as a
personal expression, we are also expressing an emotional
reaction. "Phooey" sounds just like its meaning.

Some of the nonsense songs that have come down to
us are wonderful examples of word meanings as feelings
rather than definitions. Language, usually one of the marks
of man's differences, is also a mark of his unity. In dealing with the language of the folk song, librarians provide a
readymade interior experience for our patrons that conditions
them to a better understanding of that unity.

Listening to the unintelligible words of a Chinese
mother singing a lullaby to her child and the equally difficult
lullaby of an African mother and the familiar lullaby that we
remember from childhood, reveals that language is not a
barrier but a binding force. This is another plus for folk
song in the library and in our lives.

The arts will become an increasingly important factor
in all of our lives despite the naysayers who see our civilization doomed by TV, public relations, and retouched hair-
dos. There is increasing evidence that the relationship between art and everyday living is more and more a direct
one, and that increasing attention is being paid to this important factor in important levels of our society. This is
not to say that we have done away with phony art, poor
taste in music, the solid mediocrity that still overwhelms
most of our communications media. But man-on-the-street

attention is being given to design, efforts are being made to involve more individuals in producing either beautiful sounds or beautiful daubings. Folk song has a subtle way of enhancing this encouraging facet of today's life, since folk song is generally pretty because it is unaffected. It does not try for that which it is not. Its honesty is reflected in its simplicity.

Finally, folk song and the humanities have always been at one with each other--for the art of the folk song is a mirror of the people about whom the songs were made and those who made them. Men and events come alive through folk song and even more important, it brings into focus for the researcher, for the scholar, for the serious reader, many facets of man's experience which otherwise might be lost. The Revolutionary War ceases to become a history book situation when some of the issues of the day are vividly brought forth in song. The poignancy of the Civil War strikes with the sharpness of a knife in the hearing of certain songs.

A study of the humanities gives us an opportunity to understand a little more what has made man tick and why he does, says, thinks, and sings what he does.

A line in a novel, a verse of a song, become immortal expressions of common experiences that are as valid today as they were hundreds of years ago. This is why the public library cannot afford to neglect this basic commitment to its basic responsibility, the preservation of the unity of mankind.

Techniques are important and both library and school literature will give more hints on the actual use of folk song than an individual is able to schedule.

However, first things must come first and if there is agreement that folk song can help the library in the performance of its mission, then all that is needed is for the librarian to buy a few records and start singing.

Jazz
Robert Wedgeworth

From Library Journal 88:1830-2, May 1, 1963. Reprinted by permission.

The exclusion of jazz music from library phonograph record collections constitutes a neglect of an important aspect of American civilization, not to mention a tacit dismissal of a vast array of musical talent. Traditionally, libraries in the United States have been committed to the support of "good" or classical music. My point is not to raise the more or less passé argument as to the legitimacy of jazz, which was settled a long time ago, but to raise this question: Can libraries committed to the preservation and perpetuation of American culture continue to ignore jazz?

Neil Leonard, in his Jazz and the White Americans (Chicago, 1962), states very aptly that "the old and new art should not be in competition with one another. Both have a place in our sensibilities and the acceptance of one need not involve renunciation of the other."

Although the night club is still the most common setting in which jazz may be heard, there are several performers, notably Dave Brubeck, who have increasingly sought their livelihood outside of this atmosphere. The emergence of the jazz concert as a popular setting has tended to free the musicians from the limitations of the basic 4/4 dance beat, while encouraging the development of more complex rhythmic and solo patterns. Add to this the lucrativeness of recording contracts and the result is a movement out of the realm of dancing music into that of listening, or if you wish, "art music."

An attempt should be made to have a recorded music collection reflect local, regional and national cultures, whether in a college, university, or public library. Sociologically and esthetically, recordings of jazz music provide valuable resource material for the study of twentieth-century American civilization. Recognizing this fact, several institutions already have sizable collections of recorded jazz. Obviously, it is not practical for the average library to attempt to start archival collections, but their function as information or materials centers carries with it an obligation to collect jazz as a native form of musical expression.

There are, of course, certain practical questions that arise when considering the addition of jazz to the record collection. Because of its relatively young life, jazz primarily draws upon a young audience. Since the younger audience lacks experience and is easily attracted by fads, how do we avoid collecting the more ephemeral materials? Compound this with the mass of currently available albums in the Schwann catalog and even the eager beaver collectors are somewhat dismayed.

It is interesting that several European countries have more selection tools for jazz recordings than the country in which jazz has its roots. This was pointed out in the lead editorial of the first issue of Jazz, where its founders say "we are stubborn people who refuse to believe that this great big (and rich) country can't support at least as many jazz publications as Sweden, or a few less than Great Britain or France." However, good reviews by reliable critics now appear in both the jazz-orientated periodicals, such as Down Beat, and in general reviewing sources such as Saturday Review (excellent jazz coverage), The Reporter and Harpers. These reviews and articles can provide necessary guidance for the novice.

Since it may be that the reasons for excluding jazz music from the record collection lie not so much with the music itself as with the control of circulation, it should be noted that loss and mutilation are paramount considerations in any record collection, whether it be devoted to jazz, popular, classical, or folk music.

In the discography which follows, the uppermost thought was to list some currently available albums reflecting trends and personalities in the recent history of jazz and point out some developments on the current scene. Blues recordings are not included, since Irwin Silber gives a good selection of these in his discography of American folk music. The form of entry and the abbreviations follow the Schwann LP Record Catalog. Records followed by (S) are also available in stereo.

Julian Adderly: Portrait of "Cannonball," Riv 269; With
        Nancy Wilson, Cap T 1657 (S).
Mose Allison: Local Color, Prest 7121.
Louis Armstrong: Story, 4 Col CL-851/4.
Australian Jazz Quintet: In Free Style, Beth 6029 (S).
Count Basie: And His Orchestra, Dec 8049; Basie, Rou
        52003 (S).

Bix Beiderbecke: With the Wolverines, Riv 12-123.
Art Blakey: Night at Birdland, 2 Blue 1521/2.
Clifford Brown: With Max Roach, Mer 36036.
Dave Brubeck: Jazz Impressions of USA, Col Cl-984.
Ray Charles: Genius--Soul--Jazz, Impulse 2 (S).
John Coltrane: John Coltrane, Prest 7105.
Miles Davis: At Carnegie Hall, Col CL-1812 (S); Birth of
    the Cool, Cap T-762; Milestones, Col CL-1193.
Duke Ellington: Hi-Fi Ellington Uptown, Col CL-830; In a
    Mellotone, Vic LPM 1364; Music of Ellington, Col
    CL-558.
Ella Fitzgerald: Sings Duke Ellington, 4-Verve 4010-4.
Red Garland: All Mornin' Long, Prest 7130.
Erroll Garner: Concert by the Sea, Col CL-883.
Stan Getz: West Coast Jazz, Verve 8028.
Dizzy Gillespie: Groovin' High, Savoy 12020.
Benny Goodman: Great Benny Goodman, Col CL-820 (S);
    King of Swing, 2-Col OSL-180.
Bennie Green: Blows His Horn, Prest 7160.
Chico Hamilton: Sweet Smell of Success, Dec 8614.
Coleman Hawkins: Hawk Flies High, Riv 233.
Woody Herman: Early Autumn, Verve 2030.
Al Hirt: Jazz Band Ball, Verve 1012.
Billie Holiday: Lady Day, Col CL-637.
Milt Jackson: Jackson'sville, Savoy 12080.
J.J. Johnson: Jay and Kai, Savoy 12010.
Jonah Jones: At the Embers, Vic LPM-2004.
Stan Kenton: Artistry in Rhythm, Cap T-167; Milestones,
    Cap T-190.
Modern Jazz Sextet: Modern Jazz Sextet, Verve 8611.
James Moody: Last Train from Overbrook, Argo 637 (S).
Jelly Roll Morton: Classic Piano, Riv 111.
Gerry Mulligan: Paris Concert, World 1210.
Anita O'Day: Sings the Winners, Verve 8485 (S).
Charlie Parker: Genius of Charlie Parker, 2-Savoy 12009,
    12014; Immortal Charlie Parker, Savoy 12001; Story,
    Verve 8100-3.
Art Pepper: Surf Ride, Savoy 12089.
Oscar Peterson: Recital, Verve 2044.
Oscar Pettiford: Orchestra in Hi Fi, ABC 135.
Andre Previn: Pal Joey, Contem 3543 (S).
Sonny Rollins: Big Brass, MGM 1002 (S).
George Shearing: Touch of Genius, MGM 3265.
Sonny Stitt: New York Jazz, Jazzland 71 (S).
Cal Tjader: Vibrations, Savoy 12054.
Sarah Vaughan: In the Land of Hi Fi, Mer 36058.
Joe Williams: Everyday I Have the Blues, Rou 52033 (S).

Lester Young: Lester Leaps In, Epic LN-3107.

Collections:

Classic Jazz, Vol. 1-5, Riv 112/16.
Encyclopedia of Jazz, Vol. 1-4, 4-Dec DX-140.
History of Jazz, 4-Cap T-793/6.
Jazz, Vol. 1-11, Folk 2801/11.
New Orleans Legends, Riv 119.

The Sound of Poetry
William Ready

From A. L. A. Bulletin 56:153-4, February, 1962. Reprinted by permission.

While phonograph records have been a part of library circulation for generations in the more generous of our libraries, only recently have they become a new dimension in literature. Those of us in middle age remember the cracked voice of Caruso on machines that we wound up by hand. For decades now the soaring sound of music on records has become a part of our musical heritage and has done for the composer what Andre Malraux maintains the fine art reproduction presently possible has done for the artist--make his work appreciated far beyond the walls that hold the original.

There is an argument against this that is growing in strength. Because of the sound engineers and the printing technocrats, the sound of music and the sight of painting are being removed from the original, from what the artist decided in the first place. We are taking the shadow for the substance and this can lead to catastrophe.

However, in poetry it is altogether different. It started just a few years ago when that roaring Welshman put the horn of poetry to his lips and blew it for the Caedmon sisters. It was the first time in the history of the world that millions were hearing poetry for the first time. I remember how an "Omnibus" television program was interrupted to announce the death of Dylan Thomas at St. Vincent's Hospital in the Village. Through the blurred and blotched still picture of his misspent life came the brazen glory of his voice declaiming, for the millions staring at their television sets, his noble lament for Death that had encompassed him within the hour: "Do not go gentle into that good night."

This eulogy of the dead poet was the first literary success of the phonograph world. Since that time, Caedmon has triumphed and has brought us many charming records of poets and storytellers reading their own work. Along with Caedmon, the Library of Congress, Spoken Arts Series, and others such as Angel and Riverside, have added, for our enjoyment, a great wealth of literature in a new dimension. This wealth has become a charge on us, like books, to circulate and make known.

There are now hundreds of recordings; there will be thousands very soon, with their present culmination the Caedmon Shakespeare series. But the Library of Congress recording, "An Album of Modern Poetry, " edited by Oscar Williams, with a printed text included, is really a joy and really pushes the books of these poets back on the shelves or makes references out of them, their proper role when the voice of the poet can be caught as truly as it is here. It is surprising how well so many poets and writers can read their own work. The pale, high, brave Southern voice of William Faulkner accepting his Nobel Prize transmutes the cold words of the text of his message into a stern call to action for the artist.

No editor or printer can ever do Eudora Welty justice again after you have once heard her reading (Caedmon, TC-1010) her raucous and comic story, "Why I Live at the P. O., " and her lovely tale of the old Negro woman, "A Worn Path. "

Frank O'Connor reads his own stories, "The Drunkard" and "My Oedipus Complex" (Caedmon, TC-1036), better than any author has a right to, and Alfred Knopf must be proud of this white-headed boy he has published for so long and so well.

John Betjeman made history in print twice recently, by making a best seller out of his Collected Poems and by writing his early life in blank verse and selling that well also (Summoned by Bells). Now Spoken Arts (710) has brought out "The Golden Treasury of John Betjeman" and has capped with this record his two earlier successes in print, making with the charm and the power of his voice, his own fine hat trick.

There are Eliot and Yeats, James Stephens and Masefield, all available on Spoken Arts records, and every large city and college town has a stock of them. But these recordings reach down to the primary and high school levels. To hear Walter Brennan reading "The Jumping Frog of Calaveras County" (Caedmon, TC-1027) will hush any crowded class, and Dylan Thomas' memorable rendition of his childhood, "A Child's Christmas in Wales" (Caedmon, TC-1002) will ring through the minds of the children who hear it like a bell in an underwater belfry. Every school and college in the land should possess these records even before they own the books. They can help us more to fulfil our real purpose in all things than anything else invented since the coming of print.

The Record Review
Kurtz Myers

From Library Journal 88:1813-17, May 1, 1963. Reprinted by permission.

Since 1948 I have compiled the Index of Record Reviews which is published in each quarterly issue of the Music Library Association's Notes. My indexing has covered the entire period of LP record manufacture. During this decade and a half a changing list of about 25 record reviewing periodicals has been indexed. In recent years a typical issue of Notes has contained about 2,500 review citations. During the total period of publication about 150,000 citations have been printed, and each one of these stands for a review which I have read, often more than once.

Not only have I read the review, but I have been faced with the task in each instance of trying to decide how the reviewer really felt about the recording--to reduce my idea of his idea to a symbol and, in effect, to make a recommendation by assembling a series of review citations with their attached symbols. For the Index is not content with being an index; it also attempts to incorporate features of a discography and of a buying guide, obviating (except for the most curious, and those most distrustful of my function as an intermediary between them and the reviewer) the necessity of exploring the back files of a large number of magazines, some rather specialized.

The symbol system indicates whether the reviewer judges the recording to be excellent, adequate, or inadequate, among other things. Though the system is not perfect, I remain convinced that it sorts out the really superior and inferior recordings, besides indicating the large number of safely mediocre performances. Because of length or ambiguity (what Variety would call a "no opinion" review), many reviews must be re-read a number of times before a symbol can be assigned. At the same time, many reviews must be indexed for which, in the end, there is no space in Notes.

Important categories of recordings, the very ones for which reviews are hardest to locate, are thus eliminated from the Index. Among the types of material omitted are

86

jazz, popular music, collections of so-called "semi-class-
ics," band music, seasonal music, theater music (recordings
derived from moving picture and television spectaculars, as
well as Broadway shows), humor, language instruction records, and recordings of various types of literature. Also,
a great miscellany of instructional records, and a considerable number of reissues of musical recordings which are of
solely historical interest are not published in the Index.

Taking all factors into account, I think I may claim
to have examined at least a quarter million record reviews
in the past 15 years. My view has been bifocal, simultaneously that of a private collector (since childhood) and that of
a librarian who has been concerned with recordings as library materials for 25 years. From all of this experience
might predictably come some conclusions about the adequacy
of record reviews, and specifically about their usefulness in
record selection by librarians.

Without entering upon a discussion of book reviewing,
I must express my conviction that record reviewing is quite
different. Most record reviewers are not much concerned
with content. Few "originals" appear on records (among
the classics, at least--the situation is different in the popular, jazz and folk song fields); most recordings are concerned with material previously tested, sometimes over a period
of many years. Recordings of serious music draw heavily
upon the standard repertory, with which the reader of the
review and potential purchaser of the record can be presumed to have some familiarity. Should a reviewer have in
hand a first recording of a piece of contemporary music or
a rediscovered work of the past, he may attempt to supply
background information in his review, or even attempt to
judge the composition qualitatively. Even then his approach
will be somewhat different from that of a reviewer hearing
the same piece for the first time in the concert hall. He
will award the piece some points for having gotten recorded,
aware as he is of the great amount of unrecorded musical
literature, and being himself surfeited by the fantastic amount
of re-recording of standard works. And he will be aware
that by being recorded the piece has achieved a certain im-
mortality, distinguishing it from the evanescent concert hall
performance.

Usually the chief concern of the reviewer will be not
with the value of the music per se, but rather with the quality of performance and with the adequacy of the recording
from a mechanical standpoint. He also may be concerned
with format (the adequacy of printed notes, the attractive-
ness and suitability of packaging, the congruousness of coup-

lings). His chief concern, however, is always with perform-
ance--how and how well the piece is done.

The Comparison Game

Here we come face to face with the basically comparative nature of record reviewing. Our comparisons are
not so often comparisons of one composer with another, but
rather of one performer with another, or of one performer
with himself (or performing organization with itself). Recordings are ideal material for the comparison game; they
allow us to move about geographically and in time. Rubin-
stein is measured against his own earlier recordings of the
same work; Stern is measured against Oistrakh. A romantic or "effective" interpretive approach on one disc is con-
trasted with a musicologically correct approach to the same
work on another. One generation is measured against an-
other--Price and Rethberg, Valentti and Schipa. The game,
of course, can also be played, with even greater critical
hazards, in reviewing folk music and jazz recordings.
The reviewer is also concerned with the suitability of
the artist chosen to record the work. At an earlier period
musicians usually recorded only works with which they had
had a long association and for which they had evolved a mature interpretation of some familiarity to the concert-going
public. Nowadays, in the period of the highly competitive
A and R man, exclusive contracts, and the exploitation of
young talents, we experience on recordings (particularly
opera recordings) interpretations which have not been tested
as yet in the fire of public performance, or if they have,
are still immature and lacking in distinctiveness. Some
young artists seem to be learning their repertory on records, as others are learning theirs from records--a risky
business when the models themselves are unformed. So-
called "definitive" performances are still being committed to
records nonetheless, though they seem to be lost sometimes
in the sheer volume of new recordings.
The reviewer is also inevitably concerned with the
accidentals of performance. Was the artist caught on a good
day and in a moment of inspiration? Such circumstances
may mean the difference between a faultless and a memorable performance, and they are the chief justification for the
issuance of mechanically imperfect recordings derived from
live performances and air checks.
Assessing the mechanical factors involved in recording can be most troublesome. Few reviewers can be expected to be equally qualified as music critics and acoustical

engineers. Sensitive musicians seem often to be quite in-
sensitive to mechanical crudities in recordings; perhaps they
compensate for them in the inner ear.   There is, of course,
a basic discrepancy between the kind of reproducing equipment used by the reviewer (usually unspecified) and that owned by the reader-buyer.   Furthermore I have never been
able to understand how reviewers can be so confident that
the flaws which they so often encounter on "test pressings"
will not show up in mass-produced records found in shops.
And finally there is the barrier set up by technical jargon.
The engineer-reviewer probably needs, if he is to tell you
anything specific about the mechanical quality of a recording,
a more specific trade language than the layman (librarian)
reader can understand.

Each wave of technological "advance" in recordings
seems to prompt a new concern of reviewers with mechanical factors.   In the past two decades we have experienced a
number of such waves.   Each time there comes a leveling-
off period when common standards of mechanical quality seem
to prevail, and only the cheaply produced and inadequately
manufactured recordings are singled out for criticism.   We
seem to be at such a period of development at the present
time, as the novelty and artificialities of stereo are being
absorbed and refined.   Perhaps the reviewers and readers
who are primarily sound enthusiasts have shifted their al-
legiance to tapes, now, as a rule, separately reviewed but
offering the same performances and repertory which are to
be found on discs.

Format is a matter of ever-increasing importance.
The glossier packages have become status symbols, and
jackets must now compete (as do the covers of paperbounds)
in supermarket racks.   When notes are truly informed and
contributory (and not just Late Twentieth Century puffing),
and when art work is appropriate and well reproduced, packaging can be much more than a merchandising aid.   It's a
pleasant switch once in a while when a reviewer decides to
review an outrageous jacket or some pseudo-musicological
notes rather than the bland recorded performance which they
accompany.

Two other factors may well enter into the reviewer's
evaluation--topicality and uniqueness.   In the recording field
there is now more than ever a great desire to capitalize on
news-making events--events on Broadway, on television, at
the Metropolitan, at the White House.   Andre Watts on the
Bernstein Youth Concerts telecast, the New York Philharmon-
ic opening under glass, Casals at the White House, Siepi on
Broadway or in Las Vegas, Tebaldi in (or out of) Adriana--

all these developments can be expected to be reflected in
current record releases, along with an increasing number of
memorial and anniversary releases. The reviewer is usually very responsive to this built-in mass in-ness. In large
part this is because he is a journalist writing for a readership, and he feels that novelty is attention compelling.

Uniqueness is a somewhat different matter. Here we
are concerned with the critic's predisposition toward anything which has not been done before. Obscure works, when
they appear for the first time on records, are very often
presumed to be of a value and their performance of an elo-
quence and authenticity strangely unapparent when the third
or fourth recording of the same work comes along. Similarly a recording made by the participants in a premiere is often presumed to have a special value, even though the circumstances surrounding the premiere may have been more
accidental than optimum. The reverse of this is that the
most staple works and performances (Tchaikovsky's familiar
works for orchestra, the Philadelphia Orchestra) rarely receive their due from jaded record reviewers.

Though the day of the one-volume, one-author collection of record reviews seems to have passed, two magazines currently are publishing compilations of the reviews
which have appeared in their pages within the year. These
annuals are Records in Review (available from Wyeth Press
since 1955) and Down Beat Jazz Records Reviews (available
from Maher Publications since 1956). Lippincott has produced an interesting series of annotated discographies in its
Keystone Books in Music series. Typical titles are The Collector's Bach, by Nathan Broder, The Collector's 20th-Cen-
tury Music in the Western Hemisphere by Arthur Cohn, and
The Collector's Verdi and Puccini by Max de Schauensee.

But it is to magazines one must turn for extensive
coverage of new records. The range of commercial commitment to be found among them runs from Cash Box and Bill-
board (quite a bit) to Musical Quarterly and Ethnomusicology
(not much). Less commercial and more critical than might
be expected are some of the house organs published by record stores. A classic example is the Gramophone Shop Supplement, fondly remembered. The tradition is continued by
New Records (published for the past 30 years in Philadelphia
by H. Royer Smith Co.) and The Monthly Letter from E. M.
G. (published in London for 33 years). These two magazines are especially valuable for the fullness of their discographical information, particularly for their full listings of
the contents of anthologies and of performer credits.

The greatest number of reviews appear in the month-

lies which are solely devoted to recordings and their reproduction. In addition to reviews of many types of recordings,
these magazines contain news notes about forthcoming releases, articles, interviews, discographies, and descriptions
of new equipment. The titles which come first to mind are
The American Record Guide (29th year), High Fidelity (13th
year), and HiFi/Stereo Review (10th year). Their English
equivalents are The Gramophone (40th year, the daddy of
them all) and The Gramophone Record Review (7th year).

Continental Counterparts

        Opposite numbers also exist on the Continent. Dis-
ques is published in Paris under the editorship of Armand
Panigel; it appears irregularly but has achieved 130 issues
in its new series since 1948. Its advertising pages are luxe
but restrained compared to the flamboyant advertising in Musica e Dischi, its Italian counterpart. Germany has come
late to the field but presently has two substantial record
magazines: Fono Forum (Hamburg) and Phonoprisma, a supplement to Musica (Kassel). It is worth noting that international distribution of recordings has been so facilitated by
technology and commercial alliances that many new recordings are released and reviewed simultaneously here and
abroad.
        A smaller number of records are reviewed in the gen-
eral magazines, which typically feature a department presid-
ed over by a well-known reviewer: The Atlantic Monthly
(Herbert Kupferberg), Harpers ("Discus"), The Saturday Review (Irving Kolodin), Consumers' Bulletin (Karl F. Gruen-
inger), The Nation (Robert Evett), The New Republic (B. H.
Haggin), The Reporter (Roland Gelatt and Nat Hentoff), and
Musical America (Everett Helm). These too have their opposite numbers abroad, notably The New Statesman and Nation and The Music Review. This group of magazines can
be counted on to cover the outstanding recordings of general
interest. Space limitations often result in capsule reviews,
which can be cryptic to the point of meaninglessness. Records are not always reviewed currently, often being held
back so that they can be reviewed in meaningful groups.
However, Messrs. Haggin and Kolodin, two senior figures
among record reviewers, continue to stress new releases
and the earliest review of an important new release often appears in The Saturday Review. The Sunday edition of the
New York Times also can claim membership in this group,
its coverage ranging from merely descriptive one-sentence
reviews to extensive signed reviews of notable releases.

Some other magazines carrying record reviews are specialized in their subject field and/or readership. Foremost in this group is Library Journal, emphasizing in its reviews suitability for library collections. Another important specialized periodical is Hobbies, in which Aida Favia-Artsay reviews recordings of antiquarian interest, many of them LP anthologies dubbed from acoustical discs. Corresponding information is found in The Record Collector, published monthly in England for vocal record fanciers. Other "little magazines" for vocal record collectors have come and gone, including Ross, Court & Company's recently defunct Record Collector (Canada). This ceased publication at about the same time as The Canadian Music Journal which, while it lasted, was a fine source for reviews of recordings of Canadian folk music and of contemporary works by Canadian composers. Reviews of new opera recordings will be found in the pages of Opera News (New York) and of Opera (London). Serving their own special interests through record columns are The American Organist, Down Beat, Audio, Parents, and The Musical Quarterly, a diverse quintet. Magazines in which records have received slight or inconsistent attention but which are always hopefully examined are The Journal of American Folklore, The Quarterly Journal of Speech, and the Educational Theatre Journal.

It is, of course, not necessary for the librarian to continuously examine all these reviewing periodicals. One or two magazines which attempt to cover all types of recordings on a current basis should be read and checked regularly. These might well be supplemented with Library Journal and Saturday Review. My own index in Notes, if it can be waited for, and if only the serious musical repertory is needed, can be most helpful. Sources for reviews of specialized materials--children's records for instance--can be sought out. It is probably more sound to check a few review sources consistently than to see more sources spasmodically. It is especially important to become familiar with the general critical slant of the publication, especially if the reviewing is done by a single critic.

If one is inexperienced musically, there may be a temptation to buy only enthusiastically recommended or "big name" performances. But in a library collection, space must be provided also for "adequate" performances of less frequently recorded and less virtuosic material. Users of library collections are often less fussy musically and less name-conscious, more adventurous and more unprejudiced than are private collectors. Furthermore, it is necessary in a large collection to buy quite a few recordings which go unreviewed. This is particularly true of speech recordings and of recordings of the "music between" (miscellanies by the Boston "Pops" and the Hollywood Bowl Orchestra, programs of old favorites by well-known choral groups, performances of the popular music of various foreign countries). With material of this type, one must fall back on the reputations of recording companies and of performers, or one must contrive to do one's own reviewing, a time-consuming process increasingly difficult to arrange in this day, when records are so often factory-sealed and mail-ordered.

Finally, one or two words of caution. Try to read record reviews from an institutional viewpoint. Beware the temptation to build a library record collection along the lines of a private one. Most reviews are written by pundits who got that way by being private collectors. Their reviews are written essentially for other private collectors. For this reason it is refreshing to encounter occasionally reviewers who apparently are not discophiles (Alfred Frankenstein, Nathan Broder, the reviewers of The Musical Quarterly), who regard the record only as a vessel for the conveying of the music and who do not reflect the collector's mystique.

Too often a reviewer will reveal his snobbery by dismissing a recording with "strictly for the admirers of..." (who is usually a best-selling artist). A record so dismissed may well be one which should find its place on library shelves. Our presumably anti-coterie reviewer may really be pro-coterie, and his recommendation must be further evaluated. One also should be wary of following too closely the recommendations of any one critic, however high principled. The library collection should reflect a diversity of tastes. The librarian must see his record collection as a part of the total resources of the library, and as a resource broad and comprehensive rather than special and choice. Toward this end he will find record reviews a limited (especially because of their heavy emphasis on serious music), sometimes exasperating, but always fascinating, aid.

A Music Critic Looks at Basic LP Collections
Sandor Kallai

From Library Journal 88:3802-3, October 15, 1963. Copyright 1963 by R.R. Bowker Co. Reprinted by permission.

(Editor's Note: During the past 18 months, four basic record collections have been published:
A Basic Record Library. By the publishers of the Schwann
    Long Playing Record Catalog.
"A Basic Collection of Records for a College Library," by
    David O. Lane, College and Research Libraries, Vol.
    23, No. 4, July, 1962.
"A Basic Stock List," in Gramophone Record Libraries, London, Crosby, Lockwood & Son, 1963.
Basic Library, by Robert H. Reid. Recommended by Sam
    Goody.)

One was compiled by an American librarian, one by Robert H. Reid "of the Sam Goody organization," one by the publisher of the standard discographical periodical, and the most recent by a British music librarian.

The three U.S. lists have been widely circulated and, we presume, widely used for collection building. How good are they? We decided to ask a music critic to evaluate them. Why a music critic? Because the professional critic knows the repertoire, he lives with it, it is his business. Also, like the librarian, the critic faces the task of educating his public. His job will be a good deal easier if the library in his community makes effective use of records to educate the concert-going public; for what this public hears is often largely dependent on what they want to hear. What they want to hear depends largely on how well educated their tastes are.

With one exception, these lists are entirely "classical," and it is from this point of view that they were examined by Mr. Kallai. The number of titles varies considerably. The Schwann list contains around 1,000 titles, the Sam Goody list around 900, the CRL list 300, and the British list 400.)

The four basic record repertoire lists I have been

asked to examine share a major fault--they all include Beethoven's nine symphonies.

Yes, and they unanimously approve the six Bach Brandenburg Concertos, Bizet's Carmen (but all omit his Pearl Fishers), both piano concertos of Brahms, Handel's Messiah, the Bolero of Ravel, Orff's Carmina Burana (though three of the lists show no other Orff work), and dozens of other standard compositions that constitute the backbone of today's concert and operatic fare.

The list makers, it would seem, have deliberated long and searchingly and have ended in fearlessly seconding history's judgment of what is great and deserving of perpetuation. The compiler of the British list has stated their intention well:

"What I have tried to do is to make the list both standard and representative--that is to say, I have included as many popular works as possible, since these will always be in demand. . . ."

Perhaps it is not fair to blame the list makers--theirs is an understandable emotion. They are aware that librarians are happiest when their circulation statistics are high and this can be assured by stocking the shelves with titles the public wants. But is this the fundamental reason libraries exist?

In some respects I am a typical library record patron--I use its collection a lot, and complain when I encounter worn, scratchy surfaces. I get furious when the record I want is unavailable, and positively livid if it is not part of the collection at all; the many times I've found just what I ` wanted, I forget instantly.

But, in all frankness, I must admit that I am not a rank-and-file disc borrower--I seldom use library records for recreational listening and I can't abide background music. Most times I look for works I am to be hearing soon in performance and which are not part of my fairly substantial collection.

My quarrel is with the premise that a basic library record collection should consist in the main of the best examples of the period from c.1725 to c.1900. (It is granted that these lists all give a nod to the 20th-century works that have acquired a degree of respectability, and three of them concede that some great music was created before Bach.)

Though the last century has brought libraries and their benefits happily within easy reach of a mass public, it seems to me that the needs of the serious student should be considered over those of the idle reader; the library as a repository for accumulated knowledge should take precedence over the library as a center for relaxation and fun.

As for records, the initial effort in building a useful collection should be to provide in abundance examples of historically significant music, such as that of medieval times and the Renaissance. Next most important is the music of our own day--not only that part of it that pampers conservative ears, but a comprehensive span of as many of the current trends as can be found in the catalogs, along with the compositions of recent decades that have had the profoundest effect on contemporary modes of expression.

That time will eventually quash the great majority of these creations is not the issue. They are as important a part of now as television and space exploration. They paint the age in sound; they reflect its anxieties--and its hopes.

Then comes the library's responsibility to fill the gaps in the music listener's experience. The lesser composers of other eras and the lesser works of the great ones deserve hearing. They often have meaning in the development of the art far beyond their intrinsic merit.

And finally, as a sort of luxury item, budget permitting, should come the tried and proven masterpieces.

No list exists suggesting this type of record-buying procedure and the librarian without a broad musical background might well ask how to go about it. My answer must be: leave it to those who know. Few communities are entirely without some person qualified to select music for its usefulness to the student. The librarian should consult such a person rather than rely on list makers.

Should this be impossible, a good survey of music history should provide clues for a selection of old music, and there are excellent studies of the modern field that should help in that department.

A collection built with this program in mind will bring scant thanks to the librarian and will be sure to evoke complaints from the unadventurous patron who feels deprived of a standard of what he should like. But this is precisely what ails the concert-going public nowadays. Its desire is for security when it should relish an invigorating plunge into the unusual.

The library's record collection, no matter how constituted, probably will not correct this deplorable situation, but it need not cater to it.

Classification Chaos
Gordon Stevenson

From Library Journal 88:3789-94, October 15, 1963. Copyright 1963 by R. R. Bowker Co. Reprinted by permission.

Ever since phonograph records have been widely accepted as library materials we have been trying to decide how to arrange them on our shelves so that the best interests of the library patron will be served. This report will try to show what progress has been made towards a common solution to some of the problems which have plagued us since the introduction of the LP record upset some beautiful theories of record classification.

Although there has been a consistent effort to make records accessible to their users in such a way that their full potential will be realized, there has been little agreement about how best to accomplish this. The necessity of classification has been questioned, and many librarians believe that the LP recording of music defies any logical subject or content approach to classification.

Much of our thinking has been influenced by traditional methods of arranging printed material. But whereas the physical form of the book has not changed radically in many centuries, the "record" has assumed many different shapes, sizes and speeds--it refuses to settle down. There is no reason to believe that the present form of the record will not one day give way to yet a different shape, size or speed. Any system of classification that aims to be universal must take this into account.

There are almost limitless possibilities as to how records can be arranged. A decision concerning which method to use depends on the collection, its purpose, what is in it, who is going to use it, why and how they are going to use it. Recorded sound has four uses (at least) that seem to relate to traditional functions of the library: documentation, research, education, and entertainment.

The library archives that collects and preserves all types of recorded material for research, functions quite differently from the public library. In most public libraries the record is a means to an end, and the only interest in preservation is the attempt to insure that its normal life expectancy will be reached before it is consigned to the junk heap. The use of records in a formal program of education implies still different shelving arrangements and controls.

Of course it is not all this simple, since many public and university collections serve more than one function. What is right for one library may be all wrong for another. Even one library will find that the best way to handle one collection (e.g., a student browsing collection) may not be practical for another (e.g., a historical collection of 78's).

To gather information on current trends in shelving arrangements and classification schemes, a questionnaire was sent to 473 libraries with record collections. It was obvious from the returns that an astonishing amount of initiative and imagination had been devoted to the problem. Of the 392 libraries that answered the query, only 37 indicated that their system was definitely known to be based on that of some other library.

We knew that there were at least eight ways of arranging phonograph records currently in use. What we did not know is their frequency of use, or how well they actually serve the purpose for which they were intended. Because of differences in notation and the many variable elements that may be taken into account in setting up classes and subclasses, the following tabulation can be considered no more than a general indication of what is happening in the libraries which responded.

	Open or partially open stacks	Closed stacks
Arrangement by accession number	89	59
By manufacturer's number	13	8
Adaptation of Dewey D.C.	46	6
Adaptation of L.C.	4	1
Arrangement by broad subject area	51	8
Color code used as location symbols	15	0
Schedules with a letter notation	42	0
Arranged in alphabetical order by composer, author, or title	30	3
Other systems	12	5

We did not ask for information on how satisfied librarians were with their own arrangement, assuming that if they chose a system, or invented one (as many of them did), and used it, they must like it. This was a mistake, of course, but many librarians volunteered the information. Almost everyone who commented made it a point to say that even though their method might seem a bit unusual, it was ideal for their situation, their patrons were delighted with it, and they could heartily recommend it to other librarians. Many expressed astonishment that a library would even consider a basic approach different from the one that they themselves had chosen.

Only six librarians indicated dissatisfaction with their current methods, each being dissatisfied with a different scheme. Seven librarians volunteered the information that they had switched from one scheme to another, but there was no pattern. One library, for example, found an alphabetical arrangement by composers unsatisfactory and switched to manufacturers' numbers. Another library found manufacturers' numbers unsatisfactory and switched to an alphabetical composers arrangement.

The above tabulation is deceptively neat and simple. It gives no idea of the incredible lack of uniformity among libraries that had adopted any one system. Hardly any two classed approaches seemed to be exactly the same in all details. Some libraries used Dewey for nonmusic and another scheme for music records. In some alphabetical setups, Dewey numbers were used to sub-arrange a composer's works by media, the class number being used after the composer's Cutter number. Dewey was used in one or another of its US forms and in an adaptation of the McColvin-Reeves revision of the 780's. Two libraries assigned all records to one single Dewey number, then one sub-arranged by composer, the other by accession number. Dewey was adapted to the use of records by the addition of letters, by the omission of numbers, by the displacement of the decimal point, and by the addition of the manufacturer's number. Some schedules made mnemonic use of letters, others were arbitrary.

Color codes were used in combination with Dewey, with accession numbers and with a scheme of letters. One library used 16 different colors to identify as many subject classes. Accession numbers were used within subject classes and in combination with Cutter numbers. Some libraries arranged every LP in no order other than the order in which it was processed, so Brubeck followed Mozart, the B Minor Mass was shelved next to Le Sacre du Printemps, and Beethoven's nine symphonies were scattered all over the place in any order.

One is tempted to call the total picture chaotic, but the illusion of total confusion is created more by differences in notational systems than by a multiplicity of basic approaches to the problem.

Once we have decided, for example, that all operas should be grouped together, whether we identify this class as LP782, 78.2, 7.82, 783, 210, PRM-ML1500, Bin # 13, OP, Op, O, 061, D, LO, H, M, C, Z, Zgn, the color blue, or what have you, we have at least decided that it is to the patron's advantage if we keep all operas together in one place on the shelves. Of the 302 libraries which reported open or partially open stacks, 200, or 66 percent, favored some form of classified arrangement, though the structure of these classes and subclasses, and their sequence, varied greatly.

The question of open or closed stacks is obviously a factor of paramount importance. It is at this point that most of the academic libraries part company with public libraries. The main trend in public libraries is open stacks with very liberal loan privileges. Generally speaking, university and college libraries consider records more of a long-term investment. Their use is rigidly controlled and there are few large collections thrown wide open to the potential dangers of an omniverous student public. The main functions of a public library (self-education, recreation, and entertainment) are hardly important at all in record libraries serving institutions of higher learning. In such academic communities records for recreational or noncourse-related listening are often (though not always) considered ephemeral and expendable material. As often as not they are the responsibility of a student organization or some university authority other than the library.

Whether in academic or public library, once the records are in closed stacks, there are few librarians who would recommend any attempt at subject classification (not that it isn't being done), unless it be of the most general nature.

The open stack principle remains the most favored arrangement for LP's in the public library. It is felt that nothing should separate the book or the record from the potential user. I would like to suggest that we may have been wrong in assuming that what is good for the book is also good for the record. It is interesting to compare our practices with those of British libraries in this respect. A report published this year[1] indicates the British libraries, with very few exceptions, are wedded to the "closed access"

method of shelving records. Either by choice or by necessity, 90 libraries that replied to my questionnaire shelve
their records in closed stacks. The relative merits of the
two practices should be explored further.

At least one public library has found an interesting
solution to the problem (if it is a problem), by removing the
discs from their jackets, storing them in closed stacks, and
placing the empty (but still attractive and informative) jackets in open bins for browsing. There is a lot to be said
for this idea and it deserves serious consideration. The
chief objections to it are the added expense, extra demands
on staff time, and doubled space requirements.

With records on open shelves we come to the crux of
the problem. Ideally, we would like to follow certain bibliographical principles: variant "editions" should be shelved
together, composers and authors should be arranged alphabetically, related "subjects" should be shelved together and
in a logical sequence, "listener's interest" areas, and detailed subject classifications must be considered. And, as
is the case with the book, the borrower should be able to
go directly to the shelves, by-passing the card catalog in
his first attempt to find what he wants.

It is in the nature of the LP record that none of these
procedures can be faithfully followed, and in every system
there will have to be some compromise. A beautiful, logical, well-ordered, and universal theory of record classification, based on the only thing about a record that really
counts (the sounds hidden in those little grooves), is not possible with the LP. The difficulty stems from the fact that
most LP's of music contain more than one composition, and
often two or more composers are represented. We are not
classifying monographs, but "bound withs," and this is the
flaw in any classed or alphabetical arrangement. Only one
of the two sides of the record can be used as the basis for
assigning a classification number, only one composer can be
given a Cutter number, and the record can only be shelved
in one place.

My own feeling is that a compromise must be accepted, since the only alternatives are accession number order
(which is no order at all), or a sequence based on manufacturers' numbers. The latter is the equivalent of arranging
books in alphabetical order by the name of the publisher,
with sub-arrangements by the order of publication.

The use of manufacturers' numbers (the number on
the label and in the Schwann catalog), has the endorsement
of one of the largest archives of records in the world, the
British Broadcasting Corporation. The assistant librarian

of the BBC Gramophone Library writes: "The number given
[by the manufacturer] is most important to the librarian--it
is an identification universally understood and recognized--
it is in the makers' catalogues, lists, and advertisements.
With its prefix (if it has one) it indicates what type and size
of record it is. No greater mistake can be made by a librarian than that of substituting his own numbering system
for this universal one."[2]

Other arguments in favor of this method are fast retrieval of specific titles; cataloging costs are reduced (the
"call number" is on the record, the jacket, and on printed
LC cards); the number is short and efficient; and a subject
classification of sorts emerges because of the tendency of
manufacturers to specialize (e.g., Folkways for folk music,
C.R.I. for contemporary music). If we are talking about a
closed stack collection, I cannot argue with any of this (the
BBC collection of 400,000 records is not exactly a browsing
collection!). At least one U.S. librarian regretted using
this method, even in closed stacks, because his collection
"grows unevenly in regard to labels, and shifting is a regular necessity"--a point not to be overlooked.

Shelving by accession number order is used in all
sizes and types of libraries, from the smallest to the largest, with both open and closed stack collections. Almost
38 percent of all libraries which answered my query use
this method. If all types of records are collected, categories based on physical characteristics have to be set up, and
a notation devised to define these classes. This can result
in a very large number of classes. The General Library of
the University of California (Berkeley) has developed a schedule of 36 classes for phono-discs and four for phonotapes.
Major classes are indicated by one or more letters. For
example, A designates a 12 in., single acoustic 78 rpm record; DX designates a 10 in., single electric 33 1/3 rpm
micro-groove record. Other wide-ranging collections have
developed similar schemes (with different letter prefixes, of
course).

Most reasons for using accession number order are
negative, but a few positive reasons were given: the simplicity of the numerical order (unfettered by other location
symbols) makes for fast shelving and retrieval, inventory is
simple, reserves can be checked fast, and a fixed location
eliminates much shifting.

This popular method of shelving open stack collections
of LP's was not a trend I was happy to discover. Obviously
there is a serious difference of opinion among librarians on
this point. The Cincinnati Public Library, for example, has

shelved by accession number since 1947, and its collection
has grown to over 13,000 records. How serviceable is the
method for them? It is "far from desirable." On the other
hand, the report from the Cleveland Public Library is opposite and unequivocal: "Arrangement by accession numbers
is the only practical way to arrange records." Furthermore,
the Chairman of the Music Library Association's Committee
on Classification reported that "it was the consensus of the
Committee members that shelving by accession number was
the most satisfactory method." I am inclined to believe that
it is a method that will never be acceptable to the majority
of public librarians as long as their records are in open
stacks.

If the decision is made to classify by content, the
question arises as to what relationship, if any, shall exist
between the notation chosen for records and the one used for
books. In Recordings in the Public Library (ALA, 1963),
Mary D. Pearson recommends the use of the Dewey classification because it "is the most flexible and relates best to
other library materials," a viewpoint shared by many librarians. But it has received some strong opposition ("Dewey
numbers have little meaning to patrons, the notation is too
cumbersome, etc."). I'm afraid that many librarians have
lived unhappily with Dewey's 780's and will resist any attempt to carry them over into the record collection. But
the point is far from being settled; and so many libraries
are inextricably bound to Dewey that some sort of official
recommendations for a uniform way to adapt it to records
would be most welcome.

It will be impossible here to do justice to the many
schedules using a notation based on a series of letters--
there are too many of them, they are too diverse and some
of them are too involved. I believe that the most satisfactory classification schedule (still referring to open stack collections), and one that will be useful to the largest number
of libraries, will be drawn from some of these. If there
is any one system, other than the mnemonic, that now shows
signs of being widely adopted, I failed to find it.

I gather that mnemonic letter systems can be quickly
understood by library patrons, and it makes sense to them
to look under B for band music, under O for opera, etc.
My own reservations stem from the lack of logical order
that may result. For example, the sequence Bl (ballet), Bn
(Band), Ch (chamber music), is a rather violent juxtaposition
of unrelated material.

Several libraries have been very successful in using
color codes. Some surprisingly detailed methods have been

used, but color is most often chosen as a method to quickly
sort out and identify broad subject areas, often in combination with some other system of order. One method which
showed something like a stroke of genius was the idea of using color to identify various types of records within one overall accession order. The idea is that the person interested
in, say, chamber music, can quickly spot the records he is
interested in by looking for all albums with red tabs (or
whatever color was chosen to identify chamber music).

An alphabetical arrangement by composers (using Cutter numbers) strikes me as an efficient way to organize
medium-sized collections. Mary Pearson, in her book, says
it should work with collections up to 5,000 records. Such a
system will get out of hand unless a few major divisions
(jazz, folk music, spoken word, etc.) are pulled out and arranged separately. There will be no end of headaches if
collections are interfiled by title. Collections can be placed
at the beginning or the end, or grouped by content or performer and interfiled by these groups. One librarian strongly opposed the alphabetical composers arrangement because
it may very well give the patron the false idea that all of
the music of one composer is together, which it is not.
There is no method, classed or unclassed, that will substitute for detailed composer analytics in the card catalog.

A factor that will definitely play an important part in
shaping up classification methods is the increased use of
bins or "browser boxes" of the type used in many record
stores. I would think that, for libraries that use them, they
should sound the death knell of accession order shelving (or
is this just wishful thinking?). One librarian said her circulation of records doubled within three months after she
abandoned her vertical shelves for the "browsers."

At best, shelving in vertical book-derived stacks is
compact; but it can be, and I speak quite literally, a pain
in the neck. Try shelf-reading a few thousand records (or
try to find that one you need in a hurry) with numbers like
LP-785.11 B33s92t, in lettering not much bigger than this,
and all standing on end in tight rows. This is why some librarians invented color codes, letter codes, and yes, even
accession numbers.

If I have overlooked any of the problems involved in
classifying records, I am sorry; but if nothing else, I think
I have proved that it is now time for those responsible for
the destinies of our record collections to stop going their
own separate ways, to get together to pool their experience
(of which they have accumulated much), to thrash out their
differences (which are fewer than they think), and to arrive

at not more than one system of classification that can be recommended for general adoption by all libraries with open stack collections. This is a professional responsibility that all who work with records must share.[3]

It does not make sense for every librarian who wants a record collection to have to work out his own classification schedule. It can be fascinating, even therapeutic, but it is a waste of money and time, and most of us have more important things to do. The purpose, after all, is to get the records arranged as quickly, as efficiently and as economically as possible, so we can get to the business of seeing that they are properly used.

Notes

1. Currall, H. F. J. <u>Gramophone Record Libraries</u>, London, 1963.
2. Op. cit., p. 55.
3. A step in the right direction would be for all libraries which have worked out schedules to send copies to the Special Libraries Association Classification Center (School of Library Science, Western Reserve University), so that they may be available to others for study and comparison.

Radio Active Library
Floyd M. Cammack

From Library Journal 90:4300-2, October 15, 1965. Copyright 1965 by R.R. Bowker Co. Reprinted by permission.

The idea of adopting transistor radio receivers for university library service had its beginning some years ago at Cornell. There it was my duty as a graduate assistant to deliver several lectures a week on the glories of French grammar.

Several weeks after the beginning of one full semester, I noticed that an attractive young lady, who wore a hearing aid, was not doing particularly well on the first quizzes of the season. Having made an appointment with her for a conference in my office, I suggested that in recognition of her hearing loss, she should feel free to change her seat for one nearer the front of the lecture room. It was only after she left the office that I noticed she had not been wearing the aid during our talk. Glowing with the fires of pedagogical zeal, I paid particular attention to her during the next week's lectures. It was this concern for her educational well-being that occasioned my noting that the wire descending from her hearing aid directed itself not into any of the usual places, but into a voluminous purse beside her desk. It was several unimproved quizzes later that suspicion finally dawned, and I asked her to remain one day after class to show me her hearing aid at closer range.

With the forthright calm that only a guilty woman can display when caught, she extracted from the depths of her purse the small transistor radio to which she had been listening regularly throughout my lectures, explaining with consummate poise that she had a friend who was a disc jockey on the University station and that if she were to miss his program even once, her matrimonial prospects would certainly be dashed to a most un-Gallic oblivion. After a few selected comments from me on the connection between matrimony and French grammar, the hearing aid disappeared forever, still presumably attached to its owner.

It was several years later, in connection with a Peace Corps language training program in Hawaii, that the possibility occurred for plugging students into transistorized ra-

dios for other than matrimonial purposes. The intensive
language training received by Peace Corps trainees wore the
drill instructors down to sandy inaudibility in a very short
period of time. Language laboratory equipment with its elaborate wiring and carpentry was far beyond our budget. It
was Electronic Futures' new "Transiphones" that finally provided the answer. By stringing aerials ("Learning Loops")
around several rooms in the building used for a training site
and by attaching these to EFI's small transmitter ("Teacher
Control"), we had for less than $300 what amounted to a
small broadcasting station. A standard tape recorder plug-
ged into the transmitter provided the needed input.

The trainees could check out headsets ($77-$97),
which function as battery-powered transistorized receiver-
amplifiers, for reception anywhere within range of the aerial or "loop." No complicated wiring, no cabinet work, no
installation cost, and as it turned out, virtually no maintenance costs. The equipment has continued to function so well
that other applications seemed worth exploring.

The Kresge Library at Oakland University now serves
1800 day students and 1500 night students in an attractive
new building which houses some 52,000 volumes. The faculty are a young, adventurous lot, and the Library Committee
is no exception. After a short demonstration of the equipment, it was decided to try a small, experimental installation in January 1965, to see what would happen.

The Music Department was the first to see the appli-
cability of a library broadcasting system. Listening assignments were difficult to schedule both for large and for small
classes. Students who missed scheduled performances were
hard put to make them up, and reruns for individuals were
on a catch-as-catch-can basis. If the library, which is open
from 8:00 A.M. to midnight anyway, could provide listening
facilities for both individuals and for groups, the problems
would become considerably easier to handle, and programs
could be directed to the library area where scores are available for those who wish to use them.

The English Department wished to take more advantage of dramatic and literary recordings available on campus
and of occasional broadcasts from Canada. A library-based,
listen-as-you-will system extended the accessibility of these
recordings beyond any previous limits. A professor from
the Economics Department, who is frequently away from
campus on business, now tapes his lectures for scheduled
library broadcast times when he knows he must miss a regular class period. Other departments have come up with
similar projects, but the one which shows most promise

from the library's point of view came from a member of the
Political Science Department, who set us off on the new library orientation system.

Since the receiving headsets leave the listener free
to wander at will anywhere within range of the looped aerial,
"ambulatory" courses of instruction could be taped, the faculty member suggested, on bibliographical sources in his
field. Students could be directed on a "tour" of selected
stack areas in much the same manner as is now common in
larger museums and art galleries. The faculty member
would be spared the repetitive instruction on bibliographic
sources each semester, and the library's reference staff
could then know more definitely just what type of instruction
it was expected to supplement and to extend. An even more
important advantage of the new system was its adjustability
to periods of high student motivation.

My own experience with library orientation courses
for both American and foreign students has tended to indicate
that large, general doses are absorbed only incidentally and
almost immediately forgotten. In August 1964, Shiro Saito
of the University of Hawaii Library's reference staff developed an excellent orientation course for Fulbright students
coming from Asia and the Pacific. Using diagnostic tests
adapted from the "Peabody Library Information Test," and
a series of individualized practical problems, we were generally pleased with the final test results, which tended to
support the proposition that reasonably high motivation could
be best supported with step-by-step, individual accomplishment of carefully graded projects emphasizing what industrial educators often call "hands-on" time (i. e., individual use
of machines or techniques immediately following their introduction in class). Even with a teacher-student ratio of 1:10,
it was still difficult to provide optimum supervision and individual correction, and the time lag between the introduction
of a technique and its actual use was long enough to allow
a noticeable lack of retention.

With the transiphone system it is now possible to reduce this gap to zero. Students can be directed to a certain
volume in its actual location on the shelves, and in the case,
let us say, of a periodical index, they can receive detailed
instruction in its use while actually performing a practice exercise or problem designed to accompany the taped instructions. Generalization of these instructions can be so written
to make it possible for small groups of students to be guid-
ed through the same program at the same time without dis-
turbing one another, thus preventing the limitation of a trans-
mitted program to a single individual.

While it is too early to report detailed results of this type of orientation program, its potentialities seem to be extremely varied. Subject bibliography offers numerous possibilities for experimental instruction tapes, as do such common problems as card catalog use, government documents, basic reference sources, national bibliographies, and periodical indexes. In each case, the cost of tape preparation is minimal, and access to tapes can be as flexible as program schedules will allow. Editing and updating tapes, again, provide no significant cost problems, as opposed to film, video tape, or other standard audio-visual techniques, and the number of broadcast channels can be expanded or moved by the purchase of additional transmitters, which cost less than half the price of an electric typewriter.

Music, book reviews, lectures, aids to blind students, all can be provided to groups or individuals in any portion of the library without special enclosures, wiring, and other standard costs of permanent audio receiving equipment.

The central control units consist of nothing more complicated than a record player, a tape recorder, and one or more transmitters with a single off-on switch. In the Kresge Library they are set up at the circulation desk and operated by the student attendant on duty. Eventually, programming may be handled from a central campus source and coordinated with language laboratory materials or other audiovisual sources. At the outset, however, the control center at the circulation desk allows Oakland's library users to be radio dispatched, radio controlled, and radio active at the same time.

Oral History: A New Horizon
Elizabeth I. Dixon

From Library Journal 87:1363-5, April 1962. Reprinted by permission.

Something new has been added to the field of academic research. It has been wandering into the back doors of libraries for some 15 years, introducing itself by the rather unprepossessing title of Oral History. It has been accorded the absent-minded nod that one reserves for the unimportant and has been left to make its way unobtrusively into academic circles. Here and there it has been acknowledged in a footnote; a few articles have been written about it; and once a book was written from an Oral History interview. Recognition has come but slowly.

And yet, the concept of Oral History is not new. By other names, without the technological appurtenances, the technique is as old as speech itself. Our earliest ancestors, without the gift of written symbols, were forced to communicate orally from one generation to the next. Herodotus, that "father" of historians, made use of interviews to gather material before writing his History. Down through the ages the spoken word has always been the preferred primary source material. Hubert Howe Bancroft's contributions to California history, through his interviews with early pioneers, are well known, although only one survives in its original question and answer form--the interview with Governor Frederick Low. With the advent of sound recording, such men as Charles F. Lummis set about preserving the music and language of primitive cultures. Columbia University, the Ford Foundation, and the University of California at Berkeley and at Los Angeles are all now engaged in tape recording the memoirs of various persons of prominence.

However, the uses, the dimensions of the Oral History transcription have never been really explored. The emphasis has been upon providing a substitute for the diary and the journal and ephemeral data--an ersatz offering to fulfill the hunger for primary source material. It has been pointed out repeatedly that much of the important history of the twentieth century is literally dying every day with the passing of important persons, especially those important to local

110

history--the lives of those of national or international fame
are not likely to be overlooked in documentation.

It is no longer fashionable to keep a diary, nor is
there enough time in this jet age for the travel journal. As
Doyce B. Nunis notes in his article, "The Library and Oral
History" (California Librarian, July 1961): "The future of
manuscripts . . . as a primary corpus for scholarly research would appear bleak: we shall have naught but telephone bills; travel journals on the backs of ticket envelopes
and the stubs of airplane (or rocket) tickets!" Oral History
has been proposed to relieve this bleak future by substituting
the tape-recorded memoirs of the persons who have influenced our time. Such an approach has blinded researchers
to the fact that the Oral History transcript offers not a substitute, but a totally new area of research; that it augments
other forms of manuscript material and provides opportunities for full and meaningful research.

Oral History offers to the researcher, to the scholar,
and to the merely curious, a first: a unique means of communication with the past and with the present. It offers to
each reader something he has longed for since earliest times--
conversation, direct conversation, with the people who actually took part in the shaping of an era. It offers the researcher an opportunity to pull away from nineteenth-century
methodology and become a part of the modern world through
modern technology and modern concepts of research. How
can Oral History perform such miracles? What can be done
that hasn't already been done?

Because the basic unit of transmission in Oral History is the interview, it will serve as the focal point of this
examination. Much has been written, and more has been
said, about the proper techniques to be employed in conduct-
ing the Oral History interview. We are told that the "good"
interviewer must learn all the methods for keeping the interviewee on the right track and not permitting too many digressions. The multiplicity of the warnings makes it clear
that digressions are the norm rather than the exception.
Yet, in the later editing, it is often found that these digressions give the clearest insight into the personality of the interviewee. The tape recorder, the understanding interviewer,
and the ease of the spoken word can combine to produce a
marvelously frank memoir. However, due to the many mis-
conceptions and presuppositions about the potential value of
the resulting transcript, the editor's pencil often sterilizes
the interview into a pallid, but factual, skeleton of its former lusty self. "Good" grammar and "proper" punctuation
are the leeches which draw off the strength of an erstwhile

healthy interview. The resultant memoir will still furnish
more information than the "travel journals on the backs of
ticket envelopes" for the researcher of the future, but would
it not have more impact if the real flavor of a conversation
were maintained? Must a sentence always be properly structured simply because it is to be printed on a sheet of paper?

The Oral History interviewer usually finds that, after
the initial embarrassment of having the twin discs of the tape
recorder ceaselessly turning before him, the interviewee re-
laxes; the interviewer is no longer a stranger with a machine, but has become a friend and confidante. The interview is no longer an interview but a conversation, the depth
of which is controlled only by the interest, or lack of it,
which the subject finds in the face and in the response of the
interviewer. With thorough preparation in the background of
each interviewee, the taping sessions can become true con-
versations, not just question and answer periods. As Poly-
bius once stated:

> For how is it possible to examine a person proper-
> ly...or to understand the details of his narrative,
> if one has no clear ideas about these matters?
> For the inquirer contributes to the narrative as
> much as his informant, since the suggestions of
> the person who follows the narrative guide the mem-
> ory of the narrator to each incident...

The interviewee need no longer be on guard lest he say something wrong, use incorrect grammar, or reveal some hidden
facet of a past event. He can be absolutely candid in his
observations.

Oral History might take a lesson from the great literature of our century. The literary technique of the "stream
of consciousness" has been acclaimed in such authors as
Proust, Faulkner, Joyce, Woolf, and Salinger, to name but
a few. The reader enters the brain of the fictional character and sees his thoughts in process. Few persons have the
time or the temerity to write down their thoughts as they oc-
cus, thus the stream of consciousness has remained a technique of fiction. Ben Jonson said, "Language springs out of
the most retired and inmost parts of us... No glass renders
a man's form or likeness so true as his speech." Modern
technology brings us the opportunity to render our generation's likeness for the future to see.

What, then, should be done? The optimum would appear to be the preservation of the tapes in toto--an idea
worth considering but impracticable, due to the difficulty and

expense involved in such preservation, the time involved in the listening (most interviews run more than 12 and often as much as 40 or more hours), and the awkwardness of taking accurate notes or making citations. Transcription offers more convenience in all these areas, plus the additional advantages of correct spelling of proper names, insertion of addenda where necessary, and indexing. With more sensitive editing--new styles more in keeping with the medium-- the essential elements of candor and the stream of consciousness need not be lost. The eye can learn to hear, just as the ear has listened to life, in an Oral History interview.

The potential of Oral History programs all over the United States rests on the ability of participants to recognize the power of the tools which they can leave for future researchers. A re-evaluation of the concepts of interviewing and editing must take place, rules must be rewritten, and transcripts must be provided which will make the researcher of the future feel that he is the interviewer, the other half of the conversation. With such tools, it is possible that a vital new concept of historiography will take place; sociologists, economists, etymologists, and industrial relations experts may be better able to fathom what has made our generation act and react as it has; but most of all, they will know who we were and what we were.

Language Lab in the Library
James H. Smith

From Library Journal 86:1656-7, April 15; Junior Libraries
7:20-1, April 1961. Reprinted by permission.

I recently inherited a small language laboratory consisting of four booths with mikes and earphones, and a control unit with a tape recorder and a record player in it.

I was puzzled at first as to just how to use it in connection with the concept of the library as a materials resource center. The day after the unit was installed, the
chairman of the English Department asked me if I would play
a tape recording of a lecture he had given for students who
had missed his class, and the tremendous potential of this
unit as a teaching aid struck home.

A language laboratory unit can be of tremendous significance in the areas of social science, English, and science. With such facilities in the library students can listen
to their instructor explain further an aspect of a lesson for
which he did not have enough time in class, or listen to him
elaborate on their collateral reading or a pertinent magazine
article. The student gets an extra lesson which can be of
great value to him, and the teacher is provided with that
extra lesson he did not have time to cover in class.

Let me illustrate this further. At present a biology
teacher is preparing a lecture on genetics for those students
whom he wishes to go further into the subject than the rest
of the class does in regular lessons. He is also preparing
diagrams which he will have mimeographed and placed in the
library. When students come to the library from study hall,
they will be presented with the essential diagrams and, as
the lecture is presented on the tape recorder, they will be
able to observe and mark the illustrations provided.

A social studies teacher came upon a magazine article which was extremely pertinent to the unit he was teaching. To assign the article for collateral reading was not
enough because it required his interpretation. He taped the
article with his interpretation and assigned it to his classes
to listen to during their study hall periods.

An English teacher, not having enough class time in
a unit on poetry for his students to listen to all the poems

he felt they should hear, assigned them to his students to hear in the library, and used class time for discussion of the poets.

My language laboratory unit is at present too small to fill the demand on it, and there will be greater demand next year when its potential as a teaching aid is fully realized by other departments. I am hoping to expand it into a twenty-booth unit, which will be installed on the main floor of the library. These listening booths will serve a dual purpose. In each booth a jack for earphones will be installed, and when a student wishes to hear a tape or record, earphones will be provided him and his booth switched on from the control panel. When the booths are not being used for listening, they will be used as student carrels, for those who wish to do research or reading.

The school library with listening facilities such as these can provide a very valuable service to teachers. It can provide an extra period of instruction in almost all subject fields. A tape library of teacher's discussions of collateral readings, extended lectures, reviews and makeup lessons, can provide the teacher that "little more time" that he always needs. My white elephant has proved to be a gold mine.

Language Courses on Magnetic Tape:
A New Reference Service
M. J. Harkin, A. L. A.

From Library Association Record 68:161-5, May 1966. Reprinted by permission.

The development of the spoken record on tape has had
a revolutionary effect on language learning techniques.   Students listening to the recorded dialogue of each exercise are
able to link pronunciation with the written text, thus acquiring the feeling and intonation of the language.   Most language
teachers agree that a pupil must hear the language he is
studying spoken often and well over a fairly lengthy period.
Courses on tape can help provide this wider range of linguistic experience; they can acclimatize the ear of the beginner
and add continually to the experience of the advanced student.
Shortly after the opening of the Language and Literature Library, the latest subject department in Manchester
[England] Public Libraries, it was decided to introduce language courses on tape as part of the reference service of the
new department.   Whereas the issue of language instruction
records from gramophone record libraries is a fairly well
established custom, as far as we know our reference service on tape is the first of its kind in the country.   One disadvantage of a lending service is that it can cater to only a
few people at a time.   Once the records are borrowed they
are unavailable as far as other users are concerned, and
they are often used only infrequently by the person who has
them at his home.   With a reference service it is possible
to ensure that tapes are kept in almost constant use.   In
fact the primary object is to get the most economic use out
of equipment and tapes by aiming at keeping them in use for
as long as the library is open.
The service commenced in January, 1964, as an experiment, with no publicity apart from notices in the department.   The equipment consisted of two tape recorders and
two language courses (French and German).   Bookings at
first were slow but soon gathered momentum and soon it was
impossible to accommodate all those interested in the French
course.   Even in those early days 100 percent use was frequently achieved, i. e., on some days each machine ran con-

tinuously for twelve hours.   From January 13 to March 31,
1964, the courses were in use 562 hours out of a possible
1,680 and, as the service stimulated considerable interest,
it was decided to extend it.   During the year the service
was twice extended.   A further three languages and two machines were added in June, and the service was for the first
time given some publicity in the local press.   In August another copy of the French course and two more machines
were added.   At present there are six machines in operation and five languages are represented, namely French (two
copies), German, Italian, Russian and Spanish.   In the year
April, 1964-March, 1965, of the 18,570 machine hours available, 9,004 were actually used, which means that each machine was in use an average of six hours per day.

Equipment and Courses

The service we have developed requires no structural
alterations nor indeed the alteration of any existing fittings
but only the provision of adequate table and seating accommo-
dation.

Tape Recorders.   The tape recorders are Grundig
Twin-Track Tape Recorders Model TK14.   Since, for the
purposes of this service, they are used only as "tape players," they have one simple modification: a plastic dome cap
is fitted over the recording button--a precaution against the
student erasing the lesson on the tape.   We have found these
machines to be extremely reliable and very robust.   The
various switches and controls will stand up to quite punishing
use from the most heavy-handed user.   As the controls allow for stopping, starting, and winding fast in both directions, it is possible for the student to go over the same part
of a lesson as many times as required.

Earphones.   For reasons of cost and, more important,
lack of space, the provision of individual sound-proof booths
for each student was out of the question.   The only alternative was to place the machines in the department proper, obviating interference with the work of readers using other
reference material, by arranging for the sound to be picked
up through headphones.   Obviously, with such an arrangement it is unfortunately not possible to repeat the lesson
aloud, as one does in a language laboratory.

We use the earphones issued by Grundig and find
them ideal for the purpose.   They are of the stethoscope
variety and, being light in weight, can be worn for long periods without causing fatigue; they may even be worn with the
most modish hairstyle.   When properly adjusted there is no

sound leakage whatever, and no distortion for the listener,
two very important considerations. Though of light construction, there is very little breakage in use, and fortunately,
the stethoscope part of the set, which is most likely to be
damaged, can be replaced quite cheaply. Hygiene is a problem, since the earpieces fit directly into the ear. Our solution is to wipe the earpieces, after every user, with paper
tissues dipped in an antiseptic solution. We have, in fact,
had no complaints so far on this point.

Seating Arrangements. Since each student has a separate machine it would be possible to disperse such a service to several points throughout a large room, but our experience indicates that it is better to congregate machines
and users in one area where proper surveillance, control
and guidance can be exercised by a minimum number of staff.
We find that a table measuring 2 1/2 feet by 5 feet gives
just sufficient room for three students with their three machines and attendant textbooks and notebooks.

Maintenance. The machines need surprisingly little
maintenance, which is most satisfactory because, when dealing with heavy bookings, it is important that every machine
is in running order. As might be expected, certain minor
faults develop regularly to a definite pattern, according to
the number of hours a machine has been running. The most
usual faults are (a) fracturing of the fins on the clutch tops
(i.e., the small decks on which the spools are placed) and
(b) the appearance of a certain muzziness in the quality of
the sound, caused by the accumulation of loose particles on
the recording heads. The staff are quite competent to deal
with faults of this magnitude, but for anything of a more
serious nature there is an arrangement with the local supplier who will speedily carry out whatever adjustments or
repairs are necessary.

Courses. All of the courses used so far are Linguaphone courses. Each is of approximately 50 lessons on two
spools of tape, which are used in conjunction with a number
of booklets containing the texts of the lessons, vocabularies,
explanatory notes on the grammar, and one giving good advice on the best way to tackle the course. Many people using the courses have suggested it would be helpful if sets of
the booklets were available for home reading. The Linguaphone Institute was not willing to supply extra sets for this
purpose, but agreed to our having extra sets for use in the
department as reference books. Students may use these extra booklets at times other than when they have booked a
machine. We find that many do use them either immediately
prior to, or immediately after, their booking. As a result

of the heavy use the booklets receive, it has become necessary to bind them in full cloth, in order to lengthen their
life. In fact they are best bound as soon as received because the publisher's casing and covers soon show signs of
wear.

Magnetic tape, the other component of the course, is
a much stronger material than it appears to be. Two or
three tapes have been frightfully mangled in the machines by
inexperienced students, but with care the tape can normally
be retrieved unbroken and seemingly little the worse for
wear. Each tape has a top and a bottom track, which means
that when one gets to the end of the tape, the spools must
be reversed for the continuation. [For simplification the
staff normally talk about a spool having two sides.] The
spools are clearly marked "1" and "2" and the list of lessons appearing on each side is displayed, for ease of reference, on the inside lid of the container used to store the materials.

One further piece of equipment is necessary--a tape
splicer. A lead tape is spliced on to each end of the magnetic tape to prevent undue fraying of the tape ends. This
splice is a weak link, which tends to snap from time to
time; however, with a tape splicer it is a simple task to replace the fractured splice.

At an early stage it was discovered that the very first
lesson on each course involved the staff in an excessive
amount of work. The start of the lesson was quite near the
beginning of the tape: the student had not yet had time to become familiar with the controls or achieve a certain dexter-
ity in using them; consequently, returning to the beginning of
the lesson almost invariably resulted in the tape running off
the spool. Since we find it safer not to allow the new student to re-thread tape on the spool, an assistant was quite
frequently engaged in this activity. One solution would have
been to put an excessively long lead tape on the beginning of
all the first reels. Instead, it was decided to record, on a
sufficient number of lengths of tape, some of the more important points from the "introduction to the service" given by
the staff to all new students. Splicing these lengths of tape
on before the beginning of each first lesson achieved two objectives: (a) the increased amount of tape at the beginning
of the spool allowed the inexperienced operator more latitude
when playing back over the first lesson; (b) important instructions about the use of the service were doubly under-
lined.

In order to be able to deal with the minor faults mentioned under the heading "Maintenance" it is also necessary

to have a supply of replacement clutch tops, some spare
spools, and a small screwdriver.

Booking Procedure and Statistics

At the outset it was decided that, to obtain the fullest
use of courses and equipment, casual use must be prevented
altogether. Courses, therefore, may only be used on a regular weekly basis. The smallest unit of time bookable is an
hour and this must be a regular hour on a regular day every
week for at least fourteen weeks. The fourteen-week period
was chosen arbitrarily with the intention of cutting out the
casual user and those only interested in the novelty. Although lessons are booked initially for the fourteen-week period, there is provision for the bookings to be extended for
as long as the student desires, the onus being on the student
himself to seek these extensions on every tenth visit.

Various booking routines may be devised but whatever
procedure is adopted should supply answers to the following
questions:

(a) Which of a choice of languages is available at
a particular time?
(b) What times are available on _____ day?
(c) What days are available at _____ o'clock?
(d) When will a certain hour be free?
(e) When will you have any time available?
(f) How many more lessons am I booked for?

The booking register devised for our purpose takes
the form of a ledger with a double page spread for every day
of the week. The dates are listed along the top of the page.
The double spread is split up into twelve sections representing the hours available that day. In each section the languages are listed on the left-hand side, so that on each line
in each box the name of the person booking that hour can be
added and under the date can be indicated whether or not the
student did in fact attend for his booking. All marking up
in the register is done in pencil, which is easily erased if
one person cancels a booking and another takes it up. A
simple code is used to mark the record of attendance in the
register: ✓=Present; X=Not Present; *=Advance notice of
absence given.

Running concurrently with the booking register we
have found it necessary to start waiting lists for each language. If a person cannot immediately find a place vacant
in the booking register, his name, address, telephone num-

ber, language and preferred times are noted, and, when a suitable vacancy occurs, he is offered the first option and asked to confirm the booking as soon as possible.

Since there is no shortage of interested people it is necessary to be quite strict about the way students use the course. Students persistently arriving late, for instance, may be refused permission to continue and their booking given to the next person on the waiting list. Absence without prior notification on two consecutive occasions results in automatic cancellation of all bookings, although if a student informs the library in advance that he is unable to attend for a particular hour, then his bookings are not affected.

All students starting a course are given a circular listing these and other conditions governing the use of the language courses and equipment. After reading the conditions a Declaration Form is signed, whereby the student agrees to abide by such conditions. This form, a 5 in. by 3 in. slip, then becomes a record card with the student's name printed in block capitals top left and the language he is studying printed top right. On the reverse is noted the time of the booking and the date of the fourteenth visit. Again, use is made of symbols: thus, if the student asks for his bookings to be extended on the tenth visit then the reverse of the Declaration Slip is endorsed "+" together with the new date of expiry; if, at a later date, further extensions are requested, the form is endorsed "□" together with the new date of expiry. Each period of extension is one of fourteen weeks.

Statistics. A record is kept of the number of hours actually used, which can be compared with the number of hours during which the service was available. This record is easily obtained from the booking register and we find it useful to keep separate totals for each language. The number of people who use the service during the year is worth recording. Again, we find it useful to keep separate totals for each language. In fact, a Duration Record is kept in which is noted the date each student commences his course, the date he finishes and also, wherever possible, the reason why the course was terminated.

Students

The service appeals to a wide variety of people who all have different reasons for wanting to learn a foreign language. In the case of a schoolchild or older student, a foreign language may be one of an essential number of subjects which he must master. The housewife with a grown-up fam-

ily or the retired person may simply wish to keep their
learning faculties alert and keen. Rather more pressing reasons motivate the executive, the professional worker or the
teacher, who perhaps having already a working knowledge of
a language may wish to "brush-up" because of a particular
conference, sales campaign or new job. More people are
taking continental holidays and this has given impetus to language learning, since it is generally recognized that knowing the language spoken in a foreign country leads to a much
more enjoyable holiday.

Why do these people use the service we offer? The
schoolchild and older student obviously find this a useful way
of reinforcing their class work; it is significant that the
service is especially popular with those who are preparing
for oral examinations. Housewives who, because of family
responsibilities, cannot enroll for the conventional evening
class find that they can conveniently book an hour with our
service during the day. On the other hand, older people and
retired persons, though they may have the time to go to
evening classes, frequently feel embarrassed in a class of
younger people and therefore they use our service gladly.
Those who simply need a "brush-up" type of course, would
have great difficulty in finding a conventional course suitable
to their needs since they are all at different levels of accomplishment. Using our service each person can quickly
find his individual level and start from there.

Statistics collected over the period April, 1964, to
March, 1965, show that the average number of attendances
per student was twelve. The number of people starting
courses during this period was 765 and the number finishing
courses, 607. Of the 607 who finished courses during the
year, 376 had their bookings cancelled automatically after
missing two consecutive lessons without informing the library
(42 did not in fact take up their bookings at all). The remaining 231 did inform us of their intention not to continue,
and of these 26 had completed the whole course, or as much
as was appropriate to their purpose.

Staffing and Routine

Staffing. The number of staff implicated in the running of a service of this nature will, of course, vary according to the number both of machines available and courses
offered. As far as our service is concerned, immediate responsibility is one of the duties of the "third-in-command"
of the department (A. P. T. II). A student librarian (G. D.),
as one of her duties, aids him in the clerical processes at-

tendant to the job. It is also necessary to station, at all times, an assistant at a control desk in the area where the machines are used. The duties of this assistant are as follows:

(a) Exercise general surveillance.
(b) Carry out clerical routines connected with bookings, the extension of bookings and the reduction of waiting lists.
(c) Describe the service to interested people.
(d) Explain and demonstrate the operation of the machines and the wearing of the earphones.
(e) Ensure that machines and earphones are correctly used by students. Any sound leakage or other misuse to be stopped at once.
(f) Switch off machines when they are not in use.
(g) Clean the machines regularly.
(h) Sterilize earpieces after use.
(i) Report to the senior-in-charge any fault in the machines or tapes.
(j) Generally ensure that the service is used as it was designed to be used.

Routine. When a student arrives to take up his very first booking, the routine is as follows. First, the assistant ticks his name in the booking register, indicating that he has turned up for the booking, then she shows him to a vacant machine. The make-up of the course, the contents of the booklets and the method of following the text whilst listening to the tape are all explained next. After this, the student is shown how to operate the controls of the machine and how to wear and adjust the headphones. Finally, a spool is placed on the machine and the student practices using the controls under the supervision of the assistant. We have found that female users particularly tend to hammer on the controls rather as if they were piano or typewriter keys, instead of applying the firm progressive pressure which is required. When the assistant considers that the student has grasped the technique, she retires from the scene. Before doing so, she mentions that sets of the booklets are available for reference use, and that a large amount of lending and reference material on learning foreign languages is also available.

Our experience with this service right from its very inception has been most encouraging. There has been no waning of public interest, indeed every course, every machine added resulted in more bookings and increased use.

This indicates perhaps that the time is ripe for public libraries to extend their reference services into the field of spoken records, which is not only an excellent medium for linguistic studies, but also for the communication of ideas and the presentation of imaginative literature.

World Tapes for Education--A Resource
for Elementary School Libraries
Walter W. Williamson

From Top of the News 21:311-17, June 1965. Reprinted by permission.

As the elementary school library, in its role as an instructional materials center, becomes more involved in the total program of the school, there are several problems to be solved. Probably one of the most important is the acquisition of new, significant material on a wide variety of subjects to be used by all children regardless of reading levels. Often this is difficult to achieve because of the reading content of the material, especially on international topics and the study of foreign countries. Fortunately, however, there are worthwhile sources of information for studies of this nature and World Tapes for Education is a leader in this multimedia approach to learning.

A nonprofit, international organization, World Tapes for Education has as its function the promotion of international understanding through a free exchange of information, using the medium of magnetic tape recording exchanges by classrooms, groups, and individuals. From its beginning in 1952, the result of a father's sending magnetic recorded messages to his son stationed with the Armed Service in Korea, it has become a world-wide organization, with members in more than eighty-five countries. Included in this membership are three hundred schools in the United States and two hundred schools in other countries.

World Tapes for Education offers extensive services to schools, but probably the most valuable as far as library services are concerned is the world's largest international tape library, with current material from many parts of the world on a variety of topics. For example, in one tape on different climates, a prospector in Alaska tells how it is so cold that he must heat the crankcase of his car with a flame-thrower before the engine will start. On another tape, made in an African game preserve, the park naturalist describes the actions of a family of lions as they feed on a wildebeest and in the background can be heard the snarls of the animals as they fight among themselves over the meal. Classes of

children in Australia and Hawaii tell what it is like to live
in their parts of the world and explain briefly a few historical and geographic features of their homelands.

Besides many tapes on the usual topics, there is even
one by a descendant of the Bounty mutineers in which he describes present-day life on Pitcairn Island. Also included
in the collection are several series of tapes, one with musical backgrounds describing tours through many of the principal cities of the United States, another describing life in
Africa, and a third taking the listener on a tour through English castles, some of them reputedly haunted. Through the
use of tape records, listening posts and earphones, groups
of children may listen quietly to these tapes in the library
as the normal routine continues undisturbed, or the tapes
may be used by the teacher in the regular classroom.

Classroom exchanges of tapes between schools are encouraged by WTE. For the tapes used in this exchange, the
students of a class may record information of interest to a
class in another location. The pupils may describe the community in which they live, or the school program, or a unit
of work that they have completed. In a project of this nature, the library has an important function, especially in collecting material about the school community and making this
available to the children.

To facilitate this exchange between schools, World
Tapes publishes quarterly membership lists with detailed information concerning the type of information the schools want
to exchange. Also, upon request, WTE will match schools
according to needs and interests not only within the United
States, but with schools in other countries as well.

In addition to these services, WTE also sponsors a
tape-slide section which makes available to its members programs depicting life and scenery in many different countries.
WTE operates as a coordinating agency for the various owners of shows everywhere. For the most part, the tape-slide
shows were made by persons residing in the countries shown
and authentically portray the customs and people of each
place. From Africa, for example, there is a show titled
"Amandebele, a Colorful African Tribe"; from Australia, one
named "Scenes from Tasmania"; and from Malasia, "Malayan
Scenery." These shows may be obtained directly from the
WTE members who own them at no charge except postage,
and copies may be made for the school library's permanent
collection to be used whenever there is a need.

As a direct result of WTE's emphasis on tape-slide
shows, several member schools in the Baltimore area developed their own shows to illustrate the everyday lives of the

children in their schools.   For example, in one school the
children in a third grade class interviewed the school's staff,
including the principal, vice-principal, librarian, speech specialist, cafeteria workers, and custodian, and had each person tell something about his duties.   A program done by a
sixth grade in another school described the community in
which the children lived.   Still another show took the obser-
ver on a specially conducted tour of the sights of Baltimore.
Shows of this nature have a useful place in the school library.   Not only is the planning and making of a tape-slide
show a worthwhile educational experience for children, but
also the opportunity to receive similar shows from other
children may be equally important.   The desire to know
more about the country in which the show originated is a definite stimulus for further use of the library.

Perhaps one of the best illustrations of the effective
use of a school membership in World Tapes for Education in
the Baltimore area is the program that has evolved at Hampton School, Lutherville, Maryland, under the leadership of
William Myers, a sixth-grade teacher and Mareda Nichols,
the school librarian.   Actually, however, the decision for
Hampton School to join World Tapes was made by the student
government representatives at one of their regular meetings
held in the library.   From this decision made three years
ago has developed an extensive, school-wide program for the
promotion of international understanding.

To help the children of Hampton School achieve this
aim, the student government initiated a series of monthly assembly programs on countries throughout the world.   Since
the students felt that much could be gained from the study of
underdeveloped sections of the world, they decided to present
assemblies on India, Korea, Guatemala, and China for the
first year.   Using the library's book collection, vertical file,
pictures, and filmstrips, the children collected materials on
food, customs, costumes, government, and geography of
these countries and presented this information to all the pupils of the school in the assemblies.

For the second year the student government representatives chose as the theme for the assemblies "Beauty
Throughout the World"; the students studied Samoa and other
Polynesian islands, Switzerland, and Morocco.   During the
current school year, assemblies were presented on Hungary,
Japan, Portugal, and Scotland.   Not only did the children
use all the library resources available, but they also made
use of tapes to obtain additional information.   From Scotland
came a tape especially prepared for the children of Hampton
School by two WTE members in Edinburgh, telling of life in

that part of the world.

Library displays were featured for each country chosen, and these included pictures and objects from these lands. For the most part the articles were obtained from parents who had visited these places; so much interest was aroused, however, that commercial kits of materials from foreign countries were purchased from school funds, and these were kept in the library, available to any class requesting them.

Also from these activities the children of Hampton School developed an interest in programs sponsored by UNICEF, and during Halloween they collected for that organization $777, the highest donation ever given by any elementary school. At Christmas the student government representatives organized a campaign among all the students in the school for donations to CARE instead of the usual exchange of cards.

Letter Exchange Heightens Interest

In addition to the previously mentioned activities, a letter exchange project was initiated between Mr. Myers' students and World Tape members in many different countries. From the World Tape roster lists the pupils chose the persons to whom they wanted to write and then sent letters describing themselves and the activities of the school in international education. Eighty percent of the children received replies, and all the letters were shared with everyone in the class. So much interest developed from this project that the student government representatives purchased a large photograph album with transparent pages. The letters were inserted in the album and then the book was placed in the library for everyone to read. Mrs. Nichols reported that the album has become one of the most popular books in the library, both for children and for parents.

Here are excerpts from two letters. The first came from England:

> Dear Linda,
>
> First of all, I would like to thank you for your very nice letter which I received last Friday. I was very surprised to hear from you and think it is a good idea writing to people in all parts of the world in an endeavour to promote a better understanding between people in different countries.
>
> That, of course, is one of the reasons I joined World Tapes and during the past four months since I have been a member I have spoken to people on

tape in America, Germany, Australia, and New Zealand.

Do you have tape recording facilities at your school, Linda? I see that you are actually learning letter writing at the moment, but I always think it's much more fun corresponding by tape. If you and your teacher are agreeable we could exchange tapes in the future.

The second letter came from India:

Dear Wonderful Baby Barbara,

Thank you indeed for your lovely welcome letter. Thanks, I am not a very young man. I am forty-six years young. You could be just like one of my daughters.

Of course you can try to understand the peoples of different parts of the world, and you should. I think you have taken the right step. I hope you will some day be a great woman social worker.

I am an expert equestrian, horseback rider, yes. Perhaps you may wonder if I tell you that I work in the movies and I have played in Mark of Zorro, Viva Zapata, Thief of Baghdad, Don Juan and other films in our vernacular language. Recently I played Robin Hood. So I ride a lot and sword fight a lot. That is how I make my living. I am a movie star just like Errol Flynn or Roy Rogers.

As a direct result of the letters the children wrote, several of them received tapes in return. One pupil was sent a tape from England, and, in addition to the usual description of the English countryside, was given a sample of the latest Beatle music. From Argentina came a tape of guitar music and the sound of Spanish dancing. A third pupil, who hopes some day to be a physician, received a tape from one of Portugal's leading surgeons. In addition to the tape from Portugal, the pupil also had a local telephone call from someone who was a good friend of the surgeon and had just returned from visiting him.

Mr. Myers also received tapes, some of them good enough to retain in the school tape library. One of them, done by a Belgian, took the children on a musical tour of Europe.

Of course, these personal contacts have stimulated interest in these countries, not only by the persons directly

involved, but also by other members of the class.   Everyone seemed eager to share any information he gained from
library sources, letters, or tapes, and this enthusiasm has
proved contagious.

        The Student Library Committee, also, became active
in developing international understanding and conducted a
drive to collect educational materials, including art supplies,
to send to a school in a somewhat remote section of the
Philippine Islands.   The members of the committee had been
writing to a school on Leyte, and, through an exchange of
pictures drawn by the students in both schools, learned that
the Filipino children lacked most of the art supplies needed
to conduct an effective program.   Through the committee's
efforts, enough money was raised to send a quantity of material to the Philippines.

Oratorical Contest Developed

        As a result of this increased interest in international
understanding during the first year of the project, an oratorical contest developed with the theme, "Understanding--The
Hope of Peace."   This contest proved so successful it was
continued a second and a third year, with the topics, "Com-
mitment--The Challenge of Progress" and "Tolerance in a
World of Contrast."   The library had an important part in
the preparation of the speeches and many hours were spent
collecting data.   In addition to studying the usual reference
material, the children listened to speeches of famous orators
and attempted to analyze the reasons for their superiority.
After the students had completed their speeches, they gave
them in an assembly.   The winners of the contest were selected by a panel composed of a member of a local television station, a Baltimore County elementary supervisor,
and a representative of the county speech department.

        An increased demand for library materials on other
lands resulted from the many activities for the development
of international understanding, and therefore extensive additions to the collections on that topic were made.   As the
new material was obtained, Mrs. Nichols reported that it
was used by an increasingly larger number of intermediate
pupils.

        Although the Mt. Royal Elementary School, the Knapp
Project Center in Baltimore, has just recently joined the
World Tapes for Education, extensive plans are being made
for the acquisition of many types of materials for the library
through the services offered by World Tapes.   A permanent
tape collection of approximately two hundred reels of re-

corded material on many different topics is being organized
for use in the library and in the classrooms. For the most
part, the tapes relate to social studies and literature topics,
but the library staff hopes eventually to have tapes on every
subject in the elementary curriculum.

In order to develop a comprehensive collection of material on the countries that are studied by the Mt. Royal
classes, plans are being formulated by the librarians, Idella
Nichols and Nancy Bloom, for the acquisition of tape-slide
shows from WTE members in as many countries as possible.
When the shows are received, copies of the slides and tapes
will be made, and these will become permanent additions to
the library.

Also through WTE members, plans are being made to
collect kits of worthwhile objects to show some aspects of
life in another land. Perhaps there might be included articles of children's clothing, games, toys, pictures, handmade
objects, a child's book, and taped music and information.
These will be used for display purposes in the library and
also will be available for classroom use.

In its collection WTE also has a number of tapes primarily for teachers. These consist of talks by leading educators describing teaching methods and materials. Some of
these will be obtained for use in the Knapp Project for faculty meetings, committee meetings, or individual listening.
These tapes will supplement current educational periodicals
and professional books on the teachers' shelf.

Two teachers in the Mt. Royal School have begun
classroom tape exchanges, one during an Hawaiian unit and
the other after listening to a tape from a class in a New
Zealand school. As other teachers become acquainted with
this activity, probably more will become involved in this
method of exchanging information.

For the resourceful librarians and teachers, World
Tapes for Education offers unlimited possibilities for the effective use of a wide variety of activities and materials.
Through this multimedia approach, more emphasis is placed
on inquiry and on the student's locating information to answer his own questions according to his own style of learning. Less emphasis is placed on acquiring isolated facts for
the completion of a general assignment. Through personal
contacts with persons throughout the world, the children may
learn cultural concepts based on anthropology and sociology
in addition to those from the fields of geography, history,
music, and literature. The information received is current,
an important factor in the selection of any library material.
When used effectively, WTE resources are a stimulus to

learning, a goal of any good library program.

Membership requirements and additional information about World Tapes for Education may be obtained by writing to Harry Matthews, Director, World Tapes for Education, P. O. Box 15703, Dallas, Texas, 75215.

Reading for the Blind at a New Frontier
Lee E. Grove

From A. L. A. Bulletin 55:744, September 1961.   Reprinted
by permission.

The possibility of a complete system of tape-record-
ing and playback machines for blind readers, representing a
new technological advance, is the subject of a joint investigation now under way.

Investigation of the system, which if proven feasible
can supplement the present program of Talking Books on
long-playing records, is being carried on by the Library of
Congress' Division for the Blind and Recording for the Blind,
Inc., a nonprofit organization in New York.   The latter's
program, by providing educational materials, including some
textbooks, which it records chiefly on specific request, com-
plements that of the Library, which provides material for
general, or recreational, reading.

Since most blind people do not read braille, talking
books on long-playing discs have for several decades been
the chief means of providing reading matter.   The Library's
program, carried on through 31 regional libraries, is financed by congressional appropriations and the records are
carried free of charge by the Post Office Department.   Recording for the Blind is financed chiefly by contributions
from private, nongovernmental sources.

For the two years just passed the distribution of recorded books has been supplemented by the distribution of
books on magnetic tape to blind readers having special needs
and their own tape-players.   In contrast to some 50,000
readers equipped with record-players as part of the national
free program, there are only a little more than a thousand
readers using the program who request tapes on their own
conventional tape-players.

Many more, however, have tape-players.   For example, Recording for the Blind, Inc., in a person-to-person
survey of 366 blind college students found 75 percent had
their own tape-players in addition to Talking Book machines.

While the LP records serve their purpose they have
drawbacks.   They are expensive--a minimum edition of 200
copies costs about $3000.   They are heavy and bulky--one

133

book in its container weighs nine pounds and occupies 423
cubic inches.   They are susceptible to damage by abrasion
and to breakage.

As for books recorded on the conventional magnetic
tape now in current use, they can be recorded on the present
conventional magnetic tape in less time than the present operation of making a tape and then making a disc from it, and
though the cost is less they are still expensive.   Also, the
conventional tape is not easy for blind readers to use because it has to be threaded through the play-back head and
onto the winding reel.

The proposed system represents an adaptation, with
the blind specifically in mind, of a new commercial development by CBS Laboratories.   The investigation of it is being
financed by a $50,000 grant to the Library of Congress and
a $12,000 grant to Recording for the Blind from the Council
on Library Resources, Inc.   Recording for the Blind is supplementing the council's grant with an additional $8000 from
the Lilly Foundation.

This new system has three features: encapsulated
tape, a tape-player, and duplicating apparatus which can include slave machines to permit the simultaneous duplication
of submaster tapes.

The tape is contained in an 8-ounce sealed cartridge,
occupying four cubic inches and representing eight hours of
reading--the equivalent of eight 12-inch 33 1/3 rpm records.
When placed on a spindle the recording plays automatically
and rewinds automatically.   The player is small and weighs
about seven pounds.   The cost of such a player, if placed
in mass production, would perhaps be $100 or less.

In recording a book on discs it is first recorded on
tape, then onto a lacquer disc, then to a copper "mother,"
then to a "master," then to a stamper, and finally to the
plastic discs played by the blind.   In the proposed system,
a book is read directly to a master tape, from which multiple submaster tapes would be made, which if desired could
be distributed to regional centers for direct and immediate
duplication of taped copies.

The proposed technique is expected to offer cheaper
manufacturing costs than disc recording, permitting the library book budget to stretch further.   The small bulk of the
cartridges will enable a library to store a greater number
of books in much less space and will materially lower shipping costs.   Life of the book will be longer because the tape
itself is not actually handled by the reader.   When demand
for a title has been diminished the tape can be cleared and
used again.

The investigation is expected to be completed about the first of January 1962.   Recording for the Blind, of which Burnham H. Carter is national director, is concentrating its attention on the play-back machine, while the Library's Division for the Blind, of which Robert S. Bray is chief, is giving major attention to development of the duplicating apparatus.   Time and cost studies and the reaction of blind readers to actual use will be features of the investigation.

Classification of Four-Track Tapes
Allen Cohen

From Library Resources and Technical Services 6:360-1, Fall 1962.   Reprinted by permission.

The introduction of stereophonic equipment and recordings to replace the "old" monaural way of life is manifold. We now have multiplex in tuners, and the stereo tape recorder.

For those with monaural equipment, the purchase of a stereophonic tape recorder presents certain advantages and disadvantages.

In order to record stereophonically one must have two tracks recording simultaneously.   Thus, while the old monaural tape recorders had two tracks, the stereo machine has four tracks.   This means that the person with monaural equipment can utilize all four tracks separately.   The tremendous advantage lies in economy, for a single tape can be cheaper than a single LP, and yet, depending on the speed used for recording, one can tape anywhere from six to twenty-four LP sides.

However, because so much can be gotten on a single tape, the problem arises as to how to keep track of the tracks.   One finds that the space provided on the tape box for listing recordings is both inadequate and unwieldy.   Using the box necessitates writing inside and outside the box, and eventually using loose paper when space runs out.

Thus a system was devised whereby the utilization and enjoyment from taped material could be at a maximum, so that one could get to the material desired as quickly, efficiently, and painlessly as possible.

This system utilizes both tape as a unique medium, the packaging of tape, and the mechanics of the Norelco 400 tape recorder.   The tape comes in a square-shaped box, which can stand vertically and has a space for a number. So many different things can be recorded on a single tape, that a chronological system of numbering the boxes is used. To turn on the Norelco one must press down any one of three speed keys.   (Even with machines having an "On" button, one must select the proper speed soon after putting the reels in place.)   This is an important factor in the placement of the speed number in the classification. The sequence of the four tracks recorded is another factor, and the actual place on the tape where particular material was recorded is a consideration with every tape recorder.

The classification system is as follows:

First Line.

First number: box number, e.g. 1, 2, 11, etc. A period is placed after the box number so that two- and three-digit numbers will not be confused with the numbers to follow.

Second number: speed. There are three speeds: 1 and 7/8; 3 and 3/4; 7 1/2. These become 1, 2, or 7, respectively, in the classification.

Third number: track, e.g. 1, 2, 3, 4, or any combination of those numbers, depending on the amount of tape used for a particular recording.

Second Line.

First numbers: place on tape, e.g. 234-305. (Most machines have a recording meter.)

Third, Fourth, Fifth Lines.

These lines would depend on how many tracks were used for a particular recording, and would be a continuation of the "place on tape" numbers of the second line. (see example 2)

Example 1

3.31   Carter, Elliott
234.305   Second Quartet (1959)
                       ----Julliard String Quartet. RCA Victor Red
                       Seal LM 2481.

On the first line, the first number 3 with period indicates that this recording is in Box 3. The second 3 indicates the speed that this composition was recorded at, namely 3 and 3/4. These two numbers, in this order, actually take the person from card to box to turning on the machine. The last number, number 1, indicates the track. One could not possibly get the right track without first putting the machine on. The second line indicates that this composition starts at 234 on the recording meter. Most machines come equipped with a "fast forward" speed which will bring the tape to the number required. The piece ends at 305 on the meter.

For recordings running to 2, 3, or 4 tracks, the

track or track numbers would be appended to the last number on line one. Therefore, if the above piece were recorded on two tracks, the first line number would be 3.314.
The last number is 4 and not 2, because on a stereo machine, recording monaurally, the sequence of tracks recorded is 1, 4, 3, 2. In this case, a third line would indicate
the inclusive numbers on track four where the piece was
continued. A comma placed after the last number of the
preceding line would indicate that the following line(s) is a
continuation of the same piece.

Example 2

```
8. 7143      Bach, Johann Sebastian
0-1599,           St. John's Passion.   German.
0-1772,
0-584.
```

8 stands for box number 8; 7 for speed 7 1/2; 143 for the
sequence of tracks used for recording this composition. The
next three lines correspond to tracks 1, 4, and 3, indicating
that the composition ended on track 3 at 584.

A Proposed Information Retrieval System
for Sound Recordings
C. B. Hagen

From Special Libraries 56:223-8, April 1965. Copyright by Special Libraries Association 1965. Reprinted by permission.

In my capacity as a sound engineer and librarian, I have begun at Mount St. Mary's College in Los Angeles, a project of preserving on magnetic tape important lectures, speeches, TV and radio documentaries, important newscasts, drama and theater productions, live broadcasts of local concerts and recitals, broadcasts of international music festivals, phonograph records no longer available, and other material that cannot be normally obtained on commercial recordings. This project parallels the College's program of acquiring commercial recordings, both on records and on tape. There are technical and legal[1] considerations, interesting problems of circulation and use, and so on, but this paper deals only with the information retrieval aspects.

It is immediately apparent that a system embracing such a heterogeneous collection of recordings has to be extremely flexible. The system proposed here has been designed with this goal in mind, but it can also be applied to much smaller collections, even those of the average individual collector.

Accessioning and Indexing

Each individual piece of recorded material (musical compositions, separate radio programs, a newscast, etc.) is assigned a sequential accession number. A given storage unit, such as a phonograph record or a reel of tape, is identified by limiting accession numbers, e.g. Reel 735-739.

For most commercial records or tapes the label, jacket, or box satisfactorily identifies and describes the item. For non-commercial recordings, however, a brief description has to be prepared. Ideally at the time a tape is made the recording engineer prepares for each reel an index sheet with brief descriptions of each item recorded, giving data such as composer, title, performing artists, source, date,

speed used, and so on. When available, the printed programs of events or broadcasts can be clipped and pasted onto the index sheet, with the engineer adding date, speed
used, length, and other information. Duplicate copies of
these index sheets can gradually become a sort of master
index that can be arranged by accession numbers and kept in
a separate place.

     After recording and indexing the problem of catalog-
ing has to be faced. It is in this area where I feel a very
serious situation exists because of the prevailing feelings
among librarians that special materials can be treated very
much like books. In the case of recorded materials the immense complexity and impracticality of trying to adjust standard book cataloging rules to recordings are staggering. If
standard rules are applied, in the large majority of the cases
the cost of cataloging will be much higher than the cost of
the items cataloged and a highly specialized staff will be
needed. A dramatic example of this situation was reported
some years ago when the public library of a Midwestern city
decided to fully catalog and maintain its relatively moderate
record library according to all the existing rules. This decision meant that the entire work output of eight full-time
employees--three catalogers, three skilled helpers, and two
clerical workers--was devoted to the project. The startling
fact that about as many personnel were engaged in cataloging
recordings as were usually employed cataloging books became
evident. It is pertinent at this point to remember a statement made more than 20 years ago by Archibald MacLeish,
then Librarian of the Congress:

> The profession...candidly face the fact that present
> cataloging methods are nineteenth-century methods
> devised for forms of print which no longer consti-
> tute the bulk of library accessions, and for cate-
> gories of readers who constitute a part only of pre-
> sent and potential library clienteles.[2]

     This statement becomes especially prophetic in view
of the enormous advances of modern technology. New and
improved magnetic tape recording techniques, for instance,
have reduced speeds and increased trackings, flooding the
market with thousands of previously unavilable or unknown
works and reducing costs from a few dollars to a few cents.
The very complex and meticulous cataloging rules now in existence for this type of material create an immense gap between labor costs and material costs. Faced with such a
situation many record and tape libraries have been forced to

reject or to substantially modify the standard rules; as a result, a number of isolated and often awkward systems of classification and cataloging have been created with each system geared to the peculiar problems, staff, and holdings of its own collection and, unfortunately, with great variations in quality and efficiency.

The Library of Recorded Sound at Mount St. Mary's College collects a wide variety of materials, all types contained in a conventional record or tape library plus many others. The present tendency in collections of recorded sound is precisely in this direction of a wide variety of types of materials. After a survey of its present and future development and service patterns, we have concluded that a cataloging system suited for this or similar collections should meet the following requirements:

1. The cost of cataloging should be lower than the cost of most of the items cataloged. At present the average cost of most of the individual items ranges from 20 to 80 cents. In terms of labor at the present rates for skilled technical library help (about $2 per hour) this means that 10 to 25 minutes might be spent cataloging an item. Average cataloging time, therefore, should not be more than 15 minutes per recorded item.

2. The process should be simple enough to be handled by skilled non-professional help. In our case, as in many other music libraries of this type, the only labor available is student help.

3. The system should be simple and uniform enough to withstand the high turnover of a college library operating mostly with student help.

The cards described in the system discussed below are basically catalog cards adapted for machine processing and using simplified layouts that can be handled and filled in by relatively inexpensive non-professional workers. The system has not been applied yet, and many changes may be needed, but the basic approach will remain the same--namely, to produce catalog cards rapidly and efficiently using student help. The actual application of this cataloging system to IBM cards should be extremely simple. The cards are printed with an overlay indicating clearly the spaces for all the elements to be listed, and these elements are handwritten on the cards after the material to be cataloged has been examined. The actual machine processing (keypunching, interpreting, sorting) would be done by an independent commercial service. The average fee of such services is about $5-6 per hour. As a general average several hundred cards can be processed in an hour, so the cost for the library will be only a few cents for each finished card.

Author-Title-Performer Materials

These materials are treated by what might be called a "unit" cataloging method and include such items as musical compositions and plays. The cataloging is done by handwriting the various identifying characteristics on an IBM card having the following distribution for the 80 columns of the card:

Elements	No. of Columns
Classification	7
Author	10
Title	17
Performers	20
Group card number	2
Label and catalog number	10
Source	1
Recording media	1
Media size	2
Timing	4
Accession number	6
Total	80

Some explanation is needed for some of the fields:

Classification. For recorded materials there is practically no standard classification. For printed musical scores a number of detailed schedules have been worked out in the past by major libraries and authorities in the field. The best known schedules are those prepared by Brown, Cutter, Dewey, Library of Congress, Bliss, and the British Catalogue of Music, the latter based on the faceted classification principle of Ranganathan. To illustrate the diversity of these systems, a piano sonata by Beethoven has the following classification code in the different systems:

Brown	Cutter	Dewey
C647.9	VZP	786.41

LC	Bliss	B.C.M.
M23a	VXPI	QPE

Author, title, and performer. These three elements
are handled in much the same way as in standard cataloging.
When the performer is an orchestra or choral group, a sub-
field for conductor could be created by assigning to his name
the last 6 or 8 columns of the field.

Group card number. As will be explained later,
about 20 percent of the material cataloged requires one or
more expansion cards for the same accession number. On
this field the number of such cards is placed.

Source. This indicates whether the recording comes
from a broadcast, a disc, another tape, a film soundtrack,
a live concert, and so on.

Recording media. This identifies the type of record-
ing--tape, disc, cylinder, etc. A code could be introduced
in this same column to indicate the speed of the tape or disc.

Media size. This refers to the diameter of the disc
or reel of tape.

It should be mentioned at this point that data with
only one alternative, such as stereo or monaural recording,
could be coded in terms of a binary code, one with one alternative, generally yes or no, and placed on the card as
control punches in the numeric fields. Control punches
could also be used for data with few and definite choices.
In the case of source, for example, there would only be 6
possibilities: live, broadcast, disc, tape, film, other.

This basic layout would suffice for an estimated 80
percent of the author-title-performer type of materials. As
abbreviations will be used, a single card would be enough
for most of the materials. In some cases, however, the
spaces provided cannot contain all the information it would
be desirable to include. Such cases would be two or more
authors, composer-arranger combinations, or very long
names; long titles, nicknames, or names involving complete
descriptions of keys, opus numbers, etc.; and performers
in a trio, quartet, opera, or other large work.

For material that needs more expanded cataloging,
the following distribution for 80 columns on an expansion
card or cards is proposed:

Elements	No. of Columns
Classification	7
Author	20
Title	20
Performer	21
Instrument	2

Elements	No. of Columns
Group card number (--of--)	4
Accession number	6
	—
Total	80

The fields are self-explanatory. The descriptive data are left out as they already appear on card number 1. Classification is a field that may or may not be left out depending on the use of this element. After "Performer," a field for "Instrument" may be introduced to indicate in code form the instrument that particular individual plays.

The "Group card number" field would show the number of expansion cards that have been prepared for a certain composition and would be expressed in the form "3 of 7." In an opera, for example, there are several soloists, orchestra and conductor, chorus and conductor, and at times other individuals involved. One expansion card can be assigned to each of these individuals or groups. Within the accession number, the group card number will tie all these cards together after the main entry card, which is always number 1.

At the end of the cataloging process there will be a deck of cards arranged alphabetically by author and classification. Secondary decks arranged alphabetically by titles and performers can be easily prepared. Expansion cards could be merged into these files, using perhaps some color coding. For alternate names or nicknames of works or performers or when there is more than one author or an author-arranger combination, "see" cards should be made. They could simply be standard IBM cards with the entire field assigned to an alphamerical notation, for example: Pathétique Symphony--See, Tchaikovsky, Symph. # 6 in B minor, Op. 74; or Sousa, J. P. --Stars and Stripes ballet--See, Kay, H.

Other Materials

Such items as documentaries, lectures, speeches, newscasts, commercials, or sound effects may be cataloged using the principles of coordinate or Uniterm indexing. The materials may be considered exactly like printed documents, and the process is standard for this type of indexing and generally very simple. An item is assigned an accession number, and the cataloger then selects a number of terms that describe the content of the taped material. This selection is based on the program information pasted on the index sheet. If this information is not sufficient, the cataloger may find it necessary to listen to the program or at least part of it. The Uniterms can be personal names of participants or panelists, nouns, places, trade names, dates, etc. A list of these terms can be attached to the reel or box of tape. This tracing provides a record of the terms assigned to a certain item in case other terms are added in the future, some deleted, or the program is erased.

Each term is given a card of its own where the accession numbers of all recordings dealing with that term are recorded. Searching for a given program or subject can then be done by the standard coordinate indexing procedure. As with printed materials, a simple distribution for the 80 columns of the IBM card could be made as follows:

Elements	No. of Columns
Accession numbers	60
Term	13
Term account number	6
Card number	1
	—
Total	80

The field for accession numbers occupies columns 1 through 60. Punches in this field could be made to interpret accession numbers. For example, a 3 punch in column 16 would mean accession number 163. This coding has two slight disadvantages: 1) the first accession number is 10, and 2) after the number 609 is punched, a second card is necessary. On this second card consecutive numbers can be assigned to columns 1 through 60, starting with accession number 610 to keep the continuity. These disadvantages, however, are minor compared to the conveniences and compactness of this coding method.

The field for the Uniterm is alphamerical. Thus, it can accept dates or compound names having combinations of letters and numbers.

The term account number can be a very valuable asset to the file, especially for manual alphabetical arrangement. This number can be assigned to the term at the time it is assigned a card for the first time. For this purpose a table such as the Lefinder Guide[3] may be used. This useful table is a sort of condensed dictionary of the standard English language, distributing in a very balanced way num-

bers 0000 through 9999 from A through Z. We have found
that assignment of these numbers or expansions of them (expansions, of course, can be unlimited) to Uniterms is a
most valuable asset to the files for either machine or manual alphabetical arrangement.

    The last column is reserved for card number to pro-
vide for the time when accession numbers exceed 609 and
added cards are needed to code the following numbers.

    With this dual system of cataloging recorded materi-
als, any program can, of course, utilize the two treatments
simultaneously, for example, a documentary program on the
life of a composer featuring panel discussions and musical
illustrations of his compositions. The accession number
would be the same for the entire program, and it would be
assigned both to the musical illustrations (unit cataloging
with the basic elements author-title-performers) and to the
discussion material (coordinate indexing).

General Observations

    This system, we believe, provides a fairly adequate
cataloging of materials held in a collection. One relative
disadvantage that can be cited at once is that some auxiliary
tables are needed; for example, the classification schedule
or the codes for source or instruments have to be kept in a
visible place and users have to learn to use these and similar decoding guides.

    At this point the question, "For whom are we cata-
loging?", must be considered. A number of authorities are
charging that the existing catalogs are not designed for public use and that catalogers are too tradition-oriented and
afraid to experiment. Even with the adoption of the Cataloging Code Revision the catalog's main use will probably be by
a trained staff. An administrator and librarian wrote a few
years ago:[4]

> ...I worry about the state of cataloging because I
> feel that no major breakthrough has been made in
> cataloging techniques and utilizing modern devices.
> As I understand cataloging today, it is basically
> the same as it was 50 years ago, except that we
> type our cards or Xerox them instead of writing
> them out; we've changed some rules, but the ap-
> proach is basically the same. Compare this with
> the breakthrough achieved by Henry Ford in indus-
> try with his development of the assembly line sys-
> tem of production. Standardized and interchange-

able parts, high volume of production, low unit
cost, utilizing persons with relatively little skill,
and other aspects constituted a revolution in its
way such as we need of the same stature in cataloging. More relevant to cataloging is integrated
data processing which is automation in the office.
It means that information is organized by intelligent human beings once, and thereafter handled
automatically by machines according to directions.

The system described here is aimed precisely in this
direction. It has been planned with these three objectives in
mind:
1. To tackle in a comprehensive way the so far almost insoluble problem of cataloging such difficult special
materials such as sound recordings.
2. To prepare cards with inexpensive, non-professional help who receive short training periods and are subject to high turnover.
3. To make the cards suitable for inexpensive and
fast duplication and rearrangement of fields, all of which
can be achieved by extremely fast and inexpensive machine
methods.
The system described can therefore offer, like most
mechanized methods, the following advantages:
1. The possibility of placing a maximum of usable
data on a minimum of space with a minimum of time and
labor.
2. Ease of preparing the cards due to the form-like
layouts permitting the use of cheaper non-professional labor.
3. Versatility and low cost of the system: (a) Any
later modification can be made retroactive, thanks to high
speed machine duplication of card decks and rearrangement
of fields in almost any desired way. (b) Applicable to both
large and small collections. (c) High speed machine searches. (d) Entire decks of cards can be inexpensively duplicated
and their contents printed on cards or in book form. Thus,
the catalog of an entire library can be made available either
complete or in a selective way, and periodical supplements
or cumulative catalogs can be prepared at any time. (e)
Any number of additional decks of cards can be produced and,
through shifting of the fields, organized by function of any
other elements. Thus, if the master deck is arranged by
author, three additional secondary decks can be produced inexpensively and organized by title, performers, and classification.
In closing, it should be stated that this proposed sys-

tem is by no means a definitive or polished one. It needs
a sizable pilot project--the only way to work out all the details and refinements. The layouts and operational instructions presented are basically illustrations of what can be
done in this field. What I have tried to emphasize is the
fact that mechanized methods of data handling and information retrieval are not only possible, but are an essential
need for special libraries handling sound recorded materials.

Notes

1. Regarding legal and copyright aspects the author has
    prepared a report on the subject entitled "A Report
    to the U.S. Copyright Office on the Library, Educa-
    tional and Private Uses of Recordings." A condensed
    version of this report has been recently published:
    "Copyright and the Threat to Fair Use of Sound Re-
    cordings," NAEB Journal, January-February 1965, p.
    43-71.
2. Library of Congress. Annual Report of the Librarian
    of Congress for the Fiscal Year Ending June 30, 1942.
    Washington, Government Printing Office, 1943, p. 45.
3. Lefax, Inc. Lefinder Guide. Philadelphia, 1957, 32 p.
4. Goldhor, H. "The Worries of a Public Library Admin-
    istrator." Library Resources and Technical Services,
    vol. 3, no. 2, Spring 1959, p. 119-22.

The articles in this section deal with pamphlets, art works, programmed learning courses, printed music, and maps.   These materials serve a broad range of library purposes, from recreation to research.   The pamphlet's chief values are its compactness, up-to-dateness, and economy; art works offer a unique esthetic experience; programmed learning courses, with or without teaching machines, enable the student to conduct certain types of courses for himself at his own pace; and printed music and maps need no explanation.   Nearly all types of libraries are represented in the articles in this section.

Pamphlets: Problem or Blessing?
I. Elizabeth Stafford

From Top of the News 18:21-3, May 1962.   Reprinted by permission.

"The world is so full of a number of things, I'm sure we should all be as happy as kings!"   Such happy thinking on Stevenson's part is even more true today, and this very fact presents an age-old problem and one of the greatest challenges for librarians to meet: what can one do to bring to the attention and use of our patrons increased knowledge of all the ideas and advanced thinking of the day--to make the latest information available as fast as things happen?
Industry, organizations, and publishers are doing their utmost to present these facts in concise, attractive form.   Pamphlets, many hundreds of them each year, come tumbling along to the desk of busy librarians, each in its own way demanding attention.   It matters not that various library clearing houses have been set up to help us cope with the quantities available.   We are overwhelmed.   The need to acquire timely information at its peak of interest and put it quickly into the hands of eager patrons remains constant.
Whether or not school or public librarians agree that the present emphasis on quality education has stimulated greater-than-ever demands for progress reports on activities

in wide areas, children and young people are exploring as
they never dreamed of exploring in the past. Television and
all the other mass media create interests which develop into
term papers, oral speeches, bibliographies--in short, all
kinds of assignments where there is a premium on the latest
information. The impact of modern living is felt as keenly
today in the student's life as elsewhere. Accept the obvious!
Important information, in capsule form, is the order of the
day, and we are trying to do something about it.

What of the pamphlet? Where is its impact and use
felt in greatest degree? Certainly, in the library we look
upon it as a chief source of current thinking, a medium for
exchanging ideas which is nowhere equaled or excelled.
More than 150,000 new pamphlets are published in America
each year. Most of these never reach libraries, yet they
form a pool of valuable research material that is unique and,
in the main, unduplicated by books.

Consider just a few and one readily sees the breadth
of their appeal! From a detailed discussion of United States
Trade Policy in a Changing World Economy, we move to a
report on Cybernation: The Silent Conquest, to statistics
and analysis charts on world population 1960, to information
about vaccines, their use and value to laymen, to the "Man
with a Stop-Watch" and the role of time and motion study in
industry. There is something for everyone, from newly
created careers and information about them to the latest suggestions on treasure hunting in local museums, ideas on
what to look for and how. We learn how Uncle Sam safe-
guards us and, in the same instant, a handbook on The Tape
Recorder in the Elementary Classroom attracts our attention.
All are authoritative reading materials, written by experts,
not yet in book form, but obviously worth more than a rush
article in magazines.

But should we concern ourselves seriously with the
problems of bringing all this to the attention of our young
patrons? I think so.

As we take advantage of ever-increasing opportunities
to spend our professional time working with individual students, I am sure that most of us have moments of great appreciation for the publishing companies which are giving us
such attractive, timely, yet concise treatises on a wide variety of subjects. I wonder whether we are using them to
full advantage. In my own experience, I find that we must
not always wait until boys and girls have come to us needing
materials for term papers, debates, or other assignments.
Obviously, the pamphlet is important here!

But what of the young people who confide to us that

they are just looking around, seeking to "improve each shin-
ing moment," but hoping for thought and direction we can
share so easily with our "secret weapons," the compact
ideas? Do we spend enough time with our young patrons,
spreading before them particular topics which immediately
pique other interests? Do we send them away with new
ideas, new goals, and intriguing avenues for exploring? Do
we stimulate their curiosity thus and invite them to continue
their reading in books and reference materials of weightier
proportions, simply by not overwhelming them at the outset?
Does the road wind upward all the way, yes, to the very
end? Have we been really enthusiastic about a new accumulation of brochure materials which suggest that here is an
important idea for display cases? Do we consider their usefulness for informal display in the library reading room,
where the patron can pick and choose and remain to conquer?

All of us have had frequent experiences when an in-
quiring patron might exclaim about a particularly new idea,
"What a wonderful thought in this discussion of Design for a
Planet! I'd like to know more about it. Do you have books
on the subject or are we just beginning to realize its importance in the world today?" Chances are, if it's in pamphlet form, it is a new idea for the layman.

There is no better, nor more effective, way of stimulating the thinking of young people than by making many,
many ideas important to them, important enough to stop and
take time to explore a bit. Here the pamphlet or small book
reigns supreme. The whole course of a student's life may
be changed through an idea which never occurred to him before, but he picked it up because it happened to be available
at the right time for him.

When young people are obviously browsing in particular areas of thought, we need abundant materials on the
same subject but with different approaches. Our files may
be gleaned for such pamphlets, which are then spread out in
colorful array and often attract the readers who might not
have been reached otherwise. This is an obvious truth in
subjects like vocational training, science, and social studies,
but what of the child who is attracted to the fine arts or
lesser-known interests and avocations! Again I say with conviction, the pamphlet offers excellent and appealing research
material in every imaginable field.

Then there are always the children who do not know
what they want! Here, too, the pamphlet is most helpful
with suggestions. From the use of such an ephemera, it is
then possible to present to the reader books of greater length
and, eventually, deep interest is securely established and we

may look around for other possibilities.

Occasionally, and she will do it more often if the librarian encourages her, a teacher or a group leader will borrow whole collections of pamphlets on a variety of phases of one subject or on many subjects, just to distribute and use during workshop activities. She can only do this if the pamphlets are in the library, and if she learns about them in time. I think especially of a math class which was working on problems of insurance. The library offered up an armful of small brochures which covered every interesting angle, and what a wealth of learning took place in this instance! Most books on subjects of this sort are too technical for explaining to youngsters who "don't want to learn too much."

To help us do our share of stimulating to greater curiosity and "desire for the facts," something must be done about the matter of pamphlet selection. Obviously, the enormous task of separating "the wheat from the chaff" must take place behind the scenes. From this mass of available material, subjects of greatest interest at the moment must be decided upon and the best information made available in easy, attractive style, in a way which will not only benefit the eventual patron of our libraries, but also remove much of the pressure which mounts with each mailing as it crosses the librarian's desk and poses the problem of selection.

Already the librarian has several well-known aides in her selection and evaluation of pamphlets. They are only helps, however, and their use is still time-consuming in greater degree than we like. Recently, a new and unique service has become available. This undertakes, through a National Review Board, to cull through, select, and present for purchase by libraries each month a definitive group of pamphlets which should, for the most part, appeal to various ages in a wide range of topics.

And newer yet, soon we will have opportunities to select pamphlet kits on individual subjects such as careers, social studies, gardening and the like, these possibly to be presented in such a way that they may be shelved along with books on those same subjects.

Pamphlets should never be considered a problem-- they are one of our greatest and most useful blessings. Both adults and children look to pamphlets for quick, accurate, up-to-date information when doing research on most projects.

The Information File in the Secondary School
Sister M. Thomas Eulberg

From Catholic Library World 33:101-2+, October 1961. Reprinted by permission.

Introduction. There is something of a delightful idea that the standard of a high school can be judged by the caliber of its information file, a theory--we were told in a library science class some years ago--held by a noted library school. Even if this theory seems eclectic, it emphasizes the position that the information file can play in the high school library.

Necessity. The basic reason for the existence of the information file in the secondary school lies in the value of order and system. There is always an influx into the library of reprints, pamphlets, advertising materials, pictures, brochures, and similar items of some value. Unless such fugitive material is made accessible, i.e., unless there is a place for it and it is in its place, it will be absolutely worthless. Worse, it will clutter the workroom or shelving, which should serve a better use. The working information file makes available useful and timely information and material not possible to secure in other form or at so nominal an expense.

Equipment and Location. Though ordinarily only standard furniture should be used in equipping a school library, a wooden or strong pasteboard box may be substituted until a metal file is available. All material under one heading should be enclosed in legal size (14 7/8 by 10 in.) manila folders of medium quality. Since the information file is an instrument that grows and consequently changes, the five-cut and the three-cut tabs may seem most feasible for efficient and quick guide service, even though insertion from time to time will break the regularity of the pattern. The folder tab is tagged with the subject heading, either hand lettered in ink or typed on labels prepared for pasting. Besides the file itself and the manila folders, no other special equipment is necessary.

The accepted place for the information file is near the librarian's desk, because she frequently reserves free access to the file to herself. The librarian is familiar not

only with the clippings and pamphlets but also with the arrangement of the materials. Others may remove items only
to replace them in the wrong folder, mixing and misplacing
without realizing the results--temporary loss of items and
subsequent need for reorganizing.

Material Sources. One of the most encouraging
things about the information file is that really useable data
can be obtained with practically no expense. Free and Inexpensive Learning Materials, 7th ed., Nashville, Tennessee,
Division of Surveys and Field Services, George Peabody College for Teachers, 1956, $1.00, is the best single biblio-
graphical source.

A general source includes reprints, magazines, and
newspapers. Reprints of special articles and outlines have
their value; both Compton's and World Book, for example,
have issued noteworthy reprints of encyclopedia articles.
From radio and TV stations, one can obtain speeches for
the asking. Magazines and newspapers may have their particular value. Single copies of non-indexed or duplicate magazines should be perused and clipped according to the findings. Sometimes it becomes advisable to secure a particular issue for a single valuable article a magazine contains.
Keeping newspapers in the high school library is not plausi-
ble--unless exception be made for the school paper as a local history source--while individual articles of value have
their place in the information file.

From miscellaneous sources (book jackets, calendars,
catalogs, advertisements, old text books, Christmas and
greeting cards, etc.) can be derived various collections of
interest and purpose: art-picture prints; pictures of famous
cathedrals, towers, statues, buildings; post cards of geographic import; maps; bulletin board material; and class lesson illustrations.

The thing to remember when dealing with sources is
that what is reserved must be useful, and actual circulation
of material decides utility. Again, each file should reflect
its own school's peculiar and individual activities, needs,
and services.

Preparation of Materials. A practical and serviceable
way to care for clippings of greater value is to mount them
on reverse sides of large advertising envelopes. Clippings
of lesser value may be filed without mounting. Only one
subject should be mounted per envelope so that relevant matter may be added. The name of the source, with the date,
should always be indicated for each item. Articles of several pages may be stapled. Mounts for pictures should be
uniform in size and color; gray and brown are standard.

But not all pictures should be backed. Those for use in a classroom or for bulletin display should not be mounted; most users prefer to choose their own colors to fit into a scheme they have planned. A definite set of pictures--art prints, for example--will be more accessible if labeled on the reverse side, upper left-hand corner, and arranged in the folder alphabetically by the name of the artist or title of the work. (The author labels all art pictures with a triple-line entry: artist, school of painting, and title.)

Various methods are used in mounting. Pastes have been tested and many librarians prefer a special kind. Pure rubber adhesive has two valuable features: any excess can be rubbed away; and, when the cement has been applied to one surface only, a picture can be removed without being torn. One disagreeable point is that such adhesive tends to darken the paper on which it has been used. Should one apply paste over the whole edge surface? Yes; tacking invites harm to the item one is trying to preserve. A smooth job further requires that any pasted surface be pressed until dry.

Only when too much material on a certain subject accumulates in a folder should that material be relegated to a pamphlet box on the shelf. Though it is rare that a school library will find many subjects to be given such prominence, such a likely subject will be local (civic and parish) history--material, which because it is a unique source, frequently will become increasingly valuable as time goes on.

Care should be exercised, however, in balancing the worth of fugitive material--whether for the file or for pamphlet boxes--with the labor, time, and manner of securing it, especially when such material is inexpensive. One could, all too soon, with inexpensive material, be prodigal with money which might better be directed toward one good book on the subject.

Finally, all clippings and pamphlets should be stamped with the name of the organization to which they belong; they must be marked with the subject heading assigned to them and I. F. to indicate that they have been taken from the information file.

Assigning Subject Headings and Filing. When materials, clippings, pamphlets, and pictures have been collected and reserved as worthwhile, they must be assigned to subject headings. The librarian aims first to maintain consistency with the card catalog, using Sears' List of Subject Headings, Kapsner's Catholic Subject Headings, Ball's Subject Headings for the Information File, the Standard Catalog for High-School Libraries, and the Catholic Periodical Index.

The authority list of headings used, including "see" and "see also" references under appropriate headings, may be kept on three by five inch cards or on typewritten sheets.

The usual method for filing is simply alphabetical by subject headings, guide labels on the outsides of the drawers indicating, like a set of encyclopedias, the dictionary method of arrangement.

When an article is first read and put aside for preservation, its place in the file should also be determined. If at the moment no place seems fitting, one may lay aside the clipping for a second inspection rather than prepare a new folder and run the risk of cluttering the file with too many subjects. Such second perusals make more certain the necessary discretion in adding matter to the information file.

Cataloging. For the school library one method of cataloging alone seems reasonable: the indication in the general catalog that material on a given subject will be found in the information file. Material worth preserving should be worth cataloging. Subject headings are typed on cards duplicated with this statement: "Material on this subject may be found in the information file."

Weeding. House cleaning is necessary for the information file because the average life of clippings is short and pamphlets and pictures, which frequently serve their purposes longer, may need attention. So that the file may not become unwieldy or congested, superseded matter should be discarded and worn material mended or discarded. Naturally, if all material from a folder is withdrawn, the catalog card must be withdrawn, and also the subject from the authority list.

Circulation. Now if the file is to be useful to the fullest, its contents must circulate and some provision must be made for the loan of material. Large envelopes can be used so that no loose clippings will be lost. A definite color or size of card may be chosen to tally the borrower's name, subject, amount of material charged, and the date due.

Conclusion. Something really useful sells itself. The file can be the mouthpiece of the library. If it is, the theory of the library school that the standard of the high school be judged by the caliber of its information file will no longer be a delightful challenge--it will be a challenged delight.

Keeping Up with Pamphlets
Ruth B. Ferguson and Elizabeth Ferguson

From Library Journal 86:1642-3, April 15; Junior Libraries
7:6-7, April 1961. Reprinted by permission.

Let's face it. For better or for worse public libraries are involved up to their ears in the accelerated high
school program. We are well aware of the so-called "rights
and wrongs" of this demanding situation, but we feel that,
regardless of all the theories, there is a tough and a chal-
lenging job to be done every school night of the year. All of
us who are conditioned to the satisfactions--and the difficul-
ties--of serving this student clientele know that happy feeling
when we can produce the right information at the precise
time it is requested. What actually happens, however, is
rather different. During a typical evening of operation on a
first-come, first-served basis, encyclopedias, almanacs,
etc., are being used to full capacity, and circulating material has long since vanished from the shelves. But the 20 or
30 students who were not so quick as their fellows in rush-
ing to the library all clamor for these materials, already in
use in the library or at home. To complicate matters further, they are often accompanied by a parent or parents.
As we see it, the problem is best expressed as one
of numbers--numbers of students, all with the same assignment, all pouring into the library at once, day after day,
night after night. Obviously then, it is numbers--and numbers almost entirely in our reference sources--that can and
will help to ease the situation. By necessity, therefore, we
are forced to find a more encompassing method of procedure.
One solution, while not perfect, is the "getting to
know you, learning to like you" value inherent in pamphlets.
We do not advocate substituting pamphlets (however good) for
authoritative books, but rather using them as helpful aids in
meeting the ever-increasing student requests for practical
materials. It is really amazing how wide in scope, how valid, and how useful these "thin books" have become in recent
years.
If you are concerned about the student reaction to
pamphlets, just remember that they actually are already familiar with them because in school they have seen such book-

157

lets used by the teacher, who has probably suggested that
they "write away for them."

What is involved here is simply this: evaluate, select, enlarge (and don't forget to weed) your pamphlet file
or files.

All this is much easier said than done, as we well
know. The "how-to-do" has been well set out in Norma Ireland's The Pamphlet File in School, College, and Public Libraries (Faxon 1954).   But the "doing" seems to be an off-
beat job for everybody--order librarian, cataloger, reference librarian.   And time to do the job as we would like is
hard to come by.

The best answer we can see to all these difficulties
is to streamline the procedures ruthlessly. This can be
done if you operate on one premise--pamphlets are expendable.   On this basis it is possible to simplify the operation
down to the barest of essentials, and this seems to us highly desirable.   Suppose some of the orders do get lost and
the pamphlets don't come through, or some circulated pamphlets aren't returned, and torn or worn pamphlets have to
be discarded.   All these things will happen.   But we don't
believe in acquisition, or cataloging records, or in sending
overdues.   We believe it is cheaper and better to concentrate
on keeping a continuous flow of new and replacement items
going into the files to be ready for those numbers of students.

The bare essentials, the musts, appear to be (1) a
regular program for selection; (2) a simple, efficient order
routine; (3) a basic, flexible subject heading list; (4) circulating pamphlets just as miscellaneous material; (5) frequent review of the files for weeding and noting needs.   It may be
helpful to suggest some approaches and shortcuts for ac-
complishing these chores.

Selection

Regular scanning of periodically published lists really
does the best job of keeping up-to-date on pamphlet literature.   Pamphlet publication by its very nature is fast-moving,
and static lists--no matter how attractive and authoritative--
don't keep up.   The following program is suggested as offering broad coverage of the output of both publishers and
private sources and is one that can be carried out in a reasonable minimum of time.

1) Follow and check one comprehensive pamphlet service such as the Vertical File Index (H.W. Wilson).   In this
index, for instance, it is possible to check both by title and

by subject, which makes for quick scanning; precise information for ordering is given; and, although the listings are not
reviews, they give full identification of series and frequent
informative annotations.

2) Check the Weekly List of Selected U.S. Government Publications (U.S. Govt. Printing Office). For most
pamphlet files designed for student and general reading use,
this short but amazingly varied list covers many desirable
items.

3) Pick out a few current magazines, library and popular, that carry pamphlet pages or regular lists and check
these lists as soon as the magazine is received. Such a
group might include: Booklist--"Free and Inexpensive Materials," Burroughs Clearing House--"Booklet Counter,"
Changing Times--"Things To Write For," Good Housekeep-
ing--"Booklets Worth Writing For," Library Journal--"Items
of Interest," Publishers' Weekly--"Pamphlet Listings," Wilson Library Bulletin--"Write for These."

Most of these lists are short and take but a moment
to check. All give full order information, many give other
descriptive notes. Pamphlet lists appear less regularly in
many other magazines, of course. An occasional survey of
education magazines can be quite rewarding. It pays to develop an eye for the notices.

4) Collect current publications lists of individual companies, associations, and publishers by way of a request on
your order card, and check these on receipt. If a single
pamphlet appeals to you as worthwhile, it is more than likely that that source might have others you could use. This
is a selective way to keep in touch with important lists.

Order Routine

No amount of streamlining can avoid some sort of
correspondence process for obtaining pamphlets. Some libraries use the services of a purchasing agency to handle
orders for pamphlets with prices, but they still find it necessary to send individual requests for the free items. So,
there seems to be a good case for putting the whole process
on a "separate order to each source" basis. Using the same
order forms and methods for all orders greatly simplifies
the clerical assignment.

As for order forms, the "beg card" has stood the
test of many years' use and is satisfactory to library and
publisher alike. At its simplest it is a government postal
card with a printed or mimeographed message, such as the
following sample.

Please send for use in our library
_____ (space for title)

If there is a charge, please notify before mailing
(or) If there is a charge, please bill us

Please include your catalog or price list
Address to the attention of (exact name and address)

Some libraries may prefer to incorporate these order
elements in a letter.   This has the advantage of allowing
space for a courteous introductory paragraph, for instance,
or for a listing of several titles.   The clerical handling is
the same in either case.

One addition to the order form is very desirable--a
card with slots for sending coins through the mail.   It is
highly advantageous to send these small payments with the
orders so as to cover everything in one transaction.   Billing
and all additional correspondence is time-consuming and expensive for both sides.

Classification and Circulation

Subject filing seems the obvious method for classifying pamphlets.   Authors and titles are a very minor factor--
the use of this material is practically always in terms of
"something about . . ."   Some sort of established subject
heading guide, however, is a must for several reasons.   (1)
The person who does the classifying can do it faster and
with more assurance aided by a guide.   (2) New and special
categories can be worked out better in the framework of a
good list.   (3) The guide can serve, in this simplified program, as an index to the file.   (4) It makes for consistency
and order all around.

Workable subject heading lists are readily available.
Many libraries use, for instance, a retired annual volume of
the Readers' Guide with great success.   The familiar phras-
ing of its headings has many advantages, especially with students who are concurrently being initiated into the mysteries
of "looking up an article."   And further, consistent new headings can be used as they appear in the current volumes and
written into the official guide volume.   There is an excellent
list of headings in the Ireland study already mentioned, and
this can be kept up-to-date in the same way.   The principal
thing is to adopt a list and then feel free to use it flexibly.

For student service especially, it seems desirable to

circulate pamphlets for home use.   We believe in recording
them just as miscellaneous material--and no overdues.   Experience indicates that most of them are returned as a matter of course.   Let the others be expendable.

Other Records

For a fast-moving, heavily used collection like this,
there is no need for any acquisition or shelf list records or
for cataloging individual items.   The cost in time and money
of making these records and constantly changing and cancel-
ling them is far greater than the cost of continuous replacement.   Such procedures are justified for a true reference
file containing valuable source material, but not in this case.
Catalog references to additional material available in
the files are obviously desirable, but this need can really be
well covered by a direction sign at the catalog, and also one
at the index table, saying in effect, "Additional material on
many subjects can be found in the pamphlet file located at..."

In Conclusion

The key to the successful operation of this program
is the efficient division of labor between professional and
clerical jobs.   Selection and classification are jobs worthy of
professional attention, ideally.   However, good staff people,
especially those who deal with the student public, can do a
very good job if professionals are not available.   Regular
scanning of sources, continuous ordering, prompt classifying
and filing are what produce good results.
An hour or two a week of a clerk's time will take
care of a lot of orders if there are good forms and well laid
out procedures.   Filing and the housekeeping of the files can
also be done successfully by clerks.
The real secret is for the responsible professional or
staff member to be continually aware of the file material, to
handle it, and to revise and weed continuously.

Building a Vocational Information File
Marianne Schmidt

Reprinted by permission from the Wilson Library Bulletin
33:231-2+, November 1958.   Copyright 1958 by the H. W.
Wilson Company.

From the time a child first hears the question "What
will you be when you grow up?" until he is launched on a
career, the one which is eminently right for him, there is
no more important question he has to answer.   And in today's specialized society, none more difficult.

Fortunately vocational literature has kept pace with
the growing complexity of the vocations themselves.   It is
fortunate too, considering the budget limitations of most libraries, that a great amount of useful vocational material in
pamphlet form can be gathered for the price of postcards.

There is little danger that a vocational information
file will not find users.   High school teachers assign papers
on vocational topics.   Counselors and journalists offering advice customarily point the bewildered youngster to his public
library.   The adult who feels he might be more satisfied in
another job finds his way there too.

This article, describing arrangements at Dearborn
Public Library, may be helpful to those small and medium-
sized libraries which are planning to set up a vocational file
or who are, as we were last spring, dissatisfied with present arrangements.

Vocational Information Collection

Our collection of vocational materials includes books.
These are designated by a "V" before the call number and
are shelved on top of the file which holds the pamphlet material.   Nearly all of these books have a copyright date within the last ten years.   Changes in salary estimations and in
the fields themselves make it necessary to keep a vocational
collection, books and pamphlets, well-weeded.   An exception
we make to the ten-year rule of thumb is the United States
Department of Commerce series on establishing and operating small businesses, which contains practical, specialized
material not found elsewhere.   Although these were assigned

call numbers when we received them, they could as well be
treated as pamphlets.   Most pamphlets are considered to
have served their purpose within a five-year span.
        Our vocational information file contains newspaper
clippings as well as pamphlets.   One of the local newspapers
has a regular question-and-answer feature about vocations.
Articles about shortages of workers in certain fields, about
vocational courses being conducted in the area, about persons who have been honored as outstanding in their professions provide file material also.

Handling File Material

        Our vocational pamphlet file is a supplement to the
general vertical file and the color green is used to set it
apart.   Pamphlets are kept in folders marked by a green
gummed star before the subject heading.   A green star, this
one penciled in, also appears before the subject heading on
each item to facilitate refiling.   Labels on the drawers containing the material and the one-card catalog tray containing
the index to the collection are green, too.
        We have found that subject headings in the form of the
name of the worker rather than the field of work are more
useful because this tends to be the form in which the patron
asks for information and also because it provides for natural
subdivisions of material.   Our folders containing material on
Engineering, for example, were overloaded.   We still have a
heading Engineer, which takes care of general material, but
the card labeled Engineer in the vocational file index refers
the patron to fourteen specializations in the field, from Aero-
nautical engineer to Petroleum engineer.
        We have switched therefore from the old Science Re-
search Associates headings (their present headings also use
name of workers) to those used in Occupational Literature;
an Annotated Bibliography by Gertrude Forrester, New York,
Wilson, 1953.   (A new edition appeared October 1958.)
These headings are a useful distillation of those appearing
in the U.S. Employment Service's two-volume Dictionary of
Occupational Titles, which may, however, be used to supplement it.   Aside from the obvious advantage of having a limited number of headings to work from, the bibliography listed under the headings serves also as an explanation of the
heading, in cases in which two headings seem to be equally
appropriate.   Many of the cross references used in it can
also be borrowed for the card catalog index to the file, an
inevitable appendage unless the file is going to be severely
limited in size.

We followed this procedure in changing headings:
weeded file; gave material which was retained a heading from
Forrester and checked the heading in the book; sorted material and made new folders--pages can do this; made a card
index.

Cards were stamped "Pamphlets and clippings on this
subject will be found in the vocational information file," a
subject heading placed above this, and any "see also" references below. This card file also analyzes vocational book
material, but gives only a brief description of the book since
it appears also in the public catalog.

Because the subject headings, unlike those of the general information file, did not have to conform with those of
the public catalog--or Forrester either, for that matter--
consistency was sacrificed for practicability wherever necessary. The "official" headings "Manager, Retail food" and
"Manager, Retail floral" were changed to the more direct
Grocer and Florist. It should be noted, however, that nearly all of the headings in Forrester take one directly where
he wants to go. He may consult material, for example, by
checking Sailor rather than U.S. Navy what-have-you.

We retained some of the old Science Research Associate headings which had proved their usefulness, headings
for material which is of general nature: Job Hunting; Job
satisfaction and success; Occupations, choice of.

Some few headings were improvised. Automobile
dealer was a concession to the special interest of this area.
Laborer was added as a catch-all for miscellaneous information about skilled and unskilled jobs for which we had little
material and little demand.

Building Up a File

After we weeded our three file drawers, there was
barely one drawer of pamphlet material left. Now, with new
material, we have four drawers nearly full.

Most of the material was free. The government, industry, professional organizations, trade unions, colleges and
universities provide gratis most of the answers that even the
most foresighted and demanding patron can ask. We sent
postcards with this message:

> We are building up a file, as complete as possible,
> of vocational material. This will be used particu-
> larly by young people who are in the process of
> choosing a vocation. If material is available on
> your profession, we would like to include it.

These cards, signed with the name and address of
the library, were duplicated in quantity.

Our first group of cards went out to likely-looking organizations listed in Encyclopedia of American Associations:
A Guide to the Trade, Business, Professional, Labor, Scientific, Educational, Fraternal and Social Organizations of
the United States, Detroit, Michigan, Gale Research Company, 1956. This is particularly useful for its listing of
professional organizations. It was evident from our replies
that ALA is not the only organization busy with recruiting.

Typically, the scientific organizations seem to be best
organized in their approach to vocational material. The National Science Foundation, Washington 25, D.C., sent
"Sources of Information about Scientific Careers," a mimeographed sheet which permits an easy approach to collecting
information about scientific professions. "Encouraging Future Scientists: Keys to Careers," rev. ed. 1956-1957,
available from the National Science Teachers' Association
(1201 16th St., Washington 6, D.C.), contains a good bibliography of free and inexpensive material on science-related
fields.

Most large businesses and industries in the country
can be counted on for some good material about their own
field, and a number have a series on vocations as a public
service. Second to none is the New York Life Insurance
Company, whose ads "Choosing Your Occupation" have become familiar. A set of these articles, and the hard-bound
Guide to Career Information; A Bibliography of Recent Occupational Literature, Harper, 1957, were sent to us in return for a postcard addressed to New York Life Insurance
Co., 51 Madison Avenue, New York 22.

It is impossible to list here the sources of good free
material, and of course vocational interests vary with the
community. I wonder if Dearborn is typical in this: it appears that the teen-age girls who are not going to become
models are planning to become airplane hostesses! Incidentally, Glamour magazine's Job Department, 420 Lexington
Avenue, New York 17, sent us gratis a good summary description of this field, and a lot of others too.

It is important to provide a balanced picture of a vocational field. For an objective view of many occupations
get the United States Bureau of Labor Statistics' Occupational
Outlook Handbook; Employment Information on Major Occupations for Use in Guidance, 1957. This is for sale by the
Superintendent of Documents for $4. Commercial publishers
also present an objective view of a vocation. Watch dates
on these publications, however, to keep from ordering ma-

terial that is already out-dated. Careers Research Monographs, for example, does not include dates on its listings,
except in response to a request for them. A good source
of information about such publications-for-a-price is <u>Fifty
Sources of Occupational Information</u>, available free from the
State Department of Education, Division of Vocational Education, 220 South Parsons Avenue, Columbus 15, Ohio.

To anyone building a vocational information file many
helping hands reach out. It is not difficult for libraries to
collect good material, and to make it available is well worthwhile, considering the importance of the decision it is helping to shape.

The Pamphlet in the University Library
Jack King

From Library Resources & Technical Services 10:51-6, Winter 1966. Reprinted by permission.

There will be little argument among university librarians over their libraries being overtaxed. Increasing student enrollments, the steady growth of graduate schools, and a phenomenal increase in publications necessary for research have all combined to face them with demands they cannot always fill. At the same time, scholarly research for decades to come will depend upon the solutions they find for their pressing problems.

One of these problems is the perennial one of how to handle pamphlets which come into the library. These pamphlets cover a bewildering number of subjects; they may be beautiful examples of the printing art or scarcely legible products of cheap offset printing. Their authors may be distinguished literary figures or barely literate obscurities.

The initial reaction of many librarians to pamphlets is that they are "trash." However, university librarians discover that their idea of "trash" is a faculty member's idea of research material. Librarians too frequently judge pamphlets according to standards of literary art; a faculty member may or may not use such standards. A political science professor visiting the University of Iowa libraries was delighted to discover that the library had retained a series of pamphlets whose contents consisted of totally unrelated sentences brimming with an almost incoherent hate.

Once the librarian is convinced that pamphlets are actually of value to his patrons, a major hurdle has been crossed. The potential sponsor of a pamphlet collection will do well to remember that most librarians are booklovers in the narrowest sense of the term. He may well find his colleagues as dubious of starting a collection of pamphlets as they would be of beginning a collection of worn-out light bulbs. There is little advice which can be given about overcoming this prejudice; only an active campaign of re-education, perhaps with faculty help, can erase it.

After the decision has been made to preserve pamphlets, an intelligent acquisitions program must be drawn up.

At the present time, such policies for pamphlets are usually
most unsystematic. The following procedures for a "pamphlet collection" may be only too typical. Specific pamphlet
titles are purchased when requested by the faculty. Unor-
dered pamphlets are examined by the acquisitions librarian;
unaided by any library policy, he decides if a pamphlet is
valuable. Most are rejected for permanent addition to the
collection, but some are sent to the limbo of vertical files
in the reference department. The few which do meet the
subjective standards of the acquisitions librarian are forward-
ed to the catalog department. There the cataloger decides if
they are worth cataloging. Because pamphlets frequently
lack important title page information and are very narrow in
subject content, they are frequently difficult to catalog.
Bearing all of this in mind, the cataloger rejects a few
more. The survivors are then given abbreviated cataloging:
no classification, limited subject cataloging, few if any descriptive notes. Each is bound into a large volume of inconvenient size with numerous other pamphlets on assorted subjects. The result is an addition of little research significance. The undergraduate, using the subject approach, will
seldom locate the piece; the researcher, unaware that the
library might possibly have the piece because of the miscellaneous character of the collection, never checks the catalog.
Even if the researcher did check the catalog, the library
could not provide the depth which his investigations require.
Such a policy is a poor compromise. Money is wasted on a
weak collection which cannot satisfy the needs of the patron.

However, solutions can be found to the problems of
building effective pamphlet collections. For no library is
there the possibility of collecting all pamphlet titles published
in the United States; the wealthiest could not afford to acquire and process them. Obviously, then, library policies
must be adopted which limit the pamphlets desired in the collection.

An almost endless number of plans could be adopted
to bring the costs of pamphlet collecting within the limits of
the library budget. Since the late nineteen thirties, one
such plan has been in operation at the University of Iowa,
and it has operated with considerable success in limiting
both the acquisitions and cataloging of pamphlets.

Surprisingly, perhaps, the establishment of a workable acquisitions program has been Iowa's most difficult
problem in creating a pamphlet collection. The collection
was originally designed to acquire all pamphlets distributed
in the United States by foreign governments for propaganda
purposes during World War II. Records no longer exist to

indicate how active a collecting program was maintained;
however, the collection was begun, and it was expanded to
include the pamphlets issued by various domestic groups interested in helping to shape American foreign policy.   The
attack on Pearl Harbor drastically reduced the amount of
material received, but the collection still contains the publications of various special-interest groups concerned with the
problems of drawing postwar political boundaries.

At the end of World War II the collection continued to
reflect the problems in American society.   A major such
problem was the revulsion against Communism, and this was
shortly the major theme in the acquisitions policy.   However,
other matters of concern are reflected in the pamphlets of
this period.   Some returning veterans, imbued with a cru-
sading spirit, turned to pamphleteering as a way of attack-
ing shoddy products, housing shortages, and high living costs.
Some Americans, horrified by Nazi racial and religious policies, used pamphlets to broadcast the horrors to their fellow citizens.   A few pamphlets, their authors literally
shocked to disbelief by postwar revelations, built logical arguments to "prove" that the mass murders had never happened.   Most pitiful of all are those which were lovingly
published to honor the memory of relatives killed in combat.
Sometimes these pamphlets included poems or stories written by the dead soldiers; sometimes they were simple tributes written by sad parents.

By 1950 the collection was facing a crisis: the number of pamphlets being published for American consumption
was increasing tremendously.   The problems facing the nation in foreign affairs were complicated by rising doubts
about internal security and an uneasy awareness that the
Communists in Russia were skillful politicians.   The pamphlets received indicated the confusion among Americans as
they realized the dangers of the postwar world.   At Iowa it
became obvious that a new political force was coming into
being.   Pamphlets began to challenge the views of the established political organizations in two broad areas: internal
security and foreign policy.

The mounting numbers forced the library to recon-
sider its acquisitions policy for pamphlets.   Prior to this
time, the collection had been thought of as propaganda material.   This idea stemmed from the original collection of
the propaganda materials deluging the nation prior to Pearl
Harbor, and this theme had been expanded after the war to
include propaganda from any group, foreign or domestic.
By 1950 the library could no longer afford so broad a practice.

About this time a new policy began to take form,
which was apparently more of an evolutionary matter than a
definite decision. Gradually the material published by foreign governments for popular consumption ceased to be collected. Decisions were also made to stop seeking materials
published by the business community for propaganda purposes.
Emphasis was slowly made to center on the publications primarily devoted to political matters, usually at the Federal
level. These issues included the role of government in business, the conduct of foreign affairs in the cold war, internal
security, public health, social morality, and others. An examination of the collection indicated that the major portion
of it consisted of pamphlets published by organizations outside of the "mainstream" of American politics. The policy
thus began evolving in the direction of a pamphlet collection
composed of material published by political groups other than
the two major parties. By 1964 the policy limited the collection, with one major exception, to non-socialist, political
organizations which were not related to either the Republican
or Democratic parties or any other major national organization. The exception was the continuation of the policy aimed
at bringing in pamphlets published by religious organizations
outside the major American denominations.

It is probably obvious that the acquisitions policy for
the Iowa collection has been one difficult to define adequately. For example, what is a "major, national organization"?
What is a "major, American denomination"? A serious effort was made to solve these problems. However, scholarship in political science has not produced a standard terminology to describe all ranges of political activity. Scholars
use vague terms like "fringe groups, radical right, or conservative." Yet, if a consistent acquisitions policy were to
be followed, the Iowa collection could not be adequately described by such vague terms, subject to individual interpretation.

Two different methods were used to define the collection more specifically. The first attempt was to develop a
standard set of terms for the acquisitions policy. This attempt soon foundered on the simple fact that the library staff
did not have the time to fill a major gap in American scholarship. The second method took the pragmatic approach of
stating what material Iowa did not collect. Socialist and
Communist material was not desired, because it was available at other libraries within a three-hundred-mile radius.
Publications of the Republican and Democratic organizations
were not desired since they, too, seemed readily available.
Material, even though political, published by groups whose

basic reason for existence was not political, was also excluded. If the material seemed to be borderline, it was included on the theory that it was safer to include questionable
material than risk any possibility of eliminating what would
later be found to be of significance.

The technical procedures used in the acquisitions program were relatively simple. No adequate bibliographies of
pamphlets exist, but desiderata lists were compiled from
three major sources. First was the use of the few lists
available giving the names of the small political groups;
these lists probably include one-third to one-half of the existing organizations in the country. Those listed were con-
tacted and asked to donate publications for which they were
responsible.

The second major source was the discovery of new
organizations through distributing agencies. It is a common
practice for the smaller political organizations to distribute,
not only their own publications, but also those of other
groups whose publications represent similar views. One
political organization might lead to the discovery of one or
two others, and gradually the list of contributing organizations could be built up. The third major source was the
lists prepared by bookstores specializing in the sale of current political literature. These lists often revealed new organizations, and their publications were then sought.

Most of the material received was donated by the publishing organization. Letters were written to each explaining
the importance of the Iowa collection and requesting its help
through the donation of its publications. Form letters were
never widely used, because it was felt that individually written letters achieved better results. An absolute neutrality
was maintained concerning political affairs. Organizations
were asked to help a program designed to further scholarly
research, and the results were satisfactory.

Material was purchased only when it was felt to be of
unusual significance to the collection and was unavailable
through gift. Such purchases were relatively rare and were
handled through the regular channels of the Acquisitions Department. A constant check was kept to assure the library's
remaining on the mailing lists of the donating organizations.
Claims were made when necessary, always through individually written letters. It was felt that the use of forms, even
for such routine matters as claims, would make donors less
willing to cooperate with the program.

Once the acquisitions program was operating, the
problem arose of making the material easily accessible to
the patrons without the cost of complete cataloging. During

the World War II period the collection was apparently so
small that no catalog was needed. After the War, it began
to expand rapidly, and the first problems of organization
and cataloging arose.
        The initial solution was to organize the material
through filing under the name of the publishing organization;
in cases where this was unknown, the pamphlet was filed
under Library of Congress subject headings. This system
proved to be unworkable. The first difficulty was that the
filing by the name of the publishing organization did not provide for finding the material through the names of individual
authors. A second difficulty was that the organizations frequently changed names; the changes might be due to a merg-
er but were also often brought about by a change in political
viewpoint. The third difficulty arose over the pamphlets
filed under subject headings. A pamphlet, once filed under
a specific subject heading, was unavailable under any other
subject approach. Since the contents of pamphlets are usually much more specific in subject than a book, Library of
Congress subject headings were too general to describe the
pamphlets. Thus the patron, at best, would have to guess
under which of several subject headings the pamphlet he desired was filed.
        During the Korean War a card file was started of or-
ganizations whose published material would fit the collection.
This card file was later expanded to include "see" references to carry the patron through successive organizational
name changes. A few authors' names were also entered, although no systematic policy was followed. This card file,
when combined with the services of an experienced curator,
served the patron quite well. However, illness and trans-
fers resulted in a turnover of curators rapid enough to im-
pair service to the patron. It takes one or two years for a
curator to become familiar enough with the collection to
wring the most service possible out of it. By 1962 the method of subject filing had completely broken down, and the actual filing of material consumed an extraordinary amount of
staff time.
        The first step in improving service was to file as
much material as possible under some form of author entry;
if possible, under the name of the organization whose views
it represented. If the piece seemed to represent no particular organization, it was filed under the name of the author.
If no author could be found, the piece was filed by title.
Less than five percent of the material had to be filed by
title.
        The second step was to provide some kind of catalog-

ing for the material. The patrons consisted of two distinct groups. Undergraduates used the collection for term papers and required only a few representative pamphlets on some subject. This meant a subject approach of some kind was necessary. The second group of patrons were specialists, and nearly all of their requests were for the works of some particular organization.

The problem of a subject approach was considered in two basic ways. One idea was to provide a classified list of the material; this was expected to be more quickly accomplished than standard subject cataloging. The other idea was to provide the usual subject cataloging with Library of Congress subject headings. A trial run was made with both systems, and no significant difference in work time was discovered. The classified list idea was then dropped as being too rigid.

It is debatable whether Library of Congress subject headings or a special subject list should have been used. The LC headings were decided upon, even though they frequently proved to be too general or outdated, for two reasons. It was hoped that the subject cataloging could be used when the time came to catalog the collection fully. Also the University of Iowa libraries make an effort to educate their patrons in the use of LC subject headings, which are used with practically no variation in the public catalog. It was felt that an undergraduate, skilled in the use of the public catalog, should be able to apply his training to using the pamphlet subject catalog.

For the researchers an author catalog was constructed. Most of the main entries consisted of corporate authors, since the majority of pamphlets did not list individual writers. The standard cataloging practices were followed for "see" references and added entries.

The cataloging shortcuts consisted of minimizing the number of subject headings, eliminating notes, eliminating classification, and making no searches beyond the piece being cataloged.

This system of cataloging allowed for speed, one cataloger preparing 146 titles a day. One reason for this speed was that a pamphlet cover often carries a great deal more information than does a book title page. Sixty-one percent of the pamphlets at Iowa could be cataloged by examining the covers, with only a cursory inspection of the contents. The cataloging has one major deficiency: nothing appears in the main catalog of the library to guide the patron to the collection. For the researcher this is probably not of any particular importance, but the collection could conceivably completely escape the notice of an undergraduate patron.

The pamphlet collection at Iowa is by no means ideal. However, if all university libraries set up relatively inexpensive collections on different subjects, together they would provide a cooperative effort of tremendous importance to scholarly research. Until they do, a valuable source of information about modern society is going out with the trash, and the librarian is doing a disservice to scholarship.

Don Mills Uses Dewey to Classify Pamphlets
Reginald A. Rawkins

From Ontario Library Review 50:14-15, February 1966.
Reprinted by permission.

The experiment to use a classified arrangement for
pamphlets and clippings in the Don Mills Regional branch of
North York has been in operation for nearly a year and is
proving to be an easy resource to build, use and maintain
as an integral part of the library's circulating materials.
It seems logical to arrange pamphlets in a systematic classified scheme just as we treat books, and the differences in
format and topicality should not form a barrier to this method.
Processing and storage are conducted in the following
way:

(a) An item is dated with a stamp which alternates
in colour each year--red and blue. This facilitates weeding.

(b) A Dewey number is assigned and marked in the
top left corner. The probable life of the pamphlet is anticipated by a choice of three colours
for the number. Red is used for short-term ma-
terial--up to one year--and includes many clippings. Green indicates a likely span of usefulness from 3 to 5 years. Blue is employed for
long-term or near-permanent material.

(c) A Dewey index is kept near the collection to trace
subjects. As subjects and numbers are used
they are checked, thereby providing an index of
subject holdings already housed. Synonymous
terms in Dewey are also ticked if they are appropriate.

(d) The classified pamphlet is then stored in a hanging file folder (Pendaflex); projecting tabs show
the Dewey number of each folder's contents. The
folders are in the vertical file cabinet which is
housed in the reference section.

Special procedures are necessary for certain kinds of
material. As most travel pamphlets and brochures include
historical data, we use history numbers throughout. Cana-

dian travel material is available in large quantities and is
stored in separate pamphlet boxes on the reference shelves
at 971, each province being given a single box and so labelled. The notation in the Dewey index, however, is preceded by 'P.' Other Canadian history pamphlets (including
those on historical sites, etc.) are housed in the appropriate
numbers within the pamphlet collection in the vertical file.

Pamphlets and clippings on local history are arranged
at 971.35 and subdivided by folders alphabetically, thus:

971.35   Don Mills
971.35   Toronto (city)
971.35   Markham
971.35   Toronto (Metro)
971.35   North York

Local material pertaining to a subject goes with that
subject regardless of locale, e.g. Elections, Goldenberg,
Architecture, etc. Where a subject is represented in quantity, pamphlet boxes are provided as necessary, as in the
case of travel brochures, university calendars, vocational
guidance and education curricula. To relate material scattered through the subjects to a locale, a short card index is
kept to index various aspects under Canada, Ontario, Toronto and North York; e.g., Canada--Expo 67 . . . 606.4.
Subject authorities are Dewey, Canadian Index and proper
names as they occur.

References: Synonymous terms are marked in Dewey
where appropriate. Location references are also indicated
when the material is stored in separate pamphlet boxes on
the reference shelves. 'See also' references are made within the folders if the scheme shows a need, e.g. 621.48
Atomic engineering see also 539.76 Nuclear fission.

Occasionally, a form of subject analysis is employed
referring to aspects of the subject to be found elsewhere in
Dewey; e.g., in the folder for Japan at 952, additional material is listed on a card by topic and class number for
Japanese architecture, education etc.

Advantages: What advantages have we achieved from
this form of classification? Arranging pamphlet material in
a systematic classified order is by no means rare. There
are to my knowledge public libraries in British Columbia
employing it as well as special libraries in the commercial
world. Some public libraries in Europe also use a classified arrangement.

One of the outstanding advantages in classifying pamphlets is that staff searching stock for materials on various
subjects often search in the pamphlet file with Dewey numbers already in mind.

Another very favourable result is the close juxtaposition of related subjects, which conveniently allows examination of overlapping subjects. In addition, it is also convenient very often to move back through the file from a specific topic (perhaps sparsely represented) to the broader generic term. For example, pamphlets dealing with automotive engineering will be located at 629.2. If little is available, one finds extra treatment by moving back to the broad field of engineering at 620, where some pamphlets will include treatment on automotive engineering.

The use of alphabetically arranged subject headings sometimes encourages confusion and duplication by the careless use of synonyms. A classified order eliminates this possibility because Dewey gives a number which can only be found in one place in the sequence; thus stamps can only be classified at 383 whereas alphabetical possibilities could offer the choice of stamps, philately, postage stamps, etc.

We have noticed that stock revision is much easier to control when the material is in classified order. One can readily see, for example, how strongly various subjects are represented in relation to the whole collection and where discarding or strengthening is needed. Like any other pamphlet file, weeding of out-dated material takes place almost constantly as the subject folders are consulted.

In practice, we have found that indexing with Dewey and using printed index for reference is a great time-saver in building the collection. When material is being considered for adding to the pamphlet collection, the usual criterion prevails; i.e., is the item something which is needed in terms of book collection strength in that subject? Thus the decision becomes easier when thought of in the same classification terms as those used for books.

The only essential difference between the treatment of books and pamphlets is the cataloguing process. Librarians through the years have criticized the Dewey scheme in terms of its suitability for classifying books. Similarly, many will find fault with the Dewey classification of pamphlets. In the final analysis, the same answer will apply . . . it works!

Dewey Pamphlets

A letter to the editor, sent as a reaction to the preceding article. Reprinted by permission from Ontario Library Review, June 1966, pp. 84-5.

Dear Editor:
    I was roused from lethargy when I read Mr. Rawkins' article on pamphlet files in the February issue of Ontario Library Review.
    His statement that some public libraries in British Columbia and Europe use a classified arrangement, when there has been at least one library at his own doorstep using this, stirred me to draft an opposing view.
    Nov. 1, 1965 was an historic date for our pamphlet file--Dewey was deposed. We had used Dewey classification for pamphlet material since the Main library on Eglinton Ave. West opened in 1951. At that time, with limited staff, we chose Dewey as the fastest way to process pamphlets. General subjects corresponding to the larger Dewey divisions were indicated on the dividing guide, e.g. 320--Political Science, 330--Economics, 370--Education, as a general aid for staff and public. We regarded Dewey classification as adequate but never completely satisfactory for locating material quickly and efficiently.
    We found staff would have Dewey numbers in mind for general subjects such as vocations, but did not have Dewey in mind for specific subjects such as censorship, fallout shelters, or North Atlantic Treaty Organization. To locate a pamphlet on a specific such as fallout shelters, a staff member searched frantically in the pamphlet file under a general number, or referred to the public catalogue, or library classification tool to find what number or numbers Dewey had in mind. If a librarian experienced difficulty in pinpointing a subject with resultant waste of time, what untold problems would the library patron encounter?
    Finally, last fall, staff time could be allocated to reorganizing our pamphlet file under subject headings. We chose as our guide Subject Headings for Vertical Files 1964, compiled by Toronto Public Library. Our policy is to change or add subjects which will be most effective for our requirements, using as our authorities our catalogue and ex-

perience with subject headings, Readers' Guide to Periodical Literature, and Canadian Periodical Index.

Already the five librarians in the adult department and the librarian in charge of cataloguing claim they can find material more quickly and easily. Now when we are asked for information on Canada's relations with the U.S., we find all the material in one place under Canada and the United States, or are directed to a related subject by a See Also reference on the pamphlet folder. Previously our material on this subject was scattered in three Dewey numbers: 330.971, 327.71, 338.971. In connection with our pamphlet file, we plan to have a card file of See and See Also subject references for immediate direction to the subject used and related subjects. Just as the public catalogue brings all material together under one subject though Dewey often disperses it, so material in our pamphlet file is now organized for more efficient use by staff and public.

Ruth Corner
Head, Adult Services
York Township Public Library

A Survey of Vertical Files
in California Public High School Libraries
Marie L. Graycar

From California School Libraries 37:26-7, May 1966. Reprinted by permission.

In the spring of 1965 a questionnaire on vertical files
was sent to 565 high schools listed in the section of the California School Directory titled "high schools" and having 25
or more teachers. They were sent to the librarian wherever
one was listed.
The entries returned during the month of May were
the only ones used to tabulate the results. Seventy-five percent, or 423 high schools, responded by May.
The questionnaires were first separated into enrollment categories of 500, i.e., 000-499, 500-999, 3500-4000.
Some questions were not answered by all librarians and the
percentages were figured only on those answering that particular question. A summary of the responses to the questionnaires is given below.
1. Items kept in the vertical file: General pamphlets were kept by 97%; government publications, 84%; vocational material, 84%; newspaper clippings, 57%; periodical
clippings, 48%; pictures, 47%. Other items mentioned on
the questionnaire were debating materials, drama cuttings,
college catalogs. Other items listed were biographies, book
jackets, maps, bulletin board material, embassy materials.
2. Tools used to select vertical file material: Not
too much agreement here although three-fourths used government publication lists and slightly over half used each of the
following--Booklist, Vertical File Index and Occupational
Literature. Only 44% used the Standard Catalog. Tools
mentioned but not on the questionnaire were school district
lists, pamphlet series and picture distributors' lists.
3. Subject headings used for vertical file material:
Again, little agreement was shown. The greatest percentage,
43%, used Sears List of Subject Headings; 30% used the Readers' Guide to Periodical Literature, 18% used Ireland's Pamphlet File in School, College and Public Libraries, 16% the
Vertical File Index; 7% Dewey Decimal Classification; 9%
made up their own headings.

4. Subject headings for vocational file: 29% used Wilma Bennett's Occupations Filing Plan, 25% Occupational Literature, 20% Science Research Associates, 5% their own.

5. Vocational material separate or interfiled with other vertical file material: Separate files used by 95%; only smallest schools interfiled.

6. Types of materials kept as clippings: Biographical, 74%; history, 68%; local items, 61%; geography, 59%; controversial material, 57%; vocational, 37%; science, 36%; school items, 29%; holiday items, 28%; hobbies, 22%.

7. Is accession record kept: Definitely not, said 94%.

8. Is discard record kept: Again the answer was no, this time by 96%.

9. Is card file of vertical file material kept: Not kept by 71%, kept by 28%. Many thought there should be a card file but lacked sufficient help. In some cases librarians felt "see" cards in the main card catalog constituted an adequate card file.

10. Processes used on vertical file materials: The subject heading is written on the articles by 84%, the date written by 45%, the number by 20%. Only 29% kept each item in a separate folder, while 79% kept the items loose in folders. Card and pocket was made for each item by 16%, card only by 18%.

11. Storage of items: Vertical file drawers housed the material in 96% of the libraries, 18% kept some or all items in cases on shelves and 7% kept items loose on the shelves.

12. Amount of vertical file material stored: Those housing in drawers listed an average of 11, 7 in the smallest schools to 18 in the largest. Only 18% listed the use of shelf space and the average was 20 ft. of space.

13. Where and how are vertical file materials used: 90% circulate items, with 52% limiting use to overnight, 13% giving three days, 16% one week and 15% two weeks.

14. Circulation procedures used for vertical file materials: Dotted slips made out by the student were used by 48%, 17% used pocket and card, 27% used card only, 5% listed items in notebook.

15. Estimate of average weekly circulation: Only about half the librarians answered this question. The average number of items used in the library, 54, was larger than the average number checked out, 35. The largest schools had the largest circulation by far, listing 182 items used in the library and an average of 98 checked out.

16. Types of classes using vertical file materials:

History classes used the materials in 83% of the schools; English classes, 65%; debating, 60%; journalism, 21%; drama, 19%; physical education, 15%; foreign language and mathematics, each 6%.

17. Publicity for vertical file materials: Three methods were rated high: orientation, 78%, individual reference, 77%, and assignments, 61%. Only one-fourth used displays, only 6% used school newspapers, only 4% used a library newsletter.

18. Estimated weekly time spent selecting and processing vertical file materials: The average time spent by the librarian was one hour and forty-six minutes; by the clerk, two hours and three minutes. Often it was noted that this area of work was necessarily neglected because the library was understaffed.

19. Are vertical file materials worth the time spent: Yes, said 82%; no, said 14%. Qualifying statements were often given, such as--if teachers learn to use, not with limited personnel, difficult to find good material, if we had time, for vocational materials only.

Contrary to expectations this survey has disclosed the fact that no real uniformity exists in the selection, processing, and circulation of vertical file material in California high school libraries.

A Picasso in Every Library
Donald L. Foster

Reprinted by permission from the Wilson Library Bulletin 37:58-60+, September 1962. Copyright 1962 by the H.W. Wilson Company.

No doubt the concept of a Picasso in every library is facetious. But any library that can be described as "medium-sized," or that even comes close, certainly can and perhaps should own original Picassos, Matisses and Rouaults. The Picassos referred to are neither the $100,000 paintings hanging in the Museum of Modern Art, nor their $5 reproductions sold at the corner book store, but those original works of art known as prints.

By way of definition, an original print is a work of graphic art (etching, wood-cut, lithograph, engraving, etc.), the impression of which is made from an image created by an artist on a plate, stone, wood-block, or other material. The number of impressions pulled from each plate may be a few or hundreds. It is these multiple impressions that make the print ideally suited, both economically and aesthetically, for inclusion in a library collection.

Because of the number of impressions created, prints are the least expensive of all the original works of art. The greatest names, Dürer through Picasso, can be purchased at prices ranging from $10 to $100. Of course a Dürer print, not unlike his paintings, may also reach into the thousands of dollars, depending upon the number printed, quality of impression, medium, rarity, print issue, authenticity, etc. The fact remains that excellent examples of graphic art are available for not much more than reproductions of fine quality art.

With proper care prints will last indefinitely. They do not receive the abusive treatment administered to books, nor will they become worn from use as do records and other A-V materials; and a new edition cannot make them out-of-date.

Prints not only outlast other materials, but they increase in value as the years go by. During the last recession, while the stock market took a sharp dip, the price of art works, including graphic arts, kept steadily moving up-

ward. If the library chooses wisely, it will have the satisfaction of knowing that every year its collection will increase
in value, an argument that should certainly impress any
board of directors.

Original prints in the library will inspire interest in
books about the artists and schools represented. For anyone interested in familiarizing himself with a particular artist, nothing substitutes for the study of his original works.

Print displays and exhibitions will bring added publicity to the library and afford an excellent opportunity to
focus attention upon the entire library program. Radio and
TV coverage as well as feature articles in the local papers
can be natural by-products of a graphic arts collection.
Moreover, prints are decorative. Hanging in the corridors
and above book shelves they will brighten up otherwise drab
surroundings.

Library personnel are trained to handle a variety of
materials, while the library itself, more than any other public institution, has facilities for the assembling, organizing,
storing, displaying, and loaning of prints. The library has
the added advantage of being in a position to relate the collection to lectures and A-V materials as well as to books
and periodicals.

A library print collection will allow the local museum
to concentrate on paintings, sculpture and other art forms.
Few museums have wall space for the proper display of
their paintings, not to mention prints. By specializing in
graphic art, the library need neither duplicate nor compete
with local galleries.

Specializing

Most print collections, whether they belong to public
institutions or to private individuals, specialize in a specific
area, at least in the earlier stages of development. The library can collect works in a given medium (etchings, lithographs, wood-cuts, etc.); a certain artist or group of artists united by time, place, or subject matter; or a type of
print such as book-plates, posters, book illustrations, or
maps.

Two important factors to be considered in selecting
an area of specialization are the locale and the interests of
the library's patrons. A successful print collection should,
in one way or another, reflect the community of which it is
a part.

A library might collect works of local artists or
prints typical of the region--city scenes, Western prints, or

mountain scenes, depending upon the area. A library on the
coast of Maine could collect marine prints by John Marin or
Winslow Homer, while its counterpart in the Mid-West might
concentrate on Thomas Hart Benton's farm-life scenes. Interests of the community could also be reflected through
Civil War scenes, sporting or theater prints; and the economic make-up of the area can be reflected in a concentration on such themes as transportation, mining, or fishing.

Subject specialization should not, however, overshad-
ow artistic expression, for then the print is no longer a
work of art but merely a pictorial record. In selecting
works of art, quality should always come first.

No doubt the greatest interest today is to be found in
modern prints. Nearly all of the important artists are now
working in one or more of the graphic art mediums. New
and exciting experiments are being undertaken, color is used
more freely than ever before, and the prints themselves--
no longer small, delicately rendered works of art--are today
appearing in all sizes, shapes and forms.

Selection of a specific artist or subject to collect
should be done as objectively as possible. The temptation
to "ride a hobby horse" is never greater than in the field of
art. On the other hand the library must not rely solely on
popular appeal. What is appreciated on Main Street is not
necessarily good art; and what is fashionable with critics
and connoisseurs may not be suitable for either the library
or its pocketbook. The prints most in demand are those of
the Impressionists and Post-Impressionists--which, however,
naturally command the highest prices. Collectors today,
buying with an eye to the future, are selecting German expressionists; yet, because of their depressing subject matter,
the expressionists will not appeal to many patrons. And the
library that collects heavily in avant-garde abstract-expres-
sionists will not only pay high prices but will also be running
the risk of investing in what may be a passing vogue.

Setting up the collection

It is important, therefore, that the individual or individuals in charge of the print program become thoroughly
familiar with the entire field of graphic art. Outside experts or local artists should be consulted or perhaps even
be invited to take charge of the program. Print collections
in museums and larger libraries should be viewed. Books
on prints and print collecting should be consulted, the history and methods of print production studied, and the collection itself supplemented with books and A-V materials that

relate to the artists to be represented.

Dealers should be notified of the program and their
catalogs consulted. It would be safest, at least at first, to
buy from only the larger and more reliable dealers and
avoid the auction rooms, and the smaller print and antique
shops.

Policies should be established and clearly defined for
the acquisition, mounting, care, display and possible circulation of prints. Whether the prints are to be considered as
reference materials and used only for study and display, or
are to be loaned to patrons, must be determined in the light
of circumstances in each individual library. If pictures are
to be circulated, frames must be decided upon, and carrying cases in the form of portfolios, cardboard cartons, or
other containers selected. Cases can either be obtained
from a commercial company or constructed by the library
staff.

Frames can usually be bought from a local dealer or
from wherever the prints are purchased. The cheapest and
often the most attractive method of presentation is simply to
place the mounted print between a sheet of glass and a cardboard backing, cut to the size of the print. This will not
always keep the print dust-free and is impractical for circulation purposes, but the pictures can easily be replaced and
the display rotated.

A special area should be set aside for display purposes and a departmental study room established. Prints
can be hung on the walls or placed on easels. For study
and storage purposes either portfolios or solander boxes
should be utilized.

After display and study areas have been established,
outside exhibitions might be considered. Interest in the library's collection will be greatly stimulated through loan exhibitions. They could originate from museums, other libraries, or private collections, as well as from the many traveling shows that industries are now sponsoring. Exhibitions
may also be sponsored by local artists' groups, art studios,
university art departments, or even grade and high schools.

Libraries in the region might even form a co-op, as
is currently being done with A-V materials. This could be
accomplished within the framework of an already existing
film co-op.

After a collection has been instituted, many libraries
have been able to acquire valuable gifts and bequests from
interested patrons. Because of the favorable tax deductions
offered by the government, this is becoming an ever increasing source of art works in museums, libraries and

other public institutions. Many of the country's most important library print collections, including that of the New York Public Library, have been developed as a consequence of donations.

Interest in art has been growing steadily since World War II, and since 1955 the trend has developed into a boom. This is particularly evident in the increasing volume of art books aimed at the general reader, and in the use of art objects as an important part of American home decoration. Art sales are skyrocketing, while American artists are turning out hundreds of thousands of paintings and prints every year. Museums, mushrooming in every corner of the nation, are feverishly collecting in all fields and periods, and our professional art schools, colleges and universities are greatly expanding their curriculum to include all forms of art, particularly graphic art.

As a materials center dedicated to the dissemination of culture, the library, more than most institutions, has an obligation to include art as an integral part of its program. The developing concept of the library's role in our society, coupled with the public's awakening interest in aesthetic values, presents opportunities that have only begun to be realized. Today libraries must offer patrons more than mere reflections of great art; a book or film about Picasso will not suffice. Nothing can substitute for original art; and no art form satisfies library needs as well as the print.

Perhaps there should be a Picasso in your library!

Aurora Loans Art Pictures
Eleanor Plain

From Illinois Libraries 44:151-3, February 1962. Reprinted
by permission.

In November, 1959, the Aurora Public Library joined
the growing number of libraries circulating framed reproductions of art prints.

This service started as a result of the loan of two
such collections from the Illinois State Library. The borrowed pictures proved to be so popular with patrons that the
library administration felt it should start building its own
collection.

Since Aurora was far from being a pioneer in this
field, it was possible to secure information and suggestions
on developing the collection from other libraries. Special
appreciation is due the public libraries of Wichita, Kansas,
and Rockford, Illinois, for their help in furnishing necessary
details covering the mechanics of purchasing, preparing, and
circulating framed pictures.

With this information and encouragement from colleagues, the Aurora librarian sought and received approval
from the board of directors to spend approximately five hundred dollars on an initial collection.

In selecting prints for purchase, invaluable guides
were Catalogue of Colour Reproductions of Paintings Prior to
1860 and Catalogue of Colour Reproductions of Paintings 1860
to 1959, both published by UNESCO. The prints in these
two publications were included only after careful examination
by experts of many color reproductions submitted by publishers of all countries. The criteria used by the experts in
making their selections were (1) the significance of the artist; (2) the importance of the original painting; and (3) the
fidelity of the color reproduction. For each reproduction
listed in these volumes, information is given concerning the
process used in painting, the size of the print, the name of
the printer, the publisher, and the price.

Aurora's nearness to Chicago facilitated making contacts with galleries in the Merchandise Mart, which handled
art prints of high quality. After the library had selected
and ordered its prints, a decision had to be made about the

framing, whether to have it done by the agency from which the prints were purchased or by a local dealer. Aurora has tried both ways.

When the prints were ordered to be sent already framed, delivery was delayed for several weeks. Unframed prints were received promptly and local framing took a shorter period, but several hours of staff time were spent in selecting suitable frames. Disregarding this time factor, pictures framed locally or elsewhere cost practically the same. For those unfamiliar with picture framing, it should probably be mentioned that the cost of the print is a relatively small item. The framing usually costs about three times as much as the print, the exact amount depending on the size of the picture, the width and quality of the frame selected.

Upon receipt of the thirty framed pictures in the library's initial collection, two questions arose--how to display them and how to protect them when carried to and from the library by borrowers. For display the library's small amount of uncommitted wall space was utilized, and inexpensive aluminum easels, purchased at the local art supply store and placed on tables, filing cases, and other flat surfaces, also served to bring the pictures to the attention of patrons. After the first few days, display space was no problem as all the pictures were soon in circulation.

Circulation rules had been previously determined. The pictures were to be lent to adults only, for four weeks with privilege of renewal, but the problem of carrying cases for them had not been solved. Conferences with a local carton company had shown that it would not be economically feasible, because of the varying sizes of the pictures, to order cartons made commercially. It was finally decided to purchase cardboard in suitable weight and size and make the cartons at the library. Thus far, after two years and more than 1,000 circulations, there has not been a single instance of damage to any print or frame.

From the first, the collection was enthusiastically received by the public. Framed pictures from the library now hang in many homes and offices in Aurora. There have been several instances of patrons who so enjoyed the borrowed pictures that they ordered duplicates for themselves from a local dealer.

It was interesting to note that, although traditional and modern artists were equally represented in the collection, the moderns have proved to be more popular. Pictures by Braque, Renoir, Monet, Van Gogh, Degas, Matisse, and Picasso always seem to have a long waiting list. Among American artists, works by Homer Martin, Frederick Waugh,

Lawrence Smith, William Keith, John Singer Sargent, and Andreas Feininger have been most in demand.

As the popularity of the collection increased, the library was faced with the embarrassment of having patrons make special trips to the art department to select pictures and then not find any on hand. This difficulty has now been solved in a most satisfactory manner. Colored slides have been made of all pictures in the collection. The slides are two by two and mounted for viewing in a hand viewer. Each slide is identified and numbered to correspond to the number of the framed picture. The size of the library picture is also indicated on the slide so that the patron may know whether it will fit his wall space. The cost was sixty-five cents per slide. Of course, the viewer and slides are kept in the library at all times.

There are now seventy pictures in the Aurora library's collection and regular additions are planned for the future. The public, the staff, and the library administration feel that this service is one of the most gratifying and enjoyable ever offered by the library to residents of the community.

Circulating Art Collections
Gordon Bebeau

From Wisconsin Library Bulletin 62:168, May 1966. Reprinted by permission.

If the experience of the Appleton Public Library is at
all typical, probably no service that a library can offer its
patrons will be as well received as a circulating art collection. An initial showing gives a good overview.

In 1962 the Board of Trustees decided to make use of
a trust fund of approximately $675 to begin the collection.
To this amount was added a $175 gift from a member of the
Board. The first pictures, 37 of them, were put on exhibit
in the library for two weeks in the spring of 1963. It was
announced that they would begin circulating at 9:00 a.m. on
the Monday following the last day of the exhibition, and people assembled outside the library that morning, waiting for
the doors to open. By 10:00 all of the pictures had been
charged out--even the few by artists such as Klee, Grosz
and Chagall that most people found rather startling. Storage
is no problem at Appleton!

Since that initial purchase the collection has grown to
84. Only a few are originals, gifts to the library from the
Downtown Business Men's Association following an Art Fair
for Wisconsin artists.

Good quality reproductions are relatively inexpensive,
but good framing increases the net cost to the point that the
average price of our pictures is between $25 and $35. All
of the reproductions have, so far, been acquired from a
single source, chosen for the quality of the framing rather
than for any unusual value in the reproductions themselves.
Maintenance costs have been low as damage to the pictures
has been limited to an occasional chipped frame. This kind
of damage can be repaired by a local framer at very little
cost.

This new service has been an unqualified success.
Seldom are more than two or three pictures available, and
in every month since they began circulating the collection
has "turned over" completely. (Think what your circulation
figures would be if your library's book collection would do
the same!)

Because we have attempted to cover the widest possible range of art styles our patrons often comment that they have learned to appreciate artists and styles to which they previously felt a real aversion. Probably the greatest advantage that has accrued to us has been the new friends that the library has gained through this program. The initial showing was good publicity, and gave an opportunity to see the collection and the library.

Eskimo Art in a Community College Library
Bernard C. Rink

From College and Research Libraries 25:113-4, March 1964.
Reprinted by permission.

The Mark Osterlin Library at Northwestern Michigan College has literally translated Ars gratia artis into an active program of presenting original art to its academic and civic communities. It all began when an enterprising Chicago executive donated a rare collection of Eskimo carvings to be sold for the benefit of the college library. The library, with the assistance of a committee of art-conscious citizens, then organized an Eskimo art exhibit and sale. The donated carvings were enhanced with stonecut and sealskin stencil prints from Cape Dorset, Baffin Island, Canada. Enough money was realized from the sale to subsidize a year-round art exhibit program in the library. In fact, the event was so successful that the Eskimo art exhibit and sale has now become an annual summer event. Furthermore, the Mark Osterlin library has become one of the few authorized outlets for Eskimo art in America.

The proceeds from the sale are placed by the library in a separate account labeled "Eskimo Art Fund." The benefits of this fund are manifold. The most gratifying service provided, of course, is a year-round program of original art exhibits in the library. A different art show is presented each month. The exhibitions shown have ranged from "African Sculpture," loaned by the Segy Gallery in New York, to "Painters of the Western World," from the permanent collection of the International Business Machines Corporation. Cost of rental, shipping, and insurance is covered by the Eskimo Art Fund.

In addition to subsidizing the monthly exhibits, the funds derived from Eskimo art enable the library to buy original prints and paintings. This collection now includes fifteen carvings and forty prints and paintings. These, coupled with the modest but growing fine arts collection, represent the source for a program of circulating art works to the college faculty for home or office use. Eventually, the Mark Osterlin library hopes to assemble enough prints to sponsor a traveling Eskimo art exhibit at a moderate rental

193

fee.   Prior to receipt of the Eskimo art, the college had no
art collection.

The purchase and sale of reproductions and post cards
of the great masterpieces represents further service stem-
ming from the Eskimo Art Fund.   They are bought with fund
money and sold to the students on a nonprofit basis.   Consequently, any student can familiarize himself with the classic art works by tacking them up in his room.   Since we
began selling these reproductions in the library, we have
noticed little or no mutilation of fine arts reproduction books.

This blueprint for presenting art to students and citizens represents only one way that a library can patronize
the arts and enhance the cultural environment of its users.
Much of its success originates in the excellence and popularity of Eskimo art--an art that is primitive, yet sophisticated
enough to captivate those who are exposed to it.

Some librarians no doubt object to using library
space to display and promote the fine arts.   To them it represents an intrusion on the library sanctum sanctorum.   One
must judge such projects, however, in their settings, where
specific differences overrule general library beliefs or practices.   First of all, Northwestern Michigan College is a
two-year community college without a fine arts building, located in a small city that has no art gallery or museum.
In such an area, devoid of an art gallery within several hundred miles, the display and sale of art objects in the library
assumes a cogency that would not be justified in more culturally endowed urban areas, where facilities for the preservation and presentation of art already exist.

From an academic standpoint it also befits a community college library to patronize the arts if the opportunity
arises and the space exists.   One of the most pressing tasks
of a two-year college is to provide its students with an educational and cultural experience.   Exposing the two-year student to at least a few of the cultural advantages that his
four-year counterparts enjoy will certainly assist rather than
shortchange him when he does transfer to a university, where
he will have to compete and associate with individuals who
have lived and studied in richer cultural environments.

The effects of original art display are far from immediate or measurable in a setting that has never had such
a program.   We are convinced, however, that our humble
beginning will accrue interest and eventually pay dividends--
possibly a fine arts center at Northwestern Michigan College.
At least, our hope is that Eskimo art proceeds will be par-
layed into even greater benefits for our college and community during the next decade.   A recent letter concerning our

library exhibit series, from August Heckscher, special consultant on the arts to the White House, states the challenge
we are attempting to meet: "That such an undertaking
should be carried on by a community college library is particularly interesting. The relationship of the college to the
arts--and of the arts to the community--is a big opportunity
which needs to be explored through just such initiatives as
your own. "

Experimentation with an Image Library
Dr. Stanley T. Lewis

From Special Libraries 56:35-8, January 1965. Copyright by Special Libraries Association 1965. Reprinted by permission.

This article is not intended to present theoretical or final solutions but merely to discuss new experimentation with visual data initiated during 1964 at the Art Library of Queens College, N. Y. A change of emphasis was sparked by two factors: first, the needs of instructors and students were becoming more pressing and articulate; and second, the stimulus received at the SLA New York Chapter Picture Group meetings last spring at which Bernard Karpel, Librarian of the Museum of Modern Art, gave two lectures on the themes of "Word & Image" and "The Organization of Image." A background factor was my teaching of "The Literature of the Fine Arts" course at the School of Library Service of Columbia University for a number of years.

The needs of the studio art teacher are usually not realized by a librarian because they are not often expressed directly. In part, this is the result of the artist-teacher looking upon the art library as primarily organized for the use of art historians. Usually academic libraries are top-heavy in art history, and although much of their contents are of vital interest to the studio teacher, their historical bias limits their practical value. While courses in art history depend on readings from carefully evolved bibliographies, the studio teacher has no similar bibliography. His courses are based chiefly on workshop methods and studio projects. Besides sending his students to the library occasionally to obtain specific technical data, an instructor may suggest looking at reproductions of work by a particular artist. Obviously, this is far from the central role the library could and should assume as a generator of visual ideas in studio courses. During a library-wide "self-survey" last year, we began to consider this responsibility. With a heavy enrollment in studio courses and a well-known faculty of artists at home in all media, it seemed unlikely that the library was doing all it could to serve their educational requirements.

When considering the teacher-artist's attitude towards the library, one fact was immediately apparent--the book catalog was infrequently used. An artist who entered the library rarely approached it. Normally, he would go to one of the art librarians and talk about the problem his students were working on, such as the idea of placing one transparent object over another, then ask did we have anything on it. What we were then obliged to do was the old needle-in-the-haystack searching that Mr. Karpel had indicated as the usual approach to any formal problem, i. e., indiscriminate browsing through the picture and pamphlet collections and, of course, picture books. In such areas the catalog is a blind device. Only if an entire book is written on a subject will such a traditional technique as collage appear in the catalog.

Instructors who made the most use of library materials in the studio had to go directly to the pamphlet files and wade through them, usually examining the pamphlets without bothering to look at the subject headings on the folders. In the past, they had found that the standard subject headings (based on The Art Index) had little bearing on their needs. For example, if they were looking for a particular geometric pattern, it might be found in a pamphlet on Peruvian textiles. The fact that the pamphlet was filed under "Textiles--Peruvian" didn't help them, because they couldn't know when they entered the library that an exhibition catalog in this field had exactly what they needed.

Needs and Solutions

What the artist-teacher needs is a critical collection of visual materials. He is not looking for "a picture in a book" but rather for an easily handled package of pictures in sequences. Moreover, locating the visual data itself is not the main consideration. The data have to be made accessible for actual studio use. Books are not the ideal medium-- finding ten pictures in ten large-sized books does not solve the problem, for they cannot be carried to the studio conveniently, they cannot be easily passed around or displayed, and very often they cannot be taken from the library because they are needed for art history courses.

Invariably, the teacher does not care about the actual source of the pictorial data. What he wants is the visual statement removed from its original package and transformed into groups and sequences, without the interference of the author's chain of thoughts. Pictures in books do not lend themselves to such uninhibited manipulation. Consequently,

books in multiple copies must be acquired to be clipped for
their pictorial content.

   Besides physical rigidity, part of the inadequacy of a
book is the inability of the catalog itself to cope with the
multitudinous approaches to visual form evidenced within the
art book.   The catalog--as it now stands--functions best
with problems of text.   Yet it is frequently true that the
studio teacher is either unconcerned with textual content or
finds the professional cataloger's treatment of text irrelevant
to his formal problem or educational bias.

   A more diverse collection of images than those traditionally collected in fine arts libraries is needed.   For example, the sculptor Kenneth Campbell currently has his students begin one problem by preparing large plaster models
of polyhedrons.   Instead of starting with a crude piece of
material, they start by having a perfectly realized geometric
structure to carve from.   What his students need are pictures and slides of mineralogical crystals and mathematical
forms and models.   What have to be collected, then, are
not just examples of art but all types of visual phenomena.
Many of these subjects are included in the large picture collections of public libraries, where they have always been of
great interest to artists.   What the college teacher needs is
highly selective groupings of such pictures organized in
terms of visual form.   For this purpose scientific books,
commercial and advertising publications, children's literature,
and periodicals all provide valuable materials.

   The exhibition catalog is a visual collection's major
art source.   Containing readily available and flexible image
data, the advantages of the exhibition catalog are many.
They are usually compact, so that the borrower is able to
take out a dozen or two in an ordinary circulation envelope.
Their comparatively low price makes them easy to acquire
in multiple copies, either for clipping or circulation.   Most
significantly, in subject matter they present the most intense
concentration of principles and trends with which instructors
deal.   There is hardly a demand for material on forms or
trends that we have not been able to meet by assembling a
group of catalogs.

   Moreover, they are the most important art publishing
development of recent years.   The gallery and museum catalogs, together with periodicals, are the prime means of art
communication today.   In them new theories, as well as new
art, are first introduced.   This is important, for the studio
teacher who is an artist himself is usually dealing with current trends.   Often utilizing the finest graphic techniques,
they are major tools, not only through their subject coverage

but in their frequently experimental design approach. Fortunately art catalogs, once difficult to locate, are now readily accessible to a library. Wittenborn and Company (1018 Madison Avenue, New York), long specializing in all types of visual literature, publishes occasional long listings of catalogs as well as monthly listings of new publications. The recently established Worldwide Art Catalogue Centre (250 West 57th Street, New York), which distributes only exhibition catalogs, publishes quarterly an annotated bibliography of major international catalogs, prepared by scholars.

A freely developed flexible linguistic is necessary to locate a visual document without the impediments of text-oriented subject approaches. At Queens College we are concentrating on adapting to the terminology that fits our curriculum and makes sense to our instructors, rather than creating a universally applicable system. As much as possible we prefer a teacher's terms, especially since the same visual data are often relevant to the jargon current in his classes.

Visual Materials Collection

What has emerged is a visual materials collection. We employ one card index that controls the following materials: 1) catalogs, pamphlets, posters, and those books that are more practicably located here than in the regular book collection, 2) mounted pictures, 3) mounted pictures arranged in series, 4) slides, and 5) original works of art. For the first three sections--the bulk of the collection--there is no classification. Each item is simply given an accession number. Thus the index is an elementary coordinate index, each card bearing spaces for 30 numerical entries referring to 30 individual images. Subject headings include names of artists, visual attributes, style labels, materials, subjects, institutions, and so on. In other words, any term that would lead a user to a worthwhile item is included, such as Graphic techniques: metallic effects, or Organization: force movements, centripetal thrust.

It is obvious that not every image going into the collection can be, or should be, fully indexed in visual terms. We fully index what are felt to be "overt" examples of visual qualities, having attributes so clearly illustrating visual principles that they will be used frequently as teaching tools. An item is never considered finally indexed. Additional entries can be made as the need for them becomes or is made apparent. The index's reliance on flexible terminology is its chief limitation, but cannot and should not be avoided at

this stage. Mr. Karpel's image-for-image indexing, with
each card bearing a photograph of the image referred to,
would be ideal, since there would be no possibility of mis-
understanding terms, but this would require duplication facilities not yet considered normal in library procedure. What
is important is that in our period of automation everything
is possible. What we are doing is still primitive because it
lacks the sophistication technology can bring to our problems.

While our collection should be considered as experimentation on a grass-roots level, it has already shown itself
to be of decided educational value. In dealing with visual research, any attempt to reorganize on a visual basis forces a
library collection to open up many fresh and exciting possibilities. Such redirection does not lessen the art historical
value of the collection; in fact it provides more historical
data and stimulates critical study by creating new patterns
among source materials. For the first time library materials are being used creatively in a variety of studio courses,
and some of the heaviest student users of the visual collection have turned out to be education students doing student-
teaching in the schools.

Art and art education on all levels have been redirect-
ed during this century, but a library approach has not
emerged that in any way corresponds to the new art environment or attempts to meet directly the visual needs of contemporary artists, teachers, and students. The shortcomings
are twofold: there has been a failure to respond in terms of
developing a library semantics and machinery and in establishing a collection based on new needs. The second short-
coming is largely an outgrowth of the first--without a new
terminological structure, library resources have been limited
by being fitted into the philosophical definitions of knowledge
and experience of an earlier age. While many books and
pictures in our collections are of value to the modern user
of visual material, they are made virtually inaccessible by
the classical card catalog and classification schemes. We
are too easily lulled by habit and convenience into believing
that these systems are grounded on a rational objectivity,
and we are too content to compromise and work with what
we have inherited.

Regional Art As a Library Service
Michael Ligocki

From A. L. A. Bulletin 55:882-4, November 1961. Reprinted by permission.

It is not the task of a librarian to be a curator of art works. Nor do we expect that his leisure hours be spent frequenting previews of art exhibits. Yet, year after year, at the Northern Indiana Art Salon and other local art exhibits of any consequence one can be almost certain to come upon Hardin E. Smith, librarian of the East Chicago Public Library, appraising the annual hangings with the eye of a connoisseur. He is there not for diversion but as a talent scout, and his avid perusal of the offerings may result in several one-man shows.

"We display art regularly in our libraries, " Mr. Smith may explain in the course of conversation with one or more artists during the preview. "Perhaps we can work out an arrangement for a showing of your works some month this year. "

To many artists this recognition is a greater expression of success than having some single selection picked by an artists' jury. It means that his works will appear collectively in the East Chicago libraries, mingling with the assembled art and culture of the centuries, and will be viewed by a more diverse group than any off-the-beaten-path gallery could offer. With the public at large as viewers, in an area where he lives, what artist could hope for a better gallery? After all, much great art was sponsored in surroundings as public as a church.

East Chicago's program of art exhibits began in 1955 as an experiment, and it depended largely upon pictures sent out by the Studio Guild of West Redding, Connecticut, a booking agency which sends out exhibits of original works by living artists for display.

In 1956 Mr. Smith decided to add to the program of exhibits the works of local artists, at first residents of East Chicago or persons who worked within its limits, later others from the Calumet Region. With annual exhibits of art work of local school students, selected by art teachers, the experiment gradually turned into an established program feature as a library service.

If a library is to be a center for disseminating culture, Mr. Smith believes that it should draw on sources from within its own environs as well as from a distance or from the past. As if to confirm his belief, a large picture of the Indiana dunes, painted by Frank Myslive, an artist of the Calumet Region, hangs on one wall of Mr. Smith's office, loaned by a grateful artist to add a native touch to the surroundings.

The Calumet Region is not an area with long tradition or local cultural heritage to draw upon. It is a young region which has been growing fast industrially only this last half-century and is now one of the world's largest industrial concentrations. Geographically it is like a celestial constellation, with four large cities--Gary, Hammond, Whiting, and East Chicago--surrounded by a sprinkling of towns, hamlets, and suburban areas, all situated southeast of the city of Chicago along the foot of Lake Michigan in Indiana.

Although the political limitations of the various cities are distinct, the people live, work, and play over the entire region. Its public libraries have now crystallized into about five systems, one in each of the four major cities, and the county system, which rather loosely merges the local units in the rest of the county.

In such an area a librarian has a difficult problem of focusing public interest upon the activities and facilities offered by his own system. To add to Mr. Smith's problems, East Chicago is not a homogeneous city, being divided into two almost distinct areas. The library is forced into a somewhat binary existence and operation, each of the two main branches serving a public different in interest, origin, and cultural awareness. With this art service Mr. Smith receives notice and publicity regularly in the half-dozen daily and weekly newspapers which cover happenings over the region.

"Since many people work in our steel mills and oil refineries or study at the Indiana University center, yet reside elsewhere in the region, the services of our libraries are available to these persons without fee, just as if they were residents of East Chicago proper," Mr. Smith explains. "Therefore any service, like these rotating art exhibits, which promotes the enjoyment of works of local origin, is of concern to us."

"One of the rewarding parts of our activity with art is the opportunity for publicity it affords," Mr. Smith is ready to emphasize. "It enables us to get notice and news coverage on our work and facilities far outside the area we

serve.   Since I know the artists and the nature of their
works, I write the publicity releases myself. "
         New exhibits are always available.   The problem is
selection and balance in relation to the space the library can
afford.   There have been numerous one-man shows, group
works of artists featured under some unified theme, shows
of abstract as well as traditional works, portraits, land-
scapes, water colors, casein, and sculpture.   Representa-
tion by artists or type of art has been well diversified to
satisfy and express varied tastes.
         This result has not been haphazard.   Mr. Smith has
no advisory committee in this phase of his work, but he frequently consults artists about any problems or ideas which
might contribute to better exhibits.
         For that matter, relations with the artists are har-
monious and mutually useful.   One group meets one night a
week in one of the library's rooms to hold a class in discussion and painting, open to any interested dauber regardless of professional status.   It is a self-governing group,
selecting and paying its own live models, and careful to pass
the hat around to collect enough to keep the janitor willing to
tidy up after them without grumbling over added cleaning
chores.
         Art works are not like books and other reproduced
material housed in the library to be loaned out, hence pictures must be viewed and studied on the spot, like reference
material or current periodicals.   Exhibiting art in the library is not expensive, but requires time to program and
publicize.   After several years, some of the operations have
become routine.   After an artist's or group of artists' works
have been arranged for by invitation an exhibit date is set.
The exhibits are displayed for one month, concurrently or
alternately in the two main branches, which gives all the
regular library patrons a chance to view the show and affords enough time for friends and followers of the artist's
works to view them at leisure.
         The artist delivers his paintings to the library and
agrees to pick them up some reasonable time after his exhibit is over.   While his works are in the library, it is understood they are loaned at the artist's risk and that the library has no obligation other than to exercise reasonable
care.
         Mr. Smith is planning ahead, and his library board in
1960 adopted a five-year building program, to be financed by
a tax levy amounting to $146,000 a year.   Responsible groups
or clubs are encouraged to sponsor anything of a community
nature that the library cannot undertake on its own.   Thus

the art exhibits are a step in the direction of making the
East Chicago Public Library a comprehensive cultural center, with concern for any native or local expression of that
culture.

Picasso in the Nursery
Oscar Teller

From Library Journal 89:4986-8, December 15; School Library Journal 11:36-8, December 1964. Copyright 1964 by R.R. Bowker Co. Reprinted by permission.

In the Children's Department of the New Orleans Public Library there is a prominent sign on display reading: "No Pictures Checked Out to Adults Unless Accompanied by a Child." The child may be just a story-hour visitor but he checks out his painting in the same way that his parents get their much larger reproductions in the art department upstairs. The rules are simple: the adult who accompanies the child checks out the picture on his own card, but only the child is permitted to select the painting. The service encouraging children to "choose a picture for your room" has been popular from its inception.

The practice of lending children color reproductions of important works of art is now being followed by juvenile departments in a number of libraries throughout the United States, enabling the child to develop a love for art within the framework of the same department in which he selects his books. There should be no age limit for the child who is old enough to understand story-hour tales. The only requisite is that the painting be scaled down to permit him to carry it home triumphantly and even hang it up himself. (Fathers should be reminded by librarians to choose a special spot and nail for this purpose, bearing in mind the child's own eye level, seated or standing, depending on the activity he is likely to engage in near the spot he has chosen for the painting.)

How much do you charge a child who borrows a painting? The policy varies. Denny Stephens, who was the first to experiment with children's paintings at the Hutchinson, Kansas, Public Library, called his collection "The Children's Circulating Art Library," and charged 25 cents, though Mr. Stephens thinks that in some areas 10 cents might be better. The nominal fee is intended simply to establish a feeling of responsibility while the reproduction is in the child's possession. "If so young a child parts with a comparatively large amount, we can be sure he wants the picture badly," says

Mr. Stephens. New Orleans, the second public library to
experiment with a children's art collection, has no charge
for the six-week loan period. Pictures come framed, and
have a lacquered surface so that they can be wiped with a
damp cloth.

Children respond eagerly to these art works. Displayed atop bookshelves in the children's section as well as
the general display area, the reproductions in the Nashville,
Tenn., Public Library are "in circulation rather constantly."
The Bennett C. Martin Public Library, Lincoln, Nebraska,
has over 80 percent of its works in constant circulation. At
the Mount Olivet Church Library, Minneapolis, Minn., library patrons come Sunday morning, before or after services, to take out books, recordings, and paintings as well.
Religious paintings for children's rooms are often in demand
around Christmas and Easter in both church and public libraries.

Apart from size--paintings are generally 12" x 16" or
16" x 20" for children's departments--there is generally no
difference in selection for children's and adult art collections. The Hutchinson Public Library, after an initial order
chosen with special care, used the same policy for both departments. The Savannah, Georgia, Public Library issues a
ballot in conjunction with its art exhibit encouraging patrons
to check their favorites (from No. 1 to No. 30, in order of
preference), then chooses its new collection.

Choosing the children's collection

It is important to bring the children directly into the
selection process. The adult should not project conservative
tastes upon them, but should permit them to see and select
from a full range of styles, including the contemporary. For
a selection committee I would insist upon a group of children,
with some careful guidance from an adult who is sympathetic
toward modern art, perhaps an art teacher or supervisor.
Experience has shown that children are more apt to select
nonobjective and unconventional paintings than adults.

Just a few cautions: There is a tendency on the part
of adults to give children the Blue Boy, or some other beau-
tifully dressed child, apparently most orderly in behavior.
Believe me: Murillo's street urchins are much closer to
their hearts! Portraits of present-day children, vividly
painted and without too many details (for which children's
eyes are not yet well enough developed) will arouse their interest, as will any exciting activity: games and play, fishing, riding, and other sports, circus scenes. Pictures of

animals also permit a closer, more personal relationship
with the picture. Include a large variety of subjects, and
do not admit several reproductions by the same master until
many artists are represented in the collection.

Given these preferences for subject, the range of periods is wide. Children who voted on their favorites in
twentieth-century art in 80 public schools in Winnipeg, Canada, chose Franz Marc's Red Horses for first prize, Picasso's Harlequin on a Horse for second. Other favorites have
included Bellows' Sand Cart and Lady Jean (a child dressed
as an adult), Dürer's Squirrels, Breughel's Peasant Wedding,
Marin's The Circus Elephants, Degas' Ballet Dancers.

An elementary school project

The Oak Terrace Elementary School, North Charleston, S.C., now owns 80 pictures, framed and mounted by
the school custodian with the help of the local museum
"house" framer. Each Thursday morning, during "home-
room period," the children return the borrowed reproductions to the library. Later on, the pupils are permitted to
select a picture. After being checked out it is inserted in
a canvas bag and the child is on his way home with a great
masterpiece.

How did the school start its collection? A large number of reproductions, ordered on approval, were numbered
with large figures cut from a calendar and placed on exhibit
in the school library. Each pupil from grade 1 through 7
was given a printed ballot and asked to choose the three pictures he or she would most like the school to buy. "That
was a week of excitement throughout the school," reports
the originator of the project, principal J. Howard Berry.
"To begin with, the prints were unlike anything the boys and
girls had ever encountered before, but they loved them, and
we found it necessary to select many times the number we
had originally planned to buy. Prints with the lowest number of votes were returned and arrangements were made for
payment over an extended period of time."

There is an interesting sidelight to the children's ballot. A large group of the prints selected by children was
brought to a meeting of practising Charleston artists. They
were asked, "If you were buying pictures for school children,
ages 6 through 13, which of these would you select?" In the
artists' balloting, two of the three top choices of the children
were selected by the adults.

The PTA also became involved in the Oak Terrace
picture project. The school purchased military surplus can-

vas of a thickness that could be handled on home sewing machines.   From this fabric the mothers made carrying bags
with straps of surplus webbing for the framed pictures.   The
cost is not more than 10 to 15 cents for even the largest
bag.

Mr. Berry concludes: "Attention to this phase of an
elementary school child's experience has in no way inter-
fered with our basic academic program, nor has it required
any undue expenditure that should have gone into equipment
and books.   In fact, new dimensions to our students' cultural enrichment have been provided by the use of prints."

A child's everyday experiences are usually reflected
in great art, and in selecting such pictures a closer relationship to a world of beauty and mystery is made possible.
The library, the church, the school--all make possible with
little or no cost that great luxury formerly known only to
the very rich: art for the child, in the home.

The Original Print
Robert E. Cain

From Library Journal 91:5323-6, November 1, 1966. Copyright 1966 by R.R. Bowker Co. Reprinted by permission.

"I want this one," he piped, pointing his finger at a black and white etching of lobster pots on a New England shore. The speaker, a small boy about ten years old, was choosing an original art work for his room. Pointing is bad manners, they say, but there are some messages that an index finger conveys best. A lot of pointing is being done these days at the Cary Memorial Library in Lexington, Massachusetts, where library card holders may draw on a collection of original prints by contemporary artists.

Borrowers use the prints for a variety of purposes. For many, an original print is a way of bringing zest and change to their homes. Some businessmen use them to dress up the walls of their offices. Since they can be purchased, others find them appropriate gifts and still others become so fond of the prints that they make them part of their own personal collections.

Started in 1962 with about 20 prints, the collection has grown in popularity, quality, liveliness, and size. Today, of the 150 prints currently in the collection, 100 are normally in circulation at any moment.

Under the collection's present mode of operation, artists loan prints to the library, but retain ownership. The library processes the print for circulation, takes care of the necessary bookkeeping, and provides facilities for display. When a patron wishes to borrow a print, he presents his card, registers, and pays a rental fee of $1 for each month that he wishes to keep the print. If, after living with the print for several months, he decides to buy it, the rental fees that he has paid apply toward the price of the print. Or he may return it and choose another print. All fees from rentals and sales go to the artist. Thus, by taking care of the overhead expenses of the collection, the library makes available to its public thousands of dollars worth of original art.

With many libraries already lending framed reproductions of art works to their public, it is appropriate to ask why original prints are different.

An original print is not, of course, "original" in the same sense as a painting. With a painting there is only one true original, whereas there may be as many as 50 or 75 originals of a given print. According to the Print Council of America, a print is original when it fulfills three qualifications: a) the artist himself has made the master image or plate from which the print is made; b) the print has been made from this same master image, either by the artist or according to his directions; and c) the artist himself has approved the finished print. His approval is indicated by his signature on the print. While there may be slight variations in prints within the same edition, each original print remains an authentic expression of the artist's intent because of the artist's stated approval. A reproduction, on the other hand, does not have this guarantee of authenticity and may vary from the original in color, size, medium, texture, or any of a number of other factors.

The print as a medium has its own appeal and its own special adaptability to a library collection. Prints are easily displayed, stored, framed, and matted. Unlike many oil paintings, they require no heavy, expensive frames or special lighting arrangements to bring out their beauty. Their small size makes them especially suitable for lending to homes, for they are easily carried, and they fit comfortably into the average-size room. Then too, the fact that many unframed prints may be rolled up and mailed in a mailing tube facilitates transport between artist and library and makes it possible for artists from distant parts of the country to contribute to a collection.

One of the greatest advantages of a rental collection is the flexibility it gives the borrower, for it makes possible living with a work of art and testing it out. Only by doing this does the borrower discover whether the initial appeal of the print will fade or whether the print will become a source of continuing satisfaction to him. If the relationship proves rewarding, the low cost of most prints (almost 60 percent of the Cary Library collection is priced at $40 or less) makes them available to persons of modest means.

Also significant from the library's viewpoint is the lack of a well-organized system of distributing and marketing prints. Art galleries are usually not interested, because the low price of a print means a low commission, and galleries must pay high rents for their exhibition space. Some galleries are now renting prints, but the rental fees they must charge--$4 and $5 per month--tend to limit participation in their programs to people of substantial means. Thus the artist, unless he is very well established, needs a way in which he can make his work known, and he is inclined to look on a library collection not only as a way of getting wider exposure for his work but also as a means of being repaid, in a small measure, for his efforts.

A collection of contemporary prints, then, serves the double purpose of meeting the artist's need at the same time that it makes available to library patrons art which they would probably not see otherwise. As long as the artist's need exists, he will find it to his advantage to participate in a library print program.

It is no harder for a librarian to set up a print collection than it is for him to work, as he often must, in many other fields in which he may have had little or no formal training. For basic information on the print, its history, and the techniques by which it is made and cared for, Carl Zigrosser's and Christa Gaehde's Guide to the Collecting and Care of Original Prints (Crown, 1965) provides an excellent summary in little more than 100 pages of text and illustrations. This handy little book discusses in detail the techniques for framing and matting, and lists firms which supply the necessary materials.

What it does not provide is a guide to the world of the contemporary print. The guides that exist discuss artists who are already established and people of this stature have no need to contribute to a library collection. Yet there are many artists of ability who need the public exposure that a library print collection provides. For help in finding and selecting these artists librarians can turn to a resident artist, or the staff at the nearest museum or large library. Other prime sources of prints are local or regional organizations of printmakers--e. g. Boston Printmakers--or local art societies, many of which will be listed in the American Art Directory. These organizations--and museums, too-- often sponsor print shows, which are excellent places to look for contributors.

In selecting prints for the collection, several things should be kept in mind. The type of patron that a print collection appeals to most immediately has usually been exposed to one or more courses in art appreciation. This kind of individual will respond to art that is a pattern of shapes and colors without requiring that these shapes and colors depict in literal detail a "real" object.

The type of print that has been most popular at the Cary Library has been the semi-abstract multi-colored serigraph. But there has also been a response to art that is more traditional in approach. In the final analysis, the style and medium used are much less important than the talent of the artist.

A print collection must be replenished and weeded much as any other collection of library materials. At the Cary Library approximately 120 new prints are added to the collection each year. These prints replace those that have been sold and those that have not circulated. The latter are returned to the artists.

Weeding and replenishing provide an excellent opportunity for bringing new modes of artistic expression into the collection. A collection that is constantly renewed can encourage a continuing growth in the artistic taste of its users. Merely selecting prints that are similar to those that have circulated well in the past promotes the stagnation of the collection and the frustration of its educational purpose.

Besides locating prints suitable for the collection, the library must invest approximately one hour of staff time for each new print added to the collection. Forty minutes of this hour will be devoted to the framing, matting, and hanging of the print. The other 20 minutes is devoted to all the clerical tasks involved in running the collection.

Among the clerical duties are such chores as checking the print in, noting its value for insurance purposes, and sending a letter of acknowledgment to the artist. Three information cards must also be typed for each new print. One of the cards will go on the back of the framed print, giving the artist, title, price, medium, and whatever honors the print may have won at exhibitions. Another card identifies the print when it is displayed; the third card provides the record for renting the print and noting the rental fees collected. This checkout card also indicates the price, the medium, the title, and whether the price includes frame or mat.

A library assistant can also handle such tasks as sending out rental fees to the artists twice yearly, and forwarding the check to the artist when a print is sold. Then too, once each year letters are sent to the artists requesting new prints and returning those prints which have not been active in the collection.

Besides the investment of staff time, there is the cost of materials and tools. The initial cost of materials for framing and matting varies from $9 to $14 per print. Plain black frames in three standard sizes priced from $5.20 to $6.30 are used at the Cary Library. Matching sizes of plexiglas to protect the face of the print run from $2.60 to $6.60. Sheets of matting for each print are $.98 each. Other materials (including sheets of cardboard for the

backing) add about $.50 to the processing costs of a print.
However, since the frames, plexiglas, and many of the other
materials can be used again and again, recurring material
costs after the initial expense are much lower than the $9
to $14 figure.   The total cost of the tools necessary in mat-
ting and framing will be approximately $15.

Another part of the overhead expense of a print program is an insurance policy that will cover the prints while
in the library and out on loan.   While no instances of van-
dalism have yet occurred, and none are expected to occur,
Cary Library prints have already been involved in car acci-
dents and radiator explosions.

It should be evident by now that a library which supports a print program must contribute a sizable investment
of time and money.   Costs of the Cary Library collection
over a three-year period have run about $1800 in materials
and staff time.   It is natural to ask whether the library
should take a percentage of the rental and sale fees paid to
the artists.   The legal status of most public libraries prevents them from doing this, a restriction which would not
apply to college libraries in general.   And it should be noted
that, with the present rental fees, the amount paid per print
during the course of a year ranges downward from $18, de-
pending on reuse of framing materials.   The artist who has
not made a sale (only ten percent of the collection has been
sold) does little more than meet his expenses.   Furthermore,
when a program can make available to a community art
worth many times the investment of materials and labor, the
library and the community are by far the gainers.

With libraries already circulating films, slides, records, and, in some communities, reproductions of art works,
it is but a short step to the circulation of original prints.
And it is a program much more consistent with the library's
unique role of individual service than many library-sponsored
adult education programs.

Given the low price of the print, its suitability for library circulation, and its neglect in the general art market,
it is a natural candidate for inclusion in a library collection.
Although many new art museums have sprung up across the
country in the last few years, there are still large geographical and artistic areas which they do not serve, and libraries can, for a small investment, partially fill this gap.

In a day when our cities are undertaking urban renewal, when the national cry is for "beautification," and when
the man in the street is affected by and in part controls
these efforts, a widespread sensitivity to visual beauty is
necessary so that our future environment does not become

merely a different form of wasteland. Many libraries have
long made it a practice to maintain exacting standards of
taste in their exhibits, displays, and publications. In this
way they have, by their example, served as gadflies of the
public taste. Through a collection of original prints a library can expand its important role in visual education at
the same time that it continues to offer the individual service for which it is uniquely suited.

Programmed Learning '64
Philip Lewis

From <u>Illinois Libraries</u> 46:109-15, February 1964. Reprinted by permission.

Teaching machines and programmed learning, although a relatively new field, have received a disproportionate share of attention, both in the press and in terms of research and experimentation. Only during the past five years, and particularly the last two, has this activity taken on significant momentum. During this period, the field has passed from the initial phase of over-enthusiasm to the stage of pessimism and fear, and it is only now beginning to settle down to the realization of its potential as an effective approach to learning.

Librarians and libraries will be instrumental in effecting the varied applications of this self-instructional approach. The materials lend themselves particularly well to such treatment. Because of this, personnel associated with libraries should be well grounded in information about this rapidly growing field.

Programmed Learning

Briefly stated, programmed learning is a method of organizing information in a systematic and logical way for efficient learning. The following are the steps generally employed in the construction of a program:

(1) Determine a specific objective or objectives to be attained by the learner.
(2) Identify the content, information, or skills necessary to achieve the objectives.
(3) Organize the information into learning increments or frames. These are short bits of new information that are easily learned.
(4) Arrange the increments in a logical progression for learning; that is, start with the simple and progress to the more difficult, deal with the concrete before abstract concepts, etc.
(5) Insert "cues" and "prompts." This involves sup-

plying hints and helps, by employing various techniques, to assist the learner in mastering more
difficult concepts, or to provide assistance at the
start of the sequence where it may be needed.

(6) Each increment must be accompanied by a challenge that may take the form of a question to be
answered, a problem to be solved, or a manipulation to be performed.

(7) Finally, the program must incorporate a means
of informing the learner as to the validity of his
response to each increment. Such different devices have been used for this purpose as having
the question on one page of a programmed book
and the answer on the following page, or using a
sliding mask to uncover the answer.

Initially, programs were arranged to use what is
known as the "constructed response" or "linear programming"
approach. This is a method advocated by Professor B. F.
Skinner of Harvard University. The system employs very
short increments and prompts the learner to give an answer
that has been constructed in advance. Proponents of this
method have demonstrated that a well conceived program can
result in 90 to 95 percent mastery by the average learner of
the material presented.

Some disadvantages of linear programming become apparent when this approach is employed with very bright students or those with particularly good backgrounds in the area
covered by the program. Under such circumstances, the
sequence of short steps and the necessity to respond overtly
may be boring and without intellectual stimulation. To overcome this, some recent techniques known variously as "express stops" and "leap-frogging" have been devised. In use,
if the learner successfully completes a number of increments
and reaches a green-colored frame, he is instructed to omit
all of the increments between that point and the next green
frame. If, however, he missed any increments before coming to the first green frame, he must work through all the
following increments without omission.

Dr. Norman Crowder, of Western Design Division of
U. S. Industries, is the proponent of branch programming.
This, in contrast to Dr. Skinner's system, is known as the
intrinsic approach. In this instance, the learning increments
are much larger and may run to a paragraph or even to an
entire page in length. The question that is asked is also accompanied by two, three, or even five alternate answers.
The learner must, therefore, make a choice. These alter-

nate answers are not structured, as would be typical for a
multiple-choice test question. Rather they are composed as
the result of an analysis of likely misinterpretations of the
material in the increment. If, for example, a student selects answer two, then he may be directed to turn immediately to page five. If he selects answer three, he may be
instructed to turn to page 24, etc. If his first choice is indeed the correct one, and he turns to the page involved, he
is notified of his success and is then presented with a new
increment, question, challenge, etc. If, however, he selects
a wrong answer, when he turns to the page indicated he is
informed of his error, and a remediation sequence is provided to explain away the misconcept. The learner is then
requested to return to the original increment page to select
another answer.

This branching technique makes it possible for the
able learner to progress with great rapidity. On the other
hand, the person needing more assistance will have his background reinforced.

Although the two approaches mentioned are the best
known, recent experiments have revealed many diverse techniques which indicate that this field of programmed learning
is really just beginning. For example, it is no longer a
certainty that it is necessary to require an overt response
for every increment. Nor is it known exactly what mental
mechanism the learner employs in using a program. Only
additional research and broader utilization can bring answers
to these and other questions.

Why Teaching Machines?

Up to this point, only programmed learning has been
mentioned. This has been deliberate, since the emphasis
must be placed on the program. The method of presenting
the material to the learner via a fine machine is easily ne-
gated by an imperfect or poorly planned program.

Experiments and trials have shown again and again
that most programs presently available are just as effective
in a printed book format or in a loose-leaf arrangement as
they are on a machine-presenter. In such instances, a machine should not be employed. There are, however, requirements in certain areas of learning that do make it necessary to use an electric or mechanical device along with
the program. For example, in learning various languages,
an audio track is necessary so that the student can hear accurate pronunciation of words, phrases, and sentences. In
addition, it may be desirable to allow the learner to repeat,

record, and review his efforts in learning.   Certainly a machine is indicated here.

In other instances, color, motion, and feedback may be involved; in these cases, microfilm, motion picture film, and even computer storage of information may be essential. These factors show that it is too early in the game to attempt to crystallize procedures and approaches.   Rather, it is desirable to work within a flexible framework to implement programmed learning to accommodate individual requirements.

One important problem in using machines is that the consumer is generally restricted to using the available programs that will fit the particular device--much like purchasing razor blades to fit a particular razor.   At present, this is a limiting factor, since no single publisher or manufacturer has a sufficient supply of programs to cover all subject areas and levels.

About Programs

The latest [1963] figure for the number of programs commercially available is 352.   This does not include any programs that have been evolved for private use in business, industry, and the armed forces.   However, compared with the 122 available in 1962, a great deal of activity is indicated.

Most of the programs published are in the fields of mathematics and science with some variety in social studies, language arts, modern language, business, medicine, and a miscellaneous group that ranges far and wide.

The majority of the programs are adapted to a book-type format, some are designed for either book or machine use, and some can be used on the machine only.   The various media employed include printed sheets or books, cards, discs, microfilms, filmstrips, slides, and motion pictures.

Some publishers of programs provide complete courses in algebra, geometry, Spanish, chemistry, biology, psychology, etc.   These are inclusive treatments intended to cover the particular fields.   Another approach involves the use of short programs that cover units of instruction, single concepts in learning, or the development of a particular skill. Both techniques have a place in the use of programmed learning.

In the design of a program for an entire course, it is necessary to build in unit or chapter tests to enable the teacher and the student to make progress checks, although the program is self-checking for each increment.   Some of the machines are programmed so that this evaluative function is done automatically, and the student cannot progress unless he has reached a certain level of proficiency or learning.

Short programs dealing with such topics as Molar Method in chemistry, latitude and longitude, telling time, and how to use a library card catalog have obvious advantages. A diagnostic test or pre-test can reveal areas where the student should receive information or instruction, and the short units are excellent for this purpose. It is conceivable that in the future whole courses will be broken down into separate but articulated units, and the learner will work only with those units necessary for his progress.

Programs in the Library

Since programs are not graded as stringently as are courses in schools, there is a great latitude in the use of these by persons whose ages and backgrounds vary. For example, any person who can read and understand the vocabulary of a particular program can generally master the content involved. This means that a young but able learner can deal with subjects not normally available to him through regular channels. Similarly, an adult without much educational background can use the easier programs for remediation and upgrading purposes.

It is important that libraries assemble data about the offerings, relating to such items as vocabulary level, number of increments involved, average length of time needed to complete the program, conditions under which the frames were validated, and other pertinent data. This information makes it possible for library personnel to offer effective guidance to their patrons in the use of the material.

Since some fine programs are on microfilm, filmstrips, and other media, including magnetic recorded sound tracks, consideration should be given to the acquisition of appropriate machines if there will be sufficient utilization to justify such an investment.

In some instances, small and inexpensive machines can be checked out with certain types of programs for home, study hall, or other kinds of applications.

Programmed learning lends itself to library purposes in many exciting ways. The librarian can now provide specially prepared items for self-instruction that may be more effective than any approach previously available for home study.

Agorithmic Mathetical Reinforcement;[1]
The Implications of Programmed Instruction
for the Librarian
Ralph D. Gee, F. L. A.

The Library Association Prize Essay, 1965. Reprinted by permission from Library Association Record 67:228-32, July 1965.

The normal introduction[2] to this subject starts with a history, develops into explanation, and finally notes the relevant theories of B. F. Skinner and Norman Crowder. A recent selective bibliography[3] contained about 400 references, while its second edition covers over 1, 000. There is therefore no shortage of information, and it can be found scattered throughout periodicals in diverse fields from electronics to psychology. There are, however, some general points that must be raised to mollify the cynics who feel that what they missed must be harmful to their children.

Programming of lessons has been attacked by critics who feel that the human contact of education must not be destroyed. (Few, curiously, have considered this as an argument against the library.) The value of human contact is questionable if the teacher spends too much time relaying factual data to the detriment of class discussion. The program[4] allows for pre-lecture presentation of those facts that give point to any subsequent discussion, and, in group consideration, which relate opinion and knowledge. The program can also present these facts at a pace dictated by the student's own abilities.

Many feel that programming discourages the prescribed Socratic method of teaching, and the questions of the curious student. This is so if the program is allowed to replace all forms of educational media--which would be foolish. Only bigots see the library as a usurper of the teacher's function, or the book as an obsolescence superseded by television. The program is not an alternative, but a complement. In a class, many questions remain unasked from shyness, or unanswered because of the tutor's desperation in covering the syllabus in the allotted time. A clearly written program should dispel the need for many questions normally necessary through insufficient contact between tutor and student. Any difficulties within the program should always be referred to the tutor--who most certainly should not use this type of text as the excuse to put his feet up and "leave them to it." Socratic theories are based on the impractical ideal of a low student-to-teacher ratio. Today there are too few teachers, too many students, too little time, and too much literature. The program is an admirable way of cutting a path through the bush without completely devastating the mental landscape. It also presents a possible return to the pre-Socratic Hellenistic model of single pupil instruction. Much is made of the individual differences inherent in any group of students, but I am not convinced that the size of contemporary secondary school classes recognizes these differences. The self-pacing program, on the other hand, can allow the student to pursue those parts of the course that he finds personally stimulating, after grasping the fundamentals at the fastest pace. Research on programming for individual differences, although reaching various conclusions, indicates that advantage could be made of human variation when programs are complemented by discussion or by reference to further reading.

Teaching machines

Most librarians will have encountered automated learning through a subject inquiry, although the professional implications have a much wider significance, and deserve consideration. Although the dramatic term "teaching machines" is ever coupled with programmed instruction, at present the machine is a mere display device, the program being more commonly produced in a form outwardly recognizable as a book. Following the decision to purchase, this presents the librarian with problems less easily solved. Good texts are expensive; they are often compiled by teams comprising psychologists, experienced teachers, subject experts, and professional programmers. The published text is relatively delicate. The linear[5] form demands a spiral binding in order to lie flat, ensuring comfortable use and leaving the hands free to manipulate sliding masks or to write responses on separate paper (I hope). The branching[6] form ("scrambled book") demands that the user flip backwards or forwards according to answers selected from a group of alternatives. A slow learner will therefore make more of a physical impression on a "scrambled" book than a slow reader on a conventional one; and a damaged program can be useless, since the word "program" implies pedagogic planning so that each item of information is based on what has gone immediately before.

A program will be read to bits in fewer readings than normally expected with conventional books.   More copies per
title may need to be provided, since, unlike books, programs
have an estimated completion time, and cannot be taken from
a user before he has finished--and be effective.   Economics,
however, is an irrelevant counter to provision of the new
media.   If public libraries are to follow the ideals of self-
enlightenment of the founding fathers, then programmed texts
should be represented in collections already covering the
variety of materials that are now the natural part of a library's budget.   If the cost is considered prohibitive, then
the librarian of today should review the proportionate prices
of books, now and a century ago, in terms of the price of a
loaf of bread or the average wage for a 70-hour working
week.

Evaluation

The major problem confronting all potential users of
programmed texts is evaluation.   The only true way to judge
a text is either to present it to a class and see what happens, or to complete it yourself.   The latter course may
help you to decide the value in terms of what you have
learnt, but the program may not have been written for you.
(The possible bespoke approach of the program is an advantage over the individual book, but not, of course, over the
library as a collection of individual books.)   A program designed to teach the left-handed Spanish infant to play the
Welsh harp is difficult for the ambidextrous octogenarian
Welshman to evaluate; and such hyperbole is analogous to
some highly specific programs that do exist.   One of the
criteria of a good program is stated objectives for specific
grades or types of students.   Independent program testing
and evaluation centres are badly needed, in view of the
gleaming eyes of the bandwagon chasers, but until they exist, the librarian is poorly placed to consider programs for
purchase, unless his library is that of a school or college.
In which case there are further difficulties...
Within a college, many commercial programs considered so invaluable by the publishers will be useless because they bear no relation to the syllabus, or because they
have a particular emphasis not acceptable to the particular
lecturers.   Although such aversion could be shown towards
books, a lecturer may avoid confusing the students by recommending only selected parts of certain books.   This course
is not applicable to a program, which is complete within its
own terms.

In the future, lecturing staff may well devise and duplicate their own programs; and it may be left for the library to handle and disseminate them, and to have teaching machines for students to use with any programs that the library has stored.   Unfortunately, there are many difficulties of standardization to overcome before this ideal can be seriously considered.

The relationship between university libraries and programmed learning has already been established at the University of Southern Illinois, in a well-reported experiment. [7] With large numbers of students needing induction to the library each term, the staff were pressed to provide time for efficient indoctrination into the necessary elements of library use.   The experiment considered replacing valuable library staff and time by a teaching machine, and a course was programmed and its use evaluated.   The particular program incorporated pictorial and facsimile material representing recognizable parts of the library, catalogue cards and pages from reference works.   The program was so devised that it was impossible to continue without repeated reference to the catalogue or to library shelves.   Since programmed learning is intended to provide large numbers of students with basic facts in the shortest possible time, to the student's own capabilities, there is nothing particularly revolutionary in the Illinois experiment, beyond the application that would do us well to pursue.

To adapt a now famous observation: any person introducing students to a library, who can be replaced by a machine, should be.   By removing from the library the normal noise, bewilderment, catalogue blockage, and crowded reference sections that are inflicted upon the studious users by the rushed introduction of large and garrulous classes, the inculcating program does more than release staff.

Subjects to program

The subjects lending themselves readily to programmed techniques are those with basic indisputable principles and a traditional aura of tedium; they include languages, mathematics, and physical principles.   Although this is possibly because of erroneous teaching for generations, comprehension normally relies on the ready grasp of fundamentals.   It is these which must be well grounded before tuition can cater to ideas, opinions, and applications; and it is these that can be programmed.

Consider the time spent under the late syllabus in thoughtfully playing about with red rags--and all that bull.

Cataloguing regimen seemed equivocal when studied page by page in metronomic anguish, but became clarifyingly sensible when applied within a specific library. The approximate time spent on theory at full-time courses has often been a waste in terms of later professional contact with cataloguing departments; and yet the new syllabus threatens to leave the qualified librarian under-prepared. These are disciplines which deserve research to discover programming potential; and the combined efforts of practicing cataloguers, experienced tutors, and educationists, could provide good programs and also shed more light on more efficient ways to teach a difficult subject. If the library schools of the future encompass research, perhaps they will consider this, in company with other subjects that merit a similar approach. Professional education in the past has been very lax in dealing with the processes involved in compiling bibliographies, and yet the concepts are basic enough. Those students who suffered misery in any part of the professional syllabus will probably realize that it was "programmable," and those who follow in the future will surely be delighted to find it done, and having completed their programs, to devote more time to practical drill.

　　　Programmed instructional techniques have also been suggested as an information retrieval process, where replacement of the conversational interaction of the librarian by programming is considered. [8] Lines of inquiry are pursued to their intersections by key terms representing article abstracts, which have been fed into the machine using a modified language. Whether we need our "conversational interaction" replaced is another matter.

Applied librarianship

　　　After the implications for libraries, it is time to consider the reciprocal benefits of librarians to programs. There is no reason why a program should be intrinsically complete. The Illinois experiment relied on external comprehension of the catalogue and the library shelves. Any program could incorporate more text, or be designed to utilize background reading in selected places. For example, a program on mathematics could, at the sticky places, suggest that the student refer to a pleasurable book (Gardner, Hogben, Kline, Land, Moroney, Northrop, Sawyer) in order to perceive a more refreshing vision. This is where the librarian can help. His professional ability to refer any inquirer to any stated grade of book should be offered to the programmer, who in turn should introduce students to respectable and readable titles, and ensure that less attention is paid to textbook material. My personal wish is to see the program replace, not the teacher, but the textbook--the average current standard of which is boring, and its raison d'etre pecuniary.

The librarian's professional ability applies also to handling the material. The first need is documentation, not necessarily of techniques, but of specific texts. No standard commercial or national bibliography separates them from conventional publications, and yet they demand the treatment accorded to records and films--each of which have their own tracing machinery.[9] If a librarian is asked for a programmed course in blueprint reading, one is not readily found. Carl Hendershot[10] has produced a useful list of American material, but there is nothing of a regular appearance here. The only alternative lies in the educational abstracting services, which are very delayed, and which overlook programs in technical fields because only their form makes them educational. Future cooperation between publishers, educationists, and librarians will give the darkness the light that is at present a mere flash of hope.

Cataloguing the material

Having once traced and purchased the texts, the librarian should provide useful bibliographical description. Although in book form (an important thing to mention if it is not), the program bears about the same relationship to a book as a broadcast drama to a novel, having certain things in common, but purposes unconnected. Since program bibliographies are wanting at present, the library should indicate what texts it has. Classification can achieve this, either by a dictionary catalogue entry for the bibliographical form, or by an added subject entry in "teaching methods." The catalogue should stress certain information not expected in normal description, while other usually expected data can be overlooked. Pagination is less revealing, and in linear programs is probably better ignored, these being measured in frame length, and a page can contain anything from one to one dozen frames. Basic program type should be indicated--whether extrinsic (linear) or intrinsic (branching)--since they demand different study techniques. Some may be of mixed construction. The bibliographical analogy with pagination is better expressed in terms of expected completion time which, in the more respectable programs, will be indicated by the publisher. Annotation should cover the objectives, and the specific recipient; and indication should be

given of extraneous material: sliding masks, teaching notes,
self-tests, and whether the program is designed to be "written in. " This last point must be watched, as there is a
danger that the first user will ruin it for others. Finally,
attention should be paid to significant added "author" references. An example is the TEMAC series published by the
Encyclopaedia Britannica, or the Tutor Texts of E. U. P. and
Doubleday. These are worth at least a series entry and an
entry for the Encyclopaedia, where relevant, would do no
harm. Similar treatment is valuable for the Center for Programed (sic) Instruction, or the Behavioral Research Laboratories of the U. S. Air Force and George Washington University. Using a fictitious entry, I suggest the following approach:

> CROWDER, Burrhus F. , PRESSEY, Gilbert, and
> othe rs.
> Catalog 2000: an auto-instructional text;
> prepared by the RoboTeach Systems Cor-
> poration Teaching Project.
> New York. RoboTeach Inc. 1965. 2000
> frames, suppl. vol.
>
> PedaGrammatic Texts, no. 6. (RSC-65-6)
> Linear text in special folder with some
> branching sequences and teacher's notes.
> Average completion time: 30-40 hrs.
> Teaches basic library cataloguing for those
> without previous experience. (ALA Rules.)

Added author entries should cover "RoboTeach Systems Corporation, " or "PedaGrammatic Texts, " because
these can be a program's claim to prominence. Few future
programs will be written by one person, and may be worthless without the testing facilities of large organizations,
which in this country have already advertised for programmers. This implies corporate authorship with the programmer as a mere anonym obeying the rules, and some retrieval should be possible through this source.
    If a library does not use U. D. C., classification of
the above might be limited, but in one that does, the form
approach can be made by a modification of the (07) section
covering educational form--perhaps 025. 3(075). The attention of other interested programmers can be drawn by
371. 677:025. 3 (or whatever number has been adopted for
teaching machines).
    Thus is ensured retrieval by subject, form, author,

series, and programming firm.

New tricks--new names

Some commercially exploited programs were originally produced by consultancies under contract to particular
firms. The Eastman Kodak company had several for internal training, and the company is the only way to trace them.
My flippant example could have been devised under a U. S.
Office of Education contract, or for the New York Public Library. This sort of knowledge may be the only information
that an inquirer has, and until comprehensive documentation
is available in programmed learning, the library catalogue
should ease the foreseeable problems. Education is not recognized as a field with the wealth of indexing and abstracting
of the technologies, and yet it is rapidly developing its own
technology. New technologies demand and develop their own
terminology, but programmed instruction has largely borrowed from existing fields, and ambiguity exists. The Greek
root "math" (learn) was adopted in "methetics"[11] to imply
the "technology of education. " As a portmanteau word for
the vague and cumbersome "educational technology" it indicates a much wider meaning than self-instructional texts and
machinery. Although one can readily suggest new words, it
is less easy to guarantee their semantic precision or their
future popularity. I would like to set an etymological pebble
down the slope by using another Greek root: "ago" (to lead),
which already appears in "pedagogue. " To imply the principled formulations of individual steps within a program,
AGORITHM could be used; although this is as close as a pun
to the mathematical term "algorithm, " which partly suggested it. The completed program would be an AGOGRAM.

Should some librarians consider all this better condemned to the oubliette than to the proverbial ethereal castle
which it may seem to represent, I refer them to Hendershot's
bibliography.[12] It shows an expanding interest in the United
States, represented by some 1, 000 programmed texts in print
on subjects from Yiddish customs and roller-skating safety
to Boolean algebra and transistors. Some are gimmicks,
others are sincere. A microcosm, in fact, of conventional
book production. The point is that no librarian can afford to
dismiss anything, when prejudice is the last of his functions.

Notes

1. Agorithmic mathetical: See closing paragraphs for indi-

cation of these terms.

2. Goodman, R. <u>Programmed Learning and Teaching Ma-</u>
    <u>chines.</u> English Universities Press. 2nd ed., 1964.
    This provides an excellent introduction sufficient
    enough for the present purpose.

3. Gee, R. D. <u>Teaching Machines and Programmed Learn-</u>
    <u>ing: A Guide to the Literature.</u> HERTIS. 1963.
    (Out of print. 2nd ed. in prep.)

4. I have accepted the principle adopted from the U.S. by
    the computer world in general--the spelling of pro-
    gram to indicate the specific "software" as opposed
    to the more abstract term programme implying a pol-
    icy. The participles have been built to English con-
    sistency.

5. An example of linear, or frame-by-frame consecutive
    arrangement can be seen in the TEMAC texts publish-
    ed by the Encyclopaedia Britannica.

6. The branching form first appeared in this country in the
    form of the TutorTexts of English Universities Press.
    One of the first in the series was <u>The Arithmetic of</u>
    <u>Computers,</u> by Norman Crowder.

7. McCoy, R. E. "Automation in Freshman Library In-
    struction." <u>Wilson Library Bulletin,</u> 15th April, 1961,
    and February, 1962. Reed, G. "Programmed In-
    struction: A Challenge to Librarians." <u>Pacific North-</u>
    <u>west Library Association Quarterly,</u> vol. 27, no. 2,
    June, 1963. pp. 108-112. Siefker, B. "Program-
    med Instruction on the Use of the Card Catalog."
    <u>Southeastern Librarian,</u> vol. 12, Fall 1962, pp. 149-
    152. Southern Illinois University, Educational Re-
    search Center. Study to determine the extent to
    which instruction to University freshmen in the use of
    the University Library can be turned over to teaching
    machines. <u>Final Report.</u> Carbondale, Illinois, Il-
    linois University Press. 1963. Wendt, P. R. "Pro-
    grammed Instruction for Library Orientation." <u>Il-</u>
    <u>linois Libraries,</u> vol. 45, no. 2, February, 1963.
    pp. 72-77. Wendt, P. R. and Rust, G. <u>Use Your</u>
    <u>College Library Efficiently.</u> A 530-frame program
    intended for high school and college freshmen. Pub-
    lished by the authors and the Department of Instruc-
    tional Materials, Southern Illinois University. 1964.

8. McLaughlin, G. H. "Programmed Instruction As a Model
    for Information Retrieval." <u>ASLIB Procs.,</u> October,
    1964, pp. 309-316.

9. <u>British National Film Catalogue.</u> January, 1963--
    (Monthly). <u>Library of Congress Catalog:</u> a cumula-

tive list of works represented by . . . printed cards. <u>Films</u> (quarterly with annual cumulation). <u>Music and Phonorecords</u> (semiannual, annual cumulation).

10. Hendershot, C. <u>Programmed Learning: Bibliography of Programs and Presentation Devices</u>. Published by the author; 4114 Ridgewood Drive, Bay City, Michigan, 48707. (Annual with quarterly supplements.)

11. Gilbert, T. F., of Tor Laboratories, New York, is founder of a periodical called <u>The Journal of Mathetics</u>.

12. Hendershot, C., op. cit.

Bibliography's Stepchild: The Printed Note
Donald W. Krummel

From Library Journal 90:1249-54, March 15, 1965.   Copyright 1965 by R.R. Bowker Co.   Reprinted by permission.

This report is concerned with publications devoted primarily to musical notation--texts which preserve musical rather than verbal ideas, their symbols being not words but black and white notes, together with stems, flags, accidentals, and clefs, all superimposed on the five-line stave.   Inevitably such publications find their way into a library, and happily they are doing so in such quantity as to make them a problem to librarians.

A long-standing question of terminology greets us at the outset.   Strictly speaking, a part of what we are talking about is neither "printed," "published," nor "practical" music.   Not all of it consists of "scores"; much of it is more substantial than "sheet music"; and in truth, a good share hardly deserves even to be called "music."   The problem of nomenclature is quite apart from the bibliographical matters we shall discuss here; but it does reflect on our failure to provide for wise and competent handling of this material. For present purposes, we shall use the term "musical editions," broadly distinguishing them from recordings and from books about music.

The menagerie of musical editions is inhabited by a variety of bibliographical animals.   Noblest of them all are the great historical series and sets, issued by societies and foundations, handsomely executed and bound, definitive and expensive.   Close beside them are the large scores for symphonies, concertos, major chamber works, operas, and oratorios, the product of specialized music publishers, in large full scores for conductors or in miniature scores for study. From the same publishers come performance materials--ensemble parts and solo editions, intended to be used, worn out, and retired from service, and which for this reason have often been wrongly thought not to belong in a library. Also present are arrangements and other less ambitious works for bands, large amateur choruses, and church choirs, mostly sold and distributed for group performances requiring many copies.   More personalized are the song sheets, time-

ly and ephemeral; they come both from reputable firms and
from the "song sharks" who prey on the thousands of tau-
tophonous tyros who feel compelled to express themselves in
music. Anthologies come next, ranging from collections of
hit tunes and old favorites to hymnals and songbooks, and
emanating from a wide variety of sources, from the book
trade and music publishers to fraternal, religious, and political organizations. Etudes, exercises, tutors, and instructors for student use, typically produced by music publishers,
form still another category. Last but not least come the
music education materials, including "basic series" for the
classroom, which concentrate on rudimentary skills and are
generally issued by specialized educational firms.

    These various musical editions form the heart of a
library's music collection. They are the medium necessary
to the creative musical experience; in comparison, their
cousins, recordings and books about music, are passive and
petrified, for they are post hoc manifestations of the world
of original musical sound. Composers and scholars look
forward to musical editions as the end product of their la-
bors, and performers refer back to them as the basis of
their artistry.

    Throughout history, however, musical editions have
been slighted in our book-oriented libraries. Churches and
monasteries, once having presented performances from these
materials, either discarded them or relegated them to an
organ loft or wine cellar. Universities and learned societies
commonly regarded music as unworthy of the intellectual
character of their libraries. Our great retrospective bibliographies generally ignored them altogether, and most current national bibliographies have formulated arbitrary and
often elaborate rules for excluding as many of them as possible. Such library classification schemes as Dewey and
Cutter casually acknowledged their existence by dumping them
with the books which discuss them.

    In the broadening span of today's cultural life, music
has become a larger, brighter, and more clearly defined
segment of our intellectual spectrum. Enlightened librarians,
recognizing this situation, have been quick to accept a responsibility for expanded library service. As with other bibliographical media, the librarian's problems have increased
with an information explosion. Crying out for attention are
the endless problems of matching a burgeoning bibliographical supply with a rising and more varied demand from users.
Three aspects of this problem are the basis for this report:
in ascending order of importance, the need for special treatment; the need for bibliographical control; and the need for

qualitative standards.

I. The Need for Special Treatment.

In many ways, musical editions resemble printed
books; but for a variety of reasons, a line of distinction between the two has often been found convenient.   Much confusion has resulted from the different lines that have been
drawn by publishers, distributors, librarians, bibliographers,
and performers, along various historical, national, and practical lines--in each instance with a large number of incon-
sistencies and clouded areas.   The result, at worst, is a
minor nuisance.   In moments of impatience, however, it has
been all too common a practice to overlook the practical
reasons for the distinction, laying the blame instead at the
feet of the irresponsible, uneducated, and capricious musician whose stereotype we have never completely forgotten.
We therefore mention the matter for purposes of suggesting
that most difficulties come not from an inherent irrationality
in the medium of musical editions, but from a general lack
of understanding of its characteristics.
The problem is no simple one, perhaps least of all
within the complex operations of a modern library.   As an
example, an opera vocal score may in many ways be regarded as the text to a dramatic work.   It is a book, for all in-
tents and purposes, to the library's accountant who pays for
it; to the craftsmen who bind and stamp it; to the circulation
librarian who hands it out; and to the stacks man who refiles
it.   Searchers, however, will not find it listed in the Cumulative Book Index (CBI) or Publishers' Weekly.   Acquisitions
librarians will probably save trouble by ordering it from a
music supplier rather than through the usual book-trade channels.   Catalogers will assign a main entry to the writer of
the music, not the words.   Amateur performance groups and
photoduplication departments will need to study carefully its
copyright status, insofar as its protection will be slightly
different from that covering most literary texts.
There is, I suspect, a high correlation between a
rich, solid musical diet in a library and the incidence of ul-
cers in the library's internal mechanism.   Most operations
have developed rules of thumb for telling what is and what
is not music; but few realize that a one-to-one basis for definition won't always work where other operations are concerned.   Catalogers wonder what could be simpler and more
painless than following a "half-or-more" rule, defining "music" as anything in which half or more of the text is made
up of musical notation.   The reference librarian can hardly

agree when he discovers many of his hymnbooks classed as
religion, most of his songsters as literature, and a few of
his ballads and folksongs in the geography (e.g. folklore)
class.

The status of musical editions in a library has also
been influenced by the varied functions of music subject-spe-
cialists within the total library operation.   Many European
institutions have followed the administrative practice of segregating all operations involving musical editions, placing
their acquisition, cataloging, circulation, and reference work
under one administrative unit, but locating elsewhere those
operations as they involve books about music, musical manuscripts, and recordings.   Music specialists in American libraries are more frequently found behind a special reading-
room desk, servicing related materials along with musical
editions but calling on other operating units of the library
for the various processing operations.   Some of our more
sophisticated institutions, meanwhile, appear to be adapting
a practice of military organizations which distinguishes between "line" and "staff."   The music specialist, by being re-
lieved of direct responsibility for any of the library's "line"
operations, is able to make greater use of his subject training; but he does so as an advisory "staff" member, working
only indirectly through the units which handle the actual work-
load.   Successful implementation of this plan, as with other
arrangements, depends on a favorable climate of cooperation
and on a masterly administrator--both of which require an
awareness of the diverse problems of dealing with musical
editions.

II.   The Need for Bibliographical Control.

Less than half of the world's output of musical editions is listed in national bibliographies, which originate
from scarcely more than a dozen of the world's nations.
Fortunately our best lists--the Deutsche Musikbibliographie
from Leipzig and the British Catalogue of Music--cover two
of the most productive countries.   Eastern European lists
are surprisingly adequate, more so generally than those from
Italy, France, and most of the smaller Western European nations.   In comparison with any of these, the United States
fares miserably indeed.   Our Copyright Office lists, however
immense, are poorly cataloged, incomplete, not felicitously
arranged, and next to useless for most library purposes.
The Library of Congress' Music and Phonorecords, while
fairly well cataloged, is highly selective and intermixed with
other of the Library's acquisitions.   The Notes lists cover

only publications received.

The cause of music in our national bibliographical network has been hampered by a rather arbitrary exclusion of
the output of music publishers from such trade lists as the
CBI and the Publishers' Trade List Annual. Music publishers, in turn, have never succeeded in getting together to assemble a list of their own. In all fairness we should note
that the American music publishing industry is extremely
diffuse (as noted above) and its output immense (as reflected
in the fact that the number of copyright registrations in this
country for music annually equals that for books, although
much of the music is unpublished). Economically, our music publishing industry is also chronically depressed. Engraving and printing are expensive, distribution costs are
high, competition for high-quality work is keen, especially
from Europe, and sales are usually low. Furthermore, ambitious editions always seem to be the ones that lose the
most money; and this being the case, we should be thankful
every time a firm decides to subsidize a deserving musical
edition rather than a national music bibliography.

In our changing music world--that totality of musical
operations involving composer, performer, listener, and a
variety of commercial and intermediary agents--a new function for the musical edition may be anticipated. The physical objects themselves will surely relinquish their virtual
stranglehold on our musical repertoire as new copying techniques are developed, as performance-rights concepts become increasingly sophisticated, and as relationships between
various musical participants become realigned and perhaps
simplified. But so long as the performer stands between the
composer and listener, musical editions will remain the primary means of communicating the art-work itself.

Meanwhile, our total musical repertoire grows as new
works are written and old ones are rediscovered; and musicians are constantly searching for new experiences that appear to be better, broader, or just different. The pressure
of such needs is forcing the music library to expand and to
assume a more important role. Instead of preserving a
minimum stock of musical editions and an uneven assortment
of lists and guides, the library can expect to become nothing
less than the central agency in a systematic dissemination of
the entire repertoire. This task will presuppose an adequate
bibliographical control of musical editions; and, as with book
materials, the most sensible approach to the problem involves covering current publications first, and older ones later.

III.   The Need for Qualitative Standards.

     Current bibliographies, or their equivalents, generally
answer three questions: they tell us what is new, what is
available, and what is (by various criteria) good.   Covering
the American book trade, for instance, PW and the CBI tell
us what is new, as the PTLA tells us what is available.   In
music, the Notes and copyright lists cover new publications,
while such a guide as Margaret Farish's String Music in
Print (Bowker) will tell us what, in one medium, is available.   Answering the third question--what deserves to be ac-
quired--the American book trade is covered by a network of
selective lists and reviewing media, reflecting subject areas,
degrees of specialization, and levels of interest.
     In contrast, musical editions are poorly covered by
reviewing media.   Notes is gallantly fighting for a broad, li-
brary-oriented coverage in the face of a serious space problem.   A few foreign publications and several American repertoire magazines complete the picture.   Newspaper criticism of concert performances may be flourishing; but such
journalism, like the observations of analysts and theorists,
is to the music librarian at best nothing more than a basis
for a triangulation of sorts regarding a musical edition.
     The vast profusion of musical editions makes the need
for qualitative distinctions especially timely; but more critical are the frequent assertions that our entire music publishing industry has been hopelessly corrupted by commercial-
ism.   Composers complain that they are condemned to ob-
scurity because their music is not published.   Publishers
regretfully cite their sales records to prove that the composers' music will not sell.   Judging from the immense
quantity of musical inanity coming from the industry, and
the fine works by even our best composers, which are condemned to no better existence than photocopies, the problem
is a real one indeed.   The library, permeating our cultural
life as it does, is clearly in a position to improve this situation.   Its music holdings, published, manuscript, or in
photocopy, are exempt from commercial implications except
as may be involved in performance rights.   Furthermore,
the individual editions, having been selected on qualitative
grounds and provided with expensive processing treatment,
are to this extent endorsed by a library as deserving a performer's attention.
     Few of our librarians, however, are well enough
trained, or have enough time, to do any more than rely on
other people's advice on what is worth placing in a library,
and competent advice is too seldom available.   The most

important need in music librarianship today is for an expanded base of criticism of musical editions.

Together with better reviewing media should go studies of how musical editions are used in a library. In what
ways, and to what degree, can an acquisitions program encourage new and ambitious music? Is the library obligated
to provide materials for all of the performers numbered
among its clientele--on all instruments and at all levels of
ability? Librarianship's ancient "value versus demand" controversy still plagues us when we decide between chord-or-
gan manuals and historical sets; but are the libraries with
the highest percentage of historical editions necessarily either the best or the most effective? How can a "readers'
advisory" service in music be developed? The finest tributes our music libraries receive come from performers who
recall their first acquaintance with an exciting but obscure
work in a library or through the suggestion of a librarian.
The possibilities are immense for expanded library service
through musical editions, but we have given little attention
to studies of how this can be done.

The library has gained an enviable reputation for supporting the cause of intellectual freedom and for championing
fine literature rather than pulp publications, but culturally it
is lagging badly in promoting the cause of good music. The
mandate of the library can certainly be expected to expand
to include a wider range of efforts in promoting music.
Matching the right performer with the right edition is but
part of this task. It is not inappropriate for the library to
become an impresario, especially when individual concerts
can involve an intensive study of one or two unusual works,
with repeated hearings interspersed with commentary and
criticism from composers, performers, and listeners. The
library's responsibility also involves the documentation of
local music history--especially insofar as that history may
reflect an enlightened contempt for the packaged series filled with box-office favorites, concentrating instead on the
more vital and ambitious events which may take place in
schools, churches, neighborhood centers, and private homes.

It is both trite and necessary to add concluding remarks that better music libraries are not built by solving
bibliographical problems, that what is needed is a library
staff combining musical knowledge and taste with earnest efforts. But it is only reasonable to suggest that the work of
this staff will be more productive and more rewarding when
we are aware of the special problems posed by musical editions, when the available resources are better identified, and
when better guidelines are set up for determining which of

these resources deserve to benefit from the services offered
by the library.

Music in Medium-Sized Libraries
Gordon Stevenson

From Library Journal 90:1255-8, March 15, 1965. Copyright 1965 by R.R. Bowker Co. Reprinted by permission.

"In considering whatever materials and services your library provides for its community in the area of music, how would you describe your current services? Are they adequate, inadequate, or don't you know?"

I suspect that if librarians had been asked this question before they opened their morning mail that day last November when they received our questionnaire, many more of them would have replied rather optimistically. However, by the time they read through the questions, they must have realized that "music services," as implied in the questionnaire, constituted a rather broad coverage of music materials. Some of the questionnaires that escaped the wastepaper basket had these replies: 76 librarians believe their services are inadequate, 61 give themselves a rating of adequate, and 24 do not know how they rate.

One library in New Jersey, serving a metropolitan community of over 50,000 population, has 350 books about music, no records, no printed music, and is providing adequate services. Another library, a West Virginia county library serving a population of over 60,000, has 500 books about music, 5,000 records, 1,500 pieces of music, and provides inadequate service. These self-evaluations were made by professional librarians--the first a head librarian, the second a part-time music librarian--who should be qualified to evaluate the adequacy of their work. Obviously, the important question is not whether their services are or are not adequate, but "what constitutes adequate public library music services?"

The answer to this question depends on answers to such questions as these: What public? What music? What type of library? What kind of service? Service to whom? Who decides? How do they decide?

Decisions on the library's role in our musical culture involve us in many thorny problems, some musical, some social, many involving techniques of librarianship, and they all must be solved within the framework of the library's

function, aims, and responsibilities. How much thought has
gone into these matters, I do not know; but in practice,
every public library has found its own working solutions. In
some cases this was evident in returned questionnaires with
five words written across the top: "We have no music materials." At the other extreme we find, even in many medium-sized communities, working examples of Alfons Ott's
suggestion that "the finest and most important function of the
popular (i.e. public) library is to provide an enduring and
vital rallying-point for the musical public in the broadest
sense of the term" (Music in Education, Unesco, 1955). Between the two extremes there are several large areas of
agreement. These, along with information on current practice, will someday form the basis for the establishment of
standards. With this in mind, I report here on a survey of
certain aspects of music in a group of public libraries serving communities of between 50,000 and 100,000 population.

    This particular group of libraries was chosen because
I felt that their problems are typical of those that face the
profession as a whole. Few of them are large enough to
have music departments or art and music departments; generally they must do with whatever musical knowledge they
can muster from present staffs, and the status of music in
these libraries is, more often than not, in the hands of a
chief administrator who is busy running a library.

    The following information was gathered from 174 re-
plies received from a mailing to 310 libraries throughout
the United States.

    The three basic types of library materials relating to
music are the printed word, the printed musical note, and
the sound recording. Each has its own unique set of symbols and each is used by the borrower--often by three different borrowers--in a different way and for different reasons. The librarian who collects all three types of material must consult three different sets of selection tools, find
three sources for acquisitions, and once he has the material
in hand, his problems have just begun, for he is faced with
three different physical formats, each of which presents its
own problems of processing, cataloging, storing, and handling.

    Comparatively few of our 174 libraries collect all
three types of material, possibly only a fourth of them--it
is hard to say exactly because we have to decide what constitutes a "collection of printed music" (ten titles? 100?
1000?). Happily, I can report that all libraries have at
least a few books about music. All but 27 libraries provided a count of their book holdings in the 780's. They are

smaller than expected:

Books in the 780's	No. of libraries
100 or less.	14
101-300	50
301-500	28
501-1000	38
More than 1000	17

The Standard Catalog (1959) and its Supplements 1-4 list a total of around 360 titles in the 780's. Sixty-seven (around 45 percent) of the above libraries have fewer than 350 titles in this area. During the past 12 months, 126 libraries reported adding a total of 4,832 books about music, an average of about 39 titles each. The ALA Booklist and LJ each list or review close to 60 titles annually.

Phonograph records present an entirely different picture. Thirty-three of our libraries do not have record collections and another 13 did not give us a count of their holdings. Those who did provide statistics have amassed a grand total of 191,910 records:

Records	No. of libraries
500 or less	44
501-1000	26
1001-5000	51
More than 5000	7

Annual expenditures and acquisitions reflect the growing importance of recorded sound. Last year 115 of our libraries added a total of 26,151 records. Ninety-six libraries reported their expenditures during the past 12 months, or the amounts currently budgeted for records. The total is impressive: slightly over $86,000 was spent on records by these libraries.

In the general picture, printed music hardly rates at all. Seventy-four libraries have no such collections. Those that have collections and provided statistics fall into the following groups:

Printed music	No. of libraries
100 or less	34
101-200	8
201-300	1
301-500	11
501-750	5
751-1000	6

Printed music   No. of libraries
More than 1000 12

    The total resources of these 77 libraries are 65,853 pieces of printed music; but the greater part of it is in the 18 libraries that account for over 54,000 of the reported titles. Most of the collections were static last year, or so it seems from the fact that 57 libraries reported adding 1,847 titles, and only five libraries accounted for more than 50 percent of these titles.

    There is little to go on as regards standards of quantity in this area. One would think that a general collection of various types of music could begin with 500 titles. On the other hand, E. T. Bryant (Music Librarianship, 1959) and the Canadian Music Library Association's Standards for Music Collections in Medium-sized Libraries (1959) agree that a minimum basic collection can consist of around 275 titles. According to these standards, 35 of our libraries have at least basic collections. I am not going to try to answer the question of whether more libraries should have such collections, but I think you will be interested in the reasons given for the lack of them.

    Few librarians were willing to state unequivocally that this is not a legitimate public library service. Only six came right out and said so. Twenty-three librarians felt that their communities either had no need for printed music, or if they did, they had neglected to request it from the library in any quantity that would justify the library spending money on it. Six other librarians indicated that this sort of material is available elsewhere in the community or through some cooperative arrangement with another library. Only one librarian stated that her library faced other, more pressing responsibilities. Nevertheless, this thought was implicit in many of the reasons checked. In descending order of frequency, here are the reasons why the bulk of our libraries are not collecting printed music: insufficient funds, insufficient staff, lack of a staff member qualified to organize a collection, lack of space or storage facilities, lack of selection tools and other information. Since most of these problems come up and are solved when dealing with the LP record, we are inclined to think that, though these are all perfectly acceptable excuses, the basic reasons are more complex.

    The lack of channels of information is certainly a serious problem, and with this in mind I took the opportunity to test several pet theories. I wrote: "Few of the library selection tools include printed music. Please check any of

the following which, if started, you think would be helpful in
selecting printed music for a medium-sized public library
collection." Thirty-two librarians apparently did not look
with much enthusiasm on any of my brain children. The
others provoked this response: 57 librarians thought that at
least one would be useful, 47 voted for two, and 38 were interested in all three. Here are the suggestions with the
total number of votes each received: a) the inclusion of selected music titles in the Booklist, 82; b) a few reviews of
printed music in each issue of LJ, 97; c) the compilation
and publication of a standard catalog of music, 86.

Generally speaking, our libraries either collect music
in a wide variety of performing media (e.g., piano music,
chamber music, organ music, miniature scores, popular
songs, folk music, etc.), or they collect only song books.
I expected to find many libraries with collections of miniature scores selected in conjunction with record collections,
but turned to light only two outside of the libraries with wide-
ranging general collections of music. Here and there among
the smaller collections there were some unusual types of selected performing media represented, and this seems to indicate that either there was no systematic plan or the materials had been acquired as gifts. In a half-dozen collections it was clear that selections were purposely made in
one or two specific media.

In gathering information on the organization of the materials I was chiefly interested in identifying libraries that
have music departments or art and music departments. I
was surprised to find nine music departments, two "music
rooms," one "music area," eight art and music departments,
one art-music-films department, and one library with printed music, records, and films in one department. These are
libraries with large holdings of all three types of material,
though two of them do not collect printed music. The idea
of a "music department" without printed music is an idea
that implies something quite different from what we are used
to thinking of as a music department; yet this seems to be
the direction in which we are heading. The idea of the "music room," which was quite popular about 20 years ago,
seems to be on the wane. With only three exceptions, the
foregoing departments all have at least one full-time music
librarian or art-music librarian. In the others, one staff
member devotes from 25 to 75 percent of his time to music
services.

The greater part of the libraries reported that no one
on the staff is assigned exclusive responsibility for music
services. It is impossible to spell out the percentage of

time spent on music in these libraries, but 29 libraries
gave the approximate amount of time one person spends on
music.   For the most part, it ranged from 15 to 50 percent.
In one third of the reporting libraries, the head librarian
takes the responsibility for the selection of materials, sometimes with the help of other staff members.   Otherwise, the
selection of materials can fall to about anyone on the staff:
the adult services librarian, assistant librarian, reference
librarian, cataloger, head of circulation.

Public service programs of any extraordinary interest
are few.   Three-quarters of the libraries had nothing to report.   Seven libraries have live concerts, 13 have record
concerts, six have radio programs, and three have lectures
on music.   Other activities mentioned were cooperation with
local symphony orchestras, several music appreciation
courses, and cooperation with local college music appreciation classes.   Individually considered, some of these programs are quite exciting and imaginative, but there certainly
is no overall trend.

Few librarians have made surveys, formal or informal, of music in their communities, but this is not to say
they may not know quite a bit about this aspect of community
life.   I raised the question because musicmaking, outside of
public concerts, is a private activity--it is possible that
many communities are much more musical than we think.

Fifty-five percent of the reporting libraries receive
some form of help from other libraries, principally the loan
of materials.   About the same number of libraries share
their materials.   It remains to be seen to what extent the
resources of interlibrary loan can be used to the best advantage in providing access to all types of music materials.
There is a reluctance to "get involved" with the interlibrary
loan of LP records.   The record clubs send thousands of
records through the mails every month, so fear of damage
in transit should not be a problem (what other reasons do
we have for not loaning them?).   The interlibrary loan of
printed music is going to have to be investigated further.   Is
the Interlibrary Loan Code being correctly interpreted by the
nonspecialist?   (You would be surprised at the number of librarians who call all printed music "sheet music, " whether
it's a vocal score, a miniature score, or a popular song.)
Have music librarians read it lately to see if it does reflect
their recommended policies?

I did not attempt to survey the services performed by
state libraries in supporting local library music services.
Nor did I attempt to examine the place of music materials
in regional or cooperative systems.

Before drawing any conclusions, the reader will understand that I realize that a library's contribution to the musical life of its community cannot be measured by the quantity of material it houses. The quality of material and the use to which it is put are measures of its value, and this survey was not intended to investigate such services as readers' advisor, listeners' advisor, or reference.

The survey has raised the question of what materials are necessary for adequate music services in medium-sized public libraries. The majority of responding librarians are agreed that the best way they can serve the musical interests of their communities is by providing collections of records. These collections are much larger than was to be expected. Wheeler and Goldhor, in their <u>Practical Administration of Public Libraries</u> (p. 403), write that "public library record collections average about 500 discs," but the libraries in our survey have an average of 1,500 discs; and of the 128 that provided these statistics, only 44 have fewer than 500 discs.

This great interest in records does not seem to have produced any spectacular increase in books about music. For the most part, those who go to the library in search of the printed note will be disappointed. But insofar as I was able to measure the opinions of the librarians--and I am optimistic--there is an interest in extending library service to this smaller, less vocal segment of the community.

The Cost of Imported Scores
Gordon Stevenson

From Library Resources and Technical Services 6:320-31, Fall 1962. Reprinted by permission.

Between 1926 and 1929 Breitkopf & Härtel of Leipzig published Friedrich Ludwig's edition of the musical works of Guillaume de Machaut. It was out of print for many years, then, between 1954 and 1957, it was reprinted. The new printing was considerably enhanced by the inclusion of a fourth volume containing the composer's Mass and other works omitted from the first. This was an event of some importance to music libraries, and in due course the Kansas City Public Library received notices of the new printing from the following sources:

> Associated Music Publishers. Texts. New York [1959?].
> Bärenreiter Antiquariat. Libri novi de musica. Kassel, 1958.
> Breitkopf & Härtel. Chormusik. Leipzig, 1957.
> Breitkopf & Härtel. Verlags-Verzeichnis. Wiesbaden, 1957, 1961.
> Broude Bros. Special List no. 67. New York [1958?].
> Alexander Broude. Checklist no. 11-21. New York, ?-1961.
> Ernest E. Gottlieb. Musical Literature Cat. 30. Beverly Hills, n.d.
> Musica Rara. List 20. London [1959].
> Kenneth Mummery. A Catalogue of Music...N.S. 16, 18. Bournemouth, 1959, 1960.
> Kurt B. Merlander. Catalogue no. 155, 179. Burbank, n.d. [1960].

A search through the Music Library Association's Notes, the best single U.S. source for current international music bibliography, failed to turn up any mention of the new printing. Neither was it found in the "Liste Internationale Selective" published in each issue of Fontes Artis Musicae, the review of the International Music Library Association.

According to the Music Index, no reviews of the new printing
were published in the periodicals indexed. But from California and New York, from Bournemouth and London, from Kassel, Wiesbaden, Leipzig, and even Amsterdam, dealers' and
publishers' advertisements found their way to Kansas City.
The prices ranged from a low of $25.00 to $52.50 in the
United States. The price set by Breitkopf & Härtel of Wiesbaden in 1957 was DM 127.40. Four years later the German
price had risen slightly to DM 130. The list price set by
the Associated Music Publishers, Inc., N.Y., was $8.00 a
volume ($32.00 for the set). Presumably this price should
have had some authority since Associated is the U.S. representative of Breitkopf & Härtel. The curious lack of agreement among U.S. dealers as to the price of the set, its
omission from the few generally available current bibliographies, and the importance of the dealers' catalogs as a source
of information illustrate some of the problems involved in the
acquisition of imported musical scores.

These problems are different in several respects from
those involved in the acquisition of books. This follows from
the highly specialized nature of the musical score, which is,
after all, similar to the book in only a limited physical
sense. Most music falls outside the scope of book-trade activities, and few book jobbers even attempt to offer adequate
service in this area. From production and printing to distribution and marketing the machinery of music publishing
operates independently of similar book-trade activities, and
the familiar channels of communication that librarians depend
on for current book news are practically useless for music.

A few words may be necessary to explain why imported scores are important acquisitions for U.S. libraries. A
cursory survey of E.T. Bryant's list of "a representative
but not comprehensive stock"[1] of music recommended for library purchase will reveal the large amount of standard repertory music that is not available in domestic editions. In
music there are no language barriers, so the latest scores
by leading European composers are just as important as
those by American composers. The number of domestic editions in the bibliographies of such standard works as Gustave
Reese's Music in the Middle Ages (Norton, 1940) and Music
in the Renaissance (Norton, 1954) and Manfred Burkofzer's
Music in the Baroque Era (Norton, 1947) is negligible. A
further indication of our dependence on overseas publishers
in these more specialized areas of music is evident on almost every page of Anna Harriet Heyer's Historical Sets,
Collected Editions and Monuments of Music (A.L.A., 1957).
Of over six hundred titles in Miss Heyer's bibliography, only

fifty-five were published in the United States.

Finally, for current publications, an examination of four successive issues of Notes (March, 1960 through Dec., 1960)[2] shows that of the 214 items reviewed (exclusive of thirty-five choral octavo) 127, or more than fifty percent, were published overseas. Included were scores from Germany, Canada, England, Italy, Austria, Hungary, and Spain. This is not to say that U.S. musical publications are not numerous, which they are,[3] or that they are unimportant; but, for one reason or another (e.g., copyright, composer-publisher affiliation, high printing costs, and lack of a large commercial market), U.S. publishers do not compete with European publishers in those areas covered by Miss Heyer's book and compete to only a limited extent with the type of music listed in Mr. Bryant's book and reviewed in Notes. Is it the proper business of U.S. music publishers to publish music by our composers, editors, and musicologists--this is another matter entirely, and one with which I am not concerned here.

The bulk of the Western European publications reviewed or listed in Notes find their way into the U.S. with little difficulty. They are easily acquired from any of a number of U.S. dealers and agents, from European dealers, or, in some instances, direct from the European publishers. In any case, there is a marked difference between advertised U.S. prices and the original European prices. We have come to expect this with books, and there are obvious reasons why the U.S. dealer's price should be higher. It is difficult to understand, however, why the complete musical works of William Byrd are advertised in the U.S. at $175.00 (and this is described as a "special price"),[4] when the same work is advertised by a German dealer for approximately $100.00[5] and by a British dealer for approximately $90.00.[6] To cite several other examples, Edward B. Marks, Inc., the U.S. agent for the Polish publisher of the Paderewski edition of the complete keyboard works of Chopin, advertises the set at $40.00. This is a "special anniversary offer made to libraries,"[7] and is twenty percent below the $50.00 U.S. list price. Libraries that did not take advantage of this special offer could have obtained the same edition from Europe for less than $20.00.[8] The edition of the Beethoven piano sonatas published by the Association Board of the Royal Music Schools is handled in the U.S. by Mills Music, Inc., who advertise the set at $22.50.[9] The same set is available from a British dealer for less than $9.00.[10] If the Bärenreiter edition of the keyboard works of Frescobaldi is purchased from Europe, the cost is approximately $11.25;[11] the

U. S. list price is $24. 00. [12]

That the above prices are not exceptional will be
clear from the following, which is a complete listing of all
imported music reviewed in the March, 1960, issue of Notes.
Of the fifty-five titles reviewed in this issue, thirty-nine
were published overseas. The U. S. agent for twenty-seven
of these is Associated Music Publishers, N. Y. , representing
half of the twelve publishers on the list. The dollar prices
are given as they appear in Notes. The overseas prices are
from whatever source the author could lay his hands on.
The English prices have been converted to dollars according
to the Sterling-U. S. Dollar Exchange, printed by Blackwell's
Booksellers of Oxford and distributed with their catalogs.
The German mark has been converted at the rate of DM 4
to the dollar. [13] Associated Music Publishers, Inc. , has
been abbreviated to A. M. P.

	U. S.	Overseas	
Stainer & Bell (U. S: Galaxy Music Corp.)			
Storace. No Sing, No Supper. (1959)	$13.50	55s	($ 7.70)[14]
Morley. Keyboard Works. (1959)	$ 5.00	16/12	($ 2.38)
Locke. Keyboard Suites. (1959)	$ 1.50	5s	($ .70)
Breitkopf & Härtel (U. S: A. M. P.)			
Beethoven. Supplemente zur Gesamtausgabe. Bd. I. (1959)	$10.00	DM 20	($ 5.00)
Voss. Trio. (1958)	$ 4.00	DM 8	($ 2.00)
Musica Rara (U. S: Th. Presser)			
Stamitz. Quartet, Op. 8, No. 4. (1958)	$ 2.00	8/6	($ 1.19)
Dittersdorf. Partia in D. (1958)	$ 3.25	12/6	($ 1.75)
Boccherini. Quintet, Op. 21, No. 5. (1958)	$ 3.25	8s	($ 1.12)
C. P. E. Bach. Six Sonatas. (1958)	$ 5.00	25s	($ 3.50)
Schott, London (U. S: A. M. P.)			
Blomdahl. Trio. (1956)	$ 7.50	22/6	($ 3.15)
Schott, Mainz (U. S: A. M. P.)			
Mainardi. Trio. I (1958)	$ 6.00	DM 12	($ 3.00)
Francaix. L'Insectarium. (1959)	$ 2.25	DM 4.50	($ 1.12)
Torelli. Konzert, Op. 6,			

	U.S.	Overseas	
No. I. (1958)	$ 2.00	7/6	($ 1.05)
Albinoni. Sintonia a 4. (1958)	$ 1.75	6/6	($ .91)
Schuler. Funf Orchestersatze.			
(1958)	$ 3.25	DM 6.50	($ 1.62)
Henz. Drei Dithyramben. (1959)	$ 3.75	DM 7.50	($ 1.87)
Henz. Nachstucke. (1958)	$ 3.75	DM 7.50	($ 1.87)

Suvini Zerboni (U.S: A.M.P.)
  Malipiero. Quintetto. (1958)

	U.S.	Overseas	
Malipiero. Quintetto. (1958)	$ 9.00	L.4500	($ 7.25)
Malipiero. Sonata. (1957)	$ 3.25	L.1200	($ 1.93)
Maderna. Serenata No. 2. (1957)	$12.50	L.7200	($11.60)
Petrassi. Serenata. (1959)	$ 6.75	L. 900	($ 1.45)
Pousseur. Trois Chants Sacres.			
(1958)	$ 2.25	L. 800	($ 1.29)

Universal Edition (U.S: A.M.P.)
  J.C. Bach. Floten-Konzert.

	U.S.	Overseas	
(1958)	$ 3.00	10s	($ 1.40)
Nilsson. Madchentotenlieder.			
(1958)	$ 5.00	20s	($ 2.80)
Haubenstock-Ramati. Stand-			
chen. (1958)	$ 2.00	6/9	($ .95)
Lidholm. Ritornello. (1958)	$ 6.00	20s	($ 2.80)
Krenek. Funf Lieder, Op. 82.			
(1958)	$ 1.50	5/6	($ .77)
Boulez. Improvisation sur			
Mallarme. (1958)	$ 2.50	16/9	($ 2.35)

Zenemukiado Vallalat (U.S:
    Boosey & Haekes)
  Liszt. Historische Ungarische

	U.S.	Overseas	
Bildnisse. (1959)	$ 3.50	20 For.	($ 1.70)

Bote & Bock (U.S: A.M.P.)
  Tharichen. Konzert, Op. 34.

	U.S.	Overseas	
(1956)	$ 4.00	DM 8	($ 2.00)
Krol. Concerto Grosso, Op.			
15. (1958)	$ 2.25	DM 4.50	($ 1.12)
Ballif. Fantasio, Op. 21.(1959)	$ 3.00	DM 6	($ 1.50)
Ballif. Voyage de mon Oreille.			
(1959)	$ 3.00	DM 6	($ 1.50)
Xenakis. Achorripsis. (1958)	$ 2.50	DM 5	($ 1.25)
Klebe. Konzert, Op. 29.(1958)	$ 6.00	DM 12	($ 3.00)

Moseler (U.S: C.F. Peters)

	U.S.	Overseas	
Quantz. Konzert. (1958)	$ 2.75	DM 8.40	($ 2.10)

	U.S.	Overseas	

Ricordi, New York and Milano.
  Vivaldi. Concerto, F. VI, No.
    8. (1958) $ 1.25 5s   ($ .70)

Peters-Hinrichsen, New York
  and London.
  Boyce. Concerto Grosso. (1956)$ 2.50 10/6   ($ 1.47)
  Boyce. Double Concerto. (1953)$ 2.50 (overseas price
                                       not available)

     Such a comparison as this can be very misleading un-
less one takes into account the discount received from a
U.S. dealer and the overseas postage. I can only speak
from my own experience in this matter. The Kansas City
Public Library receives a ten percent discount from its main
New York source, and assumes the postage costs. The total
U.S. list price of the above material comes to $162.25, and
is reduced to $146.02 by a ten percent discount. The over-
seas prices amount to $90.86, with approximately six per-
cent extra for postage.[15]
     At the risk of getting a bit tedious, we list below
some of the imported music reviewed or listed in the issue
of Notes one year from the above, March, 1961. This gives
a cross section of the trend in prices today. The sources
for the overseas prices are mainly British, relying heavily
on the British Catalogue of Music.

	U.S.	Overseas	

Ars Viva (U.S: A.M.P.)
  Nono. La Terra e la Com-
    pagna. (1959) $ 2.25 DM 4.50 ($ 1.25)

Bärenreiter, Kassel and New York.
  Der Mensuralkodex des Niko-
    laus Apel. Teil II. (1960) $20.00 75s   ($10.00)

Bote and Bock (U.S: A.M.P.)
  Blacher. Requiem. (1959) $10.00 DM 20 ($ 5.00)

Breitkopf & Härtel (U.S: A.M.P.)
  David. Magische Quadrate.
    (n.d.) $ 4.00 16s   ($ 2.24)

Eschig (U.S: A.M.P.)
  Martinu. Concerto pour Hautbois.
    (n.d.) $ 5.75 21s   ($ 2.94)

	U.S.	Overseas	
Eulenburg (U.S: C.F. Peters)			
Haydn. Violin Concerto. (n.d.)	$ 2.00	4/6	($ .63)
Heugel (U.S: Th. Presser)			
Milhaud. Deuxieme Concerto.			
(1958)	$ 6.00	10s	($ 1.40)
Hinrichsen (U.S: C.F. Peters)			
Crusell. Three Progressive			
Clarinet Duets. Nos. 1-2.			
(n.d.)	$ 2.00	8/10	($ 1.24)
Kneusslin (U.S: C.F. Peters)			
Danzi. Quintet, Op. 86, no.1.			
(1960)	$ 4.00	15s	($ 2.10)
Leuckart (U.S: A.M.P.)			
Boismortier. Quatre Suites,			
Op. 59. (n.d.)	$ 4.25	15s	($ 2.10)
Lienau (U.S: C.F. Peters)			
M. Haydn. Quartett. (1959)	$ 2.50	7/6	($ 1.05)
Merseburger (U.S: C.F. Peters)			
Mozart. Mozart auf der Orgel.			
Bd. I. (n.d.)	$ 4.00	17/6	($ 2.45)
Mueller (U.S: C.F. Peters)			
Zipoli. Sonate. Bd. 2. (1959)	$ 3.50	10/6	($ 1.47)
Musica Rara (U.S: Th. Presser)			
Danzi. Quartet, Op. 40, No. 3.			
(n.d.).	$ 6.50	25s	($ 3.50)
Novello (U.S: H.W. Gray)			
Mozart. Fantasia, K. 608.			
(n.d.)	$ 8.75	25s	($ 3.50)
K. Prowse (U.S: Mills Music Co.)			
Gerhard. Chaconne. (1960)	$ 2.00	7/6	($ 1.05)
B. Schott, Mainz (U.S: A.M.P.)			
Fortner. Chant de Naissance.			
(1959)	$ 3.00	DM 6	($ 1.50)

Stainer & Bell (U.S: Galaxy

	U.S.	Overseas	
Music Corp.)			
Merbecke. Domine Jesu			
Christe. (n.d.)	$ 1.00	3s	($ .42)
Arno Volk (U.S: Oxford Univ.			
Press)			
Georgii. Four Hundred Years of			
European Keyboard Music.			
(1959)	$ 6.00	35s	($ 4.90)
Zanibon (U.S: C.F. Peters)			
Cirri. Concerto, Op. 14, No.			
6. (n.d.)	$ 2.50	12/6	($ 1.75)
Zimmermann (U.S: C.F. Peters)			
Moritz. Pavane. (1960)	$ 1.50	4/6	($ .63)

In-progress series of complete works editions and historical sets constitute another important area of music acquisitions. These scores, offering a repertory of music available from no other source, are indispensable to music libraries. A handy guide to current sets is Monumenta Musica, Katalog der Musikdenkmaler und Gesamtausgaben, published by Barenreiter of Kassel in 1959. This catalog is supplemented by listings in the Musica Antiqua Recens Edita section of Bärenreiter's Libri Novi de Musica. Bärenreiter is not only one of the largest publishers of this type of material, but is also an agent and dealer for music from all over Europe. Its Monumenta Musica catalog includes both its own publications and most of the important historical sets now being published in Western Europe. Of the 103 series listed, sixty are complete works editions and forty-three are historical sets. Compositions by 390 composers are represented in a total of well over one thousand volumes.

For the purposes of this study the series listed in Monumenta Musica may be divided into three groups: (1) series published by the American Institute of Musicology, (2) those of European publishers and societies that have no official U.S. agents, and (3) series printed in Europe by publishers and societies that have an official U.S. agent. The first two will be passed over briefly. The extensive publications of the American Institute of Musicology, a non-profit organization, are subsidized and sell at prices that do not even cover the costs of production.[16] Because series in the second group do not have U.S. agents, sales in this country are not widely promoted, nor, apparently, are review

copies widely distributed.   These series do turn up from
time to time in U.S. dealers' catalogs.   The acquisitions librarian should find it interesting to compare U.S. prices
with listings in Monumenta Musica and Libri Novi de Musica,
especially Ugrino Verlag publications of works of Buxtehude,
Gesualdo and Scheidt.   It is the third group, however, that
interests us here, and it is in this group that the most interesting things happen to prices.

The U.S. prices of Italian series listed in Monumenta
Musica seem reasonable, even surprisingly low by comparison.   For example, Fabio Fano's Le Origini e il Primo
Maestro di Cappella: Matteo da Perugia lists at DM 140
($35.00), the same price listed by Ricordi's New York of-
fice, which handles the U.S. distribution.   The prices on the
various series published by the Societas Universalis Sanctae
Ceciliae, handled in the U.S. by Carl Fischer, Inc., New
York, are the same or vary only slightly from the European
prices.   In this edition Dufay's Missa L'Homme Arme lists
at DM16 ($4.00) in Monumenta Musica but sells in New York
at $3.75.

British series are listed in Monumenta Musica at German prices higher than the original.   In the trade catalog
Scholarly Editions of English Music 1400-1800 (1960) issued
by the Galaxy Music Corp., New York, the U.S. agents for
Stainer & Bell, Ltd., prices are as much as one hundred
percent higher than the British prices.   These are large sets,
running from sixteen to thirty volumes each.   The following
table gives the British, German and U.S. prices of volume
one of each series:

	British	German	U.S.
English Madrigal School.	($3.15)	DM21 ($5.25)	$ 7.00
English Lutenist Song-Writers I.	($1.74)	DM 8 ($2.00)	$ 3.75
English Lutenist Song-Writers II.	($ .90)	DM 5 ($1.25)	$ 2.25
Musica Britannica.	($5.88)	DM32 ($8.00)	$12.50

The Galaxy catalog of the Stainer & Bell import series
lists special prices for purchasers of complete sets.   For
example, the total list price of the first thirty-four volumes
of the English Madrigal School comes to $272.75.   The spe-
cial price for the complete set is $225.00, a discount of a
fraction over seventeen percent.   The total cost of this same
set as listed in Blackwell's Music Shop Catalog 723 comes to
$108.32.   The Purcell Society edition of the complete works
of Henry Purcell is published in England by Novello & Co.,

which is represented in the U.S. by the H.W. Grey Co.,
New York. Volumes 27, 28 and 29 are advertised in the
April, 1961, issue of Music and Letters at £5 5S ($14.70)
each. The U.S. prices received from the H.W. Grey Co.
in July, 1961, are $36.75 (Vol. 27), $26.25 (Vol. 28) and
$30.00 (Vol. 29).

In using Monumenta Musica as a price guide for German publications it is necessary to understand that the price
listings for Bärenreiter's own publications are given in U.S.
dollars. These prices are not, however, the prevailing European rate, but special prices set up especially for the
U.S. market. This policy was introduced by Bärenreiter
when it acquired a New York representative. To see how
this has changed the cost for U.S. libraries one has only to
compare the prevailing German and British prices with those
issued by the Baerenreiter Music Publishers of New York.
For example, the last two additions to the complete works of
Heinrich Schutz are advertised in the March, 1961, issue of
Notes at $9.50 each. The prices issued from Kassel are
DM 19.30 ($4.83) each. The British prices, listed in the
Jan., 1961, issue of The Musical Times, are 35S ($4.90)
each. Since the Bärenreiter series are so important to U.S.
libraries, we will trace the history of one of their most im-
portant publications, their edition of the complete works of
J.S. Bach.

In 1954 Bärenreiter issued from its offices in Kassel
a brochure on the nature, scope, and cost of the new Bach
edition. At that time Bärenreiter had no one exclusive agent
or clearing house in the United States, and the brochure was
widely distributed throughout the U.S. by direct mail to libraries, dealers, and individuals. The following extract
from the brochure will give some idea of the idealism of the
publisher and the cost to U.S. libraries:

> The New Bach-Edition is being offered at unusual-
> ly cheap subscription rates. The intention is that
> as many Bach lovers as possible shall be able to
> subscribe.... The annual expenditure for the sub-
> scription to the edition bound in boards can only
> be estimated roughly...but it will probably not ex-
> ceed DM 80. per annum....the total cost of a
> subscription to the musical volumes of the New
> Bach-Edition will amount to roughly DM 1200.
> spread over 15 years.[17]

In other words, the estimated yearly cost was to be approximately $20.00, and the total cost over a fifteen-year period

approximately $300.00. The cost of single volumes was to
be determined by the number of pages: "For 16 pages of
one volume: subscription price DM 1.60; a volume with 120
pages will therefore cost DM 12." The additional cost for
cloth binding was announced at DM 4. Persons or institutions interested in the set could subscribe through U.S. dealers, European dealers, or direct with the publisher.

By 1956 when Bärenreiter issued its Sonderkatalog:
Denkmaler und Gesamtausgaben der Tonkunst (the first edition of Monumenta Musica) five volumes of the new Bach edition were available. Prices were very much in line with
those anticipated by the publisher. The score of the B Minor Mass, for example, was available at DM 33 ($8.50) on
subscription and DM 42 ($10.50) as a separate. Figured at
DM 1.60 (40 cents) for each sixteen pages, and DM 4 ($1.00)
for binding, the subscription price was within 20 cents of the
anticipated price. This was typical of the prices asked by
most U.S. dealers. By 1958, however, Bärenreiter had acquired a New York "affiliate," and the U.S. distribution and
price policy for all Bärenreiter publications was changed.
We quote from a form letter sent by the office in Kassel to
its U.S. customers in January, 1958:

> I wish to inform you, herewith, that, starting im-
> mediately, the Baerenreiter-Verlag will be repre-
> sented in the United States by their newly estab-
> lished affiliate, Baerenreiter Music, New York....
> This new arrangement implies that Baerenreiter-
> Antiquariat can no longer supply you directly with
> Baerenreiter music and books.... Subscriptions
> for our editions of the works of Bach...contracted
> heretofore, will of course continue to be delivered
> at the price previously agreed upon and will be
> shipped from Kassel. All future subscriptions to
> the above editions will be received by Baerenreiter
> Music in New York.[18]

Shortly after this, Baerenreiter Music of New York
issued Old and Modern Music of Distinction, a 99-page catalog listing the bulk of Bärenreiter publications. By this time
eight volumes of scores of the new Bach edition had been published. The B Minor Mass is entered at the following prices:

Mass in B Minor	$18.50
cloth	$21.00
critical annotation	$17.50
cloth	$19.50

These prices are about one hundred percent higher than the
prices originally announced by Barenreiter.

Towards the end of 1958, after seeing the New York
prices, the Kansas City Public Library entered a subscription for the new Bach edition with the Amsterdam firm of
Swets en Zeitlinger. To date (August, 1961) sixteen volumes
of the projected eighty-volume series have been received.
It may be of some interest to compare the actual cost from
Amsterdam with information we have received on the projected cost of a subscription from New York. In a letter dated
June 25, 1961, the Baerenreiter Music Publishers informed
us that the Kansas City Public Library would receive a
twenty percent discount below the New York list prices on a
subscription to the complete set of scores (i.e., without the
separately published critical commentary) in the clothbound
edition. Column A below gives the list prices, taken from
Baerenreiter, New York, catalogs, lists, and advertisements
and from one New York dealer's catalog. Column B gives
the New York price after a twenty percent discount has been
made. The last column, C, is the actual price the Kansas
City Public Library paid to its overseas dealer.

According to this, the total list price of the sixteen
volumes in the U.S. is $247.25. At a twenty percent dis-
count the cost would be reduced to $197.80. For the same
volumes the Kansas City Public Library has, as a matter of
fact, paid $101.20. To this must be added $7.10 paid in

			A	B	C
Ser. I,	Bd.	1	$ 9.50	$ 7.50	$4.20
	Bd.	2	16.75	13.40	6.90
	Bd.	7	13.25	10.60	5.50
	Bd.	10	11.50	9.20	4.95
	Bd.	12	18.75	15.00	6.85
	Bd.	13	16.50	13.20	6.75
	Bd.	21	13.25	10.60	5.65
	Bd.	33	19.50	15.60	8.20
	Bd.	38	20.50	16.40	8.40
Ser. II,	Bd.	1	21.00	16.80	8.10
	Bd.	3	10.50	8.40	4.35
	Bd.	6	22.20	18.00	8.90
Ser. IV,	Bd.	2	9.50	7.60	4.40
Ser. V,	Bd.	4	11.00	8.80	4.70
Ser. VI,	Bd.	1	15.25	12.20	6.25
Ser. VII,	Bd.	2	18.00	14.40	7.10

postage and insurance, bringing the total cost to $108.30.
The question here, however, is not the difference between

$197.80 and $108.30, considerable as this is. The complete
works edition of this one composer is expected to run up-
wards of eighty volumes. The complete catalog of imported
music issued by Baerenreiter of New York contains over one
thousand titles. If a library needs the complete works editions of Bach, Handel, Telemann or Schutz (and what library
doesn't need them), they will have to buy the Barenreiter editions, for there are no others.

The present relationship between the Baerenreiter Music Publishers, Inc., of New York[19] and the Bärenreiter
Verlag of Kassel is confusing to say the least. In the December, 1960, issue of Notes the New York firm of G. Ricordi & Co. is listed as the U.S. agent for Bärenreiter publications. In the June, 1961, issue of Notes two Bärenreiter
publications are reviewed. In both cases the imprints contain New York and Kassel followed by G. Ricordi as the U.S.
distributor. Literature received from New York as recently
as June, 1961, indicates that the New York Baerenreiter
firm is "an affiliate" of the firm in Kassel. The Baerenreiter Music Publishers' advertisement in the June, 1961, issue of Notes uses the familiar bear and star trademark of
Bärenreiter Kassel. Yet in a letter dated July 24, 1961,
from Kassel, Herr Suck said that the New York firm is no
longer the exclusive U.S. agent for their publications and that
they would now accept orders direct to Kassel from the U.S.
It remains to be seen what effect this will have on the U.S.
prices of their music.

The reader may draw his own conclusions from the
various figures here presented, keeping in mind that there
are factors other than the cost to be considered in the total
acquisitions picture: the convenience of a single U.S. source;
the fine trade lists, bibliographies, and catalogs supplied by
some U.S. dealers and agents; the time element; and efficient
service. The differences in price may be due in part to tar-
iffs, which dealers and agents pay, but from which libraries
are exempt. According to Paragraph 1410 of the Tariff Act,
sheet music and books in sheets are dutiable at the rate of
five percent if the work is of bona fide foreign authorship,[20]
as most of the music mentioned in this article is.

This paper has hardly scratched the surface of a complex business operation, the inner workings of which are
hardly known outside the trade. It has suggested more questions than it has answered. How much music gets into the
U.S. from abroad and from what sources? How large is the
U.S. library market for imported music? Who decides what
the U.S. list prices will be and on what basis? What factors
determine which music actually goes on the U.S. market?

Notes is the chief library tool for the dissemination of information on imported music,[21] yet the bulk of the music listed
in Notes seems to be supplied by U.S. agents. What about
the music of those overseas publishers who do not have exclusive U.S. agents, or agents who choose not to supply
Notes with review copies? The present system by which
overseas publishers have exclusive U.S. agents may be the
only system that will work--but has it not given these agents
exclusive control over a tremendous block of imported music
and virtually eliminated the possibility of any domestic competition?

An interesting aspect to the music trade is the firm
that combines publishing activities with importing activities--
this is almost the rule rather than the exception. In an operation like this, do high U.S. printing costs in any way affect the list price of the firm's foreign product, the imported music? Why does some music by U.S. composers have
lower list prices overseas than it does here?[22] The information that caused this last question to be raised was one
of the most ironical sidelights encountered in preparing this
paper, and is as good a place as any to end it. The vocal
score of Irving Berlin's Annie Get Your Gun (London, 1947)
has a U.S. list price of $7.50. One special price "subject
to no further discount" is $6.75.[23] Does this sound like a
good buy? Check Blackwell's Vocal Catalogue 723 and you
will find Annie Get Your Gun lists at 15^S in English money,
or $2.10 in American money (to which you can add six per-
cent for postage).

Notes

1. Bryant, E.T. Music Librarianship. London, J. Clark
& Co., 1959, pp. 289-450.
2. Music Library Association. Notes. 2d series, 17:2
through 18:1.
3. During 1959 alone, 10,796 musical compositions were
published and copyrighted in the U.S.
4. Scholarly Editions of English Music. N.Y., Galaxy Music Corp., 1960, p. 4.
5. Monumenta Musica. Bärenreiter Antiquariat, Kassel,
1959, p. 8.
6. Kenneth Mummery. A Catalogue of Music and Books on
Music, N.S. 16. Bournemouth, 1959, p. 2.
7. Edward B. Marks Music Corp., N.Y. From letter dated
March 1, 1959. Also, Notes, 17:4, Sept., 1960, p.
523.

8. Monumenta Musica. op. cit., p. 9.
9. Notes, 17:1, Dec. 1959, p. 22.
10. Blackwell's Music Shop. Instrumental Music, Catalogue No. 714. Oxford, 1959, p. 5.
11. Ibid., p. 15.
12. Baerenreiter Music. Old and Modern Music of Distinction, Catalogue. N. Y., [1958?], p. 25.
13. The current rate of exchange is DM 3.97 to the U.S. dollar. In 1954 it was DM 4.20. Converting at DM 4., used throughout this paper, results in U.S. prices that are a few cents lower to the dollar than the official exchange rate.
14. The documentation to support these quotations is available on request.
15. Blackwell's of Oxford suggests that overseas customers figure on a surcharge of about six percent for postage and insurance (see, e.g., Catalogue No. 723).
16. "Important Notice." Musica Disciplina, 15, 1961. Inside front cover.
17. The New Bach-Edition, Kassel, Bärenreiter [1954].
18. Form letter from Bärenreiter Antiquariat, Kassel, Jan., 1958.
19. I have been unable to locate any music actually published by the Baerenreiter Music Publishers of New York.
20. Information supplied from the U.S. Customs Office by the Music Division of the Library of Congress.
21. How well Notes performs the function of a selection and acquisitions tool for librarians might well be the subject of an interesting study--not that it is by any means the consensus of opinion that Notes is primarily for librarians.
22. See, e.g., the British prices of miniature scores of works by Aaron Copland in Music and Letters 42:2, April, 1961, as compared with the U.S. prices in Boosey & Hawkes' Pocket Scores, 1960-1.
23. Direct mail advertisement from The Music Exchange, N.Y., received June, 1961.

The Problem of Maps
Lloyd A. Brown

From Library Trends 13:215-25, October, 1964. Copyright
1964 by the University of Illinois Board of Trustees. Reprinted by permission.

The Library of Congress was founded in 1800, but,
writes the historian, "the only evidence there was of an interest in the collection of maps before 1865 was the vote in
the committee, March 20, 1830, that the Librarian be instructed to procure Burr's County atlas of the State of New
York, and the best maps of the several States which were
not already in the Library; . . ."[1] This general indifference on the part of the founding fathers in Washington was
reflected in the libraries of most countries. Not only did
they lack interest in maps and atlases, they deliberately
shunned them--even when the maps were offered as gifts.
But there are sufficient if not good reasons back of this attitude of indifference to maps and atlases, reasons which go
back hundreds of years.

At the beginning of the Christian era only the brave
and the pagan indulged in geographic speculation. It was a
sin to probe the mysteries of the universe, and the explanations set forth by the church in regard to the heavens and
earth were sufficiently vague and awe-inspiring to satisfy all
but the most skeptical observers of natural phenomena.

Maps have long been associated with military intelli-
gence as well as adventure and intrigue. Because they were
potential sources of information to the enemy, it was dangerous to plot on maps and charts the location of roads and
navigable streams by which an army might approach a city.
It was equally dangerous to inform the hostile world of the
location of military objectives such as arsenals, barracks,
dockyards, and public buildings. Therefore many rulers
were afraid to make good maps and charts and even more
loathe to collect and to preserve them. Georg Kohl relates
that the Roman Emperor Augustus locked up the maps that
resulted from his extensive survey of his realm, and that he
issued only partial copies to the imperial councillors of his
provinces.

As late as the nineteenth century it was considered

an act of high treason to divulge the information on official
maps, and it is safe to say that every government agency,
both here and abroad, has maps of a confidential nature
which are guarded as carefully as international boundaries
themselves.   Sea charts, too, have been jealously guarded
for ages, especially those made during and after the discovery of the New World.   Maritime trade routes, avenues
of wealth as well as lifelines, were, and still are, vital to
certain nations, and charts which plotted the courses of merchant fleets across the seas were very important documents
indeed.   Early navigators, especially the enterprising and
venturesome Spanish and Portuguese explorers of the six-
teenth century, made a practice of weighting their charts
with lead; when their ships were boarded by the enemy, they
jettisoned charts overboard rather than let the foe profit by
their hard-earned information about the high seas.   Such a
custom was not favorable to the dissemination of geographical information, nor did it contribute to a wide appreciation
of the value and importance of maps and charts.

Map production received its first real impetus in the
fifteenth century.   Within the short period of fifty years, the
printing press was invented and developed, Ptolemy's Geographia was revived, and the New World was discovered.
But at this very time, when maps were being published in
rapidly increasing quantities to meet the demand and to keep
up with the "new discoveries" in the Western Hemisphere,
a new trend appeared which threatened and delayed for years
the systematic collecting of maps.   This was the tendency to
discard old maps for new.

It is not strange that people should assume that the
latest will naturally be the best, whether it be automobiles
or maps; but it is unreasonable, in the case of a map, to
think that because it is out of date it is of no value and
therefore should not be allowed to take up valuable space.
The best maps and charts are nearly always compilations of
data taken from earlier reliable maps or charts.   Keeping
this fact in mind, let us suppose that it is possible to produce a perfect map, embodying all the information which
could be gleaned from previously compiled sources.   Would
there be any excuse for discarding and destroying the sources
from which it was compiled?   If there were, the same reasoning applied to books and manuscripts would eliminate
most libraries and all archival collections.   And yet there
is evidence which indicates that this destructive tendency has
operated continuously for hundreds of years and still persists
to a certain extent.

Maps did not come into their own and did not attain

the dignity of "historical documents, " according to Kohl, until the beginning of the nineteenth century, when a few far-
sighted European scholars began to search musty book stalls
for the long-lost items of historical cartography.   They
found some, but many were apparently gone forever.   Baron
Charles Athenase Walkenaer (1771-1852) is usually given
credit for arousing interest in historical cartography because
of his writings and the exploitation of the remarkable collection of source material he assembled in his Paris home.
Edme Jomard contributed much toward the formation of a
branch of the Imperial Library in Paris, in which were gathered remarkable examples of early cartography which had
been forgotten and "lost" for many years.   The Polish scholar Joachim Lelewel and the Portuguese Viscomte de Santarem stimulated the interest of scholars by publishing facsimiles of important maps and charts, accompanied by learned dissertations.

The vigorous efforts of a few scholars, supported by
a generally awakened interest in antiquities, resulted in the
formation of many fine collections in the latter part of the
nineteenth century, and others have since been formed.   Today it is being constantly reasserted that the civilized world
is becoming more and more map conscious.   But, in spite
of the alleged status of maps at the present time, there has
been a definite lag between the growth of interest in the subject and the development of administrative technique.   This
situation is due, in large measure, to the traditional attitude of considering maps as minor publications and administering them as such.   As reference tools, maps are seldom
given major consideration.   As minor publications, maps are
cataloged and classified after all other material has been
taken care of, which means that they seldom receive the attention they deserve.   Maps cannot be properly administered
as adjuncts to the newspaper or periodical collection of a
library.

Taking into account these various inhibiting factors,
it is not strange that there is a lack of well established rules
and procedures governing the administration of maps and
charts, nor is it surprising that a card catalog and system
of classification are not considered essential aids to the use
of the map collection.   History proves that a casual attitude
toward ancient cartographic material is not justified, especially among the members of the library profession.

Prior to the twentieth century few, if any, maps and
charts were reproduced solely for decorative purposes.
Every decade of the past two thousand years has produced
maps and charts which were compiled and executed for the

purpose of imparting geographical information in picture
form. To the men who made them, they were not amusing
or quaint. On the contrary, such geographical products
were serious attempts to portray the earth or parts thereof,
with accuracy and clarity. If the end product happened to be
artistic, so much the better, but it was a purposeful kind of
artistry aimed to please several different audiences.

Good or bad, accurate or inaccurate, the maps of a
given period tell a story such as few written documents can
tell. Often they supplement--for the historian, the geographer, and the lexicographer--the narratives and memoirs, the
personal letters and diaries, the official pronouncements of
the famous and infamous people who have had a part in history making. Time and research have proved the validity of
Captain John Smith's often quoted statement that "it is fit"
for historians to offer to our view the stage whereon the
pageant of history is and has been acted, "for as Geography
without History seemeth a carkasse without motion; so History without Geography, wandreth as a Vagrant without a
certaine habitation. "[2]

In addition to the obvious uses of old maps and charts
--the location of obsolete towns, cities, and countries, the
spelling of proper names that have changed throughout the
centuries, the verification of political boundaries that have
long since lost their identity--old maps offer a great deal of
extra-geographical information which is not apparent to the
casual reader. Usually they serve as representative examples of current art forms: the skill of the engraver or lith-
ographer and the use or abuse of color, either as a decoration or an aid in the identification of geographical areas or
geological formations. Decorative features such as car-
touches and decorative border ornamentation often reveal the
costumes of the times, the natural resources of the area involved, and the prominent buildings (shown in profile) which
a geographer and traveler would like to know about. Only
in modern times have maps and charts been shorn of adorn-
ment in favor of more utilitarian lines and letters.

Intelligent evaluation of maps and charts is the first
and most important factor in the administration of the material. Such an obvious statement of fact would not be worth
repeating except that the true value of cartographic material
has gained recognition only by slow and painful degrees.

A favorite protective device employed by librarians
when faced with unfamiliar material such as maps and charts
which do not fit neatly into the library scheme of storing
things is to point out the prohibitive cost of maintaining the
collection. It is not a very good device, however, and does

not always represent the true state of affairs.   The importance of administrative costs dwindles with the proper appreciation of the intrinsic and extrinsic value of the material
under consideration.   For example, the great elephant folio
edition of John James Audubon's The Birds of America is
probably the largest format ever produced by a publisher in
this or any age.   These four volumes are heavy, awkward
to handle, and difficult to store.   Yet what librarian would
complain about the problems of handling or storing such
books if he were to receive them as a gift?   And what librarian would not make a strenuous effort to see that the
money was forthcoming to do it properly?

Methods of preservation and classification have been
devised throughout the years to facilitate the use of library
materials.   If the methods fail or prove inadequate for the
handling of materials such as maps, do not blame the maps;
be thankful that the day of the papyrus scroll and the cunei-
form tablet is over.

No subject could be more appropriate for discussion
today among librarians concerned with present-day working
problems than maps and map administration.   The interest
of the public in the geography of the world has increased
steadily during the past fifteen or twenty years.   It is no
longer the casual interest of neutral observers; it is the interest of persons who have come to realize that world geography is our geography, and that it is high time to learn a
little more about it.   And from official government sources
we find that today the need for maps and charts of various
parts of the world is both vital and urgent.

The interesting thing about this urgency in connection
with maps is that it seems always to have existed.   For centuries explorers, travelers, and military men have complain-
ed about the lack of good, accurate maps and charts.   George
Washington, our first military commander-in-chief, whose
field of operations extended from Quebec to St. Augustine,
found himself handicapped time and time again by the lack of
good maps of the country over which his troops had to move
and fight.

In 1813, when control of the Great Lakes was being
contested, the United States naval squadron under Oliver Hazard Perry had to depend on a few crude charts of the more
important harbors to sail by; very few of them even pretend-
ed to be accurate, and a complete set of lake charts was
nonexistent.

In 1849 there was a rush for the gold fields of California.   The road to wealth lay beyond the wilderness of the
plains and the Rockies; consequently, map makers and pub-

lishers sold out entire editions of maps and "tourist guides" in a very short time. Old maps were refurbished and corrected, more or less, and new ones were hastily drawn and then redrawn many times over. People would take almost anything in the way of a map which would show them an overland route to the riches on the other side of the mountains. The West, and the ways to get there, had not been well mapped. Up to that time there had not been an urgent need for careful surveys, and the maps which existed were full of errors. Vast areas were virtually unknown to white men. Hostile Indians and precarious transportation facilities added to the hazards of the overland route.

Sea captains sailing from New York to San Francisco were equally handicapped by the lack of good charts of the coast of South America, the Strait of Magellan, and the west coast of North America. Good charts of San Francisco were so rare as to be practically nonexistent. But so pressing was the demand for ships to carry passengers and freight to California that some captains sailed out of New York harbor with nothing more than an elementary school atlas to guide them around Cape Horn, an 18,000-mile voyage which sometimes took as long as five months.

An alternate route to California, avoiding the wilds of North America and the perils of Cape Horn, was established across Mexico. Starting at Veracruz the way led through San Blas to Acapulco on the Pacific Coast. From there, parties went by boat to San Francisco. This route cut the time to about sixty days. However, all those who took it were warned to go in parties of not less than fifty, in order to avoid the danger of attack by robbers.

The United States, you see, was still so huge that the unmapped territory in the middle and western parts of it would never be needed. Even as late as 1868 there was still a great deal to be learned about the West. In that year, while returning with General Ulysses S. Grant from a trip to the Rockies, William Tecumseh Sherman wrote his friend Admiral Bailey bemoaning the fact that there were so few good maps of the region through which they were traveling.

I mention these incidents of United States history because once again history is repeating itself, in more ways than one. Today we are faced with the same shortage of geographical and cartographical information as Christoper Columbus, George Washington, and Dwight Eisenhower faced; for, in spite of the tremendous advances which have been made in geographical and cartographical research, the information is scattered and spotty.

The geographical world has shrunk in size until it has

reached a point where we Americans can no longer ignore
any part of it. To keep informed of the affairs which concern our welfare and safety, it is not enough to be familiar
with the geography of the United States and its dependencies.
Regardless of our political sentiments regarding isolation,
and whether we like it or not, the world is closing in around
us, and it behooves us to examine it more closely--every
part of it.

Today we are obliged to recognize the importance of
small islands which used to be nothing more than tiny dots
on the map, unnamed and often poorly located with reference
to other places. The strategy of our times is a strategy of
world geography, with both sides probing the far corners of
the earth for harbors which might be useful as naval bases,
and giving careful consideration to every acre of level
ground which might be used for air bases.

The result of all this feverish activity is a growing
shortage of maps and charts. Publishers cannot keep up with
the current demand for them, and huge stocks of what the
public once considered "obsolete" maps, and which publishers
had accepted as heavy liabilities, have long since been sold
out. Cartographers are hopelessly behind in the task of keeping up with world events, and the clamor for detailed maps
of remote parts of the world continues unabated.

The shortage of geographical material extends even to
some departments of our government in Washington. Today
there are at least two departments of our government that
are engaged in surveying the map resources of the country.
Both agencies have been instituted, incidentally, since December 7, 1941. Librarians are the traditional guardians of
our cultural heritage. What about preserving our defensive
resources as well? Why should it be necessary for the federal government to make a state by state survey of our map
collections, when there might have been a union list of maps
and charts started years ago?

If maps are relegated to the library storeroom, or if
they receive only incidental consideration in the library budget and the distribution of labor within the library staff, no
other problems need be discussed. However, many librarians would like to do more with maps as reference material
if some of the other problems relative thereto could be
solved without too much trouble, and the problems are not
as overwhelming as they seem.

The problem of selection--supply and demand--is one
of the chief concerns of the reference librarian. Aside from
the limitations on all library budgets, there is always the
question of what to buy and when to buy it. On the one hand

is the theory that the appetite is created by what it is fed.
On the other hand is the theory that the librarian should
hold off buying until there is a demand for material on a
given subject.   Both schools of thought have sound, logical
reasoning behind them, and both factions have evidence to
prove the wisdom of their policies.

Let us consider briefly the policy of buying map material only when and if the need arises.   Librarians are not
the only ones who have questioned the interest of the public
in maps and charts.   A few years ago I talked with a group
of newspapermen about the use of maps in their medium, a
custom, by the way, which dates back to 1733.   These editors were not at all sure about the reactions of their readers
to maps used to illustrate a complex story.   They knew, and
every librarian knows, that the public is often unpredictable
in its tastes, and that the demand for, and response to, certain types of material may change in a very short time and
for no apparent reason.   Moreover, public wants are so
multifarious that the librarian is hard pressed to spread the
collection so that it will cover the majority of requests that
come in.

Unfortunately, demands for a new type of material
come in waves of public sentiment, and waiting for the demand to hit the library sometimes means waiting until it is
too late.   The current shortage of maps illustrates this
point.

Instead of waiting for the demand for particular types
of material to arise, many librarians prefer to dig their
wells before their public gets thirsty, following the principles
of an old Chinese proverb.   Given a specific sum of money
with which to build up a general reference collection, very
few librarians would have any difficulty in spending wisely
one to five thousand dollars--until they came to the purchase
of map material.   For example, you would all buy an una-
bridged dictionary, the United States Catalogue, the Readers'
Guide, an encyclopedia, one of several biographical dictionaries, Bartlett or some other book of quotations, etc., etc.
But sooner or later the question of geographic tools would
come up, because every library must have a few fundamental
references to cover the subject.   Now the World Almanac
will answer just so many questions and no more.   A pro-
nouncing gazetteer is extremely useful for locating and spelling geographical place names, provided such places are still
on the maps (figuratively).

The selection of map material for the collection presents an interesting problem.   Unfortunately, the A. L. A.
Book List does not contain a section on current map publica-

tions.   The American Geographical Society issues a very
useful list called <u>Current Geographical Publications</u>, which
covers geographical literature pretty thoroughly.   However,
this list does not include detailed descriptions or critical
notes, which might help the uninitiated librarian select maps
for purchase.   Two general considerations will be involved
in the selection of maps and charts for the small library:
cost and lasting value.   The safest investment in map publications is an official map published by some branch of the
United States government.   Government maps are also publications of lasting value.   They are well printed on good
paper; the type is clear, and they tell the story they were
designed to tell.   They are produced at cost, and up to a
few years ago their sale was practically unrestricted.

However, it is as difficult for the working librarian
to keep up with government map publications as with other
government documents.   But in the case of maps, the re-
ward is well worth the effort.   There is a movement afoot
to prevent wasteful duplication of effort in the federal government as well as in state and civic mapping agencies.   Just
a few years ago an organization was created, calling itself
the National Congress on Surveying and Mapping.   Its membership is composed of persons who are interested either
directly or indirectly in surveying and mapping, or in the
end products of these fields.   All sections of the country are
represented in this body, and its general purpose is to coordinate the efforts of twenty-eight federal agencies (each of
which is receiving a substantial annual appropriation) engaged
in making surveys and maps.   Another general purpose of
the Congress is to see that the material is available to those
who need or want it.   Although this National Congress is the
eighteenth attempt made by various groups over a period of
years to plan and to institute a coordinated mapping program,
there are indications that this one may actually succeed.

Meanwhile there are hundreds of excellent government
maps and surveys available to libraries at a nominal figure.
Which of these have permanent value, or the most nearly
permanent value?   Which are best adapted to the use of the
small public library?

One of the most obvious, of course, and one with
which we are all familiar, is the series of United States topographical sheets.   These maps are on a scale of one mile
to an inch, which is large enough for most needs.   They are
probably the most accurate maps of their kind that we shall
have for many years.   Frequently they combine data obtained by more than one government agency.   The maps and
charts issued by the U.S. Coast and Geodetic survey and the

charts of the Hydrographic Survey are well known and widely
used for reference in many parts of the country. The General Land Office wall map of the United States, revised from
time to time, is a boon to librarians. There are lists issued periodically by the U.S. Superintendent of Documents,
which explain the important features of each map and how it
may be used. Official maps of other countries, when and if
available, are usually well made and equally desirable.

If a librarian must be limited in the purchase of map
material, he should have a good general atlas of the world
and a few sheet maps on a larger scale of the various continents, countries, and smaller political subdivisions. A
good wall map of the world and a good-sized globe would be
highly desirable additions to any collection.

In buying sheet maps from a commercial publisher, it
is necessary only to follow a few simple rules, which also
pertain in the selection of books and other library material.
A map is supposed to convey a picture. If it does this clearly, without confusing the reader, the chances are it is a
good map. And if a map is drawn to scale, with clean lines
carefully laid down, with parallels of latitude and meridians
of longitude indicated, the chances are it will be a fairly accurate map, though not necessarily so. Whether we realize
it or not, all of us are capable of editing a map or chart
which is badly done. Good maps are almost never badly
printed!

The storage of sheet maps is an old problem which
has been simplified in recent years by the construction of
several types of map storage drawers. They now have certain things in common. They are usually narrow from top
to bottom, not more than two inches or close to it. They
measure 26 1/2" from front to back, and 43 1/2" from side
to side. They come in banks of five drawers apiece, are
interchangeable, and can be stacked high without danger.
The dimensions are arbitrary, but they are the ones that
have proved most generally acceptable among librarians who
have purchased them.

Everything said here about maps and map administration has been said before, in one way or another, and the
problems today are essentially the same as they were seventy-five or a hundred years ago. But these remarks will
have been justified if they encourage librarians to go ahead,
if they reassure the profession regarding the fundamental
value of the material, and if they help to discourage the publication of such fatalistic literature as "Floundering Among
the Maps."[3]

Notes

1. Johnston, William Dawson. History of the Library of
    Congress, 1800-1864. Washington, Government Print-
    ing Office, 1904, Vol. I, p. 340.
2. Smith, John Capt. The General History of the Ber-
    mudas, 1593-1623. In Edward Arber, ed., Captain
    John Smith, Works, 1608-1631. Birmingham, The
    English Scholar's Library, 1884, p. 625.
3. Badger, H.C. "Floundering Among the Maps," Library
    Journal, 17:375-377, 1892.

The Management of Map Collections and Libraries
in University Geography Departments
A. M. Ferrar

From Library Association Record 64:161-5, May 1962. Reprinted by permission.

The flood of maps which has become available to
Geography Departments since the war, largely owing to the
generosity of the War Office and the Directorate of Overseas
Surveys, has enlarged and widened the scope of their collections beyond anything that could have been hoped for twenty
years ago. This generosity has, however, raised some problems, among them problems of storage and management to
ensure that every sheet is readily available whenever it may
be required. In most institutions this has been tackled by
setting aside a large room for storage and consultation of
the collection, and wherever possible providing a full-time
attendant. A good deal of experience on which the arrangement of the material may be based does in fact exist, though
it has not in the past been widely available. It has been the
writer's good fortune to spend ten years working on the collections of the Royal Geographical Society[1] at a time when
the formative influences in their growth were still represented by active members of its staff, and later to have the opportunity of endeavouring to adapt its methods to the requirements of two university departments. Though the limit of
improvement has not by any means been reached, it is felt
that they have crystallized to the point where it would be
useful to make them generally available.

The arrangement of a large collection of maps is essentially a problem of filing. The first step is classification.
Maps present an easier task in this respect than books--the
approach to them in the first instance is so obviously regional. A study of several large and well established collections
has led the writer to the conclusion that it is impossible to
improve upon a simple subdivision and arrangement according
in the first place to continent, and in the second to country,
the countries within each continent being placed in alphabetical order. It is sometimes suggested that a better arrangement within each continent would be to group adjacent countries together. The principal objection to this practice is

the difficulty of dealing with countries which belong, according to some viewpoints, in one group, and according to others
in another. Few collections are so large that a strict alphabetical sequence separates any two countries within a continent by more than two or three years, and as it is not
practicable to browse in map drawers as one might browse
at a bookshelf, the gain in proximity is outweighed by increased complication. In large collections further subdivision may profitably be made into four categories: "General, "
which are maps of the whole of the country in question; "Divisional" maps covering a major portion--more than a pro-
vince--and often susceptible to designation by a compass
point; "District" maps of a recognized administrative area
such as a county, province or département, whether existing
or historical; and "Special" maps of smaller units and of
anomalous areas such as frontier zones or strip maps of
rivers, which cannot be made to fit any of the larger sections. Within these subdivisions the maps are arranged in
their drawers or other storage places in order of acquisition
and numbered.
        Having settled upon the subdivisions it is necessary to
name them, i. e., give them classification symbols, and pro-
ceeding by analogy with accepted library practice it might be
thought a good thing to arrange them in an acceptable order
and number them, or letter them, according to a decimal or
some other system. This has been tried, but territorial
changes, particularly the creation of new states, and even
simple expansion of collections, have led to the breakdown
of several such schemes. Now the principal purpose of
classification symbols is to establish a sequence for convenience in filing (or shelving) and in dealing with books they
are indispensable, but we have already seen that our material is arranged in categories of descending order of magni-
tude--continent, country, district--and that the countries within each continent are arranged alphabetically. So a clear-
cut sequence has been established without recourse to extraneous symbolism. Another purpose which they are said
to serve is as convenient "shorthand references. " As the
majority of classification symbols lack any mnemonic quality
(in the writer's view a crippling disability) and as the space
available on the margin of a map for them is not at a premium, this suggestion does not bear examination. It is
found that a much simpler and perfectly adequate method is
to use the name of the section and not introduce an arbitrary
symbol at all. For maps of countries or parts of countries
the name of the continent can, in practice, be omitted; it
may be regarded as understood. The classification symbols,

which also serve as pressmarks, will thus take forms such
as:

Africa--General 3	Europe--Div. 5
Belgium--General 4	France--Div. 9
Norway--Dist. 2	Romania--Spec. 18

    This defines not only the drawer a map will occupy,
but also its position in the drawer in relation to other maps
in the same subdivision. There is only one point at which
the application of this scheme presents any difficulty, and
that unfortunately is for the British Isles. The countries involved here are "England and Wales," "Scotland" and "Ireland." But it would be highly inconvenient (and not only to
institutions in Britain) for them to be separated by other European countries in the alphabetical sequence. The solution
is to adopt an overriding heading "British Isles" under which
maps covering more than one of these countries may be
classified and the countries themselves grouped. It is possible to call to mind comparable cases, such as Scandinavia
and the Balkans, but all of them are much less closely integrated entities and the few maps which do group them may
be classified as "Europe-Divisional." Another question is
that of once unified states which have later broken up. If a
collection includes only one or two maps of Austria-Hungary
or of pre-partition India, these may be treated as "Divisional" maps of their respective continents. But if a large number are held, it may be worth instituting special sections
for them in the alphabetical sequence of countries--though,
as a general rule, only present-day political units should be
used, and when important changes take place, the parts of
the collection affected should be reclassified.
    At this point it may be well to mention that any map
consisting of a number of sheets is treated as one map from
the point of view of classification and cataloguing. All sheets
of, say, the Ordnance Survey one-inch map of Great Britain
will thus have the same pressmark, their position in the
drawer being determined by edition and sheet number (in
series whose sheets are not numbered they are placed in alphabetical order of sheet names). In cases of this kind if a
complete set is not received at the outset, the catalogue entry is marked "incomplete" and the sheets issued later are
simply inserted in their appropriate places as and when they
come along.
    Collections in university departments are not likely,
in the foreseeable future, to reach a size which would justify
the use of this scheme in full--the numbers of maps falling

in the "Divisional," "District" and "Special" categories are
too small to warrant separation from each other. It is,
however, desirable to separate them from the "General"
maps and the best compromise is found to be to retain the
heading "Divisional" in the case of continents (there can be
no "District" maps of continents as these are by definition
countries), and in the case of countries to amalgamate the
three sections under the heading "District."

The maps being now arranged in an orderly and reasonable way, the next requirement is a catalogue giving an
adequate guide to the collection. This can best take the
form of a card index arranged in the same way as the maps
themselves. It will be found that some sections, eventually
most of them, will contain a sufficient number of cards to
make a search through the whole section laborious and it
will be felt that further subdivision is called for. The most
obvious instance is perhaps that of county maps or town
plans in the "District" section, but it also arises in "General" sections. The first is best dealt with by adding the
county or town name to the card heading and alphabetizing
the cards. In the latter case it will be found that a breakdown by map type (e.g., physical, economic, demographic)
or by date of publication--or both--is convenient. The arrangement of the maps is not modified, as the numerical
reference on the card provides a sufficient guide for locating
them.

It is important that index cards be set out in such a
way that the eye can pick out the required information rapidly and easily. The recommended layout is illustrated:

Czechoslovakia--Tatra 1921	Dist 1
Podrobna mapa Vysokych Tater	1:25,000
Prague: Zemespisny Ustav 1921	
1 sheet	

It will be noted that the card heading is in English, but the
title and publisher's name are given in the language of publication (titles in non-Roman alphabets should be transliterat-
ed). Place of publication and other details are in English.
If an individual author is involved, which is unusual for maps,
his name should be placed on the next line after the title and
the other details moved down the card to make room for it.
Scale should always be given as a "representative fraction,"
not as "1 inch to x miles," etc. It should be placed at the
right-hand end of the line bearing the title as it is an impor-

tant item of information and this position helps it to stand
out. A card bearing the suggested information, set out in
this way, tells a prospective reader all he needs to know before deciding whether he wishes to consult the map. It is
confusing if it is cluttered up with additional notes--all that
is permissible is "incomplete," "2 copies," or "see also
text on bookshelf x," etc. , and such notes should be confined
to one line and set below the body of the entry, separated
from it by at least one blank line. On consulting the card
index the only information which the prospective reader needs
to abstract in order to locate the required map is the first
word on the top line of the card and the classification symbol at the opposite end of the same line--in this case
"Czechoslovakia--Dist 1." If the map consists of a number
of sheets, as in the case of large-scale surveys, a cartographical index diagram should be filed with the map, being
placed before the first sheet. This should consist of a small
scale base map showing the position of sheet lines and just
sufficient detail, such as rivers, coastlines and towns, to indicate the area covered by each sheet. On the diagram each
sheet of which a copy is available should be crossed through
with a thin line of sharply contrasting colour, so that no detail is obscured but it is possible to see at a glance what
coverage is available.

Strictly speaking this combination of card index and
cartographical indices is all that is needed to control a collection, but there are several other records which may promote easier working. The foremost is a sheaf catalogue,
for the use of the curator rather than readers. It is ac-
commodated in a loose-leaf binder in which a sheet, boldly
headed, is devoted to each section of the collection. Each
map receives a one-line entry under column headings. The
left-hand column shows the catalogue number, the next an abbreviated title, the scale follows, then place of publication,
publisher, and date (if desired). Thus:

France--General

1	Carte de France	1:50, 000	Paris	Inst. Geog. Nat.
2				

This supplementary catalogue is worth maintaining as it may
conveniently be kept on the curator's desk and serves as a
ready reminder of half-remembered pressmarks. It also
eliminates the possibility of giving a new map the same

pressmark as one already held, but in use and temporarily
out of its storage place.

Whether an inventory, in which every sheet is entered,
should be maintained is less certain. In the principal collections, British Museum, Royal Geographical Society, etc.,
where the policy is to hold only one copy of each sheet, cartographical indices may be modified to show edition dates and
the record of holdings is complete. But in other places,
where smaller collections of more commonplace maps are
continually in use by students, or for hastily arranged displays in lecture theatres, wear and opportunities for the loss
of sheets are greater, and occasional stock checking may be
desirable. The inventory used for this is an enlarged ver-
sion of the sheaf catalogue, but it should be kept separately,
as the additional detail would otherwise vitiate the usefulness
and convenience of the catalogue. It follows the same general plan but each entry is followed by a list of the numbers
(or names) of sheets held, and the number of copies of each.

Another document to be considered is a Register of
Accessions. In contrast to the inventory, this is valuable
for large collections in which each map sheet is stamped
with the date of acquisition, and its origin may thus always
be traced. But the writer has not found it to be of any use
in small working collections.

The collection will be stored in map presses, which
should be of uniform size and design. Each drawer should
measure 45 x 30 x 2 1/2 inches. The great majority of
sheets will lie flat in it. Any larger drawer size is both
unwieldy and wasteful of space, and any smaller will neces-
sitate the folding of too many sheets. Some topographical
surveys which run to a great many sheets are small enough
for two piles to be placed side by side in the same drawer.
It is a convenience if these can be separated by a removable
plywood partition. If it is desired to do this, all drawers
should be grooved to take a partition. The necessity for uniformity arises from the fact that in the course of expansion
it will be necessary, from time to time, to move maps from
one drawer to another.

When the available storage is filled, new map presses
will be added and the collection spread out so that spare
drawers are available where expansion is taking place without any alteration to the sequence. It is with this contin-
gency in mind that we have earlier been careful to tie pressmarks firmly to maps rather than to storage places. No alteration to classification symbols is required, no matter how
much a collection grows, or whether it grows at the "beginning, " "middle" or "end. "

Each drawer should also have a fixed "hood" closing the top for about four or five inches at the back. A piece of light strawboard (or other cheap card) measuring about one inch less than the drawer size is placed on top of the maps, with its back edge under the hood. If too heavy a grade of strawboard is used, it will not be sufficiently flexible. Maps are thus protected both from dust and from being pushed out at the back of drawers. Some authorities prefer to dispense with the hood and use a double sheet of thick wrapping paper in place of the strawboard, with its folded edge at the back. The author has used both methods and prefers the former, which is also cheaper as the wrapping paper must be of good quality if it is to wear well.

It is a good thing to assemble drawers into presses each ten drawers high. This gives a continuous surface about 38 inches high which is a convenient height for working on maps (standing up) and for sorting and general use. If the working surface is not required, they may be fifteen drawers high, but not more, as it is difficult to handle a heavy pile of maps at shoulder height and dangerous to do so standing on a ladder.

Atlases, though forming part of the collection, must, of course, be stored separately, the smaller on bookshelves with fairly closely spaced vertical divisions and the larger horizontally on shelves only five or six inches apart, so that not more than two or three volumes are placed on each shelf.

A little consideration must now be given to day-to-day working. In the type of institution we are considering this will be facilitated if a distinction is drawn between two types of map collections. One is the "reference collection," which covers extensive areas of the world and in which there will, in general, be only one or two copies of each sheet, and to which all that has been said above applies. On the other hand there will be, in addition, "teaching sets" of 20 or 30 flat copies of selected sheets, and "field sets" of folded sheets for class use. The reference collection must be closely supervised, since, even if it is of only moderate size, a map in the wrong place is a much more serious inconvenience than a book on the wrong shelf. It is for all practical purposes lost. No student should be allowed to go to the map storage drawers and it is essential that no one except the curator returns sheets to their places after use. (In placing sheets in, or returning them to, their drawers care should be taken that all identification marks--pressmark, sheet number or name, and if there are several editions the date--are on the edge of the map at the front of the drawer,

so that when looking for a particular sheet, only the front
edges of sheets need be raised.) Only in exceptional circumstances will a sheet be allowed to leave the reading room
and then only for use in other parts of the same building.
The teaching and field sets may be more freely removed and
replaced by students, or a junior laboratory steward, without
danger of confusion.

A minor point that is worth mentioning is that the use
of "drafting tape" is now popular for securing tracing paper
to maps while drawings are made. There is no objection to
this as long as the maps are printed on good quality, smooth
paper which is not badly worn, and are of no great value.
But there is a risk of damage and it is far better to incul-
cate the habit of using draughtsman's weights. It may be
objected that these, being of lead and in leather covers, are
expensive. However they may be easily improvised--dis-
carded tobacco tins, typewriter ribbon tins, etc., can be
filled with lead shot, or washed gravel, or old nails, and
sealed. Even smooth pebbles of four to six inches diameter
will serve.

We have dealt at some length with the management of
map collections, but we are committed by the title of this
paper to consider also the libraries run in connection with
them. Relatively little needs to be said about these as they
are already covered by standard manuals on librarianship and
there is nothing peculiar to geographical libraries as compared with those of other subjects except the classification
system employed.

Geography is ill served by the Dewey Decimal System,
and none of the other systems in use in large general libraries is any more convenient. As a result there have been
a number of attempts to devise special systems. On account of cross-classification difficulties none of them has
been entirely successful. That of the Association of American Geographers is fairly good.[2] It has been in use (with
some modifications) at Southampton University for some time,
and it was used there in the compilation of an index to articles in a score of the foremost geographical periodicals for
the years 1935-1954. Copies of this index were subsequently
made available to other institutions and it forms a good
foundation for indexes in Geography Departments. This in
itself constitutes a not inconsiderable argument for the general adoption of this system. It is far from perfect, but the
writer knows of no other which displays such a marked improvement on it that the labour of reclassification shows a
reasonable return in increased convenience in the use of the
index. It falls into two broad divisions--"systematic" and

"regional." Combinations of letters (lower case) are used for the former and a decimal system for the latter. A combination of experience with maps and a notation inspired by that in use among chemists suggests the possibility of a radical modification in the regional section which would result in a marked improvement. For instance Am Us Ga At is as effective a symbol for "America-United States-Georgia-Atlanta" as 658.1, and it does have some mnemonic quality. Since the use of a two-letter term in place of each digit yields 26^2 terms (i.e., 676 terms) instead of ten, it abolishes at one stroke the difficulties arising from the existence of a mere ten digits, as well as the resulting built-in bias which most systems display in favour of large and/or well documented areas. (Apart from any other objections this bias is a source of weakness on account of the fact that the best documented areas of today are unlikely to be the best documented areas of a few decades hence.) The writer is pursuing experiments along these lines.

Notes

1. Crone, G.R. 1936. "The Cataloguing and Arrangement of Maps." Lib. Ass. Rec., 38, 98-104.
2. Boggs, S.W. 1937. "Library Classification and Cataloging of Geographic Material." Ann. Ass. Amer. Geogr., 27, 49-93.

Problems in the Map Room
Theodore H. Layng

From Canadian Library 18:63-6, September 1961. Reprinted by permission.

Ideally a map library should so be arranged that all maps of the same area would be filed in the same place contiguous to maps of an adjacent region. In practice, because of the many and various sizes and forms in which maps are produced, and the prior association of many of them in a series, atlas, or particular collection, such an arrangement is impossible of accomplishment. Even if it were possible it would be highly undesirable from the point of view of the map archivist or of an economist. It is good that the archivist should segregate for their better preservation the rarer items in the collection; and, in the interest of space economy, it becomes necessary to group maps for filing according to their size and form.

Only after the various filing groups have been established is it both possible and desirable to arrange items within a particular group, so that all maps of the same area are filed together. There will be exceptions of course. The map librarian in fact must learn to live within, and to rationalize, the exceptions or himself become irrational.

In most map libraries of any size maps of a particular area may be found in any one of a score or more filing groups. The ease with which the librarian will bring forth upon request all maps of whatsoever form, size, or habitat of a particular area is the true measure of efficiency in the map room. The call number of a map is therefore of paramount importance.

The call number used in the Map Division of the Public Archives serves two purposes. It locates not only a map in the filing system, but also the main descriptive entry for that map in the card system. The card system is set up by area; therefore the area classification number must always be present on the individual cards. Because of the various filing groups for maps of the same area, the area classification number is not sufficient to locate accurately a map in the files. In the call number therefore the area number is preceded by the location symbol.

The map location symbol must somehow be adjustable
not only to the existing variform filing system, but--and this
is extremely important--to the multifarious pattern of the future. The necessity of changing thousands of call numbers
with each new advance in the technique of storage must be
avoided. A small map library may face such a task with
equanimity, but as the collection increases, somewhere it
will pass "the point of no return." Conceivably in a large
map library newer and better methods of filing might be rejected on the grounds of dislocating the whole system of finding aids.

The symbols employed therefore must lend themselves
to an almost infinite amount of employment. They should be
descriptive, simple and definite. Further, no one symbol
should be actually employed until the whole system of symbols has been established lest the prior use of one forbids
the free selection of another. Every form in which a map
has been seen should be considered. Every conceivable way
of storing maps should be thought out. The methods of classification, filing and carding should be thought of as inter-
dependent processes, and will therefore all be devised before
any one is employed. In other words only when he is in
control of all the factors of filing, classification and carding
is the map librarian competent to select a set of symbols
for map location. Years of experience in a map library may
increase the measure of his competence, but that complete
competence necessary to devise an infallible and permanent
set of symbols is not likely to be attained by any one of us.

It is a risky business to lay down for critical appraisal one's own system. However, such must be the order
of things if another is to build upon and improve it. Probably the easiest way to explain the need and variety of map
location symbols is to hypothecate an accession of maps--
chiefly general maps of Newfoundland (as distinct from sec-
tional maps). The area classification number for general
maps of Newfoundland is 100.

Duplicates and second-rate material have been weeded
out, and will be placed in semi-dead storage in the subsidiary
collection. The remaining ones have been divided into two
categories, those for the general collection and those for the
special collection.

Map Number 1 is a sheet of the 1/50,000 series of
the Topographical Survey. It is the least of our problems.
The fate of this series has long been decided and the sheet
will simply be folded to fit into a standard file cabinet, where
it will be filed vertically in its proper place in the series.
It will not be catalogued as an individual map, and therefore

no map location symbol need be assigned. The published index sheet for the series is a sufficient finding aid.

In years to come, because this sheet is a first edition or because the series is closed, it will probably be
mounted and hung in vertical cabinets. The closed 7.89 and
3.95 series have already been elevated to the special collection.

Number 2 is a 1960 publication, not belonging to a
series, on good paper, and of medium size suitable for folding. It will be placed in a bank of filing cabinets reserved
for folded maps of the regular classification series. Since
it is a general map of Newfoundland its area classification
number is 100; its location symbol is F (folded). The call
number assigned is F100-1960.

Number 3 is an older map, also of Newfoundland. It
is a bit tattered, and will be mounted on cotton before it is
placed in a horizontal tray (vertical filing cabinets are reserved for maps of the special collection). There are 3
sizes of trays reserved for maps of the general collection
which are to be filed horizontally. This particular map is
small and will have the location symbol H3 (i.e. the smallest
size horizontal tray). If the map had been large it would
have the location symbol H1 or H2. The call number assigned is H3/100-1901.

Number 4 is a plan of a fort in St. John's, drawn in
1750. Since 50 is the number in the classification schedule
for a plan of a building or fort, the classification number for
a fort at St. John's, Newfoundland is 150 St. John's. There
are thousands of fortification plans and for several reasons
it has been expedient to segregate them from the collection
proper. They form a special study group, and would normally be superfluous amongst town plans. It is also convenient to keep such plans as far as possible in one place since
they are so closely related one to the other. And frankly
there are always miscellaneous sizes of filing units in a map
library, either inherited or scrounged, which lend themselves very well to the filing of "miscellaneous" groups.
The particular unit used for housing plans of military properties is designated as H4. The call number of the plan
will be H4/150 St. John's 1750.

Notice that in the case of accession number 3, the
number in the map location symbol indicated a particular
size group of maps. In number 4 the number in the symbol
represents a special group of maps of varying sizes but all
relating to military properties.

Number 5 is one of those things, a map mounted on
heavy cardboard. Obviously such a map cannot be filed with

ordinary sheet maps. There is a special bank of horizontal
trays for the express purpose of storing maps mounted on
cardboard, wallboard, tin etc. and the maps within bear the
location symbol H6. The call number of the map is H6/100-
1830, which is to say that it is filed chronologically with
other maps of Newfoundland also mounted on cardboard.

Number 6 is a new chart of the Hydrographic Service.
This particular series is filed intact in a unit labelled H5
(another "miscellaneous" unit is fully employed). The chart
does not need a call number since the published index is a
sufficient finding aid, and it will not be catalogued individually.

Number 7 is a large rolled map and by all appear-
ances it seems best to keep it in this form. It will be
placed in a cardboard tube and the location symbol will be
R (for rolled). So far, although the tube maps are of different lengths and diameters, they are all filed in the same
place. In the near future, however, it will become necessary to break the Rs into R1, R2 etc.

Incidentally if this accession had been a rare map it
would probably bear the same location. A map in a tube is
well protected and there is no need "to separate the wheat
from the chaff."

Number 8 has been published as a folded map, and
because of its similarities to an ordinary book it will be
banished to a shelf and will receive the location symbol S.
Being still another map of Newfoundland its call number will
be S100-1867, and it will so find its exact location in the
Newfoundland group of shelf maps.

Number 9 is the first candidate for the special collection in our hypothetical accession. It is a rare and beautiful sixteenth-century original and will greatly enhance the
head's office. It will be framed, and its location symbol
will be W (for wall map).

Number 10, also a special map, is of medium size
and will be hung in V1 vertical filing cases. Its call number will be V1/100-1802.

Number 11 is too large for the V1 case and will become a V2.

Number 12 is a printed chart of Newfoundland published by the Admiralty in 1820. It belongs to a special group
which the PAC designates as English charts, series 2 and
this new accession will be number 132 of the series. It dif-
fers from other series maps in the collection in that it will
receive individual notice in the card system under the "100s,"
which is its area classification number. But this number
will of course not locate the map. Actually the chart will

be placed in a unit of the same size and shape in which accession no. 10 was allocated (V1). There is scarcely room
however on the descriptive entry card, or in the profession,
for such a call number as "V1 English charts, series 2, no.
132/100-1820," nor does "V1 E.C., s. 2, no. 132/100-
1820" look any more professional.

In this case the vertical unit used for the distinct
purpose of housing Series 2 of the English Charts is designated as V12. And the location symbol of chart number 132
of the series is V12.132. The call number assigned is
V12.132/100-1820.

Number 13 is a rare 17th-century map about twelve
inches square. While it is recognized that vertical filing is
preferable to horizontal, it is not economical (or suitable) to
place such a small map in a relatively large case. Therefore number 13 will be enfolded in a paper cover and filed
in a small horizontal tray. The number of special maps allocated to a horizontal tray is kept to a minimum. It is one
of the great advantages of segregating special maps that the
number assigned to any one tray can be more easily controlled. Our latest accession will receive the call number
H12/100-1631, since H12 is the label for the small horizontal
trays designed to hold small rare maps.

Number 14 is a problem. Long ago the hazard of filing great large maps horizontally was realized. With some
reluctance many of them were dissected and hung in vertical
cases. But there are always a few--let us call them exhibition pieces--that escape the shears. They are more than
likely heavily mounted and their faces covered with transparent gauze, so that rolling them is out of the question. A
reasonable solution seems to be that such maps should be
dissected, then remounted allowing for folding seams. But
all this takes time, and meanwhile our number 14 must be
treated with extreme care because it too is a large map, and
surely it is an exhibition piece! It will be placed in one of
the large size horizontal trays, an H10 or H11, and because
of its extreme vulnerability it will probably be one of six
maps in the tray.

Number 15 is an atlas of 1870 containing a general
map of Newfoundland. This focuses another problem: how
best to file atlases. Granted it would be desirable to keep
certain groups of atlases together in one place, but again the
multi-sizes in which they have been published--and always
will be--forbids anything approaching an economical arrangement according to area, date etc. Moreover, there are
likely to be several different units employed to house a large
atlas collection; and to be forever shifting from one unit to

another in order to make way for new accessions to a particular group is a particularly unprofitable exercise. The only way of preserving the status quo seems to be to fill a case comfortably, with the atlases off their spines if possible, having some degree of regard for the related atlases in the collection. Each case should have its individual label, A1, A2, A3, etc., and each atlas within the case its own number.

All the maps in our hypothetical accession have now been assigned their call numbers, but there is still a balance of unused symbols: B for a map in a book, M for maps on microfilm, P for maps in portfolio, C for maps in solander cases etc.

Whether or not the number of necessary symbols have been exhausted, enough have been mentioned to show the problems involved, and how very necessary the map location symbol is.

Incidentally, while we were "accessioning," some negative photostats were received and must be stored. The usual size (14 x 18 inches) is filed vertically in cardboard boxes, according to the area classification number of the original map. But these are oversized negatives from another institution. They will be placed in the horizontal bank of trays labelled H8, which are reserved especially for oversized negatives.

And then there is that map of Newfoundland that was to be mounted. Put it in H100 until the bindery can take care of it.

Geography and Map Cataloging and Classification
in Libraries
Dr. Arch C. Gerlach

From Special Libraries 52:248-51, May 1961.   Copyright by
Special Libraries Association 1961.   Reprinted by permission.

In 1952 the International Geographical Union established a Commission on the Classification of Geographical Books
and Maps in Libraries.   One member was named from each
of five countries (Brazil, France, Germany, Italy and the
United States).   The chairman is Professor André Libault of
France, and the United States member is the author of this
article.   Following the death of the Brazilian member, Dr.
B. Winid of the Polish Academy of Sciences was added to
the Commission, which also has corresponding members in
several countries.   The primary purpose of this Commission
was to study classification systems for geographical and cartographical collections with a view toward recommending improvements and possibly even developing an ideal system for
those materials.   Because of the Commission's narrow scope,
it has had only partial success in achieving recognition for
geography as a discipline or identification of its works as
such in the collections of large libraries.
   The basic difficulty appears to be that librarians have
had too little contact with modern geography to recognize
works in this field when they see them, and too little understanding of maps to give them the attention they deserve as
sources of information.   It seems futile, therefore, to perfect further the classification schemes for geographical and
cartographical materials until something is done to stop the
routing of maps into storage bins and the cataloging of works
prepared by eminent geographers, primarily for use by geographers, as anthropology, economics, geology, history, political science, sociology or some other subject with which the
cataloger associates them.   We must take into account the
broader aspects of descriptive and subject cataloging that are
shortcircuiting geographical and cartographical publications.

Classification Considerations

The function of classifying a particular item in a collection involves only the assignment of a notation or call
number to designate its logical filing position within a group
of related materials. The notation may be numerals, letters
or a combination of numerals and letters. It is the basic
philosophy of the classification system, however, which determines how different groups of materials will be arranged
in relation to each other and what types of subdivisions may
be made within the groups. For example, one system might
group materials by subject, then subdivide them by areas.
Another might group materials by areas, then subdivide them
by subjects. Or, to take a more limited example, one might
classify works on military geography adjacent to political
geography in one system and to physical geography in another.
But what becomes of the work on military geography when
the librarian identifies it as military science? It is classified as military science and separated from geography.

Unfortunately for geographical and cartographical research in libraries, the widest used classification systems
do not treat geography as an independent discipline or facilitate the grouping of geographical materials together. Members of the International Geographical Union's Commission on
Classification realize that long established and widely used
classification systems for large general libraries, such as
the Dewey Decimal or Library of Congress systems, are
frozen into existing patterns by the tremendous mass of material already classified. Geographers and cartographers
may, however, work toward the establishment of alternative
schedules for use in special geography and map libraries.

Such an alternative arrangement has been provided in
connection with the 16th edition of the Dewey Decimal Classification, which was published in the United States in 1958 and
is supplemented or expanded from time to time by issues of
Decimal Classification Additions, Notes, and Decisions. The
16th edition of the Dewey Decimal Classification has incorporated a number of geographical topics proposed by Dr.
Meynen, but the basic arrangement subdivides subjects into
local or geographical areas by affixing to the number for the
subject the digits 09 followed by the number of the country,
state, city and so on. The editors realize that many subjects are treated according to various regions of the earth
that cannot be identified by the 940-999 sequence and have
recognized some of these in the 16th edition through form division 091--zones and physical regions. They are considering the possibility of a regional subdivision scheme similar

to that used by the <u>British National Bibliography</u>: continents,
islands, mountains, plains, coasts, oceans, lakes, rivers,
forests, grasslands, deserts and so on.

More important, however, is the recognition that geographers would like to have all, or nearly all, material of
a geographical nature kept together in one part of the <u>Dewey
Decimal Classification</u>. To enable such an arrangement in
special libraries there is provided in the March 1960 issue
of <u>Decimal Classification Additions, Notes, and Decisions</u>,
an expansion of 910.1 for topical geography. Libraries wishing to keep works on all fields of geography together may di-
vide 910.1 like 000.899; for example, economic geography
910.133 or physical geography 910.155 14. If desired, area
subdivisions may be added after a zero, as between 940 and
999; for example, economic geography of the United States,
910.133 073 or physical geography of the United States, 910.
155 140 73.

If similar alternative schedules for geographical and
cartographical publications can be inserted into other classification systems, real progress will be made toward organizing branch libraries and specialized card catalogs for research in those fields. Working out more detailed plans of
classification without taking into account the training and judgment of catalogers may, however, be about as ineffective as
plotting the precise distribution pattern for irrigation water
over field A and leaving the cataloger in control of the master valve through which the water may be channeled into
fields B, C, D or X. The basic problem is how to gain
recognition for geographical and cartographical works together rather than how to classify the small percentage so identified by subject catalogers.

Cataloging Considerations

The principles and techniques of cataloging as presented in the <u>Rules for Descriptive Cataloging in the Library of
Congress</u> (page 7) state: "The objectives of descriptive cataloging are: 1) to state the significant features of an item
with the purpose of distinguishing it from other items and
describing its scope, contents and bibliographic relation to
other items; and 2) to present these data in an entry which
can be integrated with entries for other items in the catalog
and which will respond best to the interest of most users of
the catalog. . . . The descriptive elements are given in the
entry in the order that will best meet the needs of users of
the catalog and will facilitate the integration of the entry in
a catalog with entries for other items. "

Careful analysis of this statement reveals three areas of interpretation that cause difficulty for geographers. First, most users of library catalogs are not geographers, so when the cataloger scatters geographical works among a wide variety of other disciplines to which they do bear some overlapping relationship, he can conscientiously maintain that the entry "will best respond to the interests of most users of the catalog." Second, whenever there is a conflict between the requirement for presentation of data in an entry "that will best meet the needs of users" and the requirement for an entry which "can be integrated in a catalog with entries for other items, " the latter principle is given priority. The catalog is the thing! Entries cannot be modified to fit different disciplines. They must conform to the standards that will expedite their integration into the catalog. Third, the subject cataloger analyzes the content of items cataloged. This requires some knowledge of the subject fields as well as the principles and techniques of cataloging. Practically no catalogers have formal training in geography at the college or university level. How, then, can catalogers recognize and identify geographical works? They can't. A multitude of doctoral dissertations in geography and monographs or books written by past presidents of the Association of American Geographers may be found cataloged in subject fields quite foreign to the authors.

To prevent the continuation of such a situation, the International Geographical Union's Commission on Classification should prepare a semi-popular, descriptive summary of modern geography for distribution to library schools. The resultant document could be distributed to library school administrators with a covering letter urging that it be made required reading for all students working toward degrees in library science.

Another report should be compiled and distributed to library associations and the principal libraries in each country, explaining and justifying in detail the need for alternate rules of entry for specialized collections, classed card catalogs and libraries wishing to keep works on all fields of geography together, subdivided by subject and area or area and subject.

Problems of Maps

Alternate rules of entry are even more essential for maps and atlases than for books, because readers in those fields characteristically approach the catalog or map files to find materials by area and subject. The American Library

Association and the Library of Congress rules for entry are
based on the supposition that maps should be cataloged like
books. The main entry for books is author-title. More
than 95 percent of map reference requests require searching
by area-subject entries. A survey of 360 map libraries in
the United States, made by a committee of the SLA Geography and Map Division in 1953, revealed that 74 percent of
the requests were by area, 24 percent by subject and a few
scattered ones were by title, publisher, scale or date.
      Clearly the objective of a catalog is to identify each
item in a collection, but for whom? The author-title entry
for books is a useful approach for catalogers and acquisitions personnel but not for map reference use, so alternate
rules of entry must be provided for control over map reference collections. A map lies in character between a book
and a picture and combines some features of both. The
main entry for cataloging maps should begin with geographical area, followed by subject, date, size or scale, publisher
or authority, and notes on edition, series, number of sheets
and classification number. The main entry heading should
be one that can be applied to every kind of map and one that
is useful in the information it provides.
      The earliest map catalog printed in America (Harvard
University, 1831) was arranged by area, with map titles listed alphabetically under areas. The printed map catalogs of
the British Museum have followed an area arrangement since
1885. A concerted effort to convince library administrators
that special provisions can be made for servicing special
form and subject materials without disrupting the general collections and catalogs seems both essential and fully justified.

Future Objectives

      The scope and objectives of the International Geograph-
ical Union's Commission on Classification should be broadened to deal with a wide variety of problems such as: 1) gaining recognition in libraries for geography as a discipline;
2) promoting more use of geographical and cartographical publications; 3) development of better bibliographic tools; 4) preparation of effective exhibits to strengthen public recognition
of work in these fields; 5) improvement of research and publication standards; and 6) monitoring the cataloging and classification of geographic and cartographic publications in libraries. The Commission could inspect at frequent intervals
the cataloging and classification of new acquisitions in selected major libraries and protest promptly and vigorously
all improper identification of geographical and cartographical

works. This monitoring function might even be extended to solicit the protests of authors and publishers when their works are improperly cataloged in other fields.

To meet the requirements of rapidly growing geography and map libraries throughout the world, two basic objectives must be achieved: 1) librarians should be better acquainted with modern geography; and 2) alternate schedules of classification for geographical and cartographical works, like the one for the new 16th edition of the <u>Dewey Decimal Classification</u>, should be created and put into use. In short, detailed classification of geographical and cartographical works is futile unless library philosophies and procedures can be broadened to recognize and provide for the selection, organization, evaluation and utilization of such works to serve specialists in those fields.

Section III.   Research Rarities

The articles in this section deal with clippings and other ephemeral materials, original manuscripts, and pictures and photographs.   These materials are usually rare and of primary--though not exclusive--interest to researchers and scholars.   Ephemera provide first-hand evidence of how events happened; original manuscripts are the actual pages written to and by famous persons; and pictures and photographs show how their subjects appeared at a given time in history.   The articles in this section relate experiences with these materials in university libraries and special libraries.

On Ephemera: Their Collection and Use
Richard C. Berner

From Library Resources and Technical Services 7:335-9, Fall 1963.   Reprinted by permission.

University and research library acquisitions policies should be geared, in part, to the methods of the intellectual disciplines they are intended to support.   This statement may appear as a truism to many, particularly as acquisitions policy relates to published materials, for in this area collecting may tend to be comprehensive and faithfully reflect research needs.   The principle is, by and large, practiced by most institutions possessing sufficient financial resources to enable them to build research collections of published materials.   However, the acquisition of these materials reflects library support of intellectual disciplines and methods at only one level, and reflects it for the most part (I suspect) without knowing it.   The theoretical implications of such library support tend to be ignored and the librarians, consequently, are inclined to restrict too severely their role in developing research collections.

Often research libraries must collect the actual raw material from which publications, as such, are produced and added to our knowledge.   To do so, they must become involved in the total research process, and, in fact, key their collecting in the process to the methods of the social scientist, historian, and humanist. The relation between historical method and collecting of raw material for the historian's use is demonstrated in this article as a case in point.

Source materials as viewed by the historian are of two broad types, primary and secondary. Primary source materials are created by the actual participants in any event or development. They include manuscripts, printed and processed or near-print items of an ephemeral nature, the more typical ephemera (leaflets, pamphlets, broadsides, and the like), and government documents. Newspapers, because of their contemporaneity, are also regarded as a primary source. Normally, manuscripts and ephemera pose, for the librarian, the most difficult problem of acquisition.

Secondary sources are, for the most part, published items written by non-participants after the event, and are inherently retrospective. By one historical method the historian will explore these before he begins to use systematically the primary sources that bear upon his subject. By his survey of secondary sources he familiarizes himself with the subject at one level: what is known about it formally at a given time. He learns what else needs to be known, he asks questions and establishes working hypotheses. He is then ready to use primary sources; which of these he uses first will depend on a number of factors unique to his particular topic and the nature of the sources available (and their coverage). These factors will not be discussed here. We can assume that he plunges in, usually with the desire to modify historical interpretation in the light of new evidence and fresh considerations. Or, more important, he may select a subject which has been ignored despite its significance. From these primary source materials he will hopefully fulfill his ambition: to tell how things really happened.

If the librarians and archivists have done a responsible job of collecting, there will be an abundance of well organized manuscripts and ephemera available. But how were they acquired? Or if not yet acquired, how can they be?

As slighted as manuscripts are by librarians, they are at least paid homage, for their importance to historians is relatively uncontested. But not ephemera, for they tend to be dismissed as "junk" mail, to be, for a moment of glory, enshrined in a vertical file that is periodically weeded of items for which there is little or no current demand. Often they are received in response to a request by the library that it be placed on the mailing list of a particular corporate body. But experience with mailing lists probably will show conclusively that the privilege does not assure the receipt of

all ephemera produced by the organization.   The privilege
is convenient but deceptive; it is unreliable.   Are there other
methods for acquiring such materials, ones that assure fuller historical documentation of a given event?   We have found
that there are.   To illustrate I will discuss the experience
of the University of Washington Library in collecting manuscripts in the field of electrical power development in the
Pacific Northwest, and show how ephemera can be collected
systematically as part of a manuscripts acquisitions program,
and why their collection should be a prime objective, not
merely a by-product activity.

Hydroelectric power is one of the great natural advantages of the Pacific Northwest; its optimum utilization has
been of economic concern throughout most of this century.
The economic, technological, and scientific features are dis-
tinctively modern, and their impact on politics and economics
and their challenge to public administrators are of vast importance.   Much of the politics of the region cannot be understood without referring to the enduring controversy between
the advocates of publicly owned power and those advocating
private ownership, and to those with different schemes for
public development.   Policies in administering the water resources of the Columbia River Basin are affected by all of
these factors, political and nonpolitical alike.   Influence on
these policies tends, more and more, to be the focus of the
respective partisans, for these policies have inter-regional
(California intertie and a national power grid) and international implications (U.S.--Canadian boundary waters) as well as
effects within the Pacific Northwest itself.   It is clear that
the University of Washington Library had and has now a special responsibility to collect the files of as many of the parties concerned as possible; and in cases where their acquisition was impractical or impossible, it was necessary to coordinate services (in this instance with the National Archives
branch in Seattle, the Bonneville Power Administration in
Portland, and Tacoma Power and Light).

The library had begun collecting in this one field in
1959, by arranging with Seattle City Light to receive the
files of James D. Ross.[1]   Since then the Manuscripts Section of the University of Washington Library has arranged
with the following agencies to be the official depository of
their files: Seattle City Light, Columbia Basin Inter-Agency
Committee, the Northwest Public Power Association, and the
Washington Public Utility Districts' Association, the latter
two groups advocating publicly owned power and charged with
the task of formulating goals, handling research and publicity, and coordinating efforts among their member organiza-

tions.

We have learned from collecting and processing these files that ephemera form an indispensable part of the documentation needed for researchers who are to tell how things really happened and how the present is unfolding.

What kind of ephemera? Well, much of that which is usually regarded as such, but in addition much that falls somewhere between manuscript material and classical ephemeras (pamphlet, leaflet, or broadside material). These marginal ephemera are normally processed material in the form of circular letters, house organs, news releases, minutes of meetings, periodical, technical or special reports, speeches, resolutions, convention proceedings, colloquia and the like. Attention is seldom given to this material by most libraries, yet it is vital to the researcher interested in showing the linkages between political action and public policy, historically or contemporaneously. Without this material, the historian's task of relating the events of his study must remain more speculative than it should, for precise chronology and interconnections depend heavily upon such documentation. With a complete file of circular letters, minutes, and the like he can trace a line of development with greater certainty. True, much will not be determined positively even from this type of material, but the basic relationships can be established. It is to manuscripts the researcher must turn to learn the more subtle aspects of his problem. But manuscripts are often more fragmentary (in a documentary sense) and many times do not provide the consecutiveness that is required. Newspaper reports help in this, but ephemera of the type mentioned lie closer to the participants in an event, and for that reason, more truly reflect their motives, their interplay, and culmination in an actual policy. Manuscripts (correspondence, memoranda, etc) of course are nearest the participants and, when available, they can reduce the speculative element in historical research to its minimum; and when they are less consecutive than they should be, serial and other ephemera produced by corporate bodies, in shaping thought and defining policies, can help fill the void in an integral manner.

Papers of the Washington Public Utility Districts' Association will illustrate the point. The Association, since its formation in 1938, has produced and still produces a number of serial-type ephemera in processed and "slick" forms, as well as separate items. To my knowledge practically none of this has been systematically collected by any library, for much of it was issued primarily for internal use. Our task is to collect it. For example: minutes of meetings are now

mimeographed for internal circulation (many of the early
ones are in manuscript form). A <u>Commissioners Letter</u> was
produced in serial form during the first ten years, first in
mimeographed form, later in slick form. <u>Public Power
News</u> began in newspaper tabloid form, but has been mimeographed and now appears in a slick edition. Mimeographed
ephemera of non-serial type are represented by news releases, reports, articles, and various forms of campaign literature reflecting the formation of public utility districts or
some aspect of the controversy between the advocates of publicly owned and privately owned power. One can see from
these illustrations the interdependence of material and how
this interdependence makes it a logical extension of a manuscripts collecting program.

   The Library's manner of collecting has been three-
fold: to become the official depository for the Washington
Public Utility Districts' Association and thus receive its office files and all of its ephemera; to contact people who have
been active in the organization for their personal files, including the above mentioned ephemera; and to become the official depository for various public utility districts in western Washington. Washington State University is following a
similar policy for public utility districts in eastern Washington.

   From this initial interest in collecting manuscripts
and ephemera relating to hydroelectric power, it was logical
to broaden the scope to include water resources generally.
As the official depository for Columbia Basin Inter-Agency
Committee manuscripts and ephemera (including processed
publications) we have become interested in ephemera produced by comparable agencies: the Missouri Basin Inter-
Agency Committee and Northeastern Resources Committee.
They are all sending us current and back files of their materials. We are also contacting private organizations, analogous to trade associations, and pressure groups. The central principle of acquisitions is clear: to fan out from a
strong core collection in every direction that is a logical extension of it; in a phrase, to build on strength.

   It is clear that the overall objective in this collecting
program is to have the research materials represent as fully
as possible the whole web of activity of these participants in
history-making. Many private power organizations have their
own archives, many of which may be opened to researchers,
ultimately, if not now. The fact that they are presently operating tends to restrict access to their files in a way that
is not true of public power bodies. However, if he is denied
access to all the documentation he feels is desirable, the re-

searcher must then stretch his imagination and be a little more speculative, but he will at least find it possible to tell more truly how things really happened.

Some mention should be made of the private collector of ephemera as a potential source for the institutional repository. Often people will collect everything they can lay hands upon if it ties in with their interests: theater programs, dissident political movements--an endless list of topics. Rich collections can be obtained from such persons, collections that could not otherwise be obtained by the repository.

Lest the reader receive the impression that the author recommends the collection of all ephemera, let it be made clear that collecting should be selective; it cannot reasonably be otherwise. Selectivity should be on the basis of the institution's educational and research objectives. However, selection should be conceived in broad terms that anticipate the future and that are dynamic in the sense that much initiative should come from the library in formulating these goals.

Notes

1. Seattle City Light's first superintendent, 1911-37, and the first administrator of BPA, 1937-39; Seattle City Light and Superintendent Ross were two of the mainstays of the national public power movement in the 1920's and 1930's.

"File 13"
L. O. Lewton

From Special Libraries 57:58, January 1966. Copyright by
Special Libraries Association 1966. Reprinted by permission.

To fulfill its function as a producer of information
the special library of a company or a research organization
must necessarily be a repository of sources of information,
but the question may well be asked "what sources and what
information is it to be a repository of?" Too many library
shelves groan under collections of non-pertinent printed matter that are often sent gratis to the library, not only from
outside sources but also from within the company, and the
librarian is too fearful or too tactful to discard such "gifts."
Mail rooms are frequently instructed to send to the library
all second and third class mail not addressed to an individual. Secretaries of administrators find it much easier to
write "To Library" on such printed matter than make a decision to consign it to a waste basket.

The library thus becomes "File 13" for the company,
and it devolves upon the librarian to wade through this "cats
and dogs" printed matter, either routing it to a possible interested person or having the courage to really consign 99
percent of it to "the circular file." Firmness in delineating
the library's fields of interest and keeping its collections
"on course" is necessary lest shelf space be consumed by
material hardly likely to be productive of the kind of information expected from the library.

In the research library of the Riker Laboratories,
Inc., a part of its Technical Literature Section, this dilem-
ma has been systematically solved by making the informational productivity of the printed matter involved the only criterion for retention, regardless of its origin or source.

Miscellaneous printed matter coming into the library
over a period of 6 months was carefully reviewed, and a
chart was maintained on the character of each, noting the
company source, whether gratis or subscribed to by another
Section, whether regularly or infrequently "donated." The
main type of material received was classified, and a color
coding system set up, using 2 x 4 inch colored cards main-

tained in front of a Rolodex Card File as follows:

> Association, institute and hospital publications--white
> Sample and miscellaneous copies of journals--green
> House organs--yellow
> Annual Reports--orange
> Material for discarding (or to be shown to librarian
> on first receipt)--pink
> Services--(to be filed in appropriate binder)--blue

A decision was then made on the disposition of each title coming in to the library more than once, and an appropriate colored card was made bearing data and source, whether to be retained and for how long or how many issues, whether to be reviewed by librarian, and if to be displayed on a special rack and how shelved. These cards are filed alphabetically in the Rolodex and are constantly consulted by the library clerk sorting such mail.

Current copies of such material, unless specially routed for someone's attention, are displayed on a rack marked "Miscellaneous and Non-circulating Journals," or on another marked "House Organs and Institutional and Services Publications." No attempt is made to log in the material, or, if it is routed, to keep track of it, or to charge it if removed from the display rack, unless at least a year's run is kept.

Periodically all new titles not appearing as yet in the Rolodex File are collected and reviewed by the librarian for making the same decisions regarding discarding, retention, and display.

When several years of some of this incoming material is to be kept, i.e., chiefly house organs, these are shelved in a special section of the journal stacks.

"This works for us" and has kept the Riker Laboratories Library, a pharmaceutical research library, from turning into a financial, an aerospace, an engineering, or "what have you" library.

Snipping Is No Snap
John R. Snider

From Focus on Indiana Libraries 20:7-8, March 1966. Re-printed by permission.

Tucked away in one of the older buildings on the campus of Indiana University in Bloomington is a little known public service that is of use to students, scholars, journalists and anyone else who wants information in depth. With the information explosion of the sixties, the serious researcher, if he intends to probe any subject with more than cursory interest, runs into the problem of what the computer expert would call "information retrieval."

The mass of material on any given subject is not the basic problem. The graduate researcher, or the high school student working on a term paper, can struggle through several months of material. Seldom, if ever, will either one read even a majority of the material available, particularly in the area of public affairs.

To be, for example, a mid-western journalist who seldom gets to Washington, D.C., where one may work with material from the state department or other governmental agencies and have access to the Library of Congress, creates the problem of having to write about such diverse subjects as urban renewal in Indiana, and, perhaps, the rise of Sukarno in Indonesia, without having a good background in the subject.

Both of these subjects are of current interest, but the background material, quotes, dates and events are not repeated in the daily news sources that the journalist will be utilizing. Books on the subjects, if available at all, will not cover all of the material in the manner he wants or needs, since publication dates are behind the most recent developments.

Another resident may want some needed information about a South American country. Perhaps he is being sent there by his employer and needs information on the economics of the country to which he has been assigned, its policies, mores and facilities for various interests he has.

The essential information all these people want is scattered throughout hundreds of publications, making the task of searching out adequate information a time-consuming task.

If each of them could search a library of three hundred publications, some monthly, some quarterly and some daily,
published here in the United States and other countries, check
into the 12,000 pamphlets, booklets and information sheets
that are available, clip out the articles that pertain to his
subject and file them, he would succeed in his task.

It is true, of course, that each of these researchers
does not have the time, nor the facilities, to do the job.

It is also true that this kind of material is not absolutely
necessary for an "adequate" article or story, but it is more
true that the more facts available, the greater the understanding of the subject, the better--the more authoritative--
the article. This means, in turn, either more money for
the article, or a better grade for the high school student.
For the third researcher, it may mean a more rapid acceptance of himself and his family in a strange country, and the
more successful completion of his assigned job.

This problem of "information retrieval" is already
done! All that our three researchers have to do is read
what pertains to their subject--in depth--and take it from
there. This information is theirs for the asking from Bob
Hattery, forty-year-old Ph.D. in International Relations who
heads up the Bureau of Public Discussion on the campus of
Indiana University.

Hattery, who is based in Owen Hall on the campus,
has several hundreds of thousands of pieces of information
on almost any subject you can name. All of it right at his
fingertips. You name it, general or specific, and Hattery or
one of his staff of eleven snipsters and reference experts
will pull hundreds of column inches of material and appropriate illustrations out of the files. It would almost appear
to be magic. It might be, because the extensive files contain some juicy bits of information on magic--black or white,
new and old, telepathy or superstition.

This crew of scissor wielders, contrary to what you
might guess, does not spend its time snipping columns from
newspapers. Less than half-a-dozen papers are snipped
apart, but almost three hundred journals and magazines find
themselves carved into pieces and filed by subject. Contemporary American publications are scanned--and snipped--as
well as English language publications from Germany, the
U.S.S.R., Peking and India. If there was a Mongolian Yak-
herder quarterly printed in English, you would find at least
some of its contents filed in the appropriate places.

The public reference service, which takes up less
space than a small public library, started in 1914. It is
not a well-known service, as evidenced by the only 5000 re-

quests on 3000 subjects during the last fiscal year. Dr. Hattery estimates that about one-third of the requests filled are
from high school students who have teachers who know about
the service, a third from citizens interested in some point
or other and the other third from those who are educators
and need more information to increase their teaching efficiency.

In talking about the future of the reference service,
which, as a function of the Bureau of Public Discussion, is
a part of the I.U. Extension Service, Hattery sees more and
more people making inquiries--more and more often. The
basic reason for this prediction is just this: as more persons receive an advanced education, the more the same people will want--and need--this kind of service. It may be for
personal information, for a talk at the local service club or
participation in one of the seminars which are sponsored by
the same Bureau of Public Discussion.

The staff in Owen Hall can probably handle three to
five times as many requests as they do now, without too
much difficulty. The main problem of acquiring and filing
information is pretty much routine, since the staff can scan,
snip and file rapidly--due to their knowledge and experience.

An inquiry, when it comes in from a new "customer,"
is studied, and analyzed to determine the exact needs of the
person making the inquiry. Is this a matter of general in-
formation--or is the "customer" more interested in some
specificity? Most recipients of what used to be called the
"package library" are quite surprised at the quality of some
of the material they receive in their first "package." The
recipient is expected to pay the return postage after the normal one-month loan period.

Manuscript Collections
Robert L. Brubaker

From Library Trends 13:226-53, October 1964. Copyright 1964 by the University of Illinois Board of Trustees. Reprinted by permission.

Manuscript resources for a study of state and local history are available in a wide variety of institutions in the United States. The largest and most important collections are in major historical societies, university libraries, a few state libraries, larger public libraries, and independent research libraries. Smaller collections can be found in a profusion of local historical societies, historical museums, historic houses, and smaller public libraries.

Collection and preservation of manuscripts have always been important functions of major historical societies. When Jared Sparks, history professor, president of Harvard, and a collector and editor of the papers of George Washington and Benjamin Franklin, wrote in 1826 about the need to save the papers of important men from further neglect and destruction, he suggested that ". . . no better plan could be adopted, than that of societies in the several states expressly established for the purpose."[1] J. Franklin Jameson, then a professor at Brown University, was thinking primarily of manuscripts when he reminded the members of the American Historical Association at the end of the century that ". . . there is no other country in the world in which the libraries of historical societies have so important a place as they have among the libraries of the United States."[2]

American historical societies began collecting manuscripts before the end of the eighteenth century. Jeremy Belknap of the Massachusetts Historical Society wrote to a friend in 1795 that he was ". . . prowling about like a wolf for the prey. . ." for manuscripts and other historical materials for that recently organized society.[3] The New-York Historical Society, the Pennsylvania Historical Society, and societies in several New England states were collecting manuscripts by the time Jared Sparks made his plea for preservation, and other societies were established in the Midwest and the South during the 1830's and 1840's.[4-6] By 1905, thirty-seven major historical societies reported to the Amer-

ican Historical Association that they had manuscript holdings,
and at least four others had deposited manuscripts in another
library.[7]
 Historical societies were the only institutions that
made a sustained effort to collect manuscripts during most
of the nineteenth century. The federal government acquired
the personal papers of a few presidents and statesmen, but
these were stored at the Department of State and (except for
some papers that were published) were not available for research. The Library of Congress acquired a few important
manuscripts after the Civil War, but the Library did not begin an active collecting program until a separate Department
of Manuscripts was created in 1897.[8-9]
 University libraries began collecting manuscripts about
1890, and became most active after about 1920. Harvard
University Library paid little attention to manuscript collecting until 1914, when the Harvard Commission on Western
History began acquiring material on western expansion.[10]
Hubert Howe Bancroft began gathering his private collection
of manuscripts and books during the 1860's, but the University of California did not acquire it until 1907.[11] Duke University Library began extensive manuscript acquisitions in
1929.[11] The Southern Historical Collection was established
as a division of the University of North Carolina Library in
1930, although J.G. de Roulhac Hamilton previously had acquired the nucleus of the collection during his years as head
of the department of history.[12] Indiana University Library
began the large scale acquisition of manuscripts during the
1950's.[13] Collections of personal papers occasionally came
to university libraries during the nineteenth century, but they
usually were unsought and rarely were processed for use.
The collecting programs that enabled the larger university libraries to rival the larger historical societies as manuscript
depositories were twentieth-century phenomena.

Survey of Holdings

 Some perspective on the different institutions that collect manuscripts can be gained through an analysis of the
statistics reported to Philip Hamer in 1960 for his A Guide
to Archives and Manuscripts in the United States.[14] Libraries provided descriptions of their manuscripts and rough estimates of their total holdings, usually by the number of manuscript pieces, but occasionally by linear or cubic feet. A
few libraries did not give estimates of total holdings. To
facilitate comparisons in this paper, linear feet have been
converted into number of pieces by assuming that there are

900 manuscript pieces per linear foot. Archival institutions have been excluded from the totals, although state historical societies that house both the state archives and a manuscript section or department are included.

The size of a library's manuscript holdings, of course, is only one indication of the importance of the library's manuscripts. One southern library, for instance, has a collection of the papers of a single iron works that is over twice as large as the entire manuscript holdings of a midwestern library that specializes in materials on the American Revolution and has one of the most important collections on the subject. Quantity and quality are obviously not synonymous, but statistics on quantity do give some indication of the manuscript resources of the various types of libraries.

Four major sections of the country are mentioned in the following discussion. The Northeast includes New England, the Middle Atlantic States, Delaware, and West Virginia. The Midwest includes the states created from the old Northwest Territory, and Minnesota, Iowa, Missouri, Kansas, and Nebraska. The South extends to Arkansas and Texas. The West includes North and South Dakota, Oklahoma, and the states farther west. As thus defined, the states in the Midwest all achieved statehood by 1867, while those in the West, except for California, Oregon, Nevada, and Colorado, did not achieve statehood until after 1888.

Thirty-three libraries reported to Hamer that they had one million or more manuscripts each. At least six other libraries that did not report totals probably had holdings as large as this, and some libraries have undoubtedly reached the one million mark since 1960. Among the libraries that probably had one million or more manuscripts in 1960 were twelve major historical societies, twenty university libraries, six major public, state and independent research libraries, and the Library of Congress.

A number of other libraries had at least 500,000 but less than one million manuscripts. These included five historical societies, two university libraries, and two other libraries.

The Library of Congress, which had over sixteen million manuscripts in 1960 and now has over twenty million, is the largest manuscript depository in the country. The New York Public Library and Yale University,[15] which had about nine million manuscripts each, appear to have the next largest accumulations. Six other libraries reported that they had at least four million manuscripts. Among these were the Historical Society of Pennsylvania, the State Historical Society of Wisconsin, and the libraries at Princeton University,

the University of Virginia, the University of Pennsylvania,
and the University of Oklahoma.

The most extensive system of manuscript collecting
by historical societies, university libraries, and a few state
and public libraries is found in the Northeast, with neither
historical societies nor university libraries clearly dominant.
Large manuscript depositories are particularly numerous in
New York and Pennsylvania. The New York Public Library,
the New York State Library, the libraries of Cornell University, the University of Rochester, and probably Columbia
University, each contain over one million manuscripts. The
New-York Historical Society has about 750,000 manuscripts.[16]
Four libraries in Pennsylvania contain at least one million
manuscripts each. These are the Historical Society of Penn-
sylvania, the University of Pennsylvania Library, the Pennsylvania Historical and Museum Commission, and the Friends
Historical Library at Swarthmore College.

Elsewhere in the Northeast historical societies are
dominant in collecting manuscripts pertaining to local and regional history, although several university libraries have extensive collections of manuscripts on other subjects. The
Massachusetts Historical Society, the Connecticut Historical
Society, libraries at Yale, Harvard, and Princeton universities, and the University of West Virginia have over one
million manuscripts, and the New Hampshire Historical Society has over 500,000 pieces. Four other historical societies
in the Northeast have less than 500,000 manuscripts, and two
did not report their total holdings.

Historical societies dominate manuscript collecting in
most of the Midwest. The Ohio Historical Society, the Western Reserve Historical Society, the Illinois State Historical
Library, the Missouri Historical Society, the Minnesota Historical Society, the Nebraska State Historical Society, the
State Historical Society of Wisconsin, and probably the State
Historical Society of Iowa each have over one million manuscripts. Indiana University, with over one million manuscripts, has the largest collection in Indiana, although some
collecting is done by the Indiana State Library and the Indiana Historical Society. The Historical Society of Michigan is
the only major historical society in the Midwest that has not
collected manuscripts. The largest manuscript depositories
in Michigan are the Michigan Historical Collections at the
University of Michigan and the Burton Historical Collection
at the Detroit Public Library, both of which contain over one
million manuscripts. The William L. Clements Library at
the University of Michigan is also highly respected for its
holdings of eighteenth and nineteenth-century manuscripts.

The only other libraries in the Midwest with one million manuscripts or more are the Newberry Library (Chicago) and the University of Chicago Library. Historical societies play a secondary role today in manuscript collecting in the South. Numerous societies were established during the nineteenth century, and those in Virginia, Maryland, South Carolina, Georgia, and Texas have had a continuous existence.[17] All of these have important accumulations of manuscripts, but they are relatively small compared to the holdings of six major university libraries and several state departments of archives and history.

The Maryland Historical Society is the only society in the South that reported over one million manuscripts in 1960. The Virginia Historical Society is highly respected for its research facilities and publications, but it had only about 500,000 manuscripts. Other major historical societies in South Carolina, Georgia, Kentucky, Tennessee, and Louisiana had considerably less than 500,000 manuscripts each.

Some southern historical societies have given their manuscripts to other institutions. The Alabama Historical Society gave its holdings to the Alabama Department of Archives and History when the latter was founded in 1901,[18] and the Mississippi Historical Society followed this example the next year when the Mississippi Department of Archives and History was established.[19] The Historical Society of North Carolina gave its manuscripts to the University of North Carolina for inclusion in the Southern Historical Collections,[12] and the Texas State Historical Association has deposited its manuscripts in the University of Texas Library.[14] The Florida Historical Society's collections are now administered by the University of South Florida Library at Tampa,[20] and the Tennessee Historical Society plans to have its manuscripts processed by the Tennessee State Library and Archives.[21]

The major impetus to manuscript collecting in the South was provided in the twentieth century by J.G. de Roulhac Hamilton, who traveled throughout the section acquiring materials for the Southern Historical Collection at the University of North Carolina. Partly because Hamilton showed what could be done, both historical societies and universities began collecting more extensively.[22] Four university libraries now have holdings of over three million manuscripts each, and two others have at least one million manuscripts. These include the University of Virginia, the University of North Carolina, Duke University, the University of South Carolina, Louisiana State University, and the University of Texas. As Thomas D. Clark stated in 1953, "The South has come a long way in 50 years in the preservation of its records."[23]

Nearly every western state has a state historical society that collects manuscripts. Many of the state universities and a few other libraries also do some collecting.
With a few important exceptions, however, all of these libraries have extremely small holdings.

In 1910 the secretary of the Nevada Historical Society
advanced several reasons for the paucity of historical materials then in western libraries. She pointed out that the West
was more recently settled, that the migratory habits of west-
erners had destroyed much that once existed, and that the
inhabitants of the region did not yet consider history important. "Unlike the East, " she continued, "we have no pros-
pect of large private endowments; unlike the central region,
we have no certain support from the State. "[24]

There is greater public and private support for western historical agencies today, but only two university libraries and an independent research library have holdings of
manuscripts comparable to those of larger libraries in the
East and Midwest.

None of the western historical societies reported having as many as 500,000 manuscripts in 1960. Only the Historical Society of Colorado and the State Historical Society of
North Dakota had as many as 400,000 manuscripts. Historical societies in California, Idaho, Montana, Oregon, and
Washington had approximately 100,000 items or less, and
societies in Nevada, Oklahoma, South Dakota, and Utah did
not report totals. The Historical Society of New Mexico deposited its manuscripts some years ago in the Museum of
New Mexico, which recently transferred them to the New
Mexico State Records Center and Archives.[25] The Wyoming
State Historical Society leaves manuscript collecting to the
Wyoming State Archives and Historical Department.

The same situation prevails in most other western libraries. The Bancroft Library at the University of California, the University of Oklahoma, and the Henry E. Huntington Library in California are each well past the one million
mark. All other western libraries, however, reported totals
of less than 500,000 manuscripts each.

Many libraries in the United States have manuscript
holdings ranging from a few items to 500,000 manuscripts.
Among these are twenty-one major historical societies. Thirteen societies reported that they had at least 100,000 but less
than 500,000, five had more than 10,000 but less than
100,000, and three had less than 5,000 manuscripts in 1960.
Twelve major historical societies gave no estimates of total
holdings.

Approximately 780 other libraries reported to Hamer

that they had less than 500,000 manuscripts in 1960. These figures do not include ethnic and religious historical societies, archival institutions, seminaries, and medical and scientific libraries. Approximately 390 of the 780 libraries are located in the Northeast, 190 in the Midwest, 110 in the South, and 90 in the West. About 260 are colleges and universities, 200 are local historical societies, 90 are historical museums or historic houses, 220 are public libraries, and less than 20 are state libraries. The vast majority have extremely small manuscript holdings. About 320 libraries reported that they have less than 1,000 manuscripts. Another 220 did not provide estimates of total holdings, but the descriptions in Hamer indicate that most of them have less than 1,000 items. Fifty libraries reported holdings as large as 25,000 manuscripts per library, and the holdings of about 200 libraries ranged from 1,000 to less than 25,000 manuscripts.

College and university libraries with moderate quantities of manuscripts are located in all sections of the country. There are approximately 75 college and university libraries in the Northeast with less than 500,000 manuscripts, 80 in the Midwest, 60 in the South, and 45 in the West. About 25 of these have over 25,000 manuscripts, 55 have holdings ranging from 1,000 to 25,000 items, 75 have less than 1,000 manuscripts, and 105 did not report estimates.

Local historical societies with manuscript holdings are located mostly in the Northeast and the Midwest. About 135 societies in the Northeast, 50 in the Midwest, 10 in the South, and 5 in the West have some manuscripts. A few societies have fairly sizeable holdings. About 10 societies have over 25,000 manuscripts each and 80 have holdings ranging from 1,000 to 25,000 manuscripts. Approximately 65 of the 90 societies that have at least 1,000 manuscripts are located in the Northeast, and 15 are located in the Midwest.

Approximately 40 historical museums and historic houses in the Northeast, 20 in the Midwest, 10 in the South, and 20 in the West have small holdings of manuscripts. Only 30 of them have as many as 1,000 items.

Public libraries with small holdings of manuscripts are also concentrated heavily in the Northeast. Approximately 135 public libraries in the Northeast, 40 in the Midwest, 25 in the South, and 20 in the West have holdings of less than 500,000 manuscripts. Only about 45 of these libraries reported that they had over 1,000 manuscripts, and about 135 public libraries reported that they had less than 1,000 manuscripts each.

Only a few state libraries collect private manuscripts.

Four state libraries in the Northeast in addition to the New
York State Library, three in the Midwest, four in the South,
and three in the West reported manuscript holdings to Hamer.
Seven state libraries either did not give estimates for their
total holdings or did not give separate estimates for private
manuscripts and archival materials.   Only one of the others
had over 25,000 manuscripts.   Five state libraries reported
total holdings of between 1,000 and 25,000 manuscripts, and
one had less than 1,000 manuscripts.

The size of the manuscript holdings of the various libraries has been affected by at least nine major factors.
The length of time that a library has collected manuscripts,
its total economic resources, and the goals of the library
with the resulting allocation of available funds are of obvious
importance.   Also of some importance are the length of time
that a state has been settled and the extent to which its inhabitants are aware that manuscript materials are important
and should be preserved.

Three factors have been crucial: whether a library
has had one or more directors who were intensely interested
in collecting manuscripts, whether the collecting program has
been active or passive in nature, and whether there are near-
by institutions with strong collections of manuscripts and vigorous collecting programs.   One can often find periods of
rapid growth or stagnation in collecting that resulted primarily from a particular individual's interest or apathy.   An institution that prepares a file of leads to possible sources of
manuscripts and employs staff members to travel through the
state to examine and acquire them will build its manuscript
holdings more rapidly than an institution that relies primarily
on chance information about the existence of manuscripts.
When other institutions are able to obtain most of the manuscripts of a region, a historical society may decide to devote
its resources to publication, a historical museum, school
services, or some of the other important functions of historical societies.   Other libraries may make similar decisions.

Finally, the quantity of a library's manuscript resources will depend on the extent to which the library seeks
bulky twentieth-century collections.   A library that specializes in eighteenth-century and early nineteenth-century manuscripts will inevitably accumulate a smaller quantity than a
library that attempts to preserve important twentieth-century
materials.

Scope of Collections

Major historical societies usually collect manuscripts

pertaining to the state in which the society is located. Some
of the early private societies followed the example of the
Massachusetts Historical Society, whose first constitution
called for the collection of manuscripts and other historical
materials that helped to ". . . mark the genius, delineate
the manners, and trace the progress of society in the United
States."[26] Most societies have since adopted a more limited
collecting policy, although they sometimes continue acquisitions in special fields of general American history in which
they are strong. The New-York Historical Society, for instance, collects primary material on slavery, travels in
America before 1850, the Civil War, naval and military history through 1898, and circus history, as well as New York
history.[27] The constitutions of most state historical societies specified from the beginning that they were to collect
manuscripts concerning their respective states, although
these limitations were frequently ignored, particularly when
there was no collecting program in a neighboring state.

Despite the statewide focus of their collection policies,
most major historical societies have sizeable quantities of
manuscripts pertaining to other states. These manuscripts
usually concern the region in which the state is located, but
frequently concern distant states. This results partly from
broader collection policies in the past, and partly from the
nature of most manuscript collections. The papers of a relatively obscure family in Illinois, for example, contain letters from a son describing an overland trip to California and
gold mining in 1849, and letters from another relative who
was a merchant in Pennsylvania. Families and individuals
move from one state to another, and men who become prominent on a national or even a state level usually correspond
with men of similar interests in other states. Few manuscript collections of any importance are exclusively concerned
with one state.

Within their geographical limitations, major historical
societies now collect manuscripts on a broad variety of subjects. At the end of the nineteenth century, professional historians criticized historical societies for being preoccupied
with the period of settlement, the colonial or territorial period, early statehood, and with political and military matters.[28] Many societies are still strongest in these areas,
but most societies now collect materials for social, intellectual, economic, agricultural, business, and recent history.
One of the most extensive collection programs has been that
at the State Historical Society of Wisconsin, which has carried out special projects to collect manuscripts pertaining to
business history, labor history, education, medicine, and

mass communications with the aid of grants from the University of Wisconsin, the Rockefeller Foundation, the state Medical Society, and the state Federation of Labor.[29]

When the Library of Congress began collecting manuscripts actively at the end of the nineteenth century, the Library sought to avoid competition with other libraries. Herbert Putnam, then the Librarian of Congress, suggested in 1901 that material pertaining to particular states or localities should be collected by local libraries, but that anything pertaining to the origin, history, and operations of the federal government should be left to the Library of Congress.[30] Later policy statements were similar, except that the Library's interests expanded beyond government and politics. A statement in 1950 expressed interest in acquiring ". . . papers of individuals or families or records of organizations that have played significant roles on a national scale, " and particularly ". . . material of national significance in such fields as government and politics, diplomatic and military affairs, literature, music, and aeronautics. . . ."[31]

Many major historical societies, nevertheless, have substantial quantities of manuscripts that are of national significance. Some of these were accumulated before the Library of Congress began collecting manuscripts on a major scale. Even today, however, many administrators do not accept, without some reservations, the thesis that state historical societies should limit themselves to materials of state or local significance.[32] Important national events or developments usually take place within particular states, and the papers of nationally prominent individuals and organizations are often vitally important to the study of a state's history. When a man has been both governor of his state and an important United States Senator, therefore, the location of his papers is likely to depend on whether a major historical society, a university, or the Library of Congress approached his heirs first. The prestige of having family papers in the Library of Congress, however, often gives that Library a decided advantage.

The collection policies of many state universities are quite similar to those of major historical societies, although universities usually acquire manuscripts concerning English and American literature as well as manuscripts concerning the history of the state or a part of the state in which the university is located. Some major private and state universities acquire manuscripts concerning a region rather than a state. Harvard, Yale, and the Bancroft Library at the University of California have important collections concerning the Far West, and the manuscripts at Duke University and

the University of North Carolina pertain to the entire South.
Many major universities also have substantial collections relating to the history of early and modern Europe, Asia, Lat-
in America, and general American history.

There is inevitably some competition in manuscript
collecting between historical societies, other libraries, and
private collectors.   There have been occasional complaints
from historical societies about competition with the Library
of Congress. [32]   A questionnaire returned by major historical
societies in 1962, however, indicated that they encounter competition with universities and other local libraries more frequently than with the Library of Congress. [33]

Cooperative agreements have occasionally been worked
out to reduce competition.   In New Jersey, for example, the
state historical society, the state university, a major public
library, and several of the larger local historical societies
agreed on specialized areas of collection. [34]   Elsewhere, the
State Historical Society of Missouri participated in a joint
collecting project with the library and the department of history at the University of Missouri. [35]   Joint collection programs between two different manuscript depositories are rare,
but informal agreements similar to the one in New Jersey
exist in other states.

Although efforts have been made to reduce competition,
there is by no means general agreement that competition is
wholly undesirable.   One undesirable consequence of competition, at least from the point of view of libraries, is that
competition increases the price of manuscripts.   (Most libraries acquire the vast majority of their manuscripts
through donations, but some manuscripts that are otherwise
unobtainable are purchased.)   Cooperative agreements are desirable because they ensure that manuscripts are placed in
the most appropriate library.   But lack of competition can
mean that the libraries in an area are neglecting their responsibilities, and that manuscripts remain in private hands,
frequently disintegrating from lack of proper care.   L. Quincy Mumford, the present Librarian of Congress, conceded in
1956 that there is considerable competition between the Library of Congress and other libraries, but he believed that
competition is ". . . healthy for the reason that it provides
the surest guarantee of the survival and preservation of historic papers. "[32]   Similar attitudes have been expressed by
administrators in historical societies and university libraries. [36-37]

Staff

          Numerous monographs have discussed the administra-
tion of manuscripts during the last several decades. Most
of this literature, however, does not attempt to discover the
extent to which recommended policies and procedures are
actually practiced by major libraries, and much of the information about specific libraries is no longer current.
          In order to obtain systematic current information, the
author sent a questionnaire to forty-seven major historical
societies and fifteen major universities. All of the major
historical societies that reported manuscript holdings to Hamer were queried. Only major university libraries with holdings of at least one million manuscripts were included.
Questionnaires also were sent to fifteen other libraries with
extensive manuscript holdings. Forty-one historical societies, fourteen university libraries, and twelve other libraries returned the questionnaire. Eleven of the responding historical societies are located in the Northeast, thirteen in the
Midwest, six in the South, and eleven in the West. 38
          Information was requested about the size of the staff
working with manuscripts, the nature of the card catalog and
other published and unpublished guides to manuscripts, and
policies on the use of manuscripts, literary rights, and
photoduplication. Most questions could be answered with one
word, but five required brief descriptions. Manuscript specialists in the various libraries filled out most of the questionnaires, but a few were answered by head librarians or
directors.
          Eighteen of the forty-one historical societies and all
of the fourteen university libraries reported that they have a
curator of manuscripts or a manuscript librarian devoting
full time to manuscripts (other titles are used in some libraries). Four of the societies with full-time manuscript
specialists are located in the Northeast, ten in the Midwest,
two in the South, and two in the West. Only two societies
with one million or more manuscripts, one in the Midwest
and one in the South, reported that they do not have a full-
time specialist. These societies and the other twenty-one
societies with smaller accumulations rely on one or more
staff members who spend part of their time on manuscripts.
In some societies one librarian does all of the work in the
library, including care of manuscripts. Eleven societies
rely partly on volunteer workers to process manuscripts, but
none relies entirely on volunteers. All but one of the university libraries have part-time student help available from
time to time, but only eight historical societies have any stu-

dent assistance.

A few libraries have had manuscript curators or librarians for long periods of time, but in most libraries this specialization is a relatively recent development.   The State Historical Society of Wisconsin has had a manuscript librarian for about sixty years, and the Historical Society of Pennsylvania has had one for about fifty years.   Libraries that have had a manuscript curator or librarian for at least forty years include the Minnesota Historical Society, the New York Public Library, the American Antiquarian Society, and the Henry E. Huntington Library at San Marino, California.   Two historical societies and one university library have had manuscript specialists for about thirty years, three historical societies and nine university libraries have had specialists for periods of ten to twenty-five years, two historical societies and one university library have had specialists for periods of five to nine years, and six historical societies have had specialists for less than five years.   A few libraries did not indicate how long they have had manuscript specialists.

The manuscript staff in most libraries is relatively small.   The State Historical Society of Wisconsin has six to eight full-time staff members for its Division of Archives and Manuscripts, and the Kansas State Historical Society has a staff of five for such a combined operation.   One university library reported that it has a full-time staff of six, one has a full-time staff of five, and two university libraries have a full-time staff of four.   Three historical societies and five university libraries reported a full-time staff of three, and four historical societies and three universities have a full-time staff of two.   The other libraries do not have a full-time assistant for the manuscript curator or librarian, although many have part-time assistants.

Most libraries undoubtedly need a larger manuscript staff than they now have.   A questionnaire circulated in 1944 to some of the larger historical societies revealed that nearly all of them had large backlogs of unprocessed manuscripts.[39]   The author's present questionnaire did not specifically ask for such information, but several societies commented that 30 percent or more of their manuscripts are not yet adequately cataloged.

The State Historical Society of Wisconsin furnishes one of the best examples of the backlog that can accumulate when a society exerts itself to obtain twentieth-century materials.   In the early 1950's, a staff of two professionals and one half-time student assistant processed from 15,000 to 25,000 pieces annually.   Because of the numerous collection projects, manuscript accessions increased to an average of

over 200,000 pieces per year during the 1950's. By revising processing methods and adding two full-time staff members and several part-time assistants, the Society was processing 300,000 to 500,000 pieces per year during the early
1960's. Nevertheless, the Society still had a large backlog
of unprocessed materials.[40]

Most libraries acquire less than 200,000 manuscript
items per year, but annual accessions of 100,000 items are
not uncommon. The papers of a single major public figure
frequently contain over 200,000 items. The small manuscript staffs characteristic of most libraries serve as a bar
to large-scale acquisition of twentieth-century materials, and
make it inevitable that most libraries will continue to have
large quantities of unprocessed manuscripts in the foreseeable future.

Catalogs

The best recent discussion of manuscript cataloging is
in Lucile Kane's A Guide to the Care and Administration of
Manuscripts.[41] Her discussion was based partly on the "Rules
for Descriptive Cataloging in the Library of Congress. . .for
Collections of Manuscripts,"[42] distributed to libraries in
1954 to help standardize cataloging and facilitate submission
of entries to the projected National Union Catalog of Manuscript Collections. Paul S. Dunkin's[43] article in an earlier
issue of Library Trends is another useful discussion of
changes in cataloging procedures. Kane and Dunkin provide
bibliographies of writings on the subject up to 1960. Several
other articles have been published since that time.[44-46]

A few decades ago the ideal, if not the reality, was
that card catalogs to manuscripts should contain at least three
cards for each manuscript piece or item in a collection.
These included cards for author, recipient, and date, and
sometimes added entries for subjects. Such a system was
suggested in manuals published by the Library of Congress in
1934[47] and by the Minnesota Historical Society in 1936.[48]

The mounting pressures of unprocessed manuscripts
soon forced most libraries to devise methods of group description for most manuscript collections. This method generally includes a main entry containing a brief description of
an entire collection, added entries for authors and subjects
(the number depending on the size, nature, and importance
of a collection), and occasionally analytical entries for particularly important individual items. A few libraries still retain the ideal of individual item cataloging for all collections,
and many libraries use this method for particularly impor-

tant collections.   Individual manuscripts that are not part of
a collection, of course, must be cataloged separately.

The "Rules for Collections of Manuscripts" distributed
by the Library of Congress suggested the form and type of
information to be included on the main entry.   Added entries
for authors, as developed by other libraries, generally consist of one card for any one author of incoming correspondence in a collection, citing the inclusive dates and the total
number of letters by that author.   Because of the large number of relatively insignificant correspondents in most collections, added entries for authors are usually prepared only
for authors of numerous letters and for single items by more
prominent correspondents.   Added entries for subjects are
generally used more sparingly than added entries for authors.

Because large manuscript collections are frequently so
complex that the main entry in the card catalog can provide
at best only a superficial description, libraries have also developed various types of more detailed guides to individual
collections, usually available at libraries in typescript, and
sometimes published for distribution to other libraries.   An
early form of guide was the calendar, which contained descriptions of individual letters or documents arranged chronologically.   Another form was the author index, listing the
specific dates rather than the inclusive dates of all letters by
each author.   A more usual form of guide today is the register, or inventory, which contains biographical data and descriptions of manuscripts by containers rather than by individual items.   Such guides sometimes contain information similar to that found in calendars and author indexes.

Main entries similar to those suggested by the Library
of Congress are used by twenty-four of the major historical
societies and nine of the universities that replied to the questionnaire.   The systems in several of these libraries, though
similar to that suggested by the Library of Congress, were
developed long before 1954.   Some libraries use the printed
cards prepared for the National Union Catalog of Manuscript
Collections and distributed by the Library of Congress.
Most of the other libraries use a system of group description utilizing a main entry and added entries, although the
form and type of information may differ from that suggested
by the Library of Congress rules.

Individual item cataloging for all collections is still
used by five major historical societies, four in the Northeast
and one in the Midwest.   One society in the Northeast uses
the collection cards provided by the National Union Catalog
of Manuscript Collections and makes temporary collection
cards until they arrive, but the society also catalogs each

piece by author, recipient, and (for the period before 1800)
date. One society has only about 1 percent of its manuscripts cataloged, but the society uses individual item cataloging for recent accessions and hopes to treat the backlog
in the same way. Another society has about 60 percent of
its manuscripts cataloged. Individual item cataloging for
some of the more important collections is used by two other
societies in the Northeast and two in the South.

Added entries for authors of incoming correspondence
are prepared by thirty historical societies and all but one of
the university libraries that answered the questionnaire. Libraries that do individual item cataloging, of course, are not
included in these totals. One society in the Northeast, one
in the Midwest, two in the South, and four in the West do
not prepare added entries for authors.

Added entries for subjects are prepared by thirty-five
of the historical societies, and all but two of the university
libraries. Six societies, however, prepare subject entries
only to a limited extent. Such entries are not prepared by
one society in the Northeast, one in the Midwest, three in
the South, and two in the West.

Twenty-five historical societies and all but one of the
university libraries have unpublished guides to manuscripts
in addition to a card catalog. Eight societies mentioned calendars, four said that they have author indexes to a few collections, and the remaining libraries have inventories, registers, or other types of unpublished guides. Some libraries
have calendars and author indexes for a few collections, but
inventories and registers for the rest. Unpublished guides
are not available in four historical societies in the Northeast,
three in the Midwest, one in the South, and eight in the West.

Replies to the questionnaire indicate that many libraries have too limited a manuscript staff even to prepare an
adequate card catalog based on the principles of group description. The situation is rarely as desperate as that at
one western historical society, where the librarian lamented
that "our manuscripts are in a deplorable condition and have
been neglected for years. I don't think any work has ever
been done on them." But eight out of forty-one societies reported that they prepare no added entries for authors, seven
societies prepare none for subjects, and sixteen have no unpublished guides to large collections. Even among the libraries that do prepare such entries and guides, the adequacy
of the card catalog varies considerably. Several librarians
commented that they consider their card catalogs for manuscripts quite inadequate. Not until funds are available for
increased staffs, however, can improvements be expected.

Manuscripts pertaining to almost any subject of research are scattered about the country, often in libraries where scholars would never think of looking.[49] For many years historical societies and other libraries have publicized recent manuscript accessions in their own journals and news bulletins, and frequently in such publications as the <u>Mississippi Valley Historical Review</u>. Many libraries have also published comprehensive guides to their entire manuscript holdings, since few scholars can take the time to look through hundreds of statements concerning annual accessions. The majority of the comprehensive guides to manuscripts have been published since 1940, although some libraries published such guides earlier.[50]

Ten of the major historical societies have published comprehensive guides to their manuscript collections. The Virginia Historical Society published a guide in 1901, which has not yet been revised. The State Historical Society of Wisconsin published one guide in 1906, a second guide in 1944, and a supplement in 1957. The Minnesota Historical Society published a guide in 1935 and a revision in 1955. Other guides were published by the Oregon Historical Society in 1940, the New-York Historical Society in 1941, the Historical Society of Pennsylvania in 1949, the Ohio Historical Society in 1953, the Kentucky Historical Society in 1955, and the New Jersey Historical Society in 1957. The South Carolina Historical Society published a guide in a ten-part series in its journal between 1944 and 1947. Other societies have published less detailed guides, usually ten to fifteen pages in length, in their journals. These guides are listed in Hamer's <u>A Guide to Archives and Manuscripts in the United States</u>.[14]

Most of the universities with one million or more manuscripts have published comprehensive guides to their holdings. The University of North Carolina, Duke University, the University of Rochester, and Louisiana State University published comprehensive guides during the 1940's, and Columbia University, Yale University, and the University of Oklahoma did so during the 1950's. Bancroft Library at the University of California, the University of Michigan, and West Virginia University have published guides since 1960. Guides have also been prepared by colleges and universities with smaller accumulations of manuscripts. Four of the major universities that answered the questionnaire, however, have never published comprehensive guides to their manuscripts.

Partly because many manuscript depositories have never been able to publish comprehensive guides to their manuscripts, it has long been apparent that a national union catalog would greatly simplify the task of locating pertinent

manuscript materials. Plans for such a catalog were developed during the early 1950's,[51] and with the aid of a grant
from the Council on Library Resources, the Library of Congress began the work that culminated in the publication of the
first three volumes of The National Union Catalog of Manuscript Collections (NUCMC) by early 1964.[52]

The usefulness of a national union catalog of manuscripts depends partly on the number of manuscript depositories that submit entries. A national union catalog of books
can be useful even though a relatively small percentage of
the total number of libraries in the country participate, because most titles will be found in at least one of the reporting libraries. Since manuscripts are unique, complete coverage can be obtained only if all manuscript depositories
participate in the project.

Most of the historical societies and university libraries that answered the present writer's questionnaire plan to
participate in the National Union Catalog of Manuscript Collections, but a few do not. Twenty-three historical societies
and nine of the universities had submitted entries by September 1963, and most of the others expect to do so in the near
future. Six historical societies and two universities said
they have no present intention of participating.

Two of the societies that do not plan to participate
are located in the Northeast, and four are in the West. One
has about 500,000 manuscripts and has had a manuscript librarian for about one year. The others have less than
100,000 manuscripts and have extremely small staffs. Both
of the universities have published comprehensive guides to
their holdings, and they apparently believe that participation
in the NUCMC is unnecessary for that reason. None of the
six historical societies has published a comprehensive guide.

The NUCMC will ease some of the burdens of scholarship immensely, even without information on the holdings of
libraries that cannot submit entries because of inadequate
staffs. Also, the NUCMC staff will probably be busy for
some years to come with processing entries submitted by libraries that are already participating. If the NUCMC is ever
to approach completeness, however, some means of assistance, through grants or otherwise, will have to be devised
for those libraries that are unable to prepare their own entries.

Use of Materials

Libraries have placed various restrictions on the use
of manuscripts in the past, usually because manuscripts are

unique, irreplaceable, and often fragile, sometimes because
of conditions imposed by donors, and occasionally because
sensational use of material might discourage potential donors
from giving other collections to a library.   Howard H. Peckham has said in an earlier issue of Library Trends that the
obligation to preserve and the need to keep out thieves and
persons who mutilate manuscripts means that a prospective
reader should be able to identify himself.   Peckham continued: "Many librarians and archivists go further: they prefer or insist that the user of manuscripts be a competent
scholar.   Their logic is that since manuscripts are non-ex-
pendable, they should be handled by as few readers as possible, and certainly the competent scholar should have priority over the idly curious, the unprepared, or the reader with
a trivial purpose. "53
     The author's questionnaire sought to ascertain the ex-
tent of this attitude by requesting a brief description of each
library's restrictions on who can use manuscripts.   Libraries were specifically asked whether manuscripts can be used
by graduate students, undergraduates, local historians, and
genealogists.
     All but two of the historical societies and all of the
university libraries indicated that they do not restrict the use
of their manuscripts to scholars and graduate students (two
groups that overlap in part), although many libraries do prefer that manuscripts be used only for serious research.
Twenty-seven historical societies and seven universities said
that any of the named categories can use manuscripts or that
there are no restrictions except those occasionally imposed
by donors.   One western historical society interpreted the
laws governing the society to mean that the society is required to allow anyone to use manuscripts under any circumstances.   Four other historical societies and five universities
indicated that there are no restrictions on any of the specified
groups of persons per se, although use of manuscripts is
limited to anyone with a "serious or legitimate interest, " a
"bona fide purpose, " a "legitimate research request, " or to
"any serious researcher. "
     Several libraries said that manuscripts are usually not
made available to genealogists, and some libraries that mentioned a serious or legitimate purpose probably discourage
genealogists from using many manuscript collections.   The
general attitude, however, appears to be similar to that of
the librarian of an eastern university, who said: "Local historians and genealogists are granted access to manuscript
collections if they appear to need them and can use them
with profit.   My experience is that local historians and gen-

ealogists show more respect for manuscripts than many advanced scholars and research workers. Why discourage them?"

The criteria mentioned by other libraries were varied. The manuscripts of one historical society in a major metropolitan area in the East are open to any adult who has proper identifying credentials, can offer a satisfactory explanation of why he is interested, and can prove through conversation that he has performed preliminary research and is familiar with his subject. One midwestern society said that journalists who are looking for a "hot story" are occasionally "restricted by subterfuge," and that certain manuscript dealers and collectors are discouraged from using collections when the staff does not have time to watch them closely.

In general, libraries with restrictions almost invariably make manuscripts available to college and university faculty, graduate students working on theses or dissertations, and others who are working on articles or books for publication, but they will examine requests for use by undergraduates and others a little more carefully before making a decision.

One important problem for libraries and users of manuscripts is the question of common-law literary property rights. In a discussion of the application of these rights to private correspondence, Ralph Shaw has said that they are the means by which the author of a letter ". . . or his heirs in perpetuity, may, under normal circumstances, prevent the publication of his letter, or, in rarer circumstances, may first publish it."[54] Unlike statutory copyright, common-law literary property rights are perpetual and are terminated only by "general publication."[55] Some courts have held that the deposit of correspondence and other unpublished writings in a library where they can be read by the general public constitutes "general publication" and terminates literary rights. Courts have not ruled consistently, however, and there has been no clear test case in the federal courts.[56]

Because of the uncertainties concerning literary rights, libraries have often been urged to request donors to dedicate to the public whatever literary rights the donor may have in a collection. Otherwise scholars must face the onerous task of locating hundreds of authors and their heirs to obtain permission to quote, or they must publish with the threat of a possible lawsuit hanging over their heads. The problem is most acute with twentieth-century collections; there is considerably less likelihood of legal action resulting from publication of earlier materials. A committee of the American Historical Association recommended in 1951 that libraries should make every effort to persuade donors to surrender literary property rights.[57] David C. Mearns, chief of the manuscript division at the Library of Congress, said in an earlier issue of Library Trends that, whenever practicable, instruments of gift should include a dedication of literary property rights.[58] Libraries have been requested to include information concerning literary rights in entries submitted to The National Union Catalog of Manuscript Collections.[42]

The vast majority of American libraries have totally ignored recommendations that they secure dedications of literary property rights. Only eight of the forty-one historical societies, two of the fourteen university libraries, and seven of the other fifteen libraries now make any attempt to secure such a statement.

Most libraries that request the surrender of literary property rights began doing so after about 1945. The Chicago Historical Society and Louisiana State University have requested surrender of literary rights for about fifteen years, the Kentucky Historical Society has done so for about thirteen years, and the State Historical Society of Wisconsin has done so for about ten years. The Buffalo Historical Society, the Ohio Historical Society, the Illinois State Historical Library, and the Utah State Historical Society have sought surrender of literary rights within the last five years. The Virginia Historical Society reported that it has made such a request for over a century.

Other historical societies will probably begin requesting surrender of literary rights during the next decade. A successful lawsuit, upheld by the federal courts, against a scholar for failing to secure permission from an author or his heirs to quote letters consulted in a library would undoubtedly spur other libraries into acceptance of the practice. To guard against such a lawsuit, however, scholars must continue to do over and over what libraries could do once and for all when a manuscript collection first enters a library.

During recent years there have been frequent recommendations that libraries permit more extensive microfilming of their manuscript collections. Most libraries have long provided researchers with photocopies of a few items or parts of collections. Many libraries, however, have been reluctant to provide a microfilm of an entire manuscript collection to another library, particularly when a collection was acquired through purchase.

A committee on manuscripts appointed by the American Historical Association urged in 1951 that ". . . it is of the utmost importance now and will be increasingly necessary

in the future to permit the filming of large groups of manuscripts in order to make them available elsewhere. [59] The
attitude of many librarians, however, was expressed by
Howard H. Peckham when he said, "I think service is carried to an unfortunate extreme when libraries willingly or in
response to a request reproduce a complete collection of
manuscripts for deposit in another library." [60] Among other
things, Peckham pointed out that a library's economic support depends partly on the number of scholars who come to
the library to use its collections. Paul Angle has suggested
elsewhere that the time may come when one library will provide a microfilm copy of a manuscript collection to another
library only on the condition that the second library recipro-
cate by microfilming one of its collections for the first library. [61]

Replies to the questionnaire indicated that policies on
photoduplication of manuscript collections have become increasingly liberal during the past decade or so. Twenty-six
of the reporting historical societies and six of the universities are willing to microfilm an entire manuscript collection or a major portion of a collection for another library,
and two other societies and one university might be willing
to do so under certain circumstances. Only seven historical
societies and five universities said that they are unwilling to
microfilm a collection for another library. Six societies and
two universities said that their governing boards have never
established a policy, or that the question is too involved to
answer in a few words, or they simply left the answer blank.

Reciprocation does make a difference with a few libraries. Twenty societies and five universities replied that
they are willing to microfilm collections for other libraries
regardless of whether there is reciprocation. Four societies
and one university, however, are willing to microfilm only
on a reciprocal basis. Two societies are willing to microfilm on a reciprocal basis and doubt whether they would on a
non-reciprocal basis. Two other societies and one university
library thought they might be willing to microfilm on a reciprocal basis, and are sure that they would not on any other
basis.

When statistics on collections actually microfilmed for
other libraries during the past five years are examined, it
becomes evident that historical societies have been more accommodating in this respect than major university libraries.
Only two of the university libraries microfilmed a collection
for another library during the five-year period, and they
microfilmed a total of only three collections. Seventeen historical societies microfilmed a total of approximately ninety

collections during the same period. The seventeen societies include four in the Northeast, seven in the Midwest, four in the South, and two in the West. Approximately twenty of the ninety collections were microfilmed on a reciprocal basis, and the rest on a non-reciprocal basis. Seven societies microfilmed one or two collections each, two societies microfilmed about five collections each, five societies microfilmed about ten collections each, and one society microfilmed about twenty collections during the five-year period.

The replies should not be interpreted to mean that any library willing to microfilm a collection for another library will honor all requests indiscriminately. Availability of technical staff imposes one limitation. Some libraries are willing to allow a local commercial firm to do the microfilming, provided that the firm can be trusted to handle manuscripts with care. Other libraries will not allow manuscripts to leave the building under any circumstances. Some libraries have their own photographic facilities, but they usually find it impossible to do all of the microfilming that other libraries might like them to do. Preparation of collections for microfilming is time-consuming, and libraries have to decide whether to use staff time for this or for working on manuscripts that cannot be used at all until they are processed. Some libraries are willing to microfilm a collection for a distant library, but they are reluctant to do so for a library within easy driving distance. Libraries occasionally refuse to microfilm manuscript collections because they have found that scholars sometimes give credit in their publications to the institution with the microfilm copy and fail to mention the location of the originals.

Most large libraries will provide photocopies of manuscripts for use on specific research projects whenever it would be difficult for the researcher to remain at the library long enough to study pertinent manuscripts adequately. All but two of the reporting historical societies and all of the universities will do a limited amount of photocopying for scholars or will have it done by a commercial firm. Libraries will rarely microfilm an entire collection or a major part of a collection for a scholar, although microfilms of large collections are occasionally available for loan.

Researchers are ordinarily expected to come to a library in person to read and to select pertinent material for microfilming. All but eight of the societies and two of the university libraries, however, will have photocopies prepared and sent in response to a request in a letter, provided that the request is sufficiently specific as to authors and dates, the items can be located in the card catalog or in other find-

ing aids, and the staff time required to locate requested material will not take more than a few hours. Manuscript
staffs will rarely read through collections to select items
pertaining to a given subject (subject entries in card catalogs
generally indicate that material pertaining to a subject can be
found in certain collections, but do not list specific letters
or documents). The amount of searching that a manuscript
staff will do often depends on a subjective judgment as to the
merit of the research project. When the amount of time required to answer a request is exorbitant, libraries will sometimes recommend outside researchers who search collections
for a fee. There is rarely a fee for the search that the library itself undertakes.

During the last two decades the quantity of manuscripts available for use by researchers has increased enor-
mously. Historical societies have expanded their collection
programs, and university libraries have gradually accepted
the responsibility of preserving manuscripts as well as printed materials.

There have been impressive advances in gaining bibliographical controls over manuscripts. Adoption of more efficient methods of processing and cataloging and larger staffs
have made it possible for most major libraries to prepare
fairly adequate finding aids for most of their manuscripts.
A substantial number of libraries have been able to publish
comprehensive guides to their manuscript holdings. Perhaps
the most important development has been the application of
the concept of a national union catalog to manuscripts.

In many respects, however, modern manuscript depositories are still in about the same predicament as King
Sisyphus of ancient Corinth. If additions to a staff and more
efficient processing procedures double the quantity of manuscripts that can be processed, acquisition of bulkier twentieth-
century collections is likely at least to triple the quantity of
accessions. If the last five years is any indication, more
libraries will add a manuscript curator or librarian to the
staff, and present staffs will be further augmented. But
manuscript staffs are not likely to see a time when the stone
stays put at the top of the hill and there is nothing further
to do.

Notes

1. Sparks, Jared. "Materials for American History," The
     North American Review, 23:277, Oct. 1826.
2. Jameson, J.F. "The Functions of State and Local His-

torical Societies with Respect to Research and Publication." In Annual Report of the American Historical Association for the Year 1897. Washington, D.C., U.S. Government Printing Office, 1898, p. 53.

3. Belknap, Jeremy. Letter to Ebenezer Hazard in 1795. Quoted in Stephen T. Riley. The Massachusetts Historical Society, 1791-1959. Boston, Massachusetts Historical Society, 1959, p. 18.

4. Van Tassel, David D. Recording America's Past: An Interpretation of the Development of Historical Studies in America, 1607-1884. Chicago, University of Chicago Press, 1960, pp. 60-66, 95-102.

5. Kane, Lucile M. "Manuscript Collecting." In William B. Hesseltine and Donald R. McNeil, eds., In Support of Clio: Essays in Memory of Herbert A. Kellar. Madison, State Historical Society of Wisconsin, 1958, pp. 33-34.

6. Whitehill, Walter Muir. Independent Historical Societies: An Enquiry into Their Research and Publication Functions and Their Financial Future. Boston, The Boston Athenaeum, Distributed by Harvard University Press, 1962, pp. 3-10, 38-41, 88-115.

7. Thwaites, Reuben Gold. "Report of Committee on Methods of Organization and Work on the Part of State and Local Historical Societies." In Annual Report of the American Historical Association for the Year 1905. Washington, D.C., U.S. Government Printing Office, 1906, Vol. 1, pp. 281-325.

8. Shelley, Fred. "Manuscripts in the Library of Congress: 1800-1900," American Archivist, 11:3-4, Jan. 1948.

9. Mearns, David C. "The Story Up to Now." In Annual Report of the Librarian of Congress, 1946. Washington, D.C., U.S. Government Printing Office, 1947, pp. 122, 123.

10. Bond, W.H. "Manuscript Collections in the Houghton Library," Autograph Collectors' Journal, 4:32-34, Spring 1952.

11. Historical Records Survey, Division of Women's and Professional Projects, Works Progress Administration. Guide to Depositories of Manuscript Collections in the United States. Columbus, Ohio, The Historical Records Survey, 1938, pp. 4, 83-84.

12. Wallace, Carolyn Andrews. "The University of North Carolina's Southern Historical Collection," Manuscripts 9:140, Summer 1957.

13. Martin, Thomas P. "A Manuscript Collecting Venture in the Middle West: Indiana: 1950-1953," American

Archivist, 17:305-312, Oct. 1954.

14. U.S. National Historical Publications Commission. A
    Guide to Archives and Manuscripts in the United
    States. Edited by Philip M. Hamer. New Haven,
    Yale University Press, 1961. (Information about the
    Texas Historical Association is on p. 584.)

15. Questionnaire concerning policies on the use and care of
    manuscripts, returned to the author by Yale Univer-
    sity Library during October 1963.

16. Whitehill, op. cit., p. 56.

17. Hamilton, J.G. de Roulhac. "Three Centuries of South-
    ern Records, 1607-1907," Journal of Southern History,
    10:24-25, Feb. 1944.

18. Going, Allen J. "Historical Societies in Alabama,"
    Alabama Review, 1:45, Jan. 1948.

19. Thwaites, op. cit., p. 291.

20. Chapman, Margaret L., executive secretary of the Flor-
    ida Historical Society. Letter dated Sept. 17, 1963.

21. O'Dell, Mrs. John, corresponding secretary of the Ten-
    nessee Historical Society. Letter dated Sept. 9, 1963.

22. Clark, Thomas D. "Preservation of Southern Historical
    Documents," The American Archivist, 16:36, Jan.
    1953.

23. Ibid., p. 35.

24. Wier, Jeanne Elizabeth. "The Work of the Western
    State Historical Society as Illustrated by Nevada." In
    Annual Report of the American Historical Association
    for the Year 1910. Washington, D.C., U.S. Govern-
    ment Printing Office, 1912, pp. 202, 206.

25. Questionnaire concerning policies on the use and care of
    manuscripts, returned to the author by the Museum of
    New Mexico for the Historical Society of New Mexico
    in September 1963.

26. Massachusetts Historical Society. "Constitution of the
    Historical Society," Collections of the Massachusetts
    Historical Society for the Year 1792. Boston, reprint-
    ed by Monroe and Francis, 1806, Vol. I, p. 1.

27. Whitehill, op. cit., pp. 57, 60.

28. Kane, op. cit., pp. 34-35.

29. McNeil, Donald R. "The Wisconsin Experiments." In
    Donald R. McNeil, ed., The American Collector.
    Madison, State Historical Society of Wisconsin, 1955,
    pp. 40-44.

30. Putnam, Herbert. "The Relation of the National Library
    to Historical Research in the United States." In An-
    nual Report of the American Historical Association for
    the Year 1901. Washington, D.C., U.S. Government

Printing Office, 1902, Vol. 1, p. 120.

31. Buck, Solon J., and Eaton, Dorothy S. "Manuscripts," The Library of Congress Quarterly Journal of Current Acquisitions, 7:25, May 1950.

32. Wall Jr., Alexander J. Letter to L. Quincy Mumford, Librarian of Congress, dated May 31, 1956, and reply by Mumford dated June 13, 1956, History News, 11: 81-84, September 1956.

33. Questionnaire concerning competition in manuscript collecting, returned to author by 31 major historical agencies in March and April 1962.

34. Lord, Clifford L., ed. Ideas in Conflict. Harrisburg, Pa., American Association for State and Local History, 1958, p. 62.

35. Atherton, Lewis E. "Western Historical Manuscripts Collection--A Case Study of a Collecting Program," American Archivist, 26:42-43, Jan. 1963.

36. Statements by Josephine L. Harper, manuscript librarian at the State Historical Society of Wisconsin, and Kenneth Duckett, curator of manuscripts at the Ohio Historical Society, in response to questionnaire concerning competition in manuscript collecting, returned to author in 1962.

37. Lord, op. cit., pp. 64, 68.

38. Questionnaire on the use and care of manuscript collections, returned to the author by 41 major historical societies, 14 university libraries, and 12 other libraries in September and October 1963.

39. Josephson, Bertha E. "How Can We Improve Our Historical Societies," American Archivist, 8:195, July 1945.

40. Harper, Josephine L. "Manuscripts at the State Historical Society of Wisconsin, 1950-60," History News, 16:77-78, April 1961.

41. Kane, Lucile M. A Guide to the Care and Administration of Manuscripts (Bulletins of the American Association for State and Local History, Vol. 2, no. 11). Madison, Wisc., American Association for State and Local History, 1960.

42. U.S. Library of Congress, Descriptive Cataloging Division. "Rules for Descriptive Cataloging in the Library of Congress, Manuscripts, Preliminary Edition, Preprint of the Rules for Collections of Manuscripts." Washington, D.C., Library of Congress, Processing Department, Descriptive Cataloging Division, 1954.

43. Dunkin, Paul S. "Arrangement and Cataloging of Manuscripts," Library Trends, 5:352-360, Jan. 1957.

44. Berner, Richard C. "The Arrangement and Description of Manuscripts," <u>American Archivist</u>, 23:395-406, Oct. 1960.

45. Jasenas, Michael. "Cataloging Small Manuscript Collections," <u>Library Resources and Technical Services</u>, 7:264-272, Summer 1963.

46. Finch, Jean L. "Some Fundamentals in Arranging Archives and Manuscript Collections," <u>Library Resources and Technical Services</u>, 8:28-34, Winter 1964.

47. Fitzpatrick, J.C., ed. <u>Notes on the Care, Cataloguing, Calendaring and Arranging of Manuscripts</u>. 3rd ed., 2nd Printing. Washington, D.C., U.S. Government Printing Office, 1934, p. 24. (This manual was first published in 1913; other editions were published in 1921 and 1928.)

48. Nute, Grace Lee. <u>The Care and Cataloguing of Manuscripts as Practiced by the Minnesota Historical Society</u>. Saint Paul, Minnesota Historical Society, 1936, p. 30.

49. <u>Where Are the Historical Manuscripts, A Symposium</u> (Bulletins of the American Association for State and Local History, Vol. 2, no. 4). n.p., American Association for State and Local History, 1950.

50. Cappon, Lester J. "Reference Works and Historical Texts," <u>Library Trends</u>, 5:369-379, Jan. 1957.

51. Land, Robert H. "The National Union Catalog of Manuscript Collections," <u>American Archivist</u>, 17:195-207, July 1954.

52. U.S. Library of Congress. <u>The National Union Catalog of Manuscript Collections, 1959-1961</u>. Ann Arbor, Mich., J.W. Edwards, 1962; U.S. Library of Congress. <u>The National Union Catalog of Manuscript Collections, 1962</u>. Hamden, Conn., The Shoe String Press, Inc., 1964; U.S. Library of Congress. <u>The National Union Catalog of Manuscript Collections, Index, 1959-1962</u>. Hamden, Conn., The Shoe String Press, Inc., 1964.

53. Peckham, Howard H. "Policies Regarding the Use of Manuscripts," <u>Library Trends</u>, 5:363, Jan. 1957.

54. Shaw, Ralph R. <u>Literary Property in the United States</u>. Metuchen, N.J., Scarecrow Press, 1950, p. 16.

55. Ibid., pp. 87-90.

56. Connor, Seymour V. "The Problem of Literary Property in Archival Depositories," <u>American Archivist</u>, 21:143, 147, April 1958.

57. Cochran, Thomas C., et al. "Report of Ad Hoc Committee on Manuscripts Set Up by the American Histor-

ical Association in December 1948," American Archivist, 14:235, July 1951.

58. Mearns, David C. "Historical Manuscripts, Including Personal Papers," Library Trends, 5:320, Jan. 1957.

59. Cochran, op. cit., p. 239. Underlining in the original.

60. Peckham, Howard H. "Aiding the Scholar in Using Manuscript Collections," American Archivist, 19:226, July 1956.

61. Angle, Paul M. "The University Library and Its Manuscript Collection," Library Quarterly, 15:129, April 1945.

Some Fundamentals in Arranging Archives
and Manuscript Collections
Jean L. Finch

From Library Resources and Technical Services 8:26-34,
Winter 1964. Reprinted by permission.

The importance of archives and manuscript collections
is increasing, and hence many libraries that would not ordinarily collect this material now find themselves in the position of having become archive or manuscript depositories.
This creates an increasing problem, for the majority of librarians are not equipped to handle this material, and the
treatment of archives as simple book units by librarians has
resulted in confusion.[1] Two institutions on the West Coast
that offer on-the-job training are the Bancroft Library, at
the University of California, Berkeley, and the University of
Washington Archives and Manuscript Collection. The American University, in Washington, D. C., and University of Denver, Colorado, offer more extensive archive courses as a
part of their curricula. In one sense of the word, many institutions which have manuscripts or archive collections offer types of in-service training; but as a whole, none of
these varieties of training is uniform.

Theodore R. Schellenberg, Assistant Archivist of the
United States and author of Modern Archives; Principles and
Techniques, has also conducted courses in archival practice
at various places in the United States. One such course offered by Dr. Schellenberg was held in San Francisco in the
summer of 1958, and the University of Washington School of
Librarianship offered an extensive course taught by him in
the summer of 1962. This course was the first ever offered
on archival principles by a United States library school.[2]

However, this type of training is ordinarily unavailable for most librarians. To the librarian who suddenly
finds himself inundated with masses of archival material, the
situation for its organization can seem almost hopeless. For
the most part, he does not know where to turn, and the temptation to leave the accumulating masses uncatalogued is great.
His alternative is often to employ book cataloging practices,
and here the situation becomes even more chaotic as the librarian soon finds this method inappropriate.

How, then, can bibliographic control over archival material be assumed if you, as a librarian, suddenly find yourself in the position of archivist with no prior training to aid you? Basically, this article is intended to aid in setting up a sound archival, or manuscript, program which can grow with the collection program.

First, this article assumes that archival training is unavailable in the area and that the librarian cannot be spared for even a summer course at Denver or the American University. Here, then, are definitions, suggestions, and a bibliography designed to outline an adaptable program of archive arrangement and maintenance. This is not an attempt at over-simplification, but merely a basic outline. As the archive program becomes more sophisticated, archival techniques may become more refined.

A basic terminology is needed for recognition. First of all, manuscripts and archives fall into the general category of records. Records, in the broad general sense, include three classes: textual or documentary; audio-visual, or still pictures, motion pictures, etc.; and cartographic, or diagrams, maps, etc. This article does not deal with the cataloging of the last two classes.

Textual, or documentary, records, may be further divided as follows: Public records are usually called an archive group, and this material is produced as a result of an activity by a corporate body with a specific goal in mind. This does not necessarily exclude the letters of private individuals but does include the works of a government agency, such as the Tennessee Valley Authority. On the other hand, private records, created for private purposes, are called manuscript collections and do include the letters of private individuals. These manuscript collections are usually designated as historical manuscripts to distinguish them from literary manuscripts. To separate these two groups a little more clearly, let us take an example. If a department of the University of Washington saved its correspondence and business dealings, these records would be public and hence would be termed an archival group. If a professor in a particular department in the University of Washington saved his correspondence over the years, these records would be private and, therefore, termed a manuscript collection.

Within either of these two groups, one will find nomenclature to distinguish each of the subgroups. Whether the nature of the collection is archival or manuscript, the collection may be composed of letters, documents, minutes of meetings, bills and records, court papers, etc. These items may fall into record items, which are any aggregation

of material which lends itself to physical integrity, such as
one folder or one volume, etc. A cumulation of these record items into a related unit within a specific group is called
a series, or a record series. A letter, whether it is one
piece or multiple sheets, is termed a piece. (This definition
of piece varies from the British usage of the word. British
terminology likens "piece" to the U.S. "item.")

Basically, any library that begins collecting manuscript
or archival material must consider two things in arranging
this material: (1) how can the arrangement of the material
be made to fit the basic needs of the researcher and (2) how
can bibliographic control of this material be most easily assumed?[3] In considering the research worker, it is necessary
to pause for a moment and imagine the type of patron the
manuscript or archive collection will serve. As this material is primary source material, it stands to reason that it
can seldom serve the casual reader or student--the material
does not lend itself to browsing. However, manuscript or
archive material does serve the serious student and scholar
who approach it for a specific reason. The nature of the material assumes that the user has already made use of secondary source material, i.e. books or articles, and knows the
nature of the archival material he is about to use. Therefore, it can be argued that any patron knows his needs.

Generally, it has been the repository's pleasure to consider its own convenience rather than that of the researcher's
in arranging material.[4] Two of the most commonly used
principles of arrangement have been the rule of provenance
(sometimes more akin to original order) and chronological order. There is something to be said for either practice.

The rule of provenance, or the maintenance of records
according to their origins or source, is German and comes
from the term Provenienzprinzip, which was the principle of
grouping public records according to their origins in public
administrative bodies. It was first expressed by Heinrich
von Sybel after he became Director of the Prussian State Archives in 1874.[5]

The rule of provenance rests on three assumptions:
(1) that the main purpose of the user is biographical; (2) that
the order given a collection by its creators is the best for
its purpose; and (3) that the given order reflects in some significant way the personality of its creator or creators.[6] To
a librarian newly turned manuscript curator much is to be
said for this principle. If the collection is in some basic
order, and the librarian is hesitant about re-arrangement, it
is best to follow this rule of provenance and simply inventory
the material so that he knows the extent of the collection and

can control it.

However, on the other side, the rule of provenance usually means that the librarian was overcome by the hugeness of the collection. This rule of provenance has much more validity with an archival group where the original order shows more to the researcher than an artificial order created by the librarian. And yet any collection reflects the workings of an original arranger and may not suit the library's or the researcher's purpose at all. The rule of provenance does not mean that the collection is in the best of all possible arrangements for maintenance or for the researcher.

The second way in which archive or manuscript collections may be handled is chronological. This is perhaps the simplest of all arrangements in that the entire mass of the collection is in one order. However, there are some very strong reasons against it. First, it affords only one approach to a collection. Letters of an important personage may be scattered through the collection, and the researcher may be misled by not knowing they exist. Correspondents do not reveal themselves easily. And finally, bibliographic control is difficult to achieve over a collection organized in this manner.

Actually, several criticisms of chronological arrangement may also apply to the rule of provenance. The rule of provenance may also scatter letters of an important person through the collection as well as conceal important correspondents. However, both of these methods are possible to use, and the librarian is the best judge of their validity. A librarian not trained in manuscript or archival practices should always keep in mind the maintenance of the collection. Is it easy to use? Can one find the material he wishes? Both of these practices are quite acceptable archival methods, and, rather than experiment, either one is fairly easy to follow.

It should be stressed that under no condition should a librarian break up a collection. By breaking up a collection, I mean that it should not be separated and housed in various areas. To do so violates one of the principle provenances of any collection, and I refer specifically to the practice sometimes followed by unknowing librarians of taking letters and binding them in volumes and treating them as book units. Also, the practice of occasionally binding letters of an important personage in the books by that person has occurred and should be avoided.

A third system of manuscript or archive arrangement that has been used is one that separates incoming correspondence from outgoing correspondence. This system has

been used quite successfully at the Bancroft Library and the
University of Washington Library Manuscript Department.
This divided system, which I shall describe, has several
points in its favor. First, it meets the needs of the researcher. Second, it is easy for the librarian to maintain
control over the collection. Third, by means of finding aids,
it pulls together all of the incoming letters of an important
personage while still affording the researcher a chronological
look at the span of the collection through the outgoing correspondence. The major difference in this type of arrangement
centers around the correspondence series. The correspondence is divided into two groups: the incoming correspondence and the outgoing correspondence. The incoming correspondence is arranged alphabetically by the writer of the letter unless he is acting as agent of another party, in which
case the letter should be filed under the name of the party
for whom he is writing. The outgoing correspondence is arranged chronologically. This system allows a double approach: through the correspondents and through the chronological time span. The usual approach to a manuscript or
archival collection is through the names of people and of organizations. The researcher does not find it difficult to refer to the incoming letter file for a particular reference he
might find in the outgoing, or chronological file.

    The alphabetical arrangement presents no major prob-
lem save for enclosures. These are normally separated
from the body of the letter and noted on the letter. The enclosures then are filed according to the form of the enclosure,
such as document, court paper, etc. The University of Washington Library Manuscript Department used this form and
filed letter enclosures in a separate file alphabetically by
sender.[7] Some libraries, however, do not favor separating
enclosures and prefer to keep them with the original letter.
Again, this is a matter of personal judgment, and the manuscript librarian must decide which method is most feasible
for him since both methods have points in their favor. Another point to be brought out in favor of the divided arrangement is that most of these author entries (at least the more
important ones) will appear in the card catalog as added entries. Certainly this type of arrangement also minimizes the
sorter's subjective judgment.

    Aside from letters, a manuscript librarian will also
find that he is dealing with court papers, minutes, speeches,
financial records, etc. These are inherent in almost any
collection. Basically, speeches and minutes usually fall into
obvious groups which can be arranged by organization or person giving the speech and can be sub-arranged chronologically.

Court papers are best arranged by case number.

Financial and business records usually take up a good part of the collection. Incoming bills should be arranged alphabetically by name of billing party, while outgoing bills should be arranged chronologically. The same division for the correspondence applies here, too. Inventories, journals, ledgers, trial balances, memoranda, etc., should be grouped by subject and arranged chronologically within that group.

The above descriptions have applied principally to large record units, but what about the small manuscript collection of only a few items? Since they are small units of one, two, or twenty items, they should be dealt with according to their intrinsic importance. The Bancroft Library handles these items as follows: each item is placed in an acid-free folder, and the face of the folder is inscribed as to who wrote the letter, to whom addressed, and a brief description of the letter. These folders were then contained in a portfolio, chronologically arranged within each alphabetical division. Hence, all the letters of John Brown would follow those of Henry Adams and would be chronologically arranged.

After the collection has been arranged, the librarian is then presented with a problem of description. An inventory or guide to the collection is mandatory. This usually lists the incoming correspondents, the dates of the letters, and the number of letters. For large collections, only the important people are listed, thus conserving some time. The chronological, or outgoing, correspondence is described only by the broad covering dates. The business records and miscellany are usually not described other than noting that this material can be found in certain carton numbers.

After the guide has been prepared, the librarian must indicate the collection in the card catalog. This can best be done by a main entry card that brings out some of the salient points of the collection and the people for whom subject entries and added entries are made. (See Appendix A.) Another method of handling the correspondents is by making analytic cards for the important authors. This latter practice has been criticized in some manuscript libraries as it involves a great deal of cataloging and time. (See Appendix B.) When they find their collection growing very rapidly and with great bulk, most libraries do not have the time to spend in this highly refined cataloging. The Bancroft Library, with its fifty-year backlog, was faced with the problem of whether or not to make analytics. After much trial and error, it has devised a simple loose-leaf binder with sheets that can be added at will and a process so simple that a clerk can perform it without much supervision. (See Appendix C.)

The general trend in most manuscript cataloging is away
from multiple tracings. The principal manuscript collections
favor a simplicity of practices, and the system adopted by
the Bancroft Library seems to be one that could be used anywhere with success.

A few additional points should be made concerning arrangement. First, the component parts of the collection,
i.e., the letters, etc., should be housed in acid-free folders.[8] Some libraries prefer to place single items in a folder, while other libraries limit the contents to five or ten letters, depending on the expandability of the folder. The folders carry the name of the author, with birth and death dates
when available, time span of the enclosed letters, and number of letters. It is thought to be good practice to stamp the
collections with a special stamp; usually, each page receives
an imprint. This task is one that can be delegated to pages
or clerks. The stamp is usually two lines as follows:

> James D. Phelan Collection
> Bancroft Library

The folders are housed in grey archival boxes,[9] either
letter or legal size. Some materials, such as financial and
business records and court papers, are usually housed in
cartons. Again, for small collections, portfolios are quite
suitable. Or, material may be wrapped and simply placed
on shelves like books. The librarian must again make a
judgment as to what is available.

One point that has not been mentioned and should be
considered is the problem of classification. Neither Dewey
nor the Library of Congress system seems quite adequate for
archival groups. Some libraries merely devise a numbering
system based on shelf-list order. The Bancroft Library has
incorporated this system into one originally planned by Hubert Howe Bancroft, the nineteenth-century historian who
bought the original collection for his private library to be
used in writing his histories. Bancroft's scheme divided his
collection into subject areas designated by letter combinations.
The present system used by the Bancroft Library is a combination of these two methods. For example, manuscript collections pertaining to Mexico go into the M-M group, followed by a shelf-list number. Thus, the complete classification
number for a collection would look like this: $\underline{\text{M-M}}$. Again,
$\overline{180}$
there is no certain way to establish a classification system
that is adequate although the Bancroft one has worked well
for that Library.

These are a few ideas that may be of help to a new manuscript or archive librarian with no prior training. The basic point in arranging any type of manuscript collection is one of judgment. If the librarian considers the need of the prospective researcher and the ease of maintaining the collection, the final judgment in arrangement becomes much clearer.

Notes

1. Mason, Philip P. "College and University Archives, 1962." The American Archivist, 26:163. April 1963.
2. Berner, Richard C. "The Management of Manuscript Collections." Library Journal, 88:1616. April 15, 1963.
3. Berner, Richard C. "The Arrangement and Description of Manuscripts." The American Archivist, 23:395. October 1960.
4. Ibid.
5. Schellenberg, Theodore R. Modern Archives; Principles and Techniques. Chicago, University of Chicago Press, 1956, p. 174.
6. Berner, op. cit. (Footnote 3), p. 398.
7. Ibid.
8. Acid-free folders, designed to safeguard the enclosed material, are a must for any manuscript or archive collection. These folders may be obtained from a number of paper companies. In the West, Crown-Zellerbach, San Francisco, California, has supplied libraries with a very excellent quality folder.
9. Grey archival boxes, in both letter size and legal size, may be obtained from the Fibredex Company of West Virginia. Prices are available on request.

Appendix A

Z-Z   Stephens, John Lloyd, 1805-1852.
116   Correspondence and Papers, 1800-1878

                 7 boxes.
                 Chiefly concerning Stephens' travels in Central
          America and his discovery of the ruins of Chichen
          Itza with Frederick Catherwood. Also, concern-
          ing construction of the Panama Railroad with Wil-
          liam Aspinwall and Stephens' activities as Minis-
          ter Plenipotentiary to Guatemala in 1838.
                 Some correspondence of Stephens' father, Ben-
          jamin Stephens, included.
                                               1800-1878.

Recto of Main Card

1. Central America--Description and Travel 2. Panama
Railroad 3. Chichen Itza 4. Guatemala--Politics and
Government

I.   Catherwood, Frederick
II.   Aspinwall, William
III. Stephens, Benjamin

Verso of Main Card

Appendix B

Catherwood, Frederick
    101 Letter(s).   1834-1849.

Z-Z   (In Stephens, John L. Correspondence
116   and Papers.   Box II)
Box II

For further information, see key to arrangement.

Analytic Card

Appendix C

Smith, John David, 1832-1900.
For manuscripts of the above, see Guides to the following:
collections:

Walker Family Papers U. of Washington Library		
Smith-Holmes Company Papers U. of Washington Library		

Cataloging Small Manuscript Collections
Michael Jasenas

From <u>Library Resources and Technical Services</u> 7:264-73, Summer 1963. Reprinted by permission.

In no other area of technical services has so little been done to establish a code of rules as in the cataloging of modern manuscripts. The tentative rules issued by the Library of Congress[1] are concerned only with the cataloging of collections or groups of manuscripts. Furthermore, many of these rules do not provide for special instances and merely suggest, in general terms, the basic procedures which the cataloger could apply to each special case by using his own judgment and imagination "according to the circumstances."

Some writers on this subject have expressed their doubts about the utility or feasibility of a single code of rules. According to Bond,[2] such a code is not possible "unless it is so detailed that it is unwieldy, or so general that it is meaningless." Mearns[3] points out that "no catalog can be, for everyone who may consult it, a precision instrument, neither can reference to entries in it be substituted for an examination of the works they describe." Libraries should, however, as Mearns himself admits, set up a catalog of manuscripts which will help the patron to eliminate from consideration those items which definitely have no relationship to his inquiry. To achieve this objective, manuscript departments in libraries attempt to establish their own manuscript cataloging patterns in accordance with the cataloging practice in other parts of their libraries. In this article an attempt will be made to bring out some of the major aspects of manuscript cataloging in repositories with relatively small holdings consisting predominantly of modern manuscripts, chiefly historical and literary in nature.

When manuscript holdings are very small, it is of course possible to record manuscripts piece by piece, entering each letter under its writer and making added entry cards for each addressee. As soon as collections grow in size, it becomes imperative to devise a new cataloging practice which would enable the processors to record newly acquired manuscripts quickly and effectively and, at the same time, not increase the catalog to enormous proportions.

Before establishing a cataloging practice which would best fit the needs of a particular library, it is desirable first to make a survey of manuscript catalogs of other libraries. In addition, a number of outstanding studies should be examined in detail, because they will supply useful information about practices followed in some of the other major collections, whose catalogs may not be available for consultation. Such a survey would no doubt provide the background needed for the establishment of the general policies and procedures of manuscript cataloging.

Even a cursory survey of manuscript catalogs shows that cataloging practices vary to a considerable extent from library to library. Some scholars who frequently use the facilities of various repositories attempt to identify a few major categories of manuscript control systems practiced by libraries. Johnston[4] groups these systems into the four types of control which may be summarized as follows:

1. A simple listing of manuscript collections in a card catalog, plus a partial list of persons whose correspondence may be found in a particular collection. Under this control system, the catalog does not indicate the number of letters of a writer nor their dates, and "there is no way of telling, until the last item in a given collection has been checked and inspected, whether or not all pertinent documents have been found."

2. A card catalog as above, plus written summaries available for all collections. Usually such summaries include some list of important subjects upon which information may be found and the important people involved as correspondents. This system provides only a partial index to the contents of the collections, even though it is an improvement over the kind of control mentioned under 1 above.

3. A card index of all correspondents for each collection, with dates of all letters indexed under the names of the letter writers. The main shortcomings of this system are that the reader must look through indexes of all collections because there is no master index, and that it does not provide any subject approach.

4. "The nearest approximation to the complete subject-person index for each collection," plus a master index for the resources of the repository as a whole. To scholars such a system is no doubt the most satisfactory of all.

The staff shortage in most libraries prohibits the establishment and maintenance of manuscript catalogs which would be detailed enough to meet adequately the needs of scholars by recording all correspondents with dates of all letters, and, at the same time, providing a satisfactory sub-

ject approach. Being faced with high costs of cataloging and
a continuous and substantial increase in manuscript holdings,
most repositories have no alternatives left but to catalog
each collection as a unit or to break down each individual
collection into several catalogable units. If the staff shortage is not too serious, the latter course will be chosen. In
doing so, the library will provide for its patrons a finding
device which, without listing on cards everything item by
item within a particular collection, will nevertheless enable
the readers to eliminate from consideration those items
which have no relationship to the object of their research.
Such a course means the establishment and maintenance of a
catalog which is a compromise between the ideal advocated
by scholars and the traditional practices of cataloging each
collection as a unit.

Once this sort of compromise has been made, the
first task one faces is to define the catalogable unit. To
make it applicable to as many cases of cataloging as possible, the catalogable unit is generally defined as that part of
a manuscript collection which contains a number of mutually
related items.[5] There are instances, however, where catalogable units may be either an entire undivided manuscript
collection, or a single manuscript which is not related to any
other item in the collection, or, finally, a single manuscript
which does not belong to any collection.

The correspondence included in a manuscript collection normally constitutes a separate catalogable unit. Sometimes letters are so numerous that it is deemed desirable to
break them down into smaller units requiring analytical entries. A collection of letters can be subdivided thus:

1. Letters written by the "principal person" (often
the one for whom the collection is named).

2. Letters written by major correspondents (i.e.,
those who are prominent enough to be included in biographical dictionaries, as well as those who are of particular significance within a manuscript collection).

3. Letters written by minor correspondents.

It is a sound policy to make a separate entry for all
the letters written by the principal person. Also, a group
of letters by a major correspondent, no matter what its size,
should be given a separate entry. If the letters written by
minor correspondents constitute a sizeable group, such a
group can be further subdivided in order to obtain more
manageable units. This group can be broken down by ad-
dressees or by subjects.

In cataloging manuscripts, the prevailing trend in
most libraries is to adhere as much as possible to the prin-

ciple emphasized in the A. L. A. Cataloging Rules for Author and Title Entries suggesting that manuscripts be entered according to the rules for printed books. When a cataloger deals with a group of letters all written by the same person, no problems are encountered in entering such a unit in accordance with the principle of entry under author. It is, however, not so easy to solve the entry problem when letters were written by various persons. In such cases there are two possibilities: (1) all letters are addressed to the same person, or (2) there is no common addressee for the whole group.

With regard to the first possibility the Library of Congress rule A1a may be adopted. This rule stipulates that "when a collection or group of papers consists of material written by or addressed to a person, family, government agency or other corporate body, it is entered under the name of the person, family, government agency, or corporate body."6 In the second case, i.e., a group of letters without a common addressee, the same Library of Congress rule can be applied in all cases when we deal both with the letters addressed to one person and with letters concerning this person. When, on the other hand, the cataloger is confronted with a unit containing letters about a person but none written to him, it is appropriate to enter this unit under the name of the person to whom the letters are related, or under the subject with which they all deal. An entry under subject seems to be, in some instances at least, in accordance with the principle of entry pointed out in the second part of the Library of Congress rule A1b, which concerns the choice of entry for collections having no common addressee. According to this rule, there may be cases when a collection can be entered under a title that "should start with key words which indicate the content of the collection or its chief characteristic."7 Such key words no doubt coincide frequently with the subject under which collections are actually entered.8

Without altering LC principles these three general rules can be set up for the choice of main entries for catalogable units or analytical entries:

1. Enter a group of letters of one writer under the writer, with added entry cards made for each addressee.

2. Enter a group of letters by various writers (minor correspondents) to one addressee under the addressee, with added entry cards made for each writer.

3. If a group of letters by various writers (minor correspondents) does not have a common addressee, enter such a group under the name of the person about whom the letters are written or to whom they may be related in some

other way; or under the subject with which they all deal; or
under the key words which indicate the contents of this unit
or its chief characteristics.   Make added entry cards for
each writer and addressee.
     An example of Rule 1 may be taken from the catalog-
ing of the Wyndham Lewis Collection at Cornell.   All letters
written by Lewis were grouped into one catalogable unit.   The
main entry card is as follows:

Example 1

LEWIS
    Lewis, Wyndham, 1882-1957
       Letters, 1895-(1941-49)-1957
       1861 items
    For holdings see Lewis Index, Pt. 1

       Letters--handwritten, carbon copies, and
    drafts--covering a very wide range of subjects
    and various phases of Lewis's life and activi-
    ties.   In addition to letters to members of his
    family, includes copies of letters to Thomas
    Stearns Eliot, Dorothy and Ezra Pound, and
    Augustus John.

As seen from the above general reference note, the detailed
record of all Lewis letters in our possession is included in
an index, which is in loose-leaf book form.   In this index all
Lewis's letters are listed alphabetically by addressee and
chronologically under each addressee.   This catalogable unit--
letters by Lewis--is considered a separate shelving unit within the Wyndham Lewis Collection.   But the arrangement of
letters belonging to this catalogable unit is, in the boxes, not
alphabetical by addressee, as in the index, but strictly chronological, thus giving us an additional approach to individual
items of this unit.
     Rule 2 may be illustrated by a catalogable unit in the
Truman Collection at Cornell.   This unit consists of letters
sent to Arthur W. Wilson, an old friend of Harry S. Truman.
The card for this unit reads as is shown below.   The general reference note on this card refers the reader to the index of the Truman Collection.   As do the indexes for other
collections, this index records all the holdings of the Truman
Collection item by item.   This unit is entered in the index
under the same heading and title as on the above card.   Individual letters of this unit are listed in the index alphabetical-

Example 2

TRUMAN
   Wilson, Arthur W.
      Letters received, 1941-61.
      9 items
      For holdings see Truman Index

      Letters to Wilson, mostly concerning his ap-
plication for an army commission, the publication of a letter written him by Truman in 1919,
the Democratic National Convention of 1960, and
reunions of the former members of the 129th
Field Artillery. Correspondents include former
White House officials George M. Elsey and
Charles G. Ross, General R. M. Danford, former chief of Field Artillery, and Cyril Clemens.
      See also:
         Truman, Harry S. Letters to Arthur W.
Wilson.

---

ly by writer and chronologically under each writer.

Rule 3, an example of which is shown below, is applied to cases whenever there are, within a collection, groups
of letters written by various minor correspondents and addressed to different persons.

Example 3

DREISER
   Dreiser, Theodore
      Letters relating to Dreiser, 1903-1959; un-
dated.
      68 items
      For holdings see Dreiser Index

      Correspondence of the University of Pennsyl-
vania, Mary Frances Dreiser Brennan and others
concerning Dreiser's family and his works, especially Sister Carrie and The Bulwark; also, concerning Dreiser's letters and their editing by
Robert Elias.

Here, also, the detailed list of the correspondents is included in the index, which, as in the two previous examples, records letters within this unit alphabetically by writer and chronologically under each writer.

As seen from the above examples, the information included on the catalog card is limited to the essential minimum. Usually a main entry card for both the collections and the other catalogable units contains the following elements:

1. <u>Location symbol.</u> If collections are arranged alphabetically by their names, the location symbols will be catchwords taken from these names. DREISER, for example, is the location symbol for the Theodore Dreiser Collection at Cornell. For miscellaneous manuscripts which do not belong to any collection, the location symbol may be MISC or just M.

2. <u>Author heading.</u> It should resemble the author headings for printed books as much as possible, and the "no conflict" rule might be a guiding principle in establishing entries for personal authors.

3. <u>Title.</u> In most cases a title for catalogable units must be supplied by the cataloger. It is customary to use standard titles followed immediately by the inclusive dates, as suggested by the Library of Congress rules,[9] for example:

> Correspondence, 1839-76.
> Letters, 1932-56.

4. <u>Collation.</u> The Library of Congress rule B3 concerning the physical description can be applied here. In most cases, as in those illustrated by the above examples of catalog cards, the term "items" is used, and a more detailed physical description (pagination, etc.) is provided only in the index.

5. <u>General reference note.</u> Such a note refers the reader to the index which records in detail the holdings of a particular collection. Usually this note reads as follows: "For holdings see . . . Index."

6. <u>Descriptive note.</u> For a collection card this note is usually compiled by applying the Library of Congress rules B5-10. Insofar as catalogable units within a collection are concerned, such a note, ordinarily contained in one paragraph, describes merely their scope and contents, mentioning the most important correspondents and major subjects of the documents included in a catalogable unit.

7. <u>"See also" references.</u> They are used to call the reader's attention to the additional documents which belong to another catalogable unit or even another collection, but which are related to the ones included in the catalogable unit being

examined by the reader.

8. <u>Tracing</u>. There is no need to trace added entries on the main entry card if an index is provided to record holdings of a collection; in such a case, only the subjects are traced, and they are usually listed on the verso of the card.

The only effective way to reduce the amount of information in the card catalog is to supplement the latter by indexes listing holdings of each catalogable unit. The indexes must be detailed enough to indicate the date and pagination of each item. Incipits are given only for undated or partially dated letters. Letters written by one person and constituting a separate catalogable unit are listed alphabetically by addressee and chronologically under each addressee within that unit. Catalogable units are arranged, in the index, alphabetically by main entry.

In addition to relieving the card catalog from excessive bulk by eliminating holdings cards, the indexes <u>ipso facto</u> take care of tracing added entries for numerous letter writers. The indexes are also indispensable tools for inventory. The maintenance of indexes should not present a serious problem because, being in loose-leaf book form, they are easily kept up to date. A sample of listings in the index to the Maurepas Collection at Cornell is shown below:

> Mailly-Nesle, Armande de la Porte Mazarin,
> marquise de.
> Letters, 1741-46.
> 9 items
> Letters to Maurepas (7)

1741	Sept. 2	2p.
[1741	Oct.]	2p.
	Oct.]	2p.
1741	Nov. 6[?]	1p.
1745	Apr. 11	3p.
1746	Feb. 16	2p.
	Feb. 21	2p.

> Letters to Salley, secretary to Maurepas (2)

1745	Apr. 12	2p.
	Nov. 23	4p.

No one strictly predominant arrangement of manuscripts exists in American libraries. Collections are arranged in one or two of the following ways: in order of accession number, alphabetically by main entries or names, geographically, chronologically, or by subject. In a reposi-

tory with relatively small and stable holdings, an alphabetical arrangement of collections on the shelves is fully satisfactory.

There are various methods of arranging manuscripts
within the collections--by form (for example, manuscripts of
an author's works, his personal correspondence, speeches,
diaries, business papers), by period, by place, by subject,
by size, or by a combination of these. There is a tendency
now to arrange manuscripts within an individual collection by
catalogable units, especially if most of the manuscripts are
of high quality and/or consist chiefly of the papers of prominent literary figures, as is the case in Cornell's Rare Book
Department. [10] For repositories using indexes to record
holdings of individual collections, it would seem most convenient to arrange catalogable units in the same order in
which they are listed in the index, i.e., alphabetically by
main entries.

A modern practice gaining ground in recent years is
to arrange the letters received by the principal person (incoming letters) alphabetically by writers and chronologically
under each writer, while the letters written by the principal
person (outgoing letters), which normally constitute a separate catalogable unit, are ordinarily arranged chronologically. [11] Whenever manuscripts are arranged chronologically,
undated manuscripts are placed at the end of the dated manuscripts. When only the year is given, the items are filed
at the end of that year; when the month and year are given,
items are filed at the end of that month. The nature of the
materials in the collection determines whether an alphabetical or a chronological arrangement should be adopted. For
the purely historical or archival material the proper arrangement is most likely to be chronological, but the literary
manuscripts would, in most cases, be arranged alphabetically by writer.

In order to keep all material within a particular collection together, bound manuscripts belonging to a collection
can be shelved (if the appropriate shelving space is available)
next to the boxes containing unbound manuscripts of that collection. These bound manuscripts are arranged alphabetically by catchwords taken from their titles. For example, in
the Shaw Collection at Cornell a bound volume containing material pertaining to the progress and publication of Bernard
Shaw's Geneva has the location symbol:

> SHAW
> Bd
> Geneva

If such a policy is adopted, bound manuscripts which do not belong to any special collection are shelved after the boxes containing miscellaneous manuscripts. They are arranged alphabetically by main entry.

Sometimes a newly acquired collection of manuscripts has an adequate arrangement which can be retained in its entirety or in part. An example of a well-organized collection is the collection of historical French documents of the eighteenth century, the Maurepas Papers, which was sold by Parke-Bernet Galleries in March 1962. Out of 754 items included in this collection, Cornell acquired 577 items grouped into 47 lots. After a careful study of the original arrangement, a large number of the existing groups of this collection were retained as catalogable units. The lots not kept as separate catalogable units were those which contained papers dealing solely with French naval affairs in the 1730's and 1740's. All these lots were grouped into one single catalogable unit.

The manuscript cataloging policies which have just been described are based on the catalogable unit device. This device is not an innovation; it is only a step forward in the development of the collection device which, in its turn, can, according to Dunkin,[12] be found in the cataloging of printed books. As an example Dunkin mentions here the practice followed by some libraries of cataloging pamphlets as collections rather than as individual items. Wilson[13] finds a similarity between a manuscript collection and a collection of essays by several authors in a Festschrift. Both a collection of pamphlets and a Festschrift present a problem which is similar to that of cataloging a manuscript collection, i.e., to what extent should its contents be analyzed? The solution of this problem depends primarily upon the function which the catalog of manuscripts is supposed to perform in aiding scholars in their research. Here, again, the same trend may be found in the development of both the cataloging of printed books and the cataloging of manuscripts: moving "steadily toward standardization and simplification with accent on the catalog as a finding list."[14] It may be added that the concept of a finding device is even more applicable to the manuscript catalog than to the catalog of printed books because, it is generally believed, the users of manuscripts, unlike many other users of a library's facilities, are quite familiar with the subjects under their investigation and are not likely to take a cataloger's word for details without examining the actual items described on catalog cards. The user of manuscripts, like the one portrayed by Bond,[15] "will expect to be led to his material, but not told all about it;"

and for this reason at least, "elaborately detailed cataloging will be wasted, because he [the reader] will rightly prefer to draw conclusions based upon his own examination."

Insofar as the description of the catalogable units is concerned, manuscript cataloging is intended to provide only the essential minimum which would enable a repository worker to locate individual items within a collection quickly and unmistakably. For this purpose, as has already been indicated, the loose-leaf indexes ancillary to the card catalog are used to record practically every item, without at the same time causing an excessive enlargement of the card catalog. While the indexes are keys to each individual collection, the card catalog listing names of all correspondents serves as a master key to all of the resources of the repository. This combination of the indexes and card catalog provides an instrument which is a considerable step toward the ideal sought by scholars in their use of manuscript collections.

Notes

1. U.S. Library of Congress. Descriptive Cataloging Division. Rules for Descriptive Cataloging in the Library of Congress: Manuscripts. Prelim. ed. [Washington] Library of Congress, 1954.
2. Bond, W.H. "Manuscripts and the Library," Library Trends, 7:513. April 1959.
3. Mearns, David C. "To Be Enduring: The National Union Catalog of Manuscript Collections." College and Research Libraries, 20:344. September 1959.
4. Johnston, Frontis W. "A Historian Looks at Archives and Manuscripts." American Archivist, 19:229-33. July 1956.
5. Cf. Martin, Dorothy V. "Use of Cataloging Techniques in Work with Records and Manuscripts." American Archivist, 18:317-36. October 1955.
6. U.S. Library of Congress, op. cit., p. 1.
7. Ibid., p. 2.
8. E.g: Michigan. University. William L. Clements Library. Guide to Manuscript Collections . . . comp. by Howard H. Peckham. Ann Arbor, University of Michigan Press, 1942, p. 159 (no. 89). Also: Virginia. University. Library. Thirteenth Annual Report on Historical Collections. [Charlottesville] University of Virginia, 1943, p. 50 ("War of 1812").
9. U.S. Library of Congress, op. cit., p. 4.

10. The majority of manuscripts kept in the Department of
    Rare Books consists of the papers of prominent liter-
    ary figures (e.g., William Wordsworth, James Joyce,
    Rudyard Kipling, Bernard Shaw), eighteenth-century
    French historical documents (Maurepas Papers), let-
    ters and other documents of the French Revolution and
    Napoleonic period, and correspondence of the leaders
    of the American anti-slavery movement. The great-
    est concentration of manuscripts at Cornell, approxi-
    mately fourteen million items, is in the Collection of
    Regional History and University Archives.
11. Cf. Burke, Robert E. "Modern Manuscript Collections
    and What to Do with Them." Manuscripts, 7:232-36.
    Summer 1955. Also: Berner, Richard C. "The Ar-
    rangement and Description of Manuscripts." Ameri-
    can Archivist, 23:395-406. October 1960.
12. Dunkin, Paul S. "Arrangement and Cataloging of Manu-
    scripts." Library Trends, 5:355. January 1957.
13. Wilson, William Jerome. "Manuscript Cataloging."
    Traditio, 12:522. 1956.
14. Dunkin, op. cit.
15. Bond, op. cit., p. 512.

Pictures in Your Company's Archives
Betty Hale

From Special Libraries 56:41, January 1965. Copyright by
Special Libraries Association 1965. Reprinted by permission.

Have you ever noticed how much a historical picture
can cost or what a job it is to find the right one? That's
because so few people made them, even fewer people saved
them, and almost no one realized the value of classifying
them and profiting from the demand for them. This is equally true of company historical pictures. The "age of illustrated communication" has caught most of us unprepared.
Today every company's history must be told and retold in a
hundred different ways, preferably with illustrations. It is
recounted to new employees, shareholders, customers; at the
time of anniversaries, ground-breakings, mergers; in welcome booklets, house publications, annual reports, dividend
enclosures, speeches, sales literature, and exhibits.

So the problem becomes how to provide patrons with
a collection of company pictures quickly and economically.
The starting point should certainly be a check of the company
history and a listing from that of the most important people,
plants, processes, products, and events. Good pictures of
the items on that list should be your primary goal.

Don't be afraid to ask for the pictures. Such a collection is of lasting value to a company. Obtain management's approval to circulate a memorandum requesting material and describing briefly what is wanted. Don't rely on
receiving much from it, however. Face-to-face persuasion
is usually necessary, too. Enlist the help of the company's
photographer, the advertising manager, the public relations
manager, and, especially, the house publication editor. He
should already have many pictures and will probably know
where to find others. He might even entrust you with the
care of his whole collection--if you promise to classify it.

Be sure to request other pictorial material besides
photographs: old advertisements, trademarks, trade cards,
sketches, letterheads, posters, labels, patents, and portraits-
of-the-founder-as-a-young-man. Make a record by subject
of the framed company pictures in individual offices.
Stamp the back of the material with library identifica-

tion; then make sure it bears the necessary "who, what, where, when and why" caption. If this data is not available, ask some employees who have been associated with the firm for a long time to supply the missing information. Once that is done, classification and filing are not difficult because you are dealing with concrete places, objects, and people. Arrange portraits alphabetically, plants and offices geographically, and products and processes by subject. If you have already classified loose documents by subject, you may prefer to incorporate pictures in the same file to save space. Being documentary, they will help to explain the written material, and vice versa. However, if the files are handled much, photos may suffer by not being filed separately.

If your company has a photo library, make arrangements to receive obsolete shots on a continuing basis but reserve the right to weed. One copy of every such picture should be stamped File Copy in large letters on the back and not allowed to leave the library. Every photograph for which there is a negative should have its negative number written on the back. If you are given any historical negatives, ask the company photographer to number and keep them for you, marking their negative envelopes "Historical" so they will not be weeded.

Should your company not have a photo library, start adding current pictures to your archives. Today's pictures are tomorrow's history--if someone has the forethought to save them.

Cataloguing a Photograph Collection
Jane Howe

From <u>Oklahoma Librarian</u> 13:8-12, January 1963. Reprinted by permission.

I.

In order to properly catalogue any collection, remember that it will grow. This is particularly true of photographs. Therefore, certain basic decisions must be made at the beginning.

1. How are the photographs to be used? As a part of the library research and reference materials? Is use to be one of free access by the public?
2. How are the photographs to be filed and housed?
3. How will they be indexed?
4. What information is to be gleaned from them? What is the significance of what is shown? Are the date, the photographer and the donor of importance?
5. How will the librarian anticipate what subjects the users will seek? How will these be gleaned from the subject card?

Specific methods given below are those employed by the Division of Manuscripts at the University of Oklahoma Library. They can be adapted to any size collection.

All photographs given to the library by a donor are housed together under his name. People like to point with pride to "my collection." And when the public knows that the library will care for photograph contributions in this fashion, it is more apt to make donations.

In this connection, it is worthwhile to keep in mind sources of obtaining important photographic items in the local area. "Historical" is an all-inclusive word, covering such subjects as people, flora and fauna, towns, machinery, rodeos, resorts, schools, industry, clothing and dress, sports, et cetera. Numerous attics and basements are cleaned out daily by young relatives who do not realize the importance or significance of old photographs.

Of course, a collection in which the donor is able to identify persons, places and events is a real "find." This is particularly true in the case of Indians and prominent persons, since tribal, political and industrial affiliation, as well as personal identification, is of major import.

The basic tools for cataloguing are subject index cards, library stamp, envelopes for negatives and glass plates, photograph identification gummed labels, manila folders, looseleaf binders, red rope folders, typing paper and carbons, and document cases of strong boxes.

Reference tools which are essential for Indian collections are Handbook of North American Indians by Frederick Hodge (2v) and The Tipi by Reginald and Gladys Laubin. The Look of the Old West by Foster Harris pictures all sorts of items in use in the American pioneer west, including uniforms of the army, transportation vehicles, luggage, clothing--in short, just what the title states. For prints dealing with Civil War subjects, Brady's photographs of that conflict are excellent sources of identification. Historical events may be identified in the American Heritage book, Great Historical Places. Specialized references on architecture, clothing and dress, local geography, local history and the like may be among the regular reference tools of any library.

Forts, Military--Larned

Description Officer's quarters, Ft. Larned, Kan. House nearest now used as private home. Fort was built in 1868 near the Santa Fe Trail to protect the Trail and to curtail Cheyenne and Comanche-Kiowa raiders.

Locale Kansas   Date 1960
Photographer Howe   Type print

Collection & File Number
                    Howe (Jane)--1
University of Oklahoma Library--Division of Manuscripts

        Photographic   Archives

```
+-----------------------------------------------------+
|              Subject Index Card                     |
|                                                     |
| Collection   Howe (Jane)--1                         |
|                 Negative                            |
| Description   Officer's quarters, Ft. Larned, Kan.  |
| House nearest now used as private home.   Built 1868.|
| Built for Santa Fe Trail protect.                   |
|                     Locale   Kansas                 |
|                     Photographer   Howe             |
|                              Date   1960            |
|                              Type   Print           |
|                                                     |
+-----------------------------------------------------+
```

```
+-----------------------------------------------------+
|       Catalog Entries   Forts, Military--Larned;    |
|          Historical Sites                           |
|     not to be removed from Mss Div OU Library       |
+-----------------------------------------------------+
```
                   (The Gummed Label)

There are printed subject indexes, but often these are too large and/or too complicated for local use. Here at the University, a subject index has been compiled for the peculiar needs of the Division of Manuscripts. Colloquial terms are used for two reasons: 1) there is not room for numerous "see" cards in the subject file, and 2) time is of the essence, usually, for the desired photographs to be found and pulled. Therefore, the student will look under outlaws not brigands and robbers, buffalo not bison, or Indians not Indians of North America.

The index is set up under wide general subjects with breakdowns, thus:

Agriculture--	Corn
	Crops
	Farms and Farming
	Irrigation
	Machinery
	Soy Beans
Animals--	Buffalo
	Burro
	Horse
	Skunk
	Wild Cat
Art--	Painting
	Sculpture

Art (cont.)--   Woodcarving
Cities and Towns--   Anadarko
                           Blanchard
                           Elk City
                           Pawhuska
                           Waurika
Clothing and Dress
Costumes
Houses and Housing
Indians (See below for breakdowns)
Law and Law Enforce-
         ment--   Jails
                           Marshals
                           Outlaws
Oklahoma--   Counties
                           Government Officials
                           History
                           Openings
Personalities--Persons are listed by last names and
    not by their nicknames unless family names are
    unknown, i.e., "Buffalo Bill" is Cody, William
    Frederick.
Ranches and Ranching
Uniforms
United States--   Air Force
                           Army
                           Government Officers
                           Uniforms

There are two major breakdowns under Indians: by
tribe and band, and by subjects. The tribal file may look
like this:

Indians--   Apache (Mescalero)
                           Arapaho (Northern)
                           Cherokee (No. Carolina)
                           Kiowa
                           Navajo
                           Pueblo (Acoma)
                           Sioux (Yanktonai)
                           Skitswish
                           Ute

For subjects, these are the categories most asked for:

Indians--   Antiquities
                           Clothing and Dress (Tribe)

Indians (cont.)--   Cradle Boards
                           Dances and Dancing
                           Houses and Housing (Tribe)
                           Social Life and Customs
                           Weapons

Accurate information is an absolute necessity in this category.
It is better to place a subject card under the general heading
of Indians--Clothing and Dress, than to list it under the
wrong tribe.
     Indian personalities are interfiled in the general Per-
sonality file. As a general rule, Christian names follow
family names. There are exceptions, but these are rare:

          American Horse
          American Horse, Tom
          Burnt All Over
          Burnt All Over, Mrs.
          Cadotte, Margaret One Bull
          Chasinghawk, Ruth
          Crazy Snake
          Tabbytite
          Towakonie Jim
          Colonel James Walkinghorse (This is the father,
               named for Colonel James)
          Colonel James Walkinghorse, Bill (This is his son)
          White Bull

New subject headings may be added as needed.

II.

     No matter how large the photograph collection, do not
attempt to work with more than 15 at one time.
     Step 1. Look through the photographs slowly to see
what the subject matter covers and note its significance to
your library patrons. Place duplicate copies and negatives
together (glass plates are stored separately). With a soft
lead pencil number lightly on the margin on the reverse side
of the photographs, in consecutive order, noting copy numbers. Never write across the back of a print with pencil or
pen, as the marks will ridge the face of the picture. Place
negatives in separate envelopes and number. Wrap glass
plates or place in heavy envelopes and number.
     Step 2. Starting back through the photographs, assign
subject headings. For personal use, set up a guide thus:

No. of Photo.	Copies	Neg. or Plate	Photographer
1.	1	Neg	Howe

Date	Locale	Description	Subject
1868	Kansas	Ft. Larned Officers' Quarters	Forts, Military Historical Sites

Here, then, is all of the information needed.   This prevents frequent handling of the prints and negatives.

Step 3.   Make an original and two carbon copies for the accession folder, subject file and shelf index.   The original is kept in a loose-leaf binder, the first carbon is placed in an accession folder, the second carbon is the shelf list and is stored with the photographs.   This is typed thus:

Howe (Jane) Collection

No.	Description	Subject Heading
1.	The officers' quarters, Ft. Larned, Kansas. Built in 1868. Neg.	Forts, Military--Larned Historical Sites
2.	The International Exposition, 1939, San Francisco. Neg.	Amusements--Fairs Architecture--Buildings
3.	Parade, Anadarko Indian Exposition, 1958. Zuni squaws carry pottery on their heads. Neg.	Amusements--Parades Cities & Towns--Anadarko Indians--Pueblo (Zuni) Indians--Art Indians--Clothing & Dress (Pueblo) Indians--Social Life & Customs
4.	Two University of Oklahoma senior members of Sequoyah Club at a club pow-wow, Jan. 1959. No Neg.	Education--O.U.--Sequoyah Club Indians--Cheyenne (Southern) Indians--Art Indians--Clothing & Dress (Cheyenne)

No.	Description	Subject Heading
5.	Jim Bodine, Taos Indian, wearing dance costume. 1958. Neg.	Bodine, Jim Indians--Pueblo (Taos) Indians--Art Indians--Costumes (Dance)

Step 4. Using the guide sheet, type subject heading cards. Place as much description on the card as is needed so photograph will not have to be pulled unnecessarily. Give all of the information as known. If personalities are identified, be sure to type a separate card for each. In the case of Indians, as that of the examples above, stress should be made for that particular subject, i.e. under Clothing and Dress, describe dresses and beadwork; under Art, detail pottery and dress decoration; under Education designate that the dance is sponsored by the Sequoyah Club and that the girl on the right is the Club Princess.

Step 5. The gummed labels are now typed. This label, which is placed on the back of the photograph, should point up the significance of the subject matter. Little-known facts are those sought by the researcher and these are more often than not to be found in local photographs. For example, if a photograph of Indian girls also gives the information that only students with at least 1/16th Indian blood may join the club, that each member must be able to speak a sentence in his tribal tongue, sing a song in it, and do a tribal dance in the "old way," and that this is the oldest Indian Club on any college campus in the country--this is very significant information. An indication of this should be on the label. The name of the collection and the number of the photograph are of prime importance. Be sure to make identical labels for negative and glass plate envelopes. Affix labels to the back of the prints. Copies need only be indicated as such and stamped with the Library Stamp.

Step 6. After photographs are dry, place not more than ten, with their negatives, in a manila folder, label it: Howe (Jane) Collection, Photographs Nos. 1-10. If the collection is small, several manila folders may be placed in a red rope folder, together with the shelf index, and then boxed.

Step 7. After the photographs are catalogued and stored, alphabetize and file subject cards. Place the accession sheet in its proper place.

As the collection grows it will become necessary to place collections in alphabetical order in their boxes. These, in turn, are numbered: A-1, A-2; H-10, H-11. A guide file is made to indicate where a certain collection is to be found: Howe (Jane) Photo: H-10.

Glass plates are labeled on the envelope and then placed in strong boxes or document cases and stored in a safe, cool place where opportunities for breakage are nil. The boxes are also labeled on the outside as to collection and the photograph number: Howe (Jane) Collection--Glass Plates, Nos. 1, 4, 6, 10-18, et cetera.

III.

Flexibility, adaptability and usage are the words for the procedures described above. Emphasis will change in each locale, but the essential foundation is the same everywhere. Sometimes it becomes necessary to return to the basic questions (Part I) to make sure they are still answerable in the light of the ever-changing overall library policy. But if relations between the library and the public are handled with common sense and persistence, the photograph collection will grow to become a very essential source of reference information for the use of all.

Pictures for Public Relations
Irene Simpson

From Special Libraries 56:39-40, January 1965. Copyright by Special Libraries Association 1965. Reprinted by permission.

. . . The role of the Wells Fargo Bank History Room has many facets--from arranging for the use of a full-size stagecoach as backdrop for fashion publicity to providing a source for a quill pen to be used in a TV show. Learning how to use pictures (how to store them and then retrieve the exact one needed) has proven for me the most stimulating aspect of working in the History Room.

The collection is very small by most standards and very specialized. We are narrow-minded in our collecting habits; we start with "Wells" and end with "Fargo." Pictures date from the period of the company's founding in 1852 and include the 1906 fire in San Francisco and the northern California area where the firm now operates its 180-branch bank system. Wells Fargo, however, never did operate in a vacuum, and this allows sufficient breadth to include pictures of 1) miners and the mines from which came the gold shipped by and deposited with Wells Fargo; 2) ships, trains, and stagecoaches on which Wells Fargo carried express, mail, and passengers; 3) portraits of many San Franciscans and early Californians who probably were (or should have been) Wells Fargo's customers; 4) San Francisco and northern California business firms; and 5) portraits of many of those employed by Wells Fargo & Co., and examples of buildings occupied by the firm.

No official records were available when the collection was started some 35 years ago, and the existence today of so much that has come to the collection seems to me incredible--and the flow appears unending. Almost every week some visitor will tell us about his grandfather or uncle or remote relation who was with Wells Fargo. A well-phrased request to borrow a portrait to be copied for our files seldom fails to bring results and often starts a family search that unearths letters, company papers, or other pictures, which are generously presented to us. At present there are around 8,500 pictures in the collection.

Some years ago a very workable system was evolved that has been the basis for organizing this growing collection. Some 15 subjects were arbitrarily established, within which we are able to file all our pictures. Each subject is subdivided as material is accepted, which creates a demand for regrouping, but the picture remains in the originally designated subject. These (and I am referring to 8 x 10 inch or smaller photographs or reproductions) are physically housed in plastic folders filed in three-ring binders. When a binder becomes too cumbersome for easy use, its contents are divided as seems appropriate, and a new binder is added in the series. For example, the section on "Banking" has now been subdivided within its designation of San Francisco banks to include binders marked: B3--San Francisco Banks A-C; B3.1--San Francisco Banks D-F; B3.2--San Francisco Banks G-M; B3.3--San Francisco Banks N-Z. This series is preceded by "B2" for photographs of banking implements, e.g., scales, and followed by "B4," a series of photographs of banks outside San Francisco.

Thus, much of the indexing is completed when a decision is first made as to where to file a photograph. If a photograph is by a named photographer or of more than one subject, e.g., a bank interior with identified men posed behind the tellers' cages, these names are added to the files. In case a grandson of one of them should visit us, we can quickly show him a picture of special interest. Charts outlining the content of the binders in general terms are used and usually suffice for a picture researcher or a visitor who "just wants to look at some pictures." However, when a researcher has a specific problem or, contrariwise, doesn't know what he wants, the challenge is greatest.

For a TV show on the San Francisco Fire Department, the picture researcher who was using other materials from our collection had us stumped with the request for a dalmatian dog--one with big spots. There is no subject heading in the collection for "dogs," so we resorted to intuition and offered a picture of the recipient of a large silver award watch who had posed with his dog at his feet--luckily, it was a satisfactory dalmatian! That picture was, and will continue to be, filed by the name of the man to whom Wells Fargo & Co. presented a watch for bravery.

One of the most frequent requests is for a "stagecoach in action," but somehow the news photographers of the 1860's and 70's just weren't thinking ahead--we're lucky to have a picture posed before a very civilized stage-stop just before departure. Or an editor wants a portrait of Charlie Parkhurst, who became famous after death when it was

learned that "Charlie" was a woman; in life "he" was just
another stage-driver who had no need to have a likeness tak-
en for his family.

Since the company sets up a number of small displays
in branch banks, the History Room has been the recipient of
some interesting objects and documents; in the measure that
pictures are used in these exhibits, I anticipate being given
usable pictures to add to the collection. For instance, some
branch managers had been given photographs of former loca-
tions and didn't know what to do with them until I made our
needs known.

Those who use the collection vary from local commercial artists who need "scrap," e.g., how does a stem-
winder watch open or how did the stage-driver hold his reins,
to a book editor searching for end papers, a cover illustration, or text photographs. When a request is for "any
means of transportation, or a San Francisco cable car, or
even a covered wagon," and a researcher leaves very pleased
to use a Wells Fargo stagecoach, we've had a good day!
When the editor requests a photograph of a Mother Lode
town in the 1860's and the one his picture researcher selects
just happens to be one with a Wells Fargo office prominently
marked, that's fine with us. In any event, as all who work
with pictures well know, the use of a photograph with accurate credits starts a recurring wave of requests, and the
fun of imaginatively providing suitable and usable pictures is
unending.

Recently the History Room unveiled a portrait of Henry Wells, whose name the company bears along with that of
William G. Fargo. For the past 25 years we have had a
handsome pastel by H. Hart of Mr. Fargo, given us by his
grandniece. Many times when asked, "Why don't you have
one of Mr. Wells," I have replied, "Because no one has
given us a suitable portrait to match Mr. Fargo." One day
I so replied to the visiting Director of Admissions at Wells
College (Aurora, New York), who immediately arranged for
us to use one of two portraits of Henry Wells hanging at the
college. With pride it was framed and hung; no longer must
we apologize for its lack. Sometimes the pictures come, as
this one, "large-size," but so long as they come and are
well used, I feel the pictures in the History Room are serving worthwhile purposes.

May We Use this Picture?--Rights and Premissions
Helen Faye

From Special Libraries 56:23-6, January 1965. Copyright
by Special Libraries Association 1965. Reprinted by permission.

In addition to understanding the problems of copyright
and public domain, the picture librarian and researcher must
understand the various kinds of ownership rights pertaining
to pictures as well as the problems of libel and invasion of
privacy in the use of pictures.

Who can give permission to reproduce a picture?
The holder of the copyright, of course. This means the library, the museum, the picture agency, or the individual
who has pictures of which he holds the rights.

Kinds of Rights

What kinds of rights or permissions exist for giving,
licensing, or selling? The most common are one-time rights,
which means the seller of the rights allows the purchaser to
reproduce a picture in multiple printings of one edition of the
publication for which it was purchased. The publisher must
not reproduce the illustration in a new edition without paying
again, and he cannot allow anyone else to use the picture.
The term "one-time rights" is sometimes phrased as "one-
time reproduction," "one-time use," or "one use only." All
restrict the user in the same way.

First rights is a term generally used only by photographers or photo agencies giving a purchaser the right to be the
first one to reproduce photographs or artwork. First rights
may be limited in time or in the nature of the publication in
which they may be used. For example, a photographer may
be commissioned by a magazine to do a picture story. The
agreement between the photographer and the magazine may
state that the magazine will be the first one allowed to publish the pictures and may also specify a time limit, so that
if the pictures are not published by the magazine within, say,
six months, the photographer may sell the pictures elsewhere. In addition, the agreement may state that the first
rights are for magazine sale only and that the photographer

may retain the right to sell first rights for book or other
use.

Second rights is the term used to cover sales after
the first rights have been exercised by the original party to
the agreement.   Usually when a publisher buys first rights,
the photographer holds the second rights, giving him the
right to sell the pictures elsewhere after the first rights have
been used.

Exclusive rights gives the purchaser the right to reproduce the picture in any publication at any time for any
purpose.   For example, a magazine commissions a photographer to spend a week photographing the Grand Canyon.   It
pays all his expenses and gives him a very adequate daily
rate of payment; in return the photographer signs over to the
magazine all rights in his pictures.   The magazine can then
use the pictures editorially, on the cover, for advertising,
and may even sell or syndicate the pictures to others.   In
buying exclusive rights the purchaser usually pays at least
twice the cost of one-time rights, often more, since the
agreement prohibits further sale of the material.

A picture may be sold with several other restrictions
or privileges as to its use.   Advertising rights give the purchaser the right to reproduce a work in an advertisement.
Since advertisements are usually repeated in several magazines or other media, and since the expected profit from the
use of the picture is presumably great, the cost of advertising rights is much greater than for other rights.

An additional form of rights involves the country where
the picture is to be published.   U.S. rights means the picture may be published in a work in the United States and its
possessions; it also means that the picture may not be published in a foreign edition of the original publication unless
additional world rights or foreign rights are bought.

To summarize, a picture bought from an agency, a
museum, or from a photographer may be bought with any of
the rights described above or combinations of any of them.
The fees for the various rights vary, and the cost increases
with the expected number of uses of the pictures and with
the presumed profit to be gained by the purchaser.

All this may sound rather formal and perhaps gives
the impression that those who sell pictures or rights to reproduce pictures have a good grasp of the legal and business
aspects of these transactions.   This, however, is not usually
the case; the average photographer often has a confused idea
of what rights he is selling.   However, the American Society
of Magazine Photographers has formulated clear definitions
and recommends certain ethical and legal practices to the

profession. Picture agencies, through their trade group, the Picture Agency Council of America, have recently begun to systemize their understanding of the rights they sell. But since there is no standard code, it is really the responsibility of the purchaser to make clear what rights he wishes to buy when he makes his request to the supplier of a picture. He should state what use is to be made of the picture, whether it is for a textbook, tradebook, magazine, or advertisement, and whether it is to be used as a cover illustration, inside the book, or whatever. It is then the supplier's responsibility to charge accordingly and to restrict the use, if necessary.

Invasion of Privacy

I will now turn to some of the pitfalls in the legal use of pictures, particularly in regard to invasion of privacy and libel. My remarks are based on ten years of working with these problems in the publishing of textbooks, of reading on the subject, and discussing these matters with lawyers. I am not a lawyer nor an expert in law, and any of my conclusions and recommendations are open to a different interpretation by the next judge or jury who tries such a case.

Let us assume that a magazine publisher is about to reproduce a photo of a crowd scene on Fifth Avenue in New York City. He has the photographer's permission and there is no violation of copyright, but how about the people in the picture? The photograph clearly shows many faces in the crowd. If this picture is used in an informational, educational way, in a magazine article, for example, and not for advertising, it may be published without regard for these people. Since they are appearing in a public place, going about the ordinary act of walking down the street, the publisher is not invading their privacy by publishing the picture. However, if this picture is used for advertising, the purchaser may have some lawsuits on his hands, for in many states the right of privacy is interpreted to protect against the exploitation of a person's name, likeness, or personality without his consent.

A second example is a photo of a man at work in a control tower at La Guardia Airport. Here again, there is no invasion of privacy in the publishing of this photo for editorial use since the person is at his normal occupation.

Since the term "invasion of privacy" is often defined as injury to a person's own feelings, a good test is to put oneself in the place of the person in the picture. How would you feel if your picture were used in this way? In particular, try to judge the picture in terms of the caption to be used with it, the text adjacent to it, and the entire context in which it will be viewed. Picture researchers and editors sometimes fail to consider the entire effect of pictures and words as they finally appear in print. The use of a picture in conjunction with text that may put an unfavorable or conspicuous light on the persons involved is always questionable. Even though a publisher may have a model release, which has been carefully worded to cover many uses of a picture, it may be not specific enough to allow use in an offensive context. It is necessary to state the exact use to which the photo is to be put if there is any chance that the use may be objectionable.

It is an invasion of privacy to use a caption or adjacent text to impute words or ideas, which may appear to be matters of a private or personal nature, to the individuals pictured. An example of this is the fictional picture story where words and a whole story line are made up to go with a set of pictures. It may be literature, but it isn't legal unless one has model releases from the subjects.

An extensive picture story covering many aspects of a person's life, even though completely true and flattering, may be considered an invasion of this person's privacy unless one has permission to do exactly this; for example, the detailed coverage given to many families by women's magazines. An exception to this is the famous person who has lost his right to privacy by his conspicuous position in public life. Political figures, actors, or other famous persons can sue for libel in some cases but seldom for invasion of privacy.

Do animals have rights of privacy? No, as every pet owner knows, dogs, cats, and other animals have little privacy in their lives; they have no legal protection against invasion of privacy. How about one's home? If a photographer takes a picture of a house while standing in the owner's potato field, he can be arrested for trespassing but cannot be prevented from publishing his picture, for buildings have no rights of privacy. Lastly, persons who are no longer living are not protected by invasion of privacy regulations.

In all the above examples the pictures are used in editorial publishing, not in advertising. For use in advertising it would be necessary to obtain releases for the pictures of the dog, cat, and house, since the owners have a right to profit from the use of their property.

Libel

        Invasion of privacy can be best understood as injury
to a person's own feelings; while libel, that spooky word, is
injury to a person's reputation or the holding him up to public ridicule. Note that the taking of a picture is not libelous; it is the publishing of a picture that makes it so. And
what is meant by publishing? By law, in the case of libel,
publication means not only printing a picture or a statement
in a book or magazine, it means even communicating the
defamation to a third person. In matters of libel, therefore,
displays, exhibitions, or showing a picture to a group or
even to your best friend could be considered publication.
        Note also that it is the publisher of the picture who
is sued, not the photographer, or the researcher, or the librarian who gave out the picture (except possibly in cases of
pictures where the actual picture content itself is libelous).
There are two reasons why it is generally the publisher who
is sued. First, the publication or showing of a picture is
what makes it a public matter, and a picture can only damage the person's reputation if it is made public. Second,
there is a strong tendency among plaintiffs to sue where the
money is, and a corporation would be considered better
game than an individual.
        Also, note that most cases of libel occur because of
the way in which a picture is used, the context in which it
is published, or what is said about it; less often is the intrinsic content of the picture libelous. Examples of pictures
with intrinsically libelous content are the candid shots that
make the subjects look ridiculous, cases of unfortunate juxta-
positions within the picture, and cases where optical distor-
tions result in an illusion of ugliness or grotesquery. Also,
of course, photos that have been retouched or faked in other
ways can make an innocent photo into a libelous one, as
every editor of the sensational press knows.
        Here are some examples of libelous pictures. A
photo of a married couple was purchased from a photo agency
and used conspicuously to illustrate a magazine article entitled "Is Your Marriage Going on the Rocks?" The couple
sued for libel and won, even though they had previously
signed a model release. As mentioned before, a signed
model release does not protect a publisher who uses a picture in an offensive way unless the model release is carefully worded to cover exactly such a use. In illustrating a
textbook on elementary school educational practices, Harcourt, Brace & World obtained the cooperation of several
teachers to pose for pictures showing good and bad teaching

practices. The model releases were carefully worded to
cover the exact use to which the pictures were to be put,
and in the captions it was pointed out that the teachers had
posed for the pictures.

Another publisher used a picture of three teen-agers
to illustrate an article entitled "Gang Boys." The jury found
the use of the picture libelous, even though the boys had
posed willingly for the picture. They had not been aware of
the exact use to which the picture was to be put.

News Photos

News photos, when current, are not considered libelous or invasions of privacy, unless the caption is worded in
such a way as to make it appear that, for example, a suspected criminal has in fact committed a crime. Interestingly, a news photo can contain a time bomb; if a photo of a
person accused of a traffic violation, for example, is published several years after the case was current, that person
may be able to sue for invasion of privacy because the case
is no longer newsworthy and he again has a right to his privacy. Well-known persons have no such rights, however.
Once a person has become a public figure, it is very difficult for him to object to the publishing of even unflattering
material about him, provided it passes the test of being
truthful or at least only fairly critical.

Conclusions

I hope I have not given the impression that a firm
body of legislation exists in which these matters are neatly
spelled out. Such is not the case; some laws do exist, but
they vary from state to state and do not cover all possible
cases. The existing body of tradition and common law,
which changes according to the times, governs these problems more than actual legislation does.

Perhaps by now it seems that the best course is to
give out no pictures for publication, display nothing but old
master drawings, and hide all photos with people in them.
However, intelligent observation of what other people are
publishing and displaying, plus your own sensibilities and
good taste, should be a fair guide to the proper and legal
use of pictures.

Section IV. Synthesis for Service
_____

    This section is reserved for articles that treat more than one nonbook material. The subject matter of these articles ranges from theoretical questions and speculations regarding the role and future possibilities of nonbook materials, to practical problems such as cataloging and storing the materials and choosing equipment needed to utilize them. Most of the questions discussed in these articles are relevant to all types of libraries.

A/V: Has It Any Future in Libraries?
      Harold Goldstein

Reprinted by permission from the Wilson Library Bulletin 36:670-3+, April 1962. Copyright 1962 by the H.W. Wilson Company.

    If we are to talk of the future of audio-visual materials in libraries, it seems to me we must first relate the past to the present.
    The practice of film usage started in the schools in the early Twenties, with ponderous equipment and poorly made materials. Its success as an extension of learning was evidenced by a swift rise in the Thirties--you may remember the ERPI company of those years and its films. Mainly the boom was in motion pictures; other lesser aids were and had been far more easily accepted. Flat pictures, mounted or otherwise, have been in libraries for a long time; phonographs and their necessary accompaniments--records-- have been with us to represent the "audio" half of the phrase for about thirty years. Here I want to stress something which was true in the past, is true today and is likely to be true in the future: a/v services in libraries seem to hinge mainly on the 16mm educational film, which has come to be the evidence of library participation in the varied field of audio-visual aids.
    Well, what else of the past? The American Library Association has been involved for more than twenty years through its Audio-Visual Committee, created in June 1940,

and through other groups whose responsibilities include the
promotion of library media and materials. Our written heritage from the past in this field includes Gerald McDonald's
book, [1] published in 1942; but precious little else has been
written by and for librarians. On the action front we have
had slow, slow growth in library acceptance of the idea of
non-print usages, some ventures among libraries in cooperative planning and activities, but relatively little success in
exploring with non-library agencies the feasibility of increased cooperation.

From the past to the present in the a/v field is a
matter of too few years. If for our present purposes I may
define the past as the years before 1946, 1947 marks the beginning of a present which extends right down into our laps.
It is therefore not surprising that the hold-backs and fail-
ures mentioned above are still with us, although there have
been some new developments. First and foremost is the continued growth of cooperative ventures to provide films for library patrons. Sometimes--perhaps even too often--this
growth was stimulated among smaller urban and sparse-pop-
ulation areas by the service-to-schools idea. I do not know
the number of cooperatives of this kind presently working
well in the country, nor is the number important in itself.
What is important is that they have solved a number of problems in one way or another so as to get on with the main
job of increasing the library's usefulness to its community.
Perhaps next in value are the increased a/v holdings of some
libraries--holdings which are not only respectable numerically but valuable in content. Let us not praise this point too
enthusiastically, however; for every new title added there are
more titles to see than all a/v librarians together could possibly preview at any given time.

Another source of strength is the increased use of
a/v aids in general adult services. Film forums, group activities and library extension activities in many forms have
come to utilize films--effectively in some places and dully in
others. The point is that such activities are increasingly a
commonplace rather than a rarity. Still another evidence of
growth stems from the library's general reorientation to its
community; as the library has widened its focus, so has the
awareness of audio-visual services broadened.

Yet we are today nagged by a lack of progress in
several areas. There is no overall professional group working constantly to narrow the gap between poor a/v work (or
none) and good service. There is also little evidence of internal coordination of a kind which would enable the entire
library staff to deal effectively with all materials. There is

a dearth of efficient tools designed to make the coordinated use of print and non-print matter as easy as the use of either type by itself. What has happened, for example, to the bible of library film knowledge--the Educational Film Guide? It has become atrophied (mainly, in my opinion, through the lack of library support) to the point where it is almost apocryphal.[2] How many libraries have a catalog of a/v materials, or any other locally created tool, of the same efficiency and completeness as their public catalog or even their shelf-list?

With us still are these problems: too much subscription to a/v activity without sufficient questioning of its spirit; a limiting of a/v services to standards well below those accepted for book services; and acceptance of a/v materials for their newness alone rather than for their intrinsic worth.

Obsession with 16mm

To me the clearest evidence of our involvement in this kind of rationale is our commitment to the idea, mentioned before, that effective library a/v programming revolves around films. Certainly the film is the most expensive, complex and difficult material to select, administer, and evaluate. No other single tool is so capable of misapplication--it's a program for Kiwanis, it's a substitute for a speaker, it's a filler-in when nothing else can be found. And, handled in this way, it's so ineffectual.

We attempt to justify the cost of films on something like a per capita use basis (if 1,000 people see a $100 film, it only costs ten cents per head to see, and you can hardly circulate a book for that). So we go after more showings to bigger audiences. This is phony. Do we worry about how many times an expensive art or craft book circulates? And if we do, can we best justify its purchase on the basis of circulation or on the hole it fills in our collection? By such concentration on 16mm film and the expensive equipment essential to its use, we have put too many of our eggs into a basket which has virtually no escape holes. Eight millimeter film is almost unknown in public libraries (or in any other kind either), although there is material available in this form of equal or greater value than much of the 16mm material we think we couldn't do without. Further, expenditure for 8mm equipment can be a minor factor, since approximately one in every ten homes in this country contains an 8mm projector.

But I digress from my main point, which is our commitment to one major medium as evidence of library a/v

activity. The lesser aids, if I may call them that, have
been relegated to some limbo of thinking which, I suppose,
considers them fitting only for school use, or at best of limited application to other purposes. I refer to slides, filmstrips, and other visual materials. One reason for this,
perhaps, is the steady development of book illustration, which
provides less reason for showing something to the reader in
addition to what is already on the pages before him. In any
case, few libraries can point with justified pride to organized
collections of materials, other than film and records, which
are aimed at supplementing the regular book collection for
the general user. Has anyone ever seen a package for John
Q. which will give him additional materials along with his
books and which can be charged out as simply as his books?

I do not want leveled at me charges that I am against
16mm films for public libraries. Rather, I want to remind
you that there are additional ways in which to consolidate the
gains of present a/v work.

Let me indicate a few such ways now used in the
schools. During the past two years or so, the National Science Foundation has presented complete physics, chemistry,
and biology courses on film. These are designed to help out
in the unequal struggle among school systems of varying resources to supply much-needed science instruction. While
these efforts are limited in a sense to classroom materials,
their effects must have made some dent on public and perhaps college library programs. Don't parents want more information about the new courses? Shouldn't public librarians
want to know more about them?

Another example from the schools is the Midwest Airborne Television Instructional Program, which began last
September to broadcast for six hours a day to six states.
It is inconceivable to me that the impact of this new instructional aid will not be felt by smaller libraries, in spite of
what seems to be scant attention to print resources in the
general guide to the TV programs. And when this impact becomes translated into demands for more supplementary books,
will we be ready to deal with it? I doubt it.

Both film programs and airborne TV are designed to
equalize school opportunities. It is precisely on the smaller
public libraries, with limited support and resources, that the
blow will fall. Who then will come to the rescue? If there
is no helping hand, I might be pessimistic enough to think
that the public library will be bypassed as a source of help
and that small libraries will suffer a further loss of support.
Let me point out that if this experiment is successful--and
it most probably will be--it will very soon be extended to

other areas of the country.

I have mentioned television; if my memory serves me right, the last audio-visual workshop for librarians was in 1958 at San Francisco and it concentrated on television. Those in attendance (less than a hundred) heard and saw the products of some hard-working librarians in the field; but those of us who were there have not yet revolutionized library acceptance of or participation in television activities. There is a parallel here with the remarks made above about the school film programs; we cannot assume that modern devices will be used by smaller institutions merely because larger institutions experiment with them. Some kind of equalizing support is needed throughout the profession. There are still hundreds of librarians who will adopt a/v services only after they've solved all their print problems. They are convinced that a/v activity is no more than an extra which cannot be justified with present limited budgets and staff (and, I may add, with their own limited conceptions of the possibilities of these services).

Eight problems

Television is a problem--perhaps the biggest one we've faced since movable type. When some high-priced TV pusher introduces an author, the fabulous demand created for this person's latest title is enough to give even Mr. Macy an apoplexy in trying to fill the requests; somehow I can't help feeling that "they" are plotting against us when it happens. But what bothers me more is that we are not able or willing to capitalize on such developments by making available, in quantity, worthwhile materials that are boosted in this way. I see this as perhaps the number one problem in my inventory: the matter of top-level coordination between libraries and the mass media to prevent avoidable crises of this kind.

Second on my list of problems is the need, mentioned above, of finding some way to equalize supplies of materials, training opportunities, and service patterns among libraries of varying resources. Until it can be more widely shown that it is possible for the smaller libraries to proceed successfully into audio-visual operations, we have failed to a certain extent in capitalizing on the nature of these materials --they are in themselves equalizers of educational opportunity, produced for mass audiences, and should not be limited by the size of the distributor-user.

Third, let me remind you that I have not mentioned a/v activities in college libraries. I cannot claim to know much about the field--there are only a baker's dozen or so of entries under the appropriate subject headings in <u>Library Literature</u> between 1952 and 1961. In 1955, Bennett reported in the January issue of <u>College and Research Libraries</u>[3] a survey of audio-visual services in college and university libraries. The majority of returns from about 1,600 institutions indicated that only about 15 percent had centralized a/v services under librarian control. While a much larger percentage of the respondents felt that the institution library ought to have such control, it was not evident at that time. How many more such libraries now have a/v operations under library direction I do not know; I somehow doubt that the number has changed significantly in the last six years. For one thing, on most campuses where there is one, the a/v operation has become big business; it is not within the present competencies or desires of librarians to direct such operations. Another problem here is the serving of schools from such a/v resources, with an attendant shortage of materials for on-campus needs. Few campuses are able to duplicate such materials, nor should they; but in the meantime the institutional library is outside the operation. The answer, it seems to me, might be cooperation between academic institutions and other types of libraries, since among small colleges the same limitations undoubtedly occur as among small public libraries. How many film circuits or cooperatives include colleges within their operating areas?

Fourth, what about school libraries and materials centers? Under the impetus of the current program to implement the new school standards, public and college librarians may suddenly find that their conception of a total materials center is sadly lacking in comparison to the schools. Will this not raise a serious question of reorganization, flexibility of service, and additional problems?

Fifth, there is the problem of encouraging the production of new a/v materials which would be closely related to library purposes and programs. There are thousands of film titles, records, etc., which we cannot now afford to buy; but even so there are many more topics of greater relevance to public library needs which might be covered if we could assure producers of an adequate market. Until we are organized in such a way as virtually to guarantee definite sales for given titles or materials, we will be forced to compromise and adapt. Film production especially is aimed at school needs, and we do not compare in any way, shape or size with school purchases across the nation.

Allied with this problem are two other questions involving present availability. One is the need to secure fuller community use of existing resources. Generally speaking, school collections of films are available only to school people; the reasons for this limitation concern administrative arrangements and I am not one to belittle the size of the problem. But I know of one community where cooperative use of school and public library resources was worked out (Freeport, Illinois) and it would seem improbable that the difficulty is entirely unsurmountable. The second aspect of this problem of availability concerns our limited view of what is proper film fare for public libraries. We shy away from classroom films for the most part because of their limited application to adult needs; but what do we buy in their place? Sponsored films of dubious relevance or value, series-type films whose content is much alike in interest area, and so on. Are these really more suitable for public library patrons than the best of the classroom films?

Sixth on my list of problems is the bibliographic organization of present and future materials. Does anyone know of a Detroit reader classification system for non-print materials? How do you relate such current information services as Facts on File to films or other non-print aids? Would we be more successful if we allowed individual use of the so-called mass media in the same way as print? How awful would it be, really, to have six different people see the same film at six different times instead of showing it to 60 all together in one room? Could we not better interrelate the six individual uses with a variety of other library materials? (Why don't I stop asking questions which I can't answer?)

Seventh is the provision of resource centers which are capable of collecting and organizing a variety of packages of a/v material to serve smaller units or specialized demands. This activity could be built on existing cooperatives but it would need a much broader scope than they provide in order to mobilize all kinds of local resources and seek out new ones. Its main purpose would be to provide the widest possible collections of non-print materials--in effect to become the regional Library of Congress of a/v operations.

Eighth--and last--is the matter of continued training and retraining in order to keep track of new developments without the delays inherent in the normal process of library change and innovation. Such a program would involve a central clearing house for such training, mobile personnel whose assignments would be the equivalent for a/v of the Library Community Project combined with a survey team. It would have a tough job in helping to equate the needs of a variety of libraries and librarians, but its usefulness might mean

the difference between total mobilization of library resources
and continuation of the creepingly slow way in which we now
climb on the a/v bandwagon.

We cannot afford another twenty-year gap between
peaks of accomplishment. One good reason why we can't
wait is the present inadequacy of budgets and staff. The
total expenditures to date are respectable, even if tremendous gulfs exist among and between libraries, and this total
expenditure could easily be lost if it is not consolidated into
a better coordinated service than we now have. The second
reason why we must move with speed is that we see before
us now the vanguard of a generation whose backgrounds include varied experiences with a/v learning. They will toler-
ate less and less our fumbling with materials strange to us
but familiar to them. At the moment they are forced to
rely on public libraries, but who can guarantee that another
agency might not arise to serve a future population in ways
we seem to minimize or avoid?

Fear of competition is not the reason I want better
a/v activities in libraries. I am conscious of the best reason in the world for wanting them: they provide the best
open door to the wide world of continuing learning and self-
education for all citizens. No other agency can provide this
total experience; no other profession can lay claim to a more
worthy objective. Why can't we achieve this objective in ten
years?

Notes

1. McDonald, Gerald D. , Educational Motion Pictures and
     Libraries (Chicago, ALA, 1942).
2. Editor's Note: For a statement regarding future publica-
     tion plans for Educational Film Guide, see the an-
     nouncement on page 692.
3. Bennett, F. "Audio-Visual Services in Colleges and
     Universities in the U.S. " College and Research Li-
     braries, January 1955, p. 12.

Fear of the Newer Media
A. W. VanderMeer

Paper presented at a conference on trade books in the schools,
sponsored by the American Book Publishers Council, held at
Harriman, New York, February 1961. From A. L. A. Bulletin 55:798-802, October 1961. Reprinted by permission.

In order to understand the impact of the newer media,
it is necessary to bear in mind the cultural climate in which
they exist. A primary characteristic of our society is the
high value placed upon the dissemination and discovery of
knowledge. Nearly everyone agrees on the importance of
education and its presumed result--the informed and effective
citizen.
A second area of agreement--this time a negative
one--is that the acquisition of information and of low-level
skills does not constitute an adequate or even a particularly
worthy aim for education. The development of scholarship,
the spirit of inquiry, the fulfillment of the individual's personal intellectual potential, and the satisfaction and development of creative ability are agreed upon as the really worthy
aims of education. Knowledge and skill acquisition are considered to be merely instrumental to the fulfillment of these
higher aims.
Given such agreement as to the value and aims of education, it seems surprising that among intellectuals there
is widespread resistance to newer media. The proponents
of the newer media profess the same kinds of aims and beliefs concerning education as do its antagonists. What, then,
are the sources of this antagonism? To a certain extent,
they are inherent in several broad characteristics of our society. In the first place, the newer media lend themselves
to the standardization of institutionalized education, and there
is a widespread antagonism toward this. Everyone assumes,
on an emotional basis, the superiority of the tailor-made
suit over one from Robert Hall, the Christian Dior original
over the dress from S. Klein's ready-to-wear, and the cus-
tom-built home over the prefabricated. Since the newer
media are quite justifiably associated with the less preferred
of these, they tend to be rejected on the same kind of emotional basis. Secondly, the newer media clearly involve me-

381

chanical means of communication, and many people view the
printed page as the mind's last refuge from the machine.
Finally, our schools of education emphasize individual differences among students to the point where we are almost
ready to apologize for having classes larger than half a doz-
en students.   Most of the newer media are quite obviously
group oriented.

However, these three characteristics of the new me-
dia--standardization, mechanization, and group orientation--
obviously are not "bad" in and of themselves.

For some, the newer media pose the threat of technological unemployment.   For others, they pose a threat of
numerous changes in teaching and publishing.   Certainly the
writings of the proponents of television, for example, have
done nothing to mitigate these threats.

Perhaps these sources of antagonism toward the newer media, together with additional ones, are summarized
best by what might be called the literate man's protest towards the mass media.   A. Whitney Griswold has said, in
this connection, "We are in danger of trading the mind's eye
for the eye's mind."   Joseph Krutch goes further and says,
in effect, that if we give the poor reader pictures, he never
will learn to read.

It is clear then, that the climate is generally antag-
onistic to the newer educational media.   In my opinion this
antagonism is unjustified, both in terms of the universal
agreements concerning the value of knowledge and the aims
of education, and in terms of the characteristics of these
media and of their potential effects on people.   While it is
nonetheless real for being so, this antagonism is primarily
an irrational, emotionalized attitude, for there is plenty of
data both in the "conventional wisdom" and in the scientific
literature on psychology and on communication to support the
contention that these negative attitudes overlook the facts of
human development and human learning.

In the first place, it is a fact that regardless of his
ultimate level of competence in the use of the printed page,
each human being goes through approximately the same
stages in developing such competence.   The road is the same
for all, that is, from learning to deal with concrete and real
situations to learning to deal with abstractions, which is the
essence of both reading and thought.   The speed at which
this road is traversed, the duration of the pauses, slow-
downs, and speed-ups along the way, and the age of starting
the journey all differ among individuals, but the route is essentially the same for all.

Second, it is obvious that the objections to newer me-

dia are just as valid for the less gifted members of our society as they are for the geniuses. Yet the objection to newer media rests on the assumption that they are detrimental.
There is nothing inherent in the use of newer media that requires all students to use them at all stages in their learning. There is nothing at all inconsistent between mass education for the many and the pursuit of excellence for the few.
As a matter of fact, an excellent case can be built on the
assumption that only through a program of mass education
can we discover those who are capable of becoming and mo-
tivated to become intellectual leaders.

    This then, in brief, is the climate in which newer
media exist. It is a climate full of antagonism, largely unjustified. If there is any lesson to be learned from all this,
it is that each of us has an obligation to think rather than
merely to react concerning the newer media.

    If we are to think about the role of trade books in a
society in which technology is becoming more and more a
part of the education process, we need to establish a few
bench marks concerning conditions of institutionalized education in this country.

Some aspects of education

    We recognize that there are three kinds of objectives
for education, whether it be institutionalized education carried on in schools or informal education carried on independently by individuals. These are the cognitive aspects, which
are concerned primarily with the development of concepts and
understandings; the affective aspects, which are concerned
with development of attitudes, tastes and appreciations; and
the psychomotor aspects, which are concerned primarily with
the development of skills, both manual and intellectual. The
newer media are relatively well-suited to some of these, and
relatively ill-suited to others.

    In order to deal with the problems of education, some
six kinds of systems have been devised and are in use.
These systems are mass presentation, individual and small
group instruction, automated teaching, human interaction, individual study, and creative activities. In the first two of
these systems, an essential element is the teacher operating
in a more or less formalized situation. In the third system,
automated teaching, the learner interacts with a specially designed program which, in its more sophisticated forms, permits him to pursue his own pace and, by his responses, to
determine the direction that the instruction takes. The
fourth of these systems, that of human interaction, presup-

poses the teacher as the less dominant figure in the learning
process, and assumes that learning may occur through the
interplay of intellects even though these intellects may not
be completely informed. The group-dynamics people emphasize this type of learning, as do those who find the "brain-
storming session" and allied techniques useful. Individual
study and creative activity are, as the name implies, the
solitary pursuit of knowledge and of activities for self-ex-
pression.

Using the newer media

It is quite clear that the impact of newer media has
been a prerequisite to the development of some of the systems just described, and that they are of greater use in promoting some types of learning than they are in promoting
others. It has been adequately demonstrated, for example,
that television, be it open-circuit, closed-circuit, or airborne, is quite effective in the mass presentation of data.
Research has shown that, when limited to the assessment of
concept development and to the imparting of information, television is at least as effective as face-to-face lecturing and
other conventional means of group teaching in which the
teacher imparts information. Furthermore, it has been amp-
ly shown through experiments at Stephens College and elsewhere that television has important potential in the presentation of affective material--artists, personages, events, and
drama. Some three hundred colleges and universities all
over the United States, for example, are offering credit in
mathematics to those who meet required work as presented
by the Continental Classroom, the characteristic element of
which is the dissemination of modern mathematics as taught
by the best instructors. The Midwest Airborne Television
Project is soon to get off the ground, and will reach with
enrichment lessons school children scattered over half a doz-
en states bordering the state of Indiana. Dozens of colleges
and universities have used closed-circuit and open-circuit
television as a regular or supplementary part of their educational program. In every case both experience and research have shown that via television we can present information, dramatize situations and events, extend the senses
so that all can see better, and multiply the influence of
gifted teachers.
On the other hand, efforts to provide interaction between the student and the television instructor have not met
with signal success. Only a beginning has been made on research to devise ways whereby the reinforcement that is so

much a part of face-to-face instruction can be presented to individuals via television. Seemingly insoluble is the problem of varying the level of difficulty and rate of presentation of information when television is being used.

It is inevitable that television will increase in its application in formal education and that it will have a continued impact upon the thinking, beliefs, and information of the general public. Not only is research going on apace to improve television in its obvious applications, but also to overcome the limitations that have thus far prevented more widespread and varied applications.

Implications for trade books

Obviously, there are implications here for the publication of trade books. In the first place, it seems to be inevitable that an increased trend in mass instruction will be counterbalanced by an increased emphasis on individual learning. The "equal and opposite reaction" principle holds here for education as well as for physics. This, to me, would indicate a trend not to more textbooks but to more trade books--books that are suited to various types of audiences, books that are intended for good readers, for readers lacking in some skills, for adult readers, for child readers, for the blue-collar worker and his children, for the white-collar worker and his children.

What television teaching makes available to authors and publishers it also makes available to the adult population. I would predict rather freely that television teaching will infect the entire population with an increased interest in further learning. Dr. Charles Hoban of the Annenberg School of Communication at the University of Pennsylvania is at present immersed in a study which should show the extent to which this prediction is true. He is studying the extent and qualities of that particular audience for educational broadcasts that consists of the occasional or casual viewers who, like eavesdroppers, look in on a program or two but who do not sign up for the course, or make a formal request for supplementary materials. This group, to my mind, is the one most interesting to book publishers, but its members have not heretofore been either identified or studied.

Teaching machines

Teaching machines, or automatic devices for self-instruction, have been proved to be well adapted to the presentation and teaching of sequential data, concepts, and principles. Lumsdaine and his associates in the American Institute for Research in Pittsburgh have demonstrated quite conclusively that these devices can make a significant contribution to the learning of science by secondary and elementary school children. At present, more than a dozen research studies aimed at various levels of students and involving various academic disciplines are being supported by the U.S. Office of Education under the National Defense Education Act of 1958. All of these so-called teaching machines have in common the characteristic of presenting information in small steps, permitting the learner to proceed at his own pace, and reinforcing correct responses while extinguishing erroneous ones. The more sophisticated machines add remedial teaching, controlled by the classes of errors the individual makes in responding to the information presented and the questions asked.

The central element of the teaching machine is the subject matter to be presented. The academic content must be divided into discrete units and placed in an appropriate sequence. This process is called programming. James Finn has said in his articles on technology and education, "He who controls the programming heartland, controls the American educational system." The question of who will take responsibility for developing the programs that machines present should be of at least passing interest to trade book publishers. This job could be done by school people, textbook publishers, trade book publishers, or by other entrepreneurs. I would not presume to state an opinion as to who should do the programming, but I am quite sure that someone will.

Language laboratories

An allied device is the language laboratory. In its simplest form, it can simply consist of a recording system which permits the student to hear recorded excerpts in a foreign tongue, to imitate these excerpts, and to compare his performance with that of the expert. Both experience and research have shown that the language laboratory can greatly facilitate the learning of a second language. Inevitably, as the teaching of the speaking and listening aspects of foreign language becomes more efficient, more people will feel that language study is within their grasp and interest. This will inevitably result in a greater demand for reading materials in other languages, especially materials that are graded to cater to people of varying degrees of competency and to people of varying ages, interests, and backgrounds.

These three major types of newer media seem certain to have important influences on the trade book field. Their impact can be thought of as reflecting two general characteristics. First, there is the mass presentation of information via television and related media such as motion pictures, filmstrips, radio, etc. Secondly, there is the impact of automated teaching devices which enable the educator to relegate to individualized instruction the many things that teachers have long dreamed of doing but, because of sheer weight of numbers of students, have been unable to do.

The three classes of media are complementary rather than competitive. Taken together, they have great promise for increasing both the efficiency and the scope of education in this country.

They may also be expected to have general kinds of impacts upon the trade book field. Anything that improves the efficiency of education will increase the demand for education. This is another way of saying that technological change has never decreased consumption but has always had precisely the opposite effect. True, the manufacturer of horseshoes did not benefit from the introduction of the automobile unless he was smart enough to change with the times and begin to manufacture lug bolts. By the same token, the publisher may be faced with the alternatives of fighting newer media or joining up with them. To me, the way is clear. To fight is to be overwhelmed; to join is to profit.

A fourth element of this impact of newer educational media is related to the distribution of trade books. The market for these books, or perhaps more accurately the customers for these books, will be found in walks of life not usually touched by avenues of advertising usually employed by publishers. Advertising will need to bring books to the attention of groups and individuals who have been largely ignored or have been considered inaccessible in the past. By the same token, some such scheme as the Book-of-the-Month Club, tremendously expanded to include categories related to age level and subject matter, will need to be introduced to assist schools and colleges in the selection of nontextbook reading materials.

In conclusion, may I commend to you a view of technological change in its historic concept. Consumption, or consumption potential, has always had a way of keeping up with production. Products change, but the needs these products satisfy change very little. Publishers of trade books are dealing with a product related to the most insatiable need of all, if there are, indeed, degrees of insatiability. I refer, of course, to the thirst for knowledge. There is a limit to how much a man can eat, how many cars he can drive, and how many suits he can wear, but there is no limit to what a man may know, and there is no quenching man's thirst for knowledge.

Organizing Library-Based A-V Materials
Joan Pressler

From School Libraries 14:43-7, March 1965.   Reprinted by permission.

While the Mt. Lebanon [Pennsylvania] school system has maintained a library in each elementary and secondary building for more than 25 years, it has been only recently that a movement has been made toward the instructional materials center concept.

Prior to 1959, paralleling the existing libraries had been an audio-visual department composed of a system coordinator and division representatives.   This department, completely separated from the book-oriented libraries, provided faculty members with nonprint materials of all types as well as the machines necessary for their use.   However, in 1959, with the opening of the new Jefferson Junior High School, funds were made available to establish the library as a center for both print and non-print materials, and to offer such materials to students and faculty members alike.   From this beginning, gradual steps have been taken to convert the remaining six libraries into similar central agencies through close cooperation between the librarians and audio-visual staff.

Presently, the audio-visual department continues to purchase and distribute films, filmstrips, overhead projector supplies, language laboratory equipment, and listening-viewing machines in general.   Record and tape collections, plus budgets for their acquisition, have been placed in the hands of the librarians; and it is anticipated that permanent filmstrip collections will be located in the libraries within the next two years.   All libraries are now equipped with record players, tape recorders, and individual filmstrip viewers which are maintained exclusively for students.   In the Jefferson Junior High School, however, there has been a greater development toward the instructional materials center objective.

In this building the library consists of (1) the main circulation room, (2) the librarian's office and workroom, (3) the professional library and project quarters, and (4) the audio-visual area.

Recent remodeling proved to be advantageous to the
library in that a new professional library near facilities for
curriculum projects was created, thus providing a room adjacent to the main library for a student audio-visual area by
refurnishing the former professional library. Here are
housed such equipment as record players, filmstrip viewers,
tape recorders, overhead projector equipment, slide projectors, and the various audio-visual collections used with these
machines. Students may use the area for general interest
reasons or for the completion of a particular class assignment.

All nonprint collections are fully cataloged and cards
filed in both the main card catalog and in the section devoted
to audio-visual materials. Color-banded cards are used to
indicate the different types; i.e., overhead projectuals (brown),
tapes (blue), phonorecords (red), mounted pictures (green),
35mm slides (orange), and filmstrips (black). The Sears
List of Subject Headings, used with books, has been adopted
for nonprint materials as well.

Two sets of cards are prepared for each item. For
a quick location of holdings, and to ease heavy demands on
the main catalog, a separate unit for nonprint materials is
maintained. Here the color-banded cards are filed in the
customary alphabetical arrangement; in addition, at the beginning of this section, a class arrangement is provided with
each type set off from the others and listed simply by call
number and main entry.

The duplicate set of cards prepared for the main catalog is filed with cards for print materials. Therefore,
when searching for holdings under a subject heading such as
"Mythology, Classical," the user has indicated to him all
books, tapes, phonorecords, slides, and mounted pictures
available. Faculty and students have found this centralized
catalog extremely valuable in the preparation of class projects.

While the selection, cataloging, and distribution of
nonprint media have increased the work of the library staff,
they have not offered any major problems. The selection
processes are highly correlated with the school's instructional program. For those purchases made through the library's
budgets, discussions are held between the librarian and faculty members. As the Mt. Lebanon system schedules regular subject group meetings (departmental meetings), these
discussion periods are frequently available. An opportunity
is given each faculty member to order whatever nonprint
item he needs and, as the budgets are adequate, the order
is normally filled.

Processing is rather simplified. As all materials
are offered to students and teachers, storage facilities are
of a type to make the collections easily accessible. A checkout system is maintained at the charging desk since the physical nature of some media prevents a card-pocket arrangement. Cataloging is done by the librarian, and no catalog
cards previously prepared are ordered.

Handling by Types

A brief explanation of procedures in the handling of
each type might prove useful to those libraries about to develop similar collections:
35mm Slides: Orange-banded cards designate the
35mm slides. The symbol "SLI" plus a running number
serves as the call number. Substantial information for cataloging purposes usually is not available, and the card description is often at a minimum. Sets are broken and each
slide treated as a separate unit. In the case of art reproductions, for the collection is concentrated on this field at
present, the main entry is by artist. As acquisitions are
now being made in other subject areas, indications point to
a general situation of main entry by title in the overall collection.
A sample of the information needed in a description
is shown below.

> SLI246 Correggio, Antonio Allegri da,
>   1494-1534 Madonna and child with infant
>   St. John.
>   Prepared in Italy, Kodak film. Ori-
>   ginal in Prado Museum, Madrid. Mc-
>   Graw-Hill, 1962 E-22 35mm; color
>   McGraw-Hill Art Book series, 24 in
>   set, with text "The High Renaissance."
>   1. Painting   2. Rennaissance
>   I. Title   II. Series

As the library has its own projection equipment for
35mm slides, students have been making considerable use of
the collection although it is a fairly recent project for the
library. Initiated at the request of the art department, it
naturally tends toward this field; however, several sets have
been purchased to supplement units in science, and to provide geographical material for the foreign language classes
in German and Spanish. This collection is expected to grow
rapidly.

Phonorecords: Originally, the Student Council supplied all listening equipment and records. Forming a Record Library Committee advised by the librarian, this group established procedures for students and faculty to request and receive items within a relatively short period of time. Popular from the beginning, the collection needed to expand rapidly, and a new library budget was created by the school administration. Now numbering more than 350 albums, the collection is substantial in a variety of subject areas.

Red-banded cards in the catalog represent the records. An alphabetical classification key plus a running number forms the call number. A few examples of this system are "Po 46" (poetry), "MC 19" (concerto), "Sp 34" (speech), "MJ 26" (jazz). The categories are broad indeed, but, as the collection will never reach thousands in number, this classification system is adequate and makes processing much faster than if the Dewey Decimal System were used. Locating records is no problem. They are arranged on 12"-deep shelves by broad category, then running number. The record request slip is designed to feature the call number of the item needed, thus making location a simple matter for the library assistant.

Basically, the same cataloging rules for print materials are applied to phonorecords. Main entry depends upon the item in hand. Generally, for music it is by composer, speech by performer, for plays by author, and so on.

The physical arrangement of material on records often makes it necessary to catalog by band or side of record rather than by the entire album. In such situations the same call number is used for the multiple entries.

The catalog card description for phonorecords is entered in the following pattern:

Record
FL 3 Hoge, Henry W.
        Spanish pronunciation-language labo-
    ratory manual. Wilmac, 1957 WRS201
        33 1/3 RPM microgroove
        2s. 12in.
        Pamphlet of exercises and practice
    material with album.
        1. Spanish language   I. Title

Mention should be made that, in addition to information entered on the shelf-list card, it is recommended that details of purchase or donation concerning records and other nonprint materials be kept in an accession book. This will also serve as a quick reference to the running number in the call number system.

Tapes: Blue-banded cards in the catalog indicate prepared tapes. These do not include those foreign language tapes used in the school's language laboratories; rather, the materials are short stories, science, and mythology.

Most tapes are purchased from transcription companies, but a few are prepared by teachers and deposited in the library. Blank tapes are also available. For either listening or recording purposes, students may reserve the equipment in the library at any time.

The call number of a tape is made by adding a running number to the symbol "T". Catalog entry is by title, with the description giving a statement of production and indicating rate, time, footage, and number of sides.

Tape
T-23 The Dewey Decimal System. Charles
Burke Company, 1964 No. 901
1s. rate 3 3/4; time 15m; feet 214
For use with the Jefferson Junior
High School Library Instruction Kit.
1. Libraries I. Jefferson Junior
High School Library series

The example given above refers to a series of tapes for use with a library instruction kit. This kit represents the library's segment of an educational guide designed to assist new students entering the system during the school year.

Composed of printed information and several transcriptions, the kit provides an explanation of the library regulations and school forms, briefly outlines the organization of the library, and discusses selected references useful in the preparation of assignments.

Either through the language arts classes or the administration office, new students are given time to become familiar with the library area and make use of the instruction kit.

Overhead Projectuals: This term is applied to slides for the overhead projector. There are nearly 200 completed slides in the library's collection at present, as well as an extensive file of master drawings deposited by teachers for safekeeping and, in some cases, to be made available to others. Since the school's developing equipment is located in the Jefferson building, a considerable number of the faculty make their own projectuals although the library does purchase company-prepared series. The collection is being supplied constantly through both sources.

Brown-banded cards are used for overhead projectuals.
The symbol "OV" plus the running number makes the call
number.   Main entry is generally by title, but this depends
upon the slide itself.   A series of art reproductions now being developed, for example, are being entered according to
artist.   The card description varies due to the techniques
used by those preparing slides, but the information required
is essentially as below:

> Projectual
> OV96   The human heart; 3 statics, 2 over-
>   lays.   Black overlay identifies the major
>   parts; 1 clear-acetate overlay for writing.
>   Prepared by Tecnifax Corp., n.d. 01345
>   1. Heart   2. Anatomy   I. Health Edu-
>   cation Department series

Projectors available to teachers are located throughout the building, but the library has its own projector and
screen.   Students may check out slides, and it is possible
for them in groups or individually to prepare slides for special class projects.   Instruction is given in such instances
by the librarian.

Mounted Pictures: This collection includes pictures
and photographs of all types, generally encased in plastic
holders or laminated.   Much in demand by teachers, they
are circulated throughout the building for a variety of uses.

The identifying symbol "PIC" is given to pictures.
This added to the customary running number forms the call
number.   Green-banded cards in the catalog indicate this collection, and the necessary information is entered on the card
in the following manner:

> Mounted Picture
> PIC434 New Amsterdam, now called New
>   York, 1667
>   14" x 10"; color
>   Colonial New York series, 8 pic-
>   tures in set.
>   1.   U.S.--History-Colonial Period
>   I.   Series

Two analytic book catalogs have been prepared to complement the card catalog by providing detailed information
about each nonprint item in the library's collections.   These
were found necessary when it became difficult to locate

quickly certain selections in the record albums not listed on catalog cards.

To illustrate, in the Reader's Digest album, "Festival of Light Classical Music," there are 12 records containing 71 selections; or in the Edward R. Murrow album, "I Can Hear It Now, 1919-1932," there are 54 transcriptions. If a faculty member needed "March of the Little Lead Soldiers" and another Will Rogers' comment on the United States Senate, the search problem was time consuming. Card analytics could have been made, but it was felt advisable to place such information directly in the classroom in the form of a printed book.

One analytic catalog is a classified listing of all selections to be found in the phonorecord collection, while the other is a similar list of the remaining nonprint collections. Each faculty member is given copies of the two catalogs at the beginning of the school year, with supplements added.

It should be noted that the library's book collection has, by far, the greater circulation, and efforts will be continued to promote its use. What progress has been made toward incorporating nonprint materials into the library complex has not diminished the value of the book collection in the educational program; rather, the tendency has been to increase interest in library services generally and make them a major aspect of school activity.

Cataloging Nonbook Materials
Doris M. Carson

The problem of cataloging nonbook materials is not
one of creating special rules but of adapting standard principles of cataloging to the special materials. In a book, the
cataloger looks to the title page for much of the information
which he will transcribe upon the catalog card, but not all
materials have title pages in the usual sense of the word.
"The whole face of a map is considered its title page" (Library of Congress Rules for Descriptive Cataloging (1949)
8:1). "Music title pages frequently do not have the distinctive character of title pages of literary works," being often
merely "a listing of some of the composer's works" or of
the works of other composers" (LC 9:3). More likely, specific data will be given on the caption or first page of the
actual score. The label on the phonograph record must be
used as a title page, supplemented by data found on the slipcase or album cover. The title page for microfilm is the
same as that of the original film. For motion pictures and
filmstrips, title page information is usually placed on introductory frames. The entire face of a slide or flat picture
serves as its title page. The amount and completeness of
the data found on these title pages or title page substitutes
vary.

Choice of Main Entry

The choice of main entry is the first decision which
must be made when one catalogs any kind of material. According to the ALA Cataloging Rules for Author and Title
Entries, main entry is made under author or title. This
general principle will apply as readily to nonbook materials
as to books. Materials can be classified under author, personal or corporate, as the source to whom responsibility for
the work can be assigned (ALA 1). If there is no author,
entry may be made under title (ALA 1). If there is no title,
one may be supplied by the cataloger (LC 3:5d). Maps, mu-

sic, and phono-recordings are usually entered under author (ALA 10; ALA 12). Microfilms are cataloged under the entry which would be chosen for the original work: author or title. Since responsibility for the intellectual and artistic content of motion pictures and filmstrips cannot generally be assigned to any one person, these are best entered under title. LC's Catalog of Cards for Motion Pictures and Filmstrips places the entire emphasis upon title entry. Slides and flat pictures also are most satisfactorily entered under title, present or supplied. Slides which are reproductions of pictures, sculptures, photographs, maps, book illustrations may be entered under the person responsible for the original.

Title Statement

The title statement of all nonbook materials follows the general principle: copy title in full or in part (LC 3:5). Only in music scores and music recordings has something been added: the conventional or filing title, whose purpose is to "identify and bring together in a systematic arrangement general and miscellaneous collections of a composer's works" (LC 9:2). The conventional title has its precedent in the similar handling of the multiple works of a single author (LC 9:2). The conventional title is not used for recordings of the spoken voice.

The general rules for noting place, publisher, and date are followed (LC 3:10; 3:11; 3:12). If the dates are not found, the abbreviation n. d. should be used to indicate that the data was considered by the cataloger and not overlooked. When possible, an approximate date should be supplied in brackets.

In most libraries, only maps noteworthy because of their age or period or other special feature will be cataloged. For this reason, the date of a map is important and a special effort to find the date should be made for any map that is worth cataloging.

If the publisher of a music score is little known, the addition of his street address will serve to make more specific the item of place in the imprint (LC 9:4B). The publisher's plate number will follow a supplied imprint date in order to make more positive the identification of the particular edition. This number is always added after the abbreviation n. d. (LC 9:4C).

The imprint for phonograph records is the publisher and serial identification. The album or record numbers, usually found on both container and disc label, are of prime

importance as they serve as positive identification of the recording.   Disc matrix numbers, if used in the absence of a
date or serial number, are analogous to plate numbers for
music scores.
        Since microfilm, facsimile, and photocopy are repro-
ductions of a work in another form, the imprint will be the
same as that used in describing the original, followed by the
imprint of the reproduction.   If the film is the original publication of the work, the imprint will, of course, describe
only the film (LC 10:4).
        Producer and date comprise the imprint for motion
pictures and filmstrips.   The imprint for slides and flat pictures will be almost impossible to secure unless a record is
kept of that data when the library acquires the particular
item.

Collation

        Collation describes the physical character of the work
in hand.   The information to be given in collation will vary
as the physical character of the material varies.   Book collation includes pages, illustrations, and height (LC 3:14).
        Map collation gives the number of maps, indicates
color or black-and-white, and the size in height and width
(LC 8:1B).   In the collation for atlases, the pages of text are
noted as well as the number of maps if the maps form a separate section in the book (LC 8:4).
        In considering the collation for music, note that if the
statement that the work is a music score does not appear
elsewhere in the description, the word "score" is used preceding the number of pages of the score given in parentheses
(LC 9:5).   Accompanying text should be indicated in the paging for the sake of clarity.   Height may be of lesser importance because there is a standard minimum size below which
a score will not be printed for performance purposes.   A
miniature or thematic score or any other peculiarity about
the form of score will, of course, be stated in the collation.
        Collation for phonodiscs includes the number of slides,
the size of the disc in inches, and the number of revolutions
per minute it is to be played.   The terms "microgroove" or
"stereophonic" will be added where appropriate.   The number of reels and speed (inches per second) describe tape recordings.   The collation for wire recordings is the number
of spools; for phono-rolls, the number of rolls.   If there is
more than one reel of microfilm to a microfilmed work, the
number of reels is given in the collation.   The collation of
the work reproduced appears in a supplementary note.

Collation for motion picture films indicates the number of minutes of running time, sound or silent, black-and-white or color, and the size in millimeters. Collation for filmstrips includes the number of frames, black-and-white or color, and the size in millimeters. A phonorecording may accompany this material. Its collation is placed following that of the filmstrip or motion picture.

The first collation item for slides and flat pictures is a statement of what the work is and how many, such as: lithograph, daguerreotype, 105 slides, etc. The height and width in inches and an indication and statement of color complete the description.

Series Notes

A series note may be given for any type of material which belongs to a series (LC 3:16). Only occasionally are series notes important in music scores. Usually they are simply a publisher's series, which should be noted, but which certainly need no entry in the catalog. The same may be said in general about series in music phonorecordings. Series for recordings of the spoken voice are more likely to be important. For microfilms, motion pictures, filmstrips, slides, and flat pictures, series notes may be included in the description. The decision to make a series card in any given case depends upon the judgment of the cataloger.

Some informative data will not fit into the limitations of the body of the formalized part of the entry. Yet the additional information is necessary for the complete description of the work in hand. Such data may be included in supplementary notes (LC 3:15). For certain of these special materials, however, there are specific items of information which must be included in notes. In some cases a definite order of notes is to be followed. For maps the first note is the scale note. If the scale is not indicated, a statement is made that it is not given (LC 8:1D). A scale note is sometimes given for atlases also (LC 8:4). Notes giving medium of performance, notation, and duration of performance are peculiar to music (LC 9:6).

For phonodiscs that have material on both sides of the disc, a note will explain the content on the reverse side if it is a work different from that on the first side. This note is the final note. Tracing is made on the back of both main entry cards for added entries respectively. This "With" note is analogous to the "Bound with" note for books (LC 7: 12). An album of a collection of discs may require a contents note, as indeed may a single disc reproducing several short works.   Analytic cards may be made when appropriate.

Critical Notes

        Explanatory or descriptive manuals, texts of plays,
or librettos of operas often accompany phonograph records.
The presence of such materials should be indicated in a note.
Critical and analytical comments may be printed on the album
container or disc slipcase.   These also may be mentioned in
a note.   Names of directors, conductors, performers (individual or group), narrators, medium of performance, duration, and the connection with other works are among those
items which should be noted.
        The first supplementary note for microfilm states that
the work is a microfilm, positive or negative.   If the film
is not 35mm in width, the width is also indicated (LC 10:4C).
A note must be included giving the collation of the original
work from which the microfilm was made.   If that information is not at hand, the length of the film in feet may be
given in its place (LC 10:4B).
        Motion pictures and filmstrips may have a note for an
accompanying guide or manual, a summary note, or a credits
note (including the performing cast).   The connection with
other works should always be noted.   Slides need a note giving source of the original.   Notes for flat pictures will be
similar in purpose to those for slides.
        In a few cases, then, certain information peculiar to
the specialized material must appear in a supplementary note.
In general, any information appropriate to the work in hand
may be mentioned.   The decision to include a note in any
given case depends upon the judgment of the cataloger.

Summary

        When cataloging nonbook materials by means of rules
established for cataloging books, the cataloger must know the
principles supporting those rules so that when he adapts them
to the special materials, his adaptations will remain conso-
nant with the principles.

                             Bibliography

American Library Association.   ALA Cataloging Rules for
        Author and Title Entries.   2nd ed.   Ed. by Clara
        Beetle.   Chicago,   1949.
Library of Congress.   Descriptive Cataloging Division.   Rules

for Descriptive Cataloging in the Library of Congress. (Adopted by the American Library Association) Washington, 1949.

_____ : Motion Pictures and Filmstrips.   2nd prelim. ed.   Washington, 1953, reprinted 1955.

_____ : Phonorecords.   2nd prelim ed.   Washington, 1964.

_____ : Pictures, Designs and Other Two-dimensional Representations.   Prelim. ed.   Washington, 1959.

Filing Miscellaneous Materials
June Berry

From Library Journal 87:818-20, February 15; School Library Journal 8:18-20, February 1962. Reprinted by permission.

We librarians file cards, books, magazines and pamphlets religiously; we preserve and protect our printed materials in shelves and files for convenience and utility. But do we keep our miscellaneous materials in good order? Or do we shove them into a drawer or cupboard or shuffle them from place to place until they are too dog-eared and dirty to use again?

Following are some solutions to the problem of "miscellaneous misfits. "

Pictures and pictorial material. Valuable pictures should be mounted on railway board, classified according to subject, and then stored in the vertical file alphabetically by their subjects. Referral cards may be placed in the card catalog to read: "Ships. Consult the picture file for illustrations. "

Book jackets are more ephemeral in nature, but enduring in value, and should not be overlooked. To care for these, we reserve drawers in the vertical file and place the jackets under Dewey classes. Fiction is subdivided into "Animals, " "Sports, " "Science Fiction" and so on. When jackets are needed for pictures or bulletin boards, they are easily located and always in good condition. In some libraries, jackets are filed in pamphlet boxes.

Larger pictures are more troublesome. If left flat, they are too large for the vertical file or standard-size shelf; if rolled, they are hard to store and catalog; and if folded, they are unsightly, and in time will tear on the creases. In our library these problems are eliminated by storing large pictures flat in a steel file. These files, called map files or blueprint cabinets, are obtainable up to 38 x 58 inches. Pictures which receive constant use should be mounted either on railway board by double-coat rubber-cement mounting, or on unbleached muslin or sheeting by the wet mounting process. (Instructions for mounting are given in the film "Wet Mounting Pictorial Materials, " produced by

Indiana University. 11 min., color.)
To direct the searcher to these materials, referral
cards corresponding to those for smaller pictures are inserted in the card catalog. Or you may prefer a separate catalog with a card for each picture.
Bulletin board materials. Miscellaneous materials
from dismantled bulletin boards and exhibits are too often
discarded or dumped into boxes. The wise librarian will
rescue the materials from every successful bulletin board.
A simple and inexpensive method of preserving this
material is in large envelopes about 12 x 15 inches. These
are large enough to store small silhouettes, ribbons, book
jackets and captions. We plan our signs or slogans so most
of them will fit into the envelopes too. Certain pictures may
be placed in the envelopes, especially those of a specialized
nature and of doubtful value in the regular picture file.
To obtain maximum value from these "exhibit envelopes," we use the following procedures for each bulletin
board, display or exhibit:
1. Photograph or sketch the completed bulletin board
or exhibit and place this in the envelope to indicate the arrangement of materials.
2. Include a 3 x 5 card on which is noted the location of other materials used in the exhibit. For example, a
map may be in the map file, a book jacket in the vertical
file, and so forth.
3. Write the subject (using standard subject headings)
in the upper right-hand corner and file the envelope upright
in a jumbo-size file or a cardboard box.
Objects and realia. Although storage of audio-visual
materials has been well publicized, the suggested procedures
pertain almost exclusively to films, filmstrips, and slides.
They ignore the miniature models, facsimiles, mock-ups,
and realia which are used in construction of exhibits and bulletin boards or circulated to patrons. Public libraries receive gifts which should be preserved, and school libraries
often collect small models made by students and teachers.
Packing many models into one large box is unsuitable;
every time the box is opened, the objects become more frayed or soiled or broken. You have to unpack several objects
to get to the one you want. And it's always on the bottom!
Breakage can be avoided by storing small objects and
models in separate cardboard boxes. We number the objects
just as we accession books. Put each model in the box
which most nearly fits, using padding to protect fragile materials. Number the box according to the number of the object and pack boxes into the shelf tightly. If no shelves are

available, large cardboard boxes may be substituted; but each
item must be packed first in its own box.

Again referral cards may be placed in the card catalog to direct your patrons to the objects.

Flat signs and captions. All small signs and captions
used on bulletin boards may be filed with the materials in
the large exhibit envelopes described earlier, since they are
usually related to that exhibit exclusively. Miscellaneous
small signs can be filed separately by subject.

An altogether different problem is presented by larger
signs, which are usually of varied sizes and shapes, of more
general nature, and therefore more widely used than small
captions. Signs such as "New Books," "Book Week" and
"Let's Read More," whether 12 x 12 inches or 2 x 4, square
or rectangular, all fit nicely into one drawer of the map file.
We have labeled the bottom drawer "Signs" on the outside to
differentiate it from the drawers containing maps, charts and
pictures.

Miscellaneous verse. Almost daily, requests come to
a library for poems of local interest or origin, which rarely
appear in anthologies, or for a poem which appears only in
one reference book, which shouldn't leave the library. We
keep a file of this verse on cards, a system which has the
advantage of being easy to shuffle and to remove for copying
or for circulating. Place the subject (which should follow
your standard subject heading guide as nearly as possible) in
the upper right-hand corner, and file alphabetically by subject. Cross-reference cards may be inserted in strategic
spots.

Loose-leaf notebooks may be substituted for cards
and, being larger, will accommodate longer poems. By
placing the subject in the upper right-hand corner and arranging the loose leaves alphabetically by subject, your notebook has the same organization as the cards described above.

Stories. Another valuable though ephemeral material
is short-short stories clipped from magazines or newspapers,
or copied from them. These offer several possibilities.
First, they may be placed in manila folders and filed in the
vertical file under "Stories." Thus, in that section, the
stories are filed alphabetically by subject--Christmas, Mothers, Thanksgiving, etc.

Some librarians prefer to file the Christmas stories
in with the Christmas poems and pamphlets under "C"; the
material on mothers under "M"; and the material on Thanksgiving in the "T's." Some librarians use loose-leaf notebooks, as for poems.

Teachers' assignments. Many of us have the problem

of hordes of children descending on the library with assignments which stump even the librarian. If teachers have failed to consult the librarian beforehand, near chaos may result. However, after the first shock, the librarian has a
vague notion what to expect and can plan for the next time.

Have you tried saving the copies of teachers' assignments and work sheets which concern the library? A special file with individual manila folders for each teacher is a
simple solution. In this folder are placed copies of reserve
lists, book lists, and the answers to hard-to-find questions,
as well as work sheets and assignments.

On each sheet we mark the date of the library visit
and any pertinent notes. The value of the file lies in the
probability that similar units are taught each year and the
same books and pamphlets will be helpful again and again.
Furthermore, this file is an aid in planning for the next
year's work, for book orders and as a record of our services to teachers.

The preceding suggestions are not the last word on
how these various materials should be handled. The methods
have worked effectively for us and we continually change and
improve upon them.

We realize many problems are involved--seemingly in-
surmountable ones for some libraries.

For example, most administrators and library boards
are horrified at the price of a map file (about $100). Do
we hear librarians say they would rather buy 30 or 40 new
books? If you need books more than you need a compact
container for maps, large pictures, posters and charts, by
all means order the books. Our file is like a typewriter;
we could survive without it, but it makes our work easier
and our library neater.

In some cases, administrators will not spend the necessary funds for a file, but will hire a carpenter and buy
the materials to build a wooden file, which is a fair substitute.

For vertical files, the best substitute is a cardboard
box about 12 x 15 inches. To protect your materials from
dust, use a typewriter cover over the box until you can afford a file.

You have no space for files? If this is a problem in
your library, you may need such files even more. A map
file will take care of large pictures, posters, charts, maps
and signs. You will also store your sheets of unused poster
paper in it. We have used the top of ours for displays of
new books, for special exhibits, for the dictionary and for
our Christmas tree.

Even with a good system, it doesn't take long to accumulate items which take up space and never receive use.
Continuous weeding is essential, for eliminating torn or
frayed articles and out-of-date materials. Inexpensive and
easy-to-obtain maps and charts should never take up space
needed for more significant and useful materials.

Filing miscellaneous materials is an oft-neglected but
necessary part of library work. When pictures, maps, objects, bulletin board materials, book jackets and similar
items are organized and filed in a careful manner, the divi-
dends are great. Like a man with money in the bank, the
librarian with all resources in proper order will be ready
for future emergencies.

Get the Monkey Off Your Back!!
Thomas W. Roberts

From Educational Screen and Audiovisual Guide 44:25+, May 1965. Reprinted by permission.

Nothing--but nothing--makes life more miserable for an audio-visual director than the job of revising and issuing a new film catalog! We sweat and fume, fuss and swear, and are completely frustrated every step of the way. Deadlines are extended again, until it seems that the job will never be completed. Wouldn't it be wonderful--we often think--if we just had some automatic way of creating a catalog! Well, there is!

We have found a way of eliminating most of our catalog headaches forever. Instead of our fingers doing the walking, we are putting the computer to work. The computer stores the information. The computer shuffles, arranges and rearranges the information. The computer adds and deletes the information. And the computer creates a tape which drives extremely high speed typesetting equipment. This high speed typesetting equipment results in the preparation of negatives for printing the catalog. To make this possible, Wayne State University has teamed up with CAFGA (Computer Applications for Graphic Arts). The CAFGA people are the Midwest representatives for Perry Publications, Incorporated. Perry Publications developed this system. Here's how the system works:

The first step is one of detailed study and consideration. You must think through all of the information about your materials that you want the computer to store--for use now and in the future. You must decide how your materials are to be listed, what information you want accessible, such as subject matter areas, grade levels, type of material, and any other detail which might be useful. The computer is a fantastic marvel which will remember anything you tell it to remember, and it will recall this information for you any time you ask. So it is most important that you spend time deciding "what" information you want stored by the computer for future use.

Next, the descriptions of the materials are typed out. This is the last time this information ever needs to be typed or proofread! This typing job is done on a special typewriter. This typewriter is only slightly different from a normal typewriter. (There are a few extra symbols, which are used to put directions into the copy for things such as type face changes from bold to italic, the end of entries, and similar functions.) However, once this manuscript is checked for accuracy, no other proofreading is ever needed--not even a check for typesetting errors. If the same descriptive information is to be used for each item year after year, no further typing or proofreading are needed. The computer will store and retrieve this information forevermore. This is made possible by an optical reader which is tied into the computer.

The manuscript is read automatically by this electronic optical reader. This unit "reads" the information that has been typed by the typewriter and converts it into computer language at the rate of 2400 characters per second. This information is converted and stored on a magnetic tape, and the tape is then ready for use on the computer.

The taped information is then fed into a properly programed computer. The computer calculates all things such as length of line, type faces, point sizes, line justification, and hyphenation. All of this is interlaced with the basic information and is stored on a master magnetic tape at the speed of 10,000 characters per second.

The final step is the typesetting and printing of the catalog. Again this is automatic and very fast. The master magnetic tape is used to make a perforated paper tape. The paper tape drives the typesetting equipment. The high speed typesetting units produce 70,000 characters per hour, leading to the development of negatives for each of the catalog. The printer then makes plates from these negatives and the catalog is in print!

Now the big bonanza comes with the revision of the catalog in subsequent years.

Each year all of us add many new films, delete some, and we always need new subject matter and alphabetical listings. This is now a simple chore with this system. To revise our catalog, we merely type the new information and the deletions. The reader "reads" this information from the manuscript into magnetic tape form. The computer then merges the "new" information with the "old" information which has been stored on the master magnetic tape. The computer automatically alphabetizes, makes up adjusted subject matter listings, and does other shuffling and rearrangements which are required in the revision. And all this at fantastic speeds--making a completely revised catalog possible in two weeks and not the usual six months.

In addition, the information which is stored on the computer tape may be used for other specialized purposes. You could direct the computer, for instance, to print out a listing of all your primary-level materials. Or you could ask for a descriptive listing of all of your materials in the area of educational psychology. Any information which is coded into the computer can be called out of the computer, making the information accessible for many kinds of purposes. This is why such careful consideration needs to be given to the planning step in the development of this system.

It must be emphasized that all of the variety of the graphic arts are available through this system--permitting various type faces and sizes, varying page layouts, and illustrations. This is not just typewriter printout from the computer. It is a revolutionary system which was developed about four years ago by Perry Publications, Incorporated. The Audio-Visual Utilization Center of Wayne State University has worked with CAFGA in the adaptation of this system to the preparation of our instructional materials catalog. This is a new technique now, but within ten years we feel it will be commonplace. The savings in money, time and convenience make this, to our mind, a certainty.

Choosing Audio-Visual Equipment
Wendell W. Simons

From Library Trends 13:503-16, April 1965.   Copyright
1965 by the University of Illinois Board of Trustees.   Reprinted by permission.

Great diversity and a rapidly changing technology
make the evaluation of audio-visual equipment a difficult task
for the average librarian.   Most of us have neither the skill
nor the means to conduct definitive tests on equipment being
considered for purchase, so we must depend upon published
specifications, a little common sense and, when available,
the reports of organizations such as the Library Technology
Project and the consumer services.   The problem is com-
pounded by a tendency among manufacturers toward planned
obsolescence.   This is more prevalent in the home-oriented
product than in the education-oriented product, but where
these markets overlap, for instance in tape recorders, record players, and slide projectors, the buyer will find a bewildering array of glamorized equipment.   Fortunately, in
these areas the buyer will also find the greatest amount of
advice from the professional evaluators.
    We are familiar with written programs for buildings.
An expensive piece of equipment should also be "programmed" before purchase, if not formally on paper, at least
mentally.   Programming is the process of delineating what
the equipment is to accomplish, what functions it must perform, and how its use is related to the general library operation.   The next step, that of drawing specifications, is
concerned with detailing the dimensions, the consistency and
quality of materials, and the technical capabilities of the
equipment.   In planning buildings these two steps are distinct
and each results in a formalized major document.   In buying
equipment we rarely formalize these steps but often merge
them into a single mental process, perhaps giving too much
attention to the manufacturer's specifications and neglecting
the very important process of thinking out what we want the
equipment to accomplish and why.
    In programming a piece of equipment, one should con-
sider such things as how large and how discriminating an
audience it must serve, who will operate it, how often and

in what surroundings it will be used, and how often it must be moved. Failure to consider these questions may result in equipment woefully inadequate or wastefully over-adequate. Advertising claims are usually based on operation under ideal conditions; in programming try to allow for the least favorable conditions that might be encountered.

The need for portability should be considered carefully; the trend in the schoolroom is against it.[1] A machine installed in a fixed position will last longer and give more trouble-free service than one subjected to constant moving. Fixed equipment means smoother operator performance as well. Power and sound connections will be properly in place; focus and volume levels will remain set from previous uses; spare and accessory parts will be near at hand. It is all too common in using portable equipment to discover at the last minute that some vital element, such as the power cord, has been left behind. However, a fixed machine that stands idle represents a wasted investment. While rule of thumb cannot cover every conceivable case, a machine used daily in one place deserves to be fixed if another can be acquired for portable work. Even two or three uses a week may be justification for fixed equipment.

Certain signs of quality design and manufacture are apparent even on the surface of a machine. Although perhaps akin to kicking the tires of a used car, a few simple observations of external detail can give a fair clue to what is within. Look for a carefully finished case. The halves should fit together properly, and the latches should meet and engage with accuracy. A metal body is certain to outlast a plastic one, and turned or cast metal parts will generally outlast those stamped from sheet metal. Try the control knobs and power switches; they should have a firm, smooth action. Power switches are notorious as the first part of a machine to break down. Use of a cheap part here may indicate shoddy design and workmanship elsewhere, where it is less easily detected. There should be easy and obvious access to lamps and tubes. Motors should run smoothly and quietly. Projectors should always be wired to prevent the lamp being on without the fan. Better projectors will allow the fan to run while the lamp is off. Any projector will heat up during operation, but it should not become so hot that you cannot lay your hand on the lamp housing, at least momentarily.

When considering a machine to be operated by the public, or by a number of untrained staff members, simplicity of operation must be a primary determinant. If only trained operators are involved, then more elaborate, sophisticated,

and delicate machinery can be considered. But added gimmicks and gadgets generally result in added operational difficulties and maintenance problems. Given two machines of
comparable ability and quality, one with four controls will
surely create more operator confusion and consequently require more maintenance than one with three controls. In
fact, if you have a machine with an unnecessary control, you
would do well to remove the control and blank off the hole.

In almost every case, some compromise must be accepted in the matter of quality. Few libraries can justify
the finest theater-quality projection equipment or the finest
broadcast-quality sound equipment. Rather a level of quality
must be chosen that will most nearly satisfy the needs and
expectations of the particular patronage within the limits of
the particular budget.

These generalized considerations boil down to three
basic rules of equipment selection, which should be applied
in this order:

1. Seek out a machine that will fulfill the particular
requirements of your program.
2. If you find a choice, then choose the one that will
be most durable and easy to maintain.
3. If there is still a choice, then choose the one that
is simplest to operate.

Listening and Recording Equipment

Listening is the most common of audio-visual activities in libraries; certainly it has been most thoroughly covered in the library literature. In the establishment of a listening facility, several very basic programming decisions
must be met head-on. Shall the equipment be phono or tape?
Monaural or stereo? Turntable or changer? Loud-speaker
or earphones? Staff-controlled or listener-controlled?
Ready-made or components? Fixed or portable? A very
carefully conceived program and specification for a language
laboratory has been published by the U.S. Office of Education.[2] This may serve as an excellent guide for the detailing of technical requirements in a complex facility, but be
sure that the real needs of your particular users are being
properly met.

There is an apparent trend toward more staff-controlled facilities, highly sophisticated machinery--ultimately becoming automated distribution systems featuring not only audio but also video material. Some academic libraries are
taking the lead in developing such systems for the self-in-

struction of college students. A session of the 1964 Library
Equipment Institute was devoted largely to this topic.[3] The
effectiveness of this electronic carrel approach has been well
demonstrated in language laboratory operations, but it is not
yet apparent that this degree of automation is the best approach to all study, nor especially to listening for pleasure.
One sometimes suspects that staff convenience has taken precedence over users' needs.

Mary Pearson has written a chapter on conventional
listening equipment that contains a great deal of practical
programming advice.[4] In 1962 the Library Technology Project (LTP) published a definitive report on fourteen earphone
record players.[5] Although most of these models are no
longer on the market, the testing methods described and the
performance standards outlined remain very pertinent. A
second study, to evaluate a more current crop of players,
is under way. The most valuable portion of the LTP report
may be, for many librarians, the clear, readable explanations of the various components that make up a record-play-
ing system. A summary of the report appears in Consumer
Bulletin.[6] Other articles in the same magazine[7-9] as well
as in Consumer Reports[10-14] are written in the language of
the layman and cover the technical ground very thoroughly.
It is interesting to note one recurring theme in the reports
of all the professional evaluators--the quality of audio equipment is directly related to cost.

Tape recorders have not received as much attention
in the library literature, but excellent articles can again be
found in Consumer Bulletin[15] and Consumer Reports.[16] Cartridge-loaded tape systems are gaining favor; libraries con-
templating a permanent collection of pre-recorded tapes
would do well to investigate cartridge equipment. Cartridges
are easier to handle and store than reels, tape wear and
breakage are reduced, and the possibility of mix-up of reels
or rewinding wrongside-out are eliminated entirely. Reel-
to-reel operation is still the only practical mode for original
recording and editing. Seven-inch reels are standard, but
in working closely with a radio station you may find need
for a professional model recorder accommodating ten and
one-half inch reels.

A recorder used by the public for playback purposes
should have its erase and record heads disconnected to eliminate the danger of accidental erasure. This is a simple operation, and the reconnection can be made at any time.

In tapes, a bargain brand can be a bad bargain. In
some cheap tapes, the oxide is poorly bonded to the plastic
base and the result is rapid wearing of the oxide coating.

This not only decreases the effective fidelity of the tape but,
more seriously, damages the heads of the recorder. Recording heads must be kept clean and oxide accumulation
watched closely. One recent development that overcomes
this problem is "sandwich" tape, a tape with a thin layer of
plastic over the oxide coating as well as behind it.

In both phonographs and tape recorders, do not be
fooled by claims of "stereo." Some so-called stereo phonographs have only the wiring for a stereo cartridge but require a new cartridge and an additional amplifier and speaker to become a functioning stereo player. Similarly, some
tape recorders have two sets of heads but only one amplifier
and speaker system. A stereo machine must have two of
each electronic component.

A good article on stereo headphones is found in Consumer Reports.[17] In either monaural or stereo facilities,
some listeners will prefer headphones to loudspeakers because of the aid in concentration or because they enjoy the
heightened binaural effect possible through phones. With
many headsets of good fidelity and great wearing comfort
now on the market, a library need not be apologetic for providing headphone listening stations in lieu of soundproofed
loudspeaker rooms.

Developments in the electronic world are promising
relief from that most despised of all technological monsters,
the screeching public address system. Unidirectional microphones, at one time a luxury item, are becoming more and
more available in the moderate and lower price ranges. Directional column speakers have been recently introduced that
direct more sound into the audience area allowing less to
spill back into the microphones. Use of these two directional elements is the best defense against acoustical feedback.
Amplifiers featuring anti-feedback devices have not been particularly effective since the problem is essentially physical
rather than electronic. The characteristics and proper placement of microphones and loudspeakers are the important
factors.

Another new approach to loudspeaking may offer a solution to feedback. A small transducer, similar in structure
and function to the driver of a loudspeaker horn, can be attached directly to a wall or ceiling, thus making a speaker
diaphragm out of the entire wall or ceiling surface. Sound
seems to emanate evenly from the entire surface and can
therefore be kept at a very low volume level. This device
is barely out of the developmental stages and not yet proven
but should bear watching.

Omnidirectional microphones are most useful for recording purposes where recording is not ancillary to a public address operation. They normally pick up from a hemispherical pattern and are ideal for musical ensembles or groups around a table. A technical explanation of microphone impedances is not in order, but generally speaking, low impedance microphones are higher in quality, fidelity, and price. They are appropriate for real high fidelity work and in situations where microphone cables run longer than fifty feet. High impedance microphones are more common and prove adequate for most purposes.

Visual and Projection Equipment

The trend in slide projectors is definitely toward remote controlled, cartridge-fed equipment, yet the old hand-operated standards are still useful. If one 2" by 2" slide projector were all that the budget would allow, then a hand-operated model would be the only practical choice since tape-bound slides will jam any automatic and most cartridges will accept only a limited choice of the many metal and plastic mounts now available.

Excellent help can again be found in Consumer Bulletin[18, 19] and Consumer Reports.[20, 21] Explanations of the several levels of automation and the various common slide sizes are included along with technical evaluations. A fully automatic, that is, a timer-activated, projector is probably of little use in a library or school situation. Remote control is of limited value unless focusing and reversing can be accomplished from the remote position.

If a library has a permanent slide collection which is organized and used in fixed sets, then the collection may lend itself to being stored in cartridges ready for use. In this case the cost of a large number of cartridges would become significant. If, on the other hand, slides are selected individually and used in differing combinations, storage in cartridges would be most impractical. Two styles of furniture are made for individual slide storage, vertical display racks and drawers resembling card catalog trays. The latter are standard items with some of the library supply houses. The display racks are designed to allow visual scanning of up to 120 slides at one time and this can be a distinct advantage over the drawer method. However, sliding the racks in and out of their cabinet tends to jiggle the slides behind one another or on to the floor. Drawer storage demands more detailed cataloging and marking; rack storage allows more casual organization of the collection.

Any slide projector intended for institutional use should

accept a variety of lenses. A very desirable feature to look
for is a provision for preheating the slides before they are
fed into the optical path. This prevents the slides from pop-
ping out of focus. Although its use is becoming more rare,
a well-equipped audio-visual service should have a 3 1/4" by
4" lantern slide projector. The larger format of the old-
fashioned slide makes it well suited to homemade transparencies, such as silhouettes or cellophane cutouts, typewritten
slides, or pencil and crayon drawings on ground glass.
Slidemaking kits are available commercially.

Filmstrip projectors commonly come in combination
with slide projectors. This is the one exception to the generalization that projectors which combine two functions usually do justice to neither. Filmstrip projectors are available
as separate units, but unless a great deal of use warrants
the single-purpose machine, combination with a hand-operated slide projector will prove more useful. The newer automatic slide projectors do not lend themselves to such combination. A filmstrip projector should be equipped to show
both single and double frame images. Double frame is the
size of the familiar 35mm slide; single frame is half that
size and is oriented across the width of the filmstrip rather
than with the length of it. Commercially made filmstrips
are always single frame, but it is very easy to make double
frame filmstrips of your own simply by taking a series of
pictures with a standard 35mm camera and specifying that
the exposed film be developed but not cut.

Be sure that the image area of the film, in passing
through the projection gate, is not scratched or rubbed by
any part of the projector; film guides and advance mechanism
should touch only the perforated edges of the film. The advance mechanism should have a positive action, moving the
film accurately one frame's length at a time. Some filmstrip projectors can be equipped with remote controlled advance; some can be controlled automatically by a tape-recorded signal.

Any kind of reader for 35mm microfilm can be used
as a filmstrip viewer. Conversely, a typical filmstrip viewer or projector, which is equipped with a sprocket advance,
can show perforated, but not unperforated, microfilm. There
are table-top filmstrip previewers with friction wheel advance that will accommodate any variety of microfilm.

Motion picture projector design has enjoyed many
years of relative stability, but some radical changes are now
occurring in the field. Xenon projection lamps have been
developed that yield a light intensity and quality comparable
to that of carbon arcs. These can be adapted to some stand-

ard movie and slide projectors for auditorium usage where the common incandescent lamp has been found wanting. While the equipment cost of a xenon installation is comparable to that of carbon arc, the operating techniques are far simpler and the safety requirements less stringent. A seventy-foot throw is recommended as the maximum for the best incandescent projection systems; xenon promises to solve the problem of amateur projection in larger spaces.

Eight millimeter has the potential to do to the sixteen millimeter market what long-play records did to the 78 rpm record. A sound-on-film 8mm movie camera and companion magnetic playback projector have brought sound to the more economical film size.[22] The spread of the medium has been slow because of the chicken-and-egg positions of the equipment buyers and the film producers. Neither party cares to move until the other has committed itself. However, the 8mm field is sure to mature in time, and many schools and libraries will find a greater wealth of filmed information available within a smaller budget. Another interesting development in 8mm is the cartridge-loaded automatic projector.[23] This has already been put to good use in a library situation for self orientation.[24] The cartridge is sealed, snapped into place with no threading, and has been demonstrated to be even childproof. The system, thus far, is limited to silent film in four-minute repeating clips.

Standard 16mm projectors are now available with self threading. This should prove extremely useful where many inexperienced people must handle equipment. If you are considering a manually threaded machine, check the complexity of the threading path and the clarity of the instructions. An automatic loop-setter is an essential accessory if not supplied as a standard fixture. Projectors come in two basic reel configurations--both reels overhead, front and back; and both reels in front, top and bottom. The latter type must be used at the front edge of a table and may be difficult to set up in a booth situation.

All major makes of sound projectors will show silent film as well as sound film so there is little need to consider a silent 16mm projector unless time-and-motion-study, stop-frame features are required. Both optical and magnetic sound systems are available from most manufacturers. Commercially made sound films have optical sound tracks, but with a magnetic projector you can add and edit your own sound track on specially prepared film. Many projectors come equipped to use as a public address system; for this purpose they will probably be inferior. You will definitely want a speaker that can be separated from the projector case for all but the very smallest audiences.

Of all projector types the opaque is the least efficient, since light is reflected from the surface to be shown rather than projected through a transparency. Because of this inefficiency, room darkening is a very critical problem and a 1,000 watt bulb is mandatory for good results. So intense a heat source can curl or scorch a book page, particularly the hard-surfaced papers found in expensive picture books. Cooling systems must, therefore, be looked at rather carefully. Opaques are large, bulky, and awkward to handle; attempts to make them more compact have not been notably successful. With a reducing attachment, an opaque can be a tremendous aid in copying pictures, maps, and charts for display purposes.

Overhead projectors are coming into widespread use by lecturers in education and industry. The trend has been boosted by the development of "instant" transparencies made on many standard photocopy machines. By means of photocopy, the overhead can now do much of what only the opaque could formerly do. The growing popularity has brought a wide variety of good machines on the market, which are more compact, simpler to operate, and lower in price. The most useful size is the ten inch by ten inch. Smaller sizes should be considered only if ease of portability is really important.

The chief advantages of an overhead projector are that it is operated by the lecturer at the front of the room and that it can be used without regard to room darkening. It is commonly used as a "blackboard," and colored inks, overlays, and motion gadgets have been developed for it. Attachments have been made for showing slides and filmstrips on an overhead, but these are not as satisfactory as the standard slide and filmstrip projectors. Overheads generally are focused by raising and lowering the lens head by means of a rack and pinion gear. Try this focusing adjustment for firm, sure movement and check its ability to hold its position on the rack without slipping.

Four kinds of projection screen surface are in general use: matte white, beaded, plain aluminized, and lenticular. Matte screens are a flat white color on an untextured surface and give extremely even reflectance over a very wide angle. Beaded screens will deliver up to twice the brilliance of a matte in the axis of the projection, and a plain aluminized or silvered screen up to three times. Both these types, however, fall off rapidly in brilliance as you move away from the center line. At about thirty degrees, they are the equal of a matte and beyond thirty degrees both continue to fall considerably below the matte standard. Lenticular screens are characterized by geometric patterns impressed in a fabric surface. These spread the reflected light over a wide horizontal angle while reducing the wasted reflectance toward floor and ceiling. While somewhat less brilliant on the center line than the best beaded screens, a good lenticular will outperform any other type from twenty degrees and beyond.[25-27] A screen performance test is easily conducted; line up sample screens or fabric swatches together so that a common image can be projected on all of them simultaneously. With the naked eye you should be able to judge which produces the best result across the width of the particular room as you walk back and forth in front of them.

For general audio-visual use, a square screen is far better than a rectangular. Opaque, overhead, and the smaller slides require the square format, and these media should be considered even when equipping a large hall primarily for movie showings. Motorized roller screens longer than fourteen feet are normally available only in nonflameproofed material because the added weight of flameproofing causes the longer rollers to sag. For large installations, a flat screen mounted in a pipe batten is the easy solution if there is loft space above the stage. If not, then the problem should be taken to a theatrical supply house rather than to an audiovisual dealer.

The use of rear projection screens is becoming widespread in installations such as the central projection facility at the University of Miami.[28] A comparison of rear and front screens indicates that the rear screen offers many operating advantages. (Staff convenience again?) Rear screens, however, cannot be viewed from as wide an angle and it is much more difficult to attain a large image. Both of these factors limit the effective audience capacity.[27] Subjectively, at least, rear screen projection seems harder on the eyes. A design team of the Battelle Memorial Institute summarily rejects the rear screen as inferior in microfilm readers.[29]

A long-time standard for projection screen sizes, one-sixth as wide as the maximum viewing distance, has been reaffirmed by recent research.[27] Interestingly enough, projector manufacturers have never standardized their lens sizes to this ratio. Normally, 16mm movie projectors are supplied with a two-inch lens; this produces a six-foot picture at thirty feet, a five-to-one ratio a little better than the standard. At the same distance a 2" by 2" slide projector requires a seven-inch lens, yet the lens commonly supplied is four or five inches. Under the same conditions, film-

strips require a five-inch lens, 3 1/2" by 4" slides a fif-
teen-and-one-half inch lens, and 2 1/4" by 2 1/4" slides a
twelve-inch lens.   Proper choice of lenses will obviate the
problem of placing projection tables in the middle of an audience.   Overhead projectors, of course, are intended for use
at the front of the room and opaque projectors must be used
somewhat near the front.   A lens of incredible length would
be needed to use an opaque from the back of a normal classroom or lecture hall.

Related to image sizes, the Army uses a minimum
standard of one-inch lettering to be viewed from thirty-two
feet, two-inch lettering from sixty-four feet, etc.[30]   This is
supposed to allow for less than perfect vision.

Projection carts are of two major types: the four-
wheeled table and the two-wheeled hand cart.   The choice depends on local geography.   Travel over longer distances, up
and down stairs, curbs, or ramps calls for the hand cart.
These will have larger wheels (and the bigger the better) and
may be tipped for easier maneuvering over vertical obstacles.
The table type will be more useful within a building with even
floors and elevators.   Either should be capable of carrying
two major items of equipment at one time plus accessory
items in some kind of rack or shelf.   Table carts can be
purchased with a dual electrical outlet and extension cord
built in.   This is a real convenience, and could be added to
the hand cart variety rather easily.   No rolling stand is better than its wheels.   Check them carefully to see that they
turn and swivel easily.

In designing facilities for projection, be sure that images will clear the heads of the front-row audience.   Include
conduits front to back to carry movie sound and slide changer cables; other conduits may be desired for public address
wiring.   In a stepped or raked hall, under-floor conduit is
an absolute necessity; cables cannot be strung down stairs.
Light and screen controls should be duplicated front and back.
Any hall rating a sloped floor also rates an electric screen.
Specify the type that has an automatic cutoff at the full-up
and full-down positions.   Enclosed projection booths are not
particularly appropriate or useful until audience capacity goes
beyond 200 or 300.   They often become a nuisance in a small
situation, especially if portable equipment is moved in and
out frequently.   There are some excellent recent studies on
designing audio-visual facilities.[31-34]

Librarians, historically, have had little hand in the
development of audio-visual equipment; they have adopted
standardized equipment from the schools and industry.   Humboldt Leverenz and Malcolm Townsley, writing separately on

the topic The Design of Instructional Equipment, came to the same conclusion--there needs to be closer communication between the user and the designer of audio-visual equipment.[35] By analyzing program requirements carefully, librarians may be in a position to inform manufacturers of the shortcomings of ready-made equipment and perhaps shape the development of more useful machinery.

Among the dozens of texts and handbooks in the field of audio-visual education, James Finn's Audio-Visual Equipment Manual[36] is recommended as most useful for understanding the functioning of optical and electronic devices on a quasi-technical level. The diagrams of particular makes and models are now outdated, but the basic information remains valid. A more up-to-date text by James W. Brown, Richard B. Lewis, and Fred F. Harcleroad has an appendix treating the same kind of information in briefer form.[37]

The best guide to current equipment is the Audiovisual Equipment Directory,[38] an annual publication. It covers every conceivable category of audio-visual device, even to television and teaching machines, with a photograph, performance specifications, price, weight, and accessory list for each item. Appendices list furniture items, graphic materials, miscellaneous accessories, projection lamp specifications, and trade names. New equipment is described each month in a special section of Educational Screen and Audiovisual Guide,[39] and free literature is also noted. Some of these new items may appear in the "Products and Equipment" department of Library Journal[40] or the "Goods and Gadgets" department of the ALA Bulletin.[41]

The audio-visual press is full of evaluative information on films, filmstrips, recordings, and all varieties of materials. Reams have been written evaluating the usefulness and importance of various A-V devices, but there is virtually nothing in print evaluating equipment per se except in the popular consumer magazines and the Library Technology publications. Use these as a guide and then kick the tires.

Notes

1. Wyman, Raymond. "Let's Stop Calling It Portable," Audiovisual Instruction, 7:26-27, Jan. 1962.
2. U.S. Office of Education. Bulletin. No. 37, 1963 (OE-21024). Pp. 106-119.
3. American Library Association, Library Equipment Institute, held in St. Louis, Mo., in 1964.

4. Pearson, Mary D. Recordings in the Public Library.
    Chicago, American Library Association, 1963, pp.
    43-54.
5. American Library Association, Library Technology Pro-
    ject. The Testing and Evaluation of Record Players
    for Libraries. Chicago, American Library Associa-
    tion, 1962.
6. "Record Players for Libraries and Schools," Consumer
    Bulletin, 46:12-14, March 1963.
7. "High-Fidelity Stereo Sound with Separate Components,"
    Consumer Bulletin, 46:21-26, Nov. 1963.
8. "Stereo Record Players," Consumer Bulletin, 45:25-28,
    June 1962.
9. "Stereo Record Players," Consumer Bulletin, 46:2+,
    Dec. 1963.
10. "Automatic Record Changers," Consumer Reports, 27:
    20-23, Jan. 1962.
11. "Portable Stereo Phonographs," Consumer Reports, 27:
    290-293, June 1962.
12. "Portable Stereo Phonographs," Consumer Reports, 28:
    116-120, March 1963.
13. "Stereo Amplifiers," Consumer Reports, 27:454-459,
    Sept. 1962.
14. "Turntables With Arms," Consumer Reports, 29:435-439,
    Sept. 1964.
15. "Stereo Tape Recorders," Consumer Bulletin, 45:25-28,
    May 1962.
16. "Stereo Tape Recorders," Consumer Reports, 28:538-
    545, Nov. 1963.
17. "Stereo Headphones," Consumer Reports, 28:481-485,
    Oct. 1963.
18. "Slide Projectors," Consumer Bulletin, 44:20-21, Sept.
    1961.
19. "Slide Projectors," Consumer Bulletin, 45:6-12, Feb.
    1962.
20. "Projectors for Large Slides," Consumer Reports, 28:
    78-82, Feb. 1963.
21. "Slide Projectors," Consumer Reports, 26:614-619, Nov.
    1961.
22. "Fairchild 8mm Sound Movie Equipment," Consumer Bul-
    letin, 44:2+, Sept. 1961.
23. "Once Over--Now, an Instant Movie Projector," Consum-
    er Reports, 27:372-373, Aug. 1962.
24. Gerlach, Vernon S., and Farnbach, Irene. "How to
    Teach Library Skills Without Really Being There,"
    Library Journal, 89:921-922, Feb. 15, 1964.
25. Hurley, Mel. "Screen Standards for Today's Projection,"

Motion Picture Herald, 125:34+, June 13, 1959.
26. "Choosing the Right Projection Screen," Consumer Reports, 29:232-234, May 1964.
27. University Facilities Research Center. Space for Audio-Visual Large Group Instruction. Madison, University Facilities Research Center with the Educational Facilities Laboratories, 1963, pp. 6-9.
28. Tharp, Charles Doren. Learning and Instructional Resources Center. Coral Gables, University of Miami, 1963.
29. Walkup, L. E., et al. "The Design of Improved Microimage Readers for Promoting the Utilization of Microimages." In National Microfilm Association. Proceedings, of the Eleventh Annual Meeting and Convention, 1962. Annapolis, National Microfilm Association, 1962, Vol. XI, p. 287.
30. U.S. Army Command and General Staff College. Style Manual and Editing and Publishing Services (Instruction circular 3). Fort Leavenworth, Kansas, 1959, p. 127.
31. Texas University. An Auditorium Teaching Facility. Austin, University of Texas, 1963.
32. Chapman, Dave, Inc. Design for ETV: Planning for Schools with Television. New York, Educational Facilities Laboratories, 1960.
33. De Bernardis, Amo., et al. Planning Schools for New Media. Portland, Ore., U.S. Department of Health, Education, and Welfare, Office of Education, 1961.
34. Rensselaer Polytechnic Institute, School of Architecture. New Spaces for Learning. Troy, New York, 1961.
35. Leverenz, Humboldt W., and Townsley, Malcolm G. The Design of Instructional Equipment: Two Views (National Education Association of the United States, Technological Development Project Occasional Paper, No. 8). Washington, National Education Association, pp. 25, 48.
36. Finn, James D. The Audio-Visual Equipment Manual. New York, Dryden Press, 1957.
37. Brown, James W., et al. A-V Instruction: Material and Methods. 2d ed. New York, McGraw-Hill, 1964.
38. Audio-visual Equipment Directory. Fairfax, Va., National Audio-visual Association, Inc. (Annual).
39. "New Equipment," Educational Screen and Audiovisual Guide, regular feature.
40. McConkey, Thomas W. "Products and Equipment," Library Journal, regular feature.
41. "Goods and Gadgets," ALA Bulletin, regular feature.

Recent Developments in Instructional Technology
Philip Lewis

From Illinois Libraries 47:107-13, February 1965. Reprinted by permission.

Some of the important progress in the materials field
in recent years is directly attributable to the National Defense Education Act under Title III. Although funding was
available only for the mathematics, science and foreign language fields, the resulting influences were far-reaching.
With the broadening of this Act to include history, geography,
language arts, and other services, even greater advances are
anticipated commencing this year. The addition of Title XI,
to provide institutes for librarians and audio-visual specialists, is a most significant piece of legislation designed to
assist these practitioners in keeping pace with the media
field.

During the past five years an almost overwhelming
number of technological devices, materials, and facilities
were made available for educational and instructional purposes. In many instances the hardware developments so far
outstripped the production of materials for use with the equipment that progress in adopting the new techniques was hin-
dered. This point has particular application to the field of
teaching machines and programed learning, although a close
parallel may be drawn from the development of the language
laboratory.

The Shift from Aids

Despite these growing pains, much progress has been
made, and the beginning of a real revolution in the use of
instructional technology, A-V materials, and other teaching
tools is evident. This trend is due to recognition of the fact
that instructional materials and equipment are not used with
optimum effectiveness when they are employed simply as aids.
Rather, they must be involved as integral parts of total instructional plans. For example, an educational motion picture showing should not be scheduled only if time permits.
If the film has been selected to serve an identified need that
cannot be accomplished better in any other way for a given

424

situation, then the screening is a must.   This same philosophy can assist in the selection and development of instructional facilities, based on a thorough analysis of local needs,
so that coordinated resources result rather than a mere accumulation of equipment and materials.

Recent Developments

Although some really new devices have appeared on
the market, most of the innovations are the result of modifications or combinations of previously available items. The
list that follows is of necessity limited, but should provide
an overview of these developments.

The Language Laboratory is available in so many
forms and arrangements that it is difficult to properly define
this facility.   The complete laboratory usually includes individual booths for students and a programing and control console for the teacher or laboratory assistant.   Recent trends
in design are toward remote control of equipment to allow
all recorders and playbacks to be removed from student
booths.   Also, automatic features permit dialing or pushbut-
ton access to prerecorded materials.   Perimeter Laboratories
are appearing with greater frequency.   These latter installations are generally located around some of the walls in foreign language classrooms to provide the teacher with greater
flexibility in the use of the equipment.

The Learning Laboratory resulted from the findings
that the techniques employed with language laboratories were
equally valid and applicable to many other curriculum areas.
For example, speech correction, speech therapy, listening
for music appreciation, vocabulary development for science,
etc., are all possible with such facilities.   Such broad applications make it economically possible for small schools to
consider adding a lab, where this would not be feasible for
language learning alone.

The Language Lab as a Programing Center takes advantage of the multi-channel program sources in the lab to
feed audio lines installed in adjacent or scattered listening
areas.   These include classrooms, carrells, the library and
study halls.   In this way, passive listening facilities are provided at very little additional cost.

Expanding the Usefulness of the Intercommunication
System through proper engineering is a simple but fruitful
approach.   Many schools have intercom facilities which are
used principally as a paging or message-carrying network.
In some instances AM/FM and shortwave tuners and phonographs have been added to extend the services.   However,

the installation of extra circuits and accessories permits the
existing equipment to become extremely versatile. The addition of several tape playbacks and recorders allows teachers in classrooms to request prerecorded programs for reproduction over the local loudspeaker system. Also, remote
recording of classroom discussions may be accomplished at
the control console at the request of the teacher. In this
instance the overhead speakers perform as microphones. In
a similar manner central dictation facilities can be provided
to permit teachers to dictate letters and other communications over the intercom to automatic recording devices for
later transcription by the pool stenographer. By means of
appropriate plug-in jacks at the front and back of each classroom, it is possible to connect phonographs and motion picture projectors locally to utilize the overhead speakers for
better audio reproduction.

The Communications Center represents the consolida-
tion of the Language Laboratory, the Learning Laboratory,
the Intercommunication System and other technological devices into a coordinated design to serve the special needs of
the entire school or campus. A center of this kind supplies
electronically programs that have been prerecorded in the
form of tapes, records, films, filmstrips and videotapes to
classrooms, study halls, libraries, seminar rooms and study
carrells. This approach represents the latest thinking toward supplying materials for self-directed study approaches
as well as for small and large group learning arrangements.
Specific services include stenographic dictation at different
speeds or technical, legal, or medical sequences which can
be selected according to need. The incorporation of television circuits makes possible the transmission of visuals of
all kinds including data and records remoting. This total
development will take on more and more functions as experimentation goes forward and represents one of the most exciting and promising facilities designed to assist the program
of education.

The Videotape Recorder, since its inception little
more than a decade ago, carried a price tag that made it
impossible for all except the largest educational institutions
to consider its use. About two years ago a real break-
through occurred in this connection with the production of a
miniaturized, solid-state device. It is now possible to buy
such a machine at about one-fifth to one-third of the price
of the commercial counterpart. In addition, prototypes have
been built, and others are under development which will be
of the same size as audiotape recorders. These will become available during the next two to three years and will

cost as little as $600 per unit. Some of the present appli-
cations of the small VTR's include recording lessons and
programs off-the-air for future and repeated replay; portable
recording in classroom and field situations for subsequent replay over distribution systems; recording of students in
speech classes for slow-motion replay and diagnosis and similar approaches can be used with athletic teams and other
skill development situations; recording of student teachers in
classroom situations for use in follow-up evaluation sessions.
Future applications will incorporate frame-by-frame recording of data and student records as a substitute for microfilming. Random access attachments will enable the user to
locate and reproduce data in seconds. Similarly, procedures
processed can be animated through the means of the single
frame technique. TV receivers will come equipped with videotape decks so that while one program is being viewed, another can be recorded on a different channel. The future
expansion of the use of videotape recorders will provide one
of the most flexible educational tools.
Responder Systems now on the market take various
forms. Some work with colored lights, others with meters,
and still others are hooked up to computers. In essence,
however, they all make it possible for the teacher to know
immediately both the group and the individual reactions of
her class to the presentation in progress. Thus, the teacher need not wait until the fifth-week marking period to determine that certain students did not master specific areas of
the work covered during that time. There is the significant
opportunity to reteach at the moment when reinforcement and
review is vital.
Multi-media Instructional Systems may be used with
small or large groups of learners, although the latter situation has been more popular to this date. The idea behind
this movement is to coordinate the use of many types of
audio and visual presentations so that each medium is employed in a way that will best exploit its potential in a given
instructional situation. Auditoriums are fitted with TV, motion picture, filmstrip, and slide projectors that are remote
controlled and preprogramed. In operation, the motion picture sequence may appear on the screen for a few minutes.
If a difficult concept is involved, a slide may be projected
on a second screen to explain a term or to show a closeup.
Many other combinations are possible. Some multi-media
systems are also integrated with responder facilities.

Technological Systems Are Varied

There is no single approach to the design of a communication system for learning. Each facility must develop
as a result of the needs and the program of the individual
institution. Also, all of the items to be acquired need not,
and preferably should not, be provided at the outset. The
additions should be made as the faculty and the student body
are ready to receive the innovations. Such systems should
relieve teachers of the routines of arranging for equipment
and programing and should provide students with resources
for self-study procedures. Equally important is the provision for proper and continuous maintenance to insure trouble-
free operation. Interestingly, such systems are not prohib-
itively expensive if they are planned and installed (the basic
distribution network) at the time of construction of a new
building, or if this is done when an existing building is
scheduled for remodeling.

Index to Authors

Bebeau, Gordon, 191
Berner, Richard C., 292
Berry, June, 402
Brown, Lloyd A., 260
Brubaker, Robert L., 303

Cain, Robert E., 209
Cammack, Floyd M., 106
Carson, Doris M., 396
Cohen, Allen, 136
Corner, Ruth, 178
Cushman, Jerome, 77

Dixon, Elizabeth I., 110

Eulberg, Sister M. Thomas, 153

Faye, Helen, 367
Ferguson, Elizabeth, 157
Ferguson, Ruth B., 157
Ferrar, A.M., 271
Finch, Jean L., 332
Foster, Donald L., 183

Gee, Ralph D., 220
Gerlach, Arch C., 286
Goldstein, Harold, 373
Goshkin, Ida, 34
Graycar, Marie L., 180
Grove, Lee E., 133

Hagen, C.B., 139
Hale, Betty, 354
Hanna, Edna Frances, 44
Harkin, M.J., 116
Holloway, George M., 16
Howe, Jane, 356
Howser, Ray E., 20

Jasenas, Michael, 342

Kallai, Sandor, 94
King, Jack, 167
Krummel, Donald W., 230

Lang, Paul Henry, 39
Layng, Theodore H., 280
Lewis, Philip, 215, 424
Lewis, Stanley T., 196
Lewton, L.O., 298
Ligocki, Michael, 201
Limbacher, James L., 27

Myers, Kurtz, 86

Plain, Eleanor, 188
Pressler, Joan, 389

Rawkins, Reginald A., 175
Ready, William, 84
Rink, Bernard C., 193
Roberts, Don L., 66
Roberts, Thomas W., 407

Schmidt, Marianne, 162
Simons, Wendell W., 410
Simpson, Irene, 364
Smith, James H., 114
Snider, John R., 300
Stafford, I. Elizabeth, 149
Stevenson, Gordon, 97, 238, 245
Stines, Ruth, 72

Teller, Oscar, 205

VanderMeer, A.W., 381

429

Wedgeworth, Robert, 80
White, F.A., 24
Williamson, Walter W., 125

Index to Subjects

accession record, 181
acid-free folders, 338
acquisition of:
    audio-visual equipment, 410
    ephemera, 296-7
    imported scores, 245-59
    manuscripts, 310-3
    musical editions, 236
    pamphlets, 159-60, 167-71
    pictures, 354, 364, 366
    recordings, 53-4
acquisition policies, 292
acquisitions lists, 51
adapters for phonographs, 49
administration of:
    audio-visual collections, 389-95
    manuscript collections, 314-6
    map collections, 263-4, 268-9, 271-9
    music collections, 233
    record collections, 74
adult education--films, 16-9, 20-3
adults and films, 29
advertisements, 354
advertising materials, 153
"advertising rights," 368
age-levelitis, 31
agogram, 227
agorithm, 227
aims see objectives
Akron Public Library, 35-8
ALA see American Library Association
ALA Booklist see Booklist
ALA Bulletin, 421
alphabetical arrangement of recordings by composers, 104
American Art Directory, 211
American Film Festival, 32
American Geographical Society, 268
American Historical Association, 303-4, 323-4
American Institute of Musicology, 252

431

American Library and Book Trade Annual, 63-4n
American Library Association, 15n, 19n, 58, 63-4n, 69, 396,
  400n, 421-2n
    Audio-Visual Committee, 17, 373-4
    Audio-Visual Workshops, 32
    cataloging of recordings, 69
The American Organist, 92
American Record Guide, 67-8, 75, 91
American Society of Magazine Photographers, 368
American University (Washington, D.C.), 332
amplifiers, 414
analytic book catalogs of audio-visual materials, 394-5
anthologies, musical, 231
Appleton Public Library (Wisconsin), 191-2
archival practice--courses, 332
archives, 332-41
archives and recordings, 97-8
arrangement of:
    archives, 332-41
    correspondence, 335-6
    manuscripts, 332-41, 349-51
    miscellaneous materials, 402-6
    pictures, 355
    recordings, 392
    See also   alphabetical arrangement; cataloging; classi-
               fication; classified arrangement; chronologi-
               cal arrangement; storage.
arrangement principles, 334-5
arrangements, musical, 230
art
    bibliographies, 199
    classification, 200
    Eskimo, 193-5
    graphic, 183-7
    interest in, 187
    original, 199
    publicity, 202-3
    regional, 201-4
    See also   art reproductions; paintings; pictures;
               prints; visual forms.
art and music departments, 242
art catalogs, 198-9
art exhibits, 189, 193-4, 201-4
art history in libraries, 196
art in public libraries, 183-7, 200-4
art in visual materials collection, 199
Art Index, 197

art reproductions, 188, 189, 191-2, 391
art reproductions in libraries, 188-90, 191-2, 193-5, 196-200
art sale, 193-4
articles, 154, 163, 296
artists and the library, 196-7, 201, 203, 209-11, 366
Associated Music Publishers, 245
Association of American Geographers, 278
Atlantic Monthly, 91
atlases, 269, 284
atmosphere and recordings, 55
Audio, 92
audio-visual aids in adult services, 374
audio-visual department in school system, 389-95
audio-visual diseases, 31
audio-visual equipment, 410-23
Audio-visual Equipment Directory, 421
Audio-visual Equipment Manual, 421
audio-visual holdings, 374
audio-visual librarians, 28, 32
audio-visual librarianship training, 20-1, 379-80
audio-visual materials, 376, 378, 379, 389-95
audio-visual reference aids, 32
audio-visual technology, 424-8
audio-visual work--professionalization, 27
An Auditorium Teaching Facility, 423n
Aurora Public Library (Illinois), 188-90
author approach to pamphlets, 173
author headings--manuscripts, 348
author index of manuscripts, 317
automated distribution systems, 412-3
automated teaching, 383-4

background music (recordings), 61
Baerenreiter Music Publishers, 252-7
Ball, M.O., 155
Bancroft, Hubert Howe, 338
Bancroft Library (University of California), 332-9
Bärenreiter Antiquariat, 245
Bärenreiter Verlag of Kassel, 252-7
"A Basic Collection of Records for a College Library," 94
Basic Library (recordings), 94
Basic Library of Classical LP's, 54
basic-record-collection guides, 68
A Basic Record Library, 94
"Basic Series" (music), 231
"A Basic Stock List" (recordings), 94

Bauer, Roberto, 52
BBC Gramophone Library, 102
Beetle, Clara, 400n
beg cards, 159-60
Belknap, Jeremy, 327n
Bennett, F., 380n
bibliographic control of:
    archives, 334
    audio-visual materials, 379
    manuscripts, 326, 334
    printed notes, 233-4
    See also cataloging; classification; retrieval; union
        catalogs.
bibliographic forms of printed notes, 230-1
bibliographies of:
    art works, 199
    audio-visual equipment, 420-3
    children's recordings, 53
    films, 21, 32
    information file, 154
    jazz recordings, 81
    language recordings, 52
    nonmusical recordings, 52
    paintings, 188
    pamphlets, 158-9
    printed notes, 235, 245-6
    recordings, 50-2, 67-8, 75, 90-2, 94
    subject headings, 155
    vertical file materials, 180
    vocations, 163
Bieneman, Dorothy, 63-5n
Billboard--record reviews, 90
biographies, 180
Blackwell's Music Shop, 259n
blind readers, 133-5
Blue Book of A-V Materials, 54
book jackets, 180, 402
The Booklist, 17, 32, 159, 180, 240
books, geographical--cataloging and classification, 286-9
books about music, 231, 239-40
books in visual materials collection, 199
books of art, 197-8
books of music, 231
"bound withs," 101
box list (films), 37
branch programming, 216, 221
Breitkopf and Härtel, 245

British Catalogue of Music, 233, 250
British National Bibliography regional subdivision scheme, 288
broadsides, 293
brochures, 153
Broude, Alexander, 245
Broude Bros., 245
Brown, James W., 421
browsing bins, 60
browsing boxes, 104
Bryant, Eric Thomas, 63-4n, 241, 258n
Buck, Solon J., 329n
bulletin board materials, 154, 180, 403
Bureau of Public Discussion (Indiana University), 301-2
Burkfzer, Manfred, 246
Burroughs Clearing House--"Booklet Counter," 159
business records see records, financial and business.

CAFGA, 407-9
calendar guide to manuscripts, 317
California. University. Library, 110, 332-9
California Gold Rush, 264-5
California public high school libraries, 180-2
call numbers of maps, 280-5
campaign literature, 296
Canadian Periodical Index, 179
captions, 355, 404
the card catalog and art works, 197-8, 200
card file of vertical file materials, 181
card index of map collection, 274-5
card index of visual materials collection, 199
career file see vocational file
Carnovsky, L., 76n
cartographic records see records, cartographic; maps; charts.
cartographical index diagram, 275
cartography, historical, 262
cartridges for storing slides, 415
Cary Memorial Library (Lexington, Mass.), 209-14
Cash Box, 90
catalog card elements--manuscripts, 348-9
catalog cards for:
        archives, 340-1
        audio-visual materials, 390
        manuscripts, 340-1, 346-7
        maps, 274-5
        photographs, 357-8
        stereophonic tapes, 137-8

catalog of audio-visual materials, 375
Catalog of Cards for Motion Pictures and Filmstrips, 397
catalog of films--preparation, 407-9
catalogable units, 344-52
cataloging of:
  archives, 337-8
  audio-visual materials, 390
  ephemera, 299
  festscriften, 351
  films, 396-401
  filmstrips, 396-401
  geographical materials, 286-91
  information file, 156
  manuscripts, 316-8, 337-8, 342-53
  maps, 274-5, 280-5, 396-401
  microfilms, 396-401
  nonbook materials, 396-401
  overhead projectuals, 394
  pamphlets, 168, 171-4, 175-7, 178-9, 351
  photographs, 356-63, 394
  pictures, 365, 394, 396-401
  printed notes, 396-401
  programmed courses, 225-6
  recordings, 58, 68-9, 140-1, 147, 392, 396-401
  slides, 391, 396-401
  tapes, 137-8, 393
Cataloging Rules for Author and Title Entries (ALA), 345, 396
catalogs in vertical files, 180
catalogs in visual materials collection, 199
catalogs of other libraries--recordings, 51
Catalogue of Colour Reproductions of Paintings 1860 to 1959, 188
Catalogue of Colour Reproductions of Paintings Prior to 1860, 188
Catholic Periodical Index, 155
Catholic Subject Headings, 155
censorship of films, 30
Changing Times, 159
charts, 283 See also geographical materials; maps.
The Chesterfield Shops, 54
children and art, 205-8
children's international activities, 128-32
Children's Reading Service, 54
Children's Record Center, 54
Children's Record Critique, 53
Children's Record Reviews, 53
children's recordings see recordings for children.

chronological arrangement--manuscripts and archives, 334-5
circular letters, 295
circulation of:
    art reproductions, 189, 191-2
    clippings, 302
    filmstrips, 25
    maps, 277-8
    original prints, 186
    paintings to children, 205-8
    pamphlets, 160-1
    recordings, 45, 57, 69-70
    slides, 25
    vertical file materials, 181
Clark, Thomas D., 328n
classification of:
    art works, 200
    filmstrips, 25
    four-track tapes, 136-8
    geographical materials, 286-91
    manuscripts, 338
    maps, 271-4, 280-5, 289-90
    pamphlets, 160, 175-7, 178-9
    photographs, 358-60
    pictures, 355
    programmed courses, 226
    recordings, 58, 69, 73, 97-105, 142
classroom exchanges of tapes, 126
clipping file, 301-2
clippings, 154, 163, 180, 181, 300-2
closed stacks--recordings, 100-1
Clough, Francis F., 52
Code for Cataloging Music and Phonorecords, 58, 69
collation, 348, 398-9
The Collector's Bach, 90
The Collector's Twentieth-Century Music in the Western Hem-
    isphere, 90
The Collector's Verdi and Puccini, 90
College and Public Libraries--vertical files, 180
college libraries
    art reproductions, 193-5, 196-200
    audio-visual materials, 378
    standards, 13
    See also university libraries.
colleges and film circuits, 378
colored catalog cards, 59, 99, 103-4, 298-9, 390-4
Columbia University, 110
commercials, 144-6

Commiskey, Margaret, 21
Commission on the Classification of Geographical Books and
    Maps in Libraries, 286
common-law literary rights, 322-3
communication, 39-40, 381-2
communications center, 426
community college libraries, 194-5
community needs
        films, 17-8, 20, 28
        music, 50, 75
        recordings, 45
community use of audio-visual materials, 378-9
company libraries, 354-5, 364-6
composer analytics in card catalog, 104
Computer Applications for Graphic Arts (CAFGA), 407-9
computerized film catalog, 407-9
concerts sponsored by libraries, 75
condition cards for films, 36
"Constitution of the [Massachusetts] Historical Society, " 328
"constructed response, " 216
consumer magazines and audio-visual equipment, 421
consumer services, 410
Consumers' Bulletin, 91
Continental Classroom, 384
controversial films see films, controversial.
controversial material as clippings, 181
cooperation, interlibrary, with respect to:
        art prints, 186
        audio-visual materials, 374, 377-9
        cataloging of recordings, 47
        films, 34-8
        manuscript collections, 313, 323-5
        pamphlet collections, 174
        record collections, 45, 47
        See also central processing; film circuits.
coordinate index, 144-6, 199
copyright and pictures, 367-72
copyright lists of musical editions, 235
correspondence, 335-6, 344-52
correspondence as ephemera, 295
correspondence as literary property, 322-3
correspondence as records, 333
correspondence exchange project, 128-9
cost of:
        films, 30
        imported scores, 245-59
        record collection, 74
        See also discounts; prices.

courses see programmed courses.
court papers, 333, 336-7
critical notes, 400
critics, 28
Crowder, Norman, 216, 220
Cuming, C.J., 52
Cumulative Book Index, 234
Currall, H.F.J., 105n
Current Geographical Publications, 268

Darrell, R.D., 52
dealers and printed notes, 245-59
dealers and recordings, 53-4, 68
dealers' catalogs--art prints, 186
Dearborn Public Library, 162-6
debating materials, 180
Delaunay, 52
Denver. University. Library, 332
depositories, 296, 332
descriptive note--manuscripts, 348
desiderata lists, 171, 354
Deutsche Musikbibliographie, 233
Dewey Decimal Classification and:
        geographical topics, 287-8, 291
        pamphlets, 175-7, 178-9
        recordings, 99, 103
        vertical files, 180
diagrams as records, 333
Dictionary of Occupational Titles, 163
discard record for vertical files, 181
discographies see recordings--bibliographies.
discounts
        music scores, 250
        recordings, 75
        See also cost; prices.
phonograph records see recordings.
display areas for art prints, 186
display racks for slides, 415
displays see art exhibits; exhibits.
Disques, 91
documentaries (sound recordings)--cataloging, 144-6
documentary records see records, documentary.
documents, 180, 293, 333
Don Mills Regional Branch Library (North York, Ontario),
    175-7
donations see gifts.
Down Beat, 81, 92

Down Beat Jazz Records Reviews, 90
drama cuttings, 180
drawers for slides, 415

earphones, 117
East Chicago Public Library, 201-4
Edison, Thomas A., 72
Edison cylinder, 72
education, 381-8
education and programmed learning, 220-1
education and recordings, 98
education and technological change, 387-8
Education Index, 52
Educational Film Guide, 375
educational media, 381-8, 424-8
educational methods, 383-4
Educational Screen and Audio-visual Guide, 32, 54, 75, 421
educational TV see television.
Educational Theatre Journal--record reviews, 92
Educator's Guides to Free Films and Filmstrips, 32
EFLA cards, 32
EFLA workshops, 32
electronic carrell, 413
electronic revolution, 73
embassy materials, 180
Encyclopedia of American Associations, 165
engravings, 183
ephemera, 292-9
Eskimo Art Fund, 193-4
etchings, 183
Ethnomusicology, 90
evaluation of:
        films, 27
        programmed courses, 222-3
        See also bibliographies; selection.
evaluators, 28, 410
"exclusive rights"--pictures, 368
exhibition (art) catalogs, 198-9
exhibits, 61, 128, 371
"express stops, " 216

Facts About Film, 22
Facts About Projection, 22
Farish, Margaret, 235
federal aid for instructional technology, 424
festschriften--cataloging, 351
Fifty Sources of Occupational Information, 166

file cabinets, 405
file of local resources, 51
filing cards for recordings, 59
film as a medium, 28
film catalog, 35, 37, 407-9
film circuits, 34-8, 374, 378
film collection, 28, 36
film cooperatives see film circuits.
Film Culture, 32
Film Daily, 32
Film Facts, 32
film forums, 32, 374
Film News, 32, 75
film projectors, 416-8
Film Quarterly, 32
Film Review Digest, 32
film screening committees, 17, 31
film societies, 32
Film Society, 32
Film Utilization, 20-1
Film World, 32, 75
Films, 229n
films
        acquisition, 36
        administration problems, 375
        age levels, 31
        audiences, 29
        bibliographies, 21, 32
        cataloging, 396-401, 407-9
        censorship, 30
        condition, 35
        content, 29
        controversial, 30
        cost, 30
        8mm., 417
        evaluation and criticism, 27
        inspecting and screening, 36
        library policies, 37
        narration, 28-9
        presentation, 28
        programs, 18, 32
        publicity, 18-9, 37
        repairs, 36
        selection, 17-8, 21, 28, 33, 35, 36
        16mm. educational, 373
        standards, 28
        subjects, 28, 37

films (cont.)
      techniques, 29
      theatrical, 32
      use, 17-8, 29
Films and Filming, 32
films and library activities, 374
films as records, 333
films as visual media, 31
Films for Libraries, 17
films for programmed learning, 218
films in audio-visual department, 389
films in libraries, 16-9, 20-3, 29, 34, 38
Films in Review, 32
filmstrips
      cataloging, 396-401
      circulation, 25
      classification, 25
      equipment, 390, 416
      maintenance, 25
      storage, 25
      use, 24
filmstrips in audio-visual department, 389
filmstrips in libraries, 24-6, 376
financial records see records, financial and business.
Finn, James D., 421
"first rights"--pictures, 367-8
The FM and Fine Arts Guide, 51
folk song, 77-9
Fono Forum--record reviews, 91
Fontes Artis Musicae, 245
Ford Foundation, 110
"foreign rights"--pictures, 368
Forrester, Gertrude, 163
frames, 186, 188-9, 191
Free and Inexpensive Learning Materials, 154
Friedlander, Madeline S., 21

Gaehde, 211
Gee, R.D., 228n
geographers and Library of Congress cataloging rules, 289
Geographia, 261
geographical libraries, 278
geographical materials, 286-91
gifts of:
      art prints, 186-7
      photographs 356-7
      printed matter, 298

gifts of: (cont.)
  recordings, 46
globes, 269
Good Housekeeping, 159
Goody, Sam, 54, 94
Gottlieb, Ernest E., 245
government documents see documents.
The Gramophone--record reviews, 91
The Gramophone Record Review, 91
Gramophone Shop Encyclopedia, 52
Gramophone Shop Supplement, 90
graphic arts see art, graphic.
Great Historical Places, 357
group activities and films, 374
A Guide to Archives and Manuscripts in the United States,
  304, 319
Guide to Career Information, 165
A Guide to the Care and Administration of Manuscripts, 316
Guide to the Collecting and Care of Original Prints, 211
guides to manuscript collections, 317-8, 337

Hamer, Philip M., 304, 319
Hampton School (Lutherdale, Maryland), 127-30
Handbook of North American Indians, 357
Harcleroad, Fred F., 421
Harper's, 81, 91
Harris, Foster, 357
Harry Futterman Fund, Inc., 47
Hattery, Bob, 301
headphones, 414
Heyer, Anna Harriet, 246
hi-fi listeners, 42
Hi-Fi/Stereo Review, 54, 67-8, 75, 91
High Fidelity, 67-8, 75, 91
high school libraries
  information file, 153-6
  language lab, 114-5
  pamphlets, 157-61
  vertical files, 180-2
historians and ephemera, 293, 295-7
historical houses--manuscript collections, 303-31
Historical Records, 52
historical research, 295
historical sets (music), 230, 252
Historical Sets, Collected Editions and Monuments of Music,
  246
historical societies, 303-31

history, preservation of, 110-3
history, U.S., and maps, 264-5
history of discographies, 51-2
history of recordings, 72
Hoban, Dr. Charles, 385
Hobbies, 92
hobby material as clippings, 181
Hodge, Frederick, 357
holiday items as clippings, 181
Hot Discography, 52
house organs, 295
housing see storage.
Hydrographic Survey charts, 269

Illinois Public Libraries, 20-3, 74-6
Illinois State Library, 73
image data, 198-9
image-for-image indexing, 200
image library, 196-200
Imperial Library (Paris), 262
index cards, 274-5, 357-8
index of manuscripts, 346, 349, 352
Index of Record Reviews, 52, 68, 86
index to articles in geographical periodicals, 278
indexes to record reviews, 68
indexes to recordings, 51-2
indexing of recordings, 139-40
indexing of visual materials collection, 199
Indiana University (Bloomington), 300-2
information file, 153-6
information retrieval see retrieval.
informational productivity as criterion, 298
institutes for librarians and audio-visual specialists, 424
instructional materials center, 125, 378-9, 389
instructional technology, 424-5
intercommunication facilities, 425
interlibrary loan, 51, 243
Interlibrary Loan Code, 243
International Geographical Union, 286, 289
International Index--recordings, 52
International Tape Library, 125
interviews on tape, 110-3
invasion of privacy--pictures, 369-72
inventories--arrangement, 337
inventory of manuscripts, 317
inventory of map collection, 276
Iowa. University. Library, 168-74

Ireland, Norma, 158

Jameson, J. F., 326-7n
Jasenas, Michael, 330n
jazz, 80-3
Jefferson Junior High School (Mt. Lebanon, Pa.), 389-95
Jomard, Edme, 262
The Journal of American Folklore, 92
journals, 337
junior college libraries, 13

Kane, Lucile M., 316
Kansas City Public Library, 245-59
Kapsner, O. L., 155
Kresge Library (Oakland University), 107-9
Krone, Beatrice, 53

labels, 57, 354, 360, 362-3
Landers Film Reviews, 32
Lane, David O., 94
The Language and Literature Library, 116
language courses on magnetic tape see taped language
                                          courses.
language laboratories, 114-5, 386, 389, 412, 425
language recordings see recordings, language; taped lan-
                                  guage courses.
Laubin, Reginald and Gladys, 357
the law and pictures, 367-72
Leading Film Discussions; A Handbook to Help Discussion
    Leaders to Use Films and to Set Up and Conduct a Film
    Discussion Workshop, 21
leaflets as ephemera, 293
"leap-frogging, " 216
learning laboratory, 425
"learning loops, " 107
learning to read, 382
lectures (sound recordings), 144-6
ledgers, 337
Lefinder Guide, 145
Lelewel, Joachim, 262
letterheads in picture collection, 354
letters see correspondence.
Leverenz, Humboldt W., 420-1
Levin, Abner, 54
Lewis, Richard B., 421
libel--pictures, 369-72
librarians and audio-visual materials, 377

librarians and programmed learning, 224-5
librarians as art connoisseurs, 201
the library and printed notes, 235-7
the library as a:
      clearing house of information, 51
      cultural center, 193-5, 204
      depository, 296
      educational institution, 72, 77
      materials resource center, 114
library broadcasting system, 107
"Library Classification and Cataloging of Geographic Material," 279n
library concerts, 61
Library Equipment Institute, 413
library extension activities and films, 374
Library Journal
      books about music, 240
      "Items of Interest," 159
      "Products and Equipment" department, 421
      record reviews, 54, 68, 75, 92
Library of Congress, 133-5, 148, 329-30, 352, 396-401
Library of Congress
      list of recordings, 75
      manuscripts, 304
      maps, 260
      Catalog, 228-9n
      catalog cards for recordings, 58, 69
      cataloging rules and geographers, 289
      rules for descriptive cataloging see Rules for Descriptive Cataloging in the Library of Congress.
      subject headings and pamphlets, 173
library orientation and programmed learning, 223
library restrictions on manuscript use, 320-3
library science education and programmed learning, 224
library semantics, 200
Library Services Act, 45
Library Technology Project, 410, 413
Library technology publications and audio-visual equipment, 421
Libri Novi de Musica, 245, 252
"linear programming," 216
Linguaphone language courses, 118
listening programs in libraries, 42, 73, 75, 115, 389, 412-5
literary property
      manuscripts, 322-3
      pictures, 367, 72
Literary Property in the United States, 330n

<u>Literature and Music as Resources for Special Studies</u>, 53
lithographs, 183
loan exhibitions, 186
location symbols, 281-5, 348
<u>The Long Player</u>, 52, 54
<u>The Look of the Old West</u>, 357
loudspeakers <u>see</u> speakers.
LP recordings <u>see</u> recordings, long-playing.

McDonald, Gerald D. , 374
magnetic tape <u>see</u> tapes.
main entry for nonbook materials, 396-7
maintenance
       filmstrips, 25
       recordings, 45-6
       tape recorders, 118
Manchester Public Libraries, 116-24
manuscript collections, 303-4, 310-20, 332
manuscript control systems, 343
manuscript holdings--survey, 304-11
manuscript librarians, 314-5
"Manuscripts, " 329n
manuscripts
       acquisition, 310-3
       arrangement, 332-41, 349-51
       bibliographic control, 326, 334
       cataloging, 316-8, 337-8, 342-53
       classification, 338
       description, 337
       historical, 333, 350-1
       indexes, 346, 349, 352
       kinds, 333
       literary, 333, 350-1
       microfilming, 323-5
       restrictions on use, 320-3
       storage, 338, 350-1
       subject-person index, 343
       subjects, 311-2
       terminology, 333-4
       use, 334
       written summaries, 343
       <u>See also</u> archives; records.
"Manuscripts and the Library, " 352n
manuscripts as literary property, 322-3
manuscripts as primary source materials, 293, 295
manuscripts in state historical societies, 303-4
manuscripts in university libraries, 303-4, 332-41

map catalogs, 290
map collections, 260-2, 263-4, 268-9, 271-9
map file cabinets, 405
map library, 280-5
maps
        cataloging, 274-5, 280-5, 396-401
        circulation, 277-8
        classification, 271-4, 278-9, 280-5, 289-90
        library problems, 281-5
        location symbols, 280-5
        reference collections, 277-8
        selection, 266-9
        series, 281-2
        storage, 269, 276-7
        teaching sets, 277-8
        See also atlases; charts; geographical materials;
            globes.
maps as records, 333
maps as reference tools, 262
maps in information file, 154
maps in map library, 280-5
maps in public libraries, 260-70
maps in university geography departments, 271-9
maps in vertical files, 180
Mark Osterlin Library (Northwestern Michigan College), 193-5
Marks, Edward B., Music Corporation, 258n
mass media, 377, 381-8
memoirs, 110
memoranda, 295, 337
Merlander, Kurt B., 245
microfilms, 218, 323-5, 396-401, 416
microphones, 414-5
Midwest Airborne Television Instructional Program, 376, 384
minutes of meetings, 295, 333, 336
miscellaneous materials, 402-6
mnemonic letter notations--recordings, 103
model releases--pictures, 370-2
models (objects)--storage, 403-4
Modern Archives; Principles and Techniques, 332
The Monthly Letter from E. M. G., 90
Monumenta Musica, 252-4, 258n
motion pictures see films.
Mount Lebanon School System (Pennsylvania), 389-95
Mount Royal Elementary School (Baltimore, Md.), 130-2
Mount St. Mary's College (Los Angeles), 139-48
mounting, 154, 186
multi-media instructional systems, 427

Mumford, L. Quincy, 329n
Mummery, Kenneth, 245
museums, 184, 198, 303-31
music
        bibliographies, 241-2, 246
        popular literature of, 41
        publishing, 234
        scholarly literature of, 40
        selection tools, 241-2
music activities of public libraries, 243
Music and Phonorecords, 229n, 233
music collections--standards, 241
music departments in public libraries, 242
music groups, local, 51
music in libraries, 40, 50, 238-44
Music in the Baroque Era, 246
Music in the Middle Ages, 246
Music in the Renaissance, 246
Music Index, 52, 246
music librarianship, 74
Music Librarianship; A Practical Guide, 63-4n, 241, 258n
music materials, 238-44
music publishers, 234, 245-59
The Music Review--record reviews, 91
music scores see printed notes; scores.
music services in public libraries, 238-44
Musica--record reviews, 91
Musica Disciplina, 259
Musica e Dischi, 91
Musica Rara, 245
Musical America, 75, 91
musical editions see printed notes; scores.
musical literature, 40
Musical Literature, 245
The Musical Quarterly--record reviews, 90, 92
The Musical Times, 254
Myers, William, 127-30

The Nation, 91
National Congress on Surveying and Mapping, 268
National Defense Education Act, 386, 424
National Science Foundation films, 376
National Union Catalog--recordings, 58, 67
National Union Catalog of Manuscript Collections, 316-7, 320
New Orleans Public Library, 205-8
New Records, 90
The New Republic--record reviews, 91

The New Statesman and Nation, 91
New York Times, 32, 68, 75, 91
news releases as ephemera, 295
newscasts (sound recordings)--cataloging, 144-6
newspapers and maps, 267
newspapers as ephemera, 293
nonbook materials
    cataloging, 396-401
    collation, 398-9
    critical notes, 400
    main entries, 396-7
    physical description, 398-9
    purposes, 14
    series notes, 399-400
    title page, 396-7
    title statement, 397-8
Northwestern Michigan College Library, 193-5
notational systems--recordings, 100, 102-3
Notes, 52, 68, 86, 233, 235, 245, 247-52, 258
NUCMC, 320

Oak Terrace Elementary School (N. Charleston, S. C.), 207-8
Oakland University Library, 107-9
Objectives and Standards for Special Libraries, 13
Occupational Filing Plan, 181
Occupational Literature, 163, 180-1
Occupational Outlook Handbook, 165
Ohio Valley Regional Film Library, 35-8
Oklahoma. University. Library, 356-63
Old and Modern Music of Distinction, 255
One-Spot Record Finder, 54
open stacks--recordings, 100-1
Opera, 92
Opera News, 51, 92
oral history, 110-3
oratorical contest, 130
original prints in public libraries, 183-7, 209-14
overhead projectors, 389-90, 418
overhead projectuals, 393-4

"package library," 302
paintings, 183, 188-90, 205-7
pamphlet collections, 158, 174
Pamphlet File in School, 180
The Pamphlet File in School, College, and Public Libraries,
    158
pamphlet sources--card file, 172

pamphlets
        acquisition, 159-60, 167-71
        bibliographies, 158-9
        cataloging, 168, 171-4, 175-7, 178-9, 351
        circulation, 160-1
        classification, 160, 175-7, 178-9
        desiderata lists, 171
        Dewey Decimal Classification, 175-7, 178-9
        expendability, 158
        political, 168-74
        processing, 175
        reader guidance, 151
        selection, 152, 158-9
        series, 180
        storage, 175
        use, 150-2, 173
        values, 149-52
pamphlets and research, 167
pamphlets in libraries, 149-52, 167-74, 175-9
pamphlets in vocational file, 163
Panigel, Armand, 91
Parents, 92
Pearson, Mary D., 413
Peckham, Howard H., 330n, 352n
performing media in public libraries, 242
periodicals and image data, 198
permissions to use pictures, 367-72
phonograph needles, 67
Phonograph Record Libraries: Their Organization and Practice, 76n
phonograph records see recordings.
phonographs, 40, 42, 49, 390, 410, 414
The Phonolog, 53
Phonolog system, 73
Phonoprisma--record reviews, 91
photo library, 355
photocopies of manuscripts, 325
photographs
        cataloging, 356-63, 394
        classification, 358-60
        index cards, 357-8
        literary property rights, 367-72
        processing, 360-3
        reference information, 363
        shelf list sample, 361-2
        subject headings, 358-61
        See also pictures.

photographs in audio-visual department, 394
photographs in picture collection, 354-5
photographs in university library, 356-63
picture distributors' lists, 180
pictures
    acquisition, 354, 364, 366
    arrangement, 355
    captions, 355
    cataloging, 365, 396-401
    classification, 355
    legal rights to use, 367-72
    processing, 355
    publishing, 371-2
    retrieval, 365-6
    sources, 198
    storage, 365, 402
    subject headings, 365
pictures and libel, 369-72
pictures and public relations, 364-6
pictures as literary property, 367-72
pictures as records, 333
pictures in audio-visual department, 394
pictures in books, 197
pictures in company library, 364-6
pictures in information file, 153-4
pictures in vertical file, 180
pictures in visual materials collection, 199
Planning Schools for New Media, 423n
poetry recordings, 73, 84-5
poets, 84-5
Polart Index of Record Reviews, 68
popular music, 42
portraits in picture collection, 354
posters, 199, 354
preservation see maintenance.
prices
    recordings, 68
    scores, 245-59
    See also cost; discounts.
primary source materials, 110, 293, 334
print collections, 212-3, 184-5
Print Council of America, 210
printed matter in special libraries, 298-9
printed notes, 230-6, 240-1, 396-401
    See also music; music materials; scores.
prints
    authenticity, 210

prints (cont.)
    circulation, 186
    exhibitions, 184
    insurance, 213
    processing, 212-3
    selection, 185, 211
    sources, 211
    See also art; art reproductions; original prints;
        paintings; pictures.
prints as a medium, 210
prints in information file, 154
processing of:
    bulletin board materials, 403
    pamphlets, 175
    photographs, 360-3
    pictures, 355
    recordings, 57, 139
    vertical files, 181
    See also cataloging; storage.
programmed courses, 215-226
programmed learning, 218, 224-5
programmed learning and the library, 215-9, 220-9
programmers and education, 386
programming center, 425
projection carts, 420
projection screens, 418-20
projectors see film projectors; filmstrip projectors; over-
        head projectors; slide projectors.
propaganda and pamphlets, 169
Ptolemy, 261
the public and:
    art prints, 184-5
    cataloging of recordings, 146
    films, 27
    maps, 267
    music, 41
    musical recordings, 42
    recordings, 73, 96
public libraries
    art reproductions, 188-90, 191-2
    audio-visual cooperation, 377
    films, 16-9, 20-3, 29
    filmstrips, 24
    manuscript collections, 303-31
    maps, 260-70
    music, 50
    music materials, 238-44

public libraries (cont.)
      music scores, 245-59
      music services, 238-44
      original prints, 183-7, 209-14
      paintings, 188-90
      pamphlets, 175-7, 178-9
      printed notes, 240-1
      recordings, 72-6, 240
      regional art, 201-4
      slides, 24
      standards, 13
Public Library Service; A Guide to Evaluation with Minimum
  Standards, 13
public relations, 16-9, 364-6
publicity
      art, 192, 202-3
      films, 18-9, 37
      original prints, 184
      recordings, 60-1
      vertical file materials, 182
Publishers' Trade List Annual, 234
Publishers' Weekly, 159

The Quarterly Journal of Speech, 92
Queens College Art Library, 196-200

radio program sponsored by library, 75
radio systems in university library, 106-9
reader guidance, 151, 224-5, 236
Readers' Guide to Periodical Literature, 52, 160, 179, 180
reciprocal borrowing privileges--recordings, 47
reciprocation in manuscript sharing, 324-5
record clubs, 68
record collections, 45, 47, 67, 74, 92-3, 95-6
The Record Collector, 92
record librarians, 74
record players see phonographs.
Record Ratings, 52
recorded books for the blind, 133-5
recording companies and libraries, 75
Recording for the Blind, Inc., 133, 135
recordings
      acquisition, 53-4
      arrangement, 98-103, 392
      audience, 72-3, 75
      basic collection, 46
      bibliographies, 50-2, 67-8, 75, 90-2, 94-6

recordings (cont.)
  care, 54-6, 70-1
  cataloging, 47, 58, 68-9, 140-1, 392, 396-401
  cataloging system, 147
  circulation, 42, 45, 47-8, 57, 60, 69-70
  classification, 58, 69, 73, 97-105
  cleaning, 56, 70
  dealers, 53-4
  discounts, 75
  distributors, 54
  economy reprints, 54
  8 rpm, 49
  ephemeral, 51
  evaluation, 86-93
  format, 87, 89
  45 rpm, 48
  gifts, 46
  interlibrary loans, 51
  kinds, 73
  kinds of reproduction, 41
  language, 52
  library programs, 75
  long-playing, 39, 46, 48, 66
  maintenance policy, 50
  mechanical adequacy, 87-9
  monophonic, 66
  musical, 231
  nonmusical, 52, 73
  prices, 68
  processing, 57
  publicity, 60-1
  reciprocal borrowing privileges, 47
  reference service, 43
  retrieval, 139-48
  reviewing, 87-93
  reviews, 43, 52, 67-8, 86, 87-90
  selection, 41-2, 49-51, 51-2, 66
  services, 51
  78 rpm, 46, 48, 51, 66
  16 rpm, 48
  sound reproduction, 48
  spoken, 48-9
  stereophonic, 46, 49, 66
  storage, 54-6, 59, 69-71
  See also folk song; jazz; music; music materials;
      poetry; record collections; tapes.
recordings and library purposes, 95-7

recordings for children, 53
recordings in libraries, 39-43, 44, 72-6, 240, 244
recordings of local interest, 46
records
 cartographic, 333
 documentary, 333
 financial and business, 333, 336-7
 historical, 333
 phonograph see recordings.
 private textual, 333
 public textual, 333
 series, 334
 See also archives; manuscripts.
Records in Review, 90
recreational materials, 50
reels for tape recorders, 413
Reese, Gustave, 246
reference service
 clippings, 301-2
 language courses on tape, 116-24
 recordings, 43
Register of Accessions for maps, 276
register of manuscripts, 317
Reid, Robert H., 94
religious groups, 51
rental collections of prints, 210-1
rental of:
 original prints, 209, 213
 paintings to children, 205
 recordings, 47
The Reporter, 81, 91
reports, 295-6
repository (library) see depository.
reprints, 153-4
research, 111, 167, 292-7, 381
research libraries, 292-7, 303
researchers, 300-1, 334, 366
resource centers--audio-visual materials, 379
responder systems, 427
retrieval of:
 clippings, 300-2
 films, by computer, 407-9
 pictures, 365-6
 programmed courses, 226-7
 recordings, 139-48
 See also bibliographic control; cataloging; classification; documentation; indexing.

reviewers, 28
reviews of:
    children's recordings, 53
    jazz, 81
    printed notes, 235
    recordings, 52, 68, 86, 87-93
    tapes, 68
rights (literary property)--pictures, 367-72
rights of privacy--pictures, 370-2
Riker Laboratories Inc., 298-9
Rolodex Card File, 299
rotation of films, 34-8
    See also film circuits.
rotation of recordings, 47
Royal Geographical Society, 271
rule of provenance, 334-5
Rules for Collections of Manuscripts, 317
Rules for Descriptive Cataloging in the Library of Congress,
    288, 342, 396, 400-1
Rules for Descriptive Cataloging in the Library of Congress:
    Manuscripts, 329n, 342, 352

sale of art works, 193-4, 209
Santarem, Viscomte de, 262
Saturday Review, 75, 81, 91
Schellenberg, Theodore R., 332
Scholarly Editions of English Music, 253
school libraries
    audio-visual materials, 378-9, 389-95
    pamphlets, 149-52
    standards, 14
schools and audio-visual materials, 376
schools and TV, 376
Schwann Artist Listing, 59
Schwann Long-Playing Record Catalog, 50, 52, 54, 67, 73, 75
science clippings, 181
science courses on film see filmed science courses.
Science Research Associates, 164, 181
scores--musical, 40, 51, 230, 245-59
"scrambled book," 221
Screen Facts, 32
screens, projection see projection screens.
searching service--manuscripts, 326
Sears List of Subject Headings, 155, 180, 390
"second rights"--pictures, 368
secondary source materials, 293
"see also" references--manuscripts, 348

selection of:
    audio-visual equipment, 410-23
    children's recordings, 53
    films, 17-8, 21, 28, 35
    maps, 266-9
    nonprint materials, 390
    paintings for children, 206-7
    pamphlets, 158-9
    prints, 185, 211
    recordings, 41-2, 49-52, 66
    See also acquisition; bibliographies; evaluation; reviews.
selections of jazz recordings, 81-3
series notes for nonbook materials, 399-400
serigraphs, 211
sheaf catalogue of maps, 275-6
sheet music see printed notes.
shelf list of photographs--content, 361-2
shelving see arrangement; storage.
Siefker, B., 228n
Sight and Sound, 32
signs--storage, 404
Skinner, B. F., 216, 220
slide projectors, 390, 415-6
slides
    cataloging, 391, 396-401
    circulation, 25
    storage, 25, 415
    use, 24
slides in audio-visual department, 391
slides in libraries, 24, 376
slides in visual materials collection, 199
slides of art reproductions, 190, 391
Smith, Hardin E., 201
Sonderkatalog, 255
sound effects, 51, 144-6
sound projectors, 417
soundproof cubicles, 42
sound reproduction, 48
source materials see primary source materials; secondary source materials.
sources of ephemera, 296-7
"Sources of Information About Scientific Careers," 165
sources of prints, 211
sources of vocational material, 165-6
Southampton University, 278
Sparks, Jared, 303

speakers, directional column, 414
speakers--selection, 414-5
special libraries, 13, 298-9, 354-5, 364-6
speeches, 144-6, 295, 336
the spoken word on tape, 110-3, 116-24
staffing, 242-3, 314-6
Standard Catalog, 180, 240
Standard Catalog for High School Libraries, 155
standards for:
    films, 28
    libraries, 13
    music collections, 241
    musical editions, 235-6
Standards for College Libraries, 13
Standards for Junior College Libraries, 13
Standards for Music Collections in Medium-Sized Libraries, 241
Standards for School Library Programs, 14
state consultant service--recordings, 45
state libraries--manuscript collections, 303
state library loans of recordings, 45
stereophonic recordings see recordings, stereophonic.
Sterling - U.S. Dollar Exchange, 248
storage of:
    archives, 338
    book jackets, 402
    bulletin board materials, 403
    captions, 404
    clipped stories, 404
    ephemera, 299
    filmstrips, 25
    flat signs, 404
    manuscripts, 338, 350-1
    maps, 269, 276-7, 281-5
    miscellaneous materials, 402-6
    objects and realia, 403-4
    pamphlets, 175
    pictures, 365, 402
    recordings, 54, 56, 59, 69-71
    slides, 25
    teachers' assignments, 404-5
    vertical files, 181
story hours, 61
String Music in Print, 235
student audio-visual area, 390
student library committee, 130
students and art works, 194

studio art teachers, 196-7
Studio Guild (West Redding, Conn.), 201
stylus, 67
subject headings for:
    art works, 197
    information files, 155
    pamphlets, 160, 173, 178-9
    photographs, 358-61
    pictures, 365
    vertical files, 180
    visual materials collection, 199
    vocational files, 163-4, 181
Subject Headings for the Information File, 155
Subject Headings for Vertical Files, 178
survey of:
    arrangement of recordings, 98-103
    manuscript holdings, 304-11
    map collections, 266
    music in public libraries, 238-44
    vertical files in high schools, 180-2
Sybel, Heinrich von, 334

talking book machines, 133
Talking Books for the Blind, 49, 133-4
tape recorded books, 134-5
tape recorded language courses, 116-24
tape recorders, 136, 390, 410-3
tape-slide shows for children, 126
tape splicer, 119
tape systems, cartridge-loaded, 413
tapes
    cataloging, 393
    classification, 136-8
    equipment, 117
    kinds, 393
    physical characteristics, 413-4
    reviews, 67
tapes about foreign countries, 125-6
tapes as teaching aids, 114-5
tapes for international understanding, 125-32
tapes for library orientation, 108-9
tapes for the blind, 133-5
tapes in audio-visual department, 389, 393
tapes in elementary school library, 125-32
teaching aids, 114-5
teaching and TV, 384-5
teaching machines, 215-8, 221-2, 385-6

teaching machines (cont.)
    See also programmed courses; programmed learning.
Teaching Machines and Programmed Learning: A Guide to
    the Literature, 228n
teaching methods, 383-4
technological change and education, 387-8
technological unemployment, 382
teenagers and films, 29
television and libraries, 377
television and teaching, 384-5
television circuits, 426
television instruction, 384-5
television program sponsored by library, 75
terminology for archives and manuscripts, 333-4
terminology for visual materials collection, 199-200
Texts (Associated Music Publishers), 245
Thomas, Dylan, 84
Thomson, Elizabeth, 53
The Tipi, 357
titles for nonbook materials, 396-8
Tooze, Ruth, 53
Townsley, Malcolm G., 420-1
tracing--manuscripts, 349
trade books and mass media, 385, 387
trade cards, 354
trademarks, 354
transducer, 414
"Transiphones," 107-8
transistor radios in libraries, 106-9
trial balances--arrangement, 337

UNESCO. Catalogue of Colour Reproductions..., 188
union catalog of films, 18
union list of maps and charts, 266
United States Government
        Coast and Geodetic Survey maps, 268
        Department of Manuscripts, 304
        Directorate of Overseas Surveys, 271
        General Land Office map, 269
        Library of Congress see Library of Congress.
        maps, 268
        Office of Education, 64-5n, 386, 412
        Superintendent of Documents and maps, 269
        War Department, 271
"U.S. rights"--pictures, 368
Uniterm indexing of recordings, 144-6

university libraries
    acquisition policies, 292
    archives, 332-41
    audio-visual materials, 378
    ephemera, 292-7
    manuscripts, 303, 332-41
    pamphlets, 167-74
    photographs, 356-63
University of California Library (Berkeley), 110, 332-9
University of Denver, 332
University of Iowa Library, 168-74
University of Oklahoma Library, 356-63
University of Southern Illinois, 223
University of Washington Library, 294-7, 332-9
unpublished materials and research, 292-7
unpublished writings as literary property, 322-3

Variety, 32
Verlags - Verzeichnis, 245
vertical file cabinets, 405
Vertical File Index, 158, 180
vertical file materials, 180-2
videotape recorders, 426
viewing equipment, 415-20
visible file, 25
visual forms
    bibliographic control, 199-200
    critical collection of, 197
    kinds, 198
    See also art; art reproductions; paintings; pictures;
        prints.
vocational file, 162-6
vocational literature, 162-3
vocational materials, 163-6, 180-1

Walkenaer, Charles Athenase, Baron, 262
warping of recordings, 71
Washington. University. Library, 294-7, 332-9
Wayne State University, 407-9
weeding, 298, 406
Wells Fargo Bank, History Room, 364-6
WERM, 52
Wilson Library Bulletin, 159
Wittenborn and Company, 199
woodcuts, 183
"world rights"--pictures, 368
World Tapes for Education, 125-32

The World's Encyclopedia of Recorded Music, 52
Worldwide Art Catalogue Center, 199

Xenon projection lamps, 416-7

York Township Public Library, 178-9

Zigrosser, 211

DATE DUE

DE 13 '69			
NOV 1 0 1977			
MAR 2 1 1978			
NOV 16 1978			

GAYLORD   PRINTED IN U.S.A.